DAZZLING DARKNESS

JAMES HARPUR

Dazzling Darkness

The Lives and Afterlives of the Christian Mystics

HURST & COMPANY, LONDON

First published in the United Kingdom in 2025 by
C. Hurst & Co. (Publishers) Ltd.,
New Wing, Somerset House, Strand,
London, WC2R 1LA

© James Harpur, 2025

All rights reserved.

Printed in Scotland by Bell & Bain Ltd, Glasgow

The right of James Harpur to be identified as the author of this
publication is asserted by him in accordance with the Copyright,
Designs and Patents Act, 1988.

A Cataloguing-in-Publication data record for this book is available
from the British Library.

ISBN: 9781911723905

www.hurstpublishers.com

JAMES HARPUR was educated at Trinity College, Cambridge, and is a Visiting Research Fellow at the Centre for Medieval and Renaissance Studies, Trinity College Dublin. He has published ten books of poetry, including *The Gospel of Gargoyle; The White Silhouette*; *Angels and Harvesters*; *The Oratory of Light* (poems written in the spirit of St Columba); and *The Gospel of Joseph of Arimathea*. He has also published a translation of the poems of Boethius (*Fortune's Prisoner*) and two verse memoirs: *The Examined Life*, an odyssey through boarding school; and *The Magic Theatre*, an account of student life at Cambridge in the late 1970s. He has won many prizes for his work, including the UK National Poetry Prize, the Michael Hartnett Prize, and the Vincent Buckley Award. His debut novel, *The Pathless Country*, won the J. G. Farrell Award and was shortlisted for the John McGahern Prize. His non-fiction works include *The Pilgrim Journey*, a history of pilgrimage in the West.

For Jan-Erik Guerth,
friend and fellow pilgrim,
with affection and gratitude

There is in God, some say,
A deep but dazzling darkness, as men here
Say it is late and dusky, because they
     See not all clear.
O for that night! where I in Him
Might live invisible and dim!

         —Henry Vaughan, from "The Night"

CONTENTS

List of Illustrations	xi
Acknowledgements	xv
Preface	xvii
Introduction	1
1. First Seeds	9
2. Deserts and Monasteries	25
3. The Early Middle Ages	47
4. The Twelfth Century	63
5. Preachers and Poets: The Franciscans	85
6. Holy Women: The Beguines	105
7. Mystics of the Rhineland	123
8. The Flame of English Mysticism	143
9. Women Mystics of Italy and Sweden	159
10. Eastern Orthodox Mysticism	171
11. Mystics of Spain	195
12. Protestant Mystics of the Seventeenth Century	209
13. Early Modern French Mystics	241
14. Light and Reason	263

CONTENTS

15. Romantics, Nature Mystics, and Transcendentalists	277
16. Modern Voices	297
Epilogue	317
Appendix: Poems Inspired by the Mystics	323
Notes	337
Bibliography	359
Index	375

LIST OF ILLUSTRATIONS

1. Plotinus, standing on the right, debates the finer points of philosophy with his pupil Porphyry in this 15th-century French illuminated manuscript. Public domain, via Wikimedia.

2. Hirsute from her time as a solitary in the desert, Mary of Egypt accepts the gift of a cloak from Zosima the priest to cover her nakedness. Public domain, via Wikimedia.

3. Martin of Tours, enlisted to fight in the Roman army, prepares to confront the enemy armed with only a wooden cross. This fresco is by the 14th-century Italian painter Simone Martini. Public domain, via Wikimedia.

4. Gregory of Nyssa, shown in this 11th-century mosaic in St Sophia Cathedral in Kyiv, was, and still remains, a major mystical thinker in the Orthodox Church. Public domain, via Wikimedia.

5. Dionysius the Areopagite is one of the first mystics to be associated with the approach to divine reality known as the *via negativa*, the negative way. Public domain, via Wikimedia.

6. Bernard of Clairvaux looks suitably ascetic in this painting by the 16th-century Spanish artist, Juan Correa de Vivar. Public domain, via Wikimedia.

7. With her scribe Volmar in attendance, Hildegard receives divine inspiration in her cell. From her work, *Scivias*. Public domain, via Wikimedia.

8. Hildegard of Bingen's painting, from her *Book of Divine Works*, shows a schematic world divided into four simultaneously occurring seasons. Public domain, via Wikimedia.

LIST OF ILLUSTRATIONS

9. This fresco of Francis of Assisi at the abbey of Subiaco, near Rome, is the oldest known depiction of the saint, painted, perhaps, before his death in 1226. Public domain, via Wikimedia.

10. Before her birth, Clare of Assisi was predicted to bring forth "a clear light that will illumine the world." Fresco by the 14th-century Italian painter Simone Martini. Public domain, via Wikimedia.

11. Marguerite Porete's *Mirror of Simple Souls* includes dialogues involving the figures of Love, Soul, and Reason. The manuscript here shows text from Chapter 35 of the book. Public domain, via Wikimedia.

12. Originally founded in 1245, the beguinage in Bruges no longer houses beguines but instead now functions as a Benedictine convent. Public domain, via Wikimedia.

13. Meister Eckhart, shown in this fresco from Santa Maria Novella in Florence, said, "The eye with which I see God is exactly the same as the eye with which God sees me." Public domain, via Wikimedia.

14. The Dominican Henry Suso turned from extreme austerities to a gentler form of mystical life, fully appreciative of the wonders of nature. Public domain, via Wikimedia.

15. *The Book of Margery Kempe* relates the author's pilgrimages and mystical experiences. The first line shown here (from Chapter 18) reads "steadfastly believe that the Holy Ghost dwelleth in his soul. And …" Public domain, via Wikimedia.

16. Bridget of Sweden was told by a divine voice that she would gather flowers from which people everywhere would "receive medicine." Public domain, via Wikimedia.

17. Catherine of Siena believed a combination of humility, self-knowledge, faith, and perseverance would lead the soul to union with God. Public domain, via Wikimedia.

18. John Climacus described the monk's path to God in terms of ascending a ladder on which he is assailed by demons and encouraged by angels. 12th-century icon from the Monastery of St Catherine, Mount Sinai. Public domain, via Wikimedia.

LIST OF ILLUSTRATIONS

19. Saint Gregory of Palamas was a leading proponent of hesychasm, the Orthodox tradition of mystical prayer. Public domain, via Wikimedia.

20. Sergius of Radonezh—shown here surrounded by depictions of his life in this 17th-century icon from Yaroslavl—was a mystical forest hermit who became the patron saint of Russia.

21. Teresa of Ávila receives inspiration from the Holy Spirit in the form of a dove. A copy of a painting by the Baroque Spanish artist Jusepe de Ribera. Public domain, via Wikimedia.

22. John of the Cross is associated with the "dark night of the soul"—an austere conception belying his reputation as a warm, cheerful man. Public domain, via Wikimedia.

23. Jacob Boehme believed that the "creaturely will" could be overcome only by the "grace of self-denial." Public domain, via Wikimedia.

24. For George Fox, founder of the Quakers, the divine inner light was the central spiritual reality of existence. Public domain, via Wikimedia.

25. The title page from John Bunyan's *The Pilgrim's Progress*. Bunyan is shown asleep and dreaming while his hero Christian is making his way to the Celestial City. Public domain, via Wikimedia.

26. Francis de Sales described contemplation as "simply the mind's loving, unmixed, permanent attention to the things of God." Public domain, via Wikimedia.

27. Blaise Pascal ended his account of the mystical experience he had on November 23, 1654, with the words "Joy, joy, joy, tears of joy." Public domain, via Wikimedia.

28. François Fénelon advocated a state of "holy indifference" in which grace enables the soul to desire only what God desires for it. Public domain, via Wikimedia.

29. The founder of Methodism, John Wesley said that all his strength "lay in keeping my eye fixed upon Him and my soul waiting on Him continually." Public domain, via Wikimedia.

LIST OF ILLUSTRATIONS

30. William Blake's typically visionary painting shows "Jacob's Ladder," with angels ascending and descending to and from heaven. Public domain, via Wikimedia.

31. William Blake said that on one occasion in his youth, he was watching haymakers in the fields when he suddenly saw angels walking among them. Public domain, via Wikimedia.

32. Ralph Waldo Emerson, the American Transcendentalist, believed the "inner light" worked "to bring the universe into the possession of a single soul." Public domain, via Wikimedia.

33. Thérèse of Lisieux's memoir *The Story of a Soul* became a spiritual classic. For her, "the most beautiful thoughts are nothing without good works." Public domain, via Wikimedia.

34. Charles de Foucauld's hermitage can still be seen near the Hoggar Mountains in the stark landscape of southern Algeria. Public domain, via Wikimedia.

35. On one occasion when Simone Weil was reciting George Herbert's poem "Love (III)," she said that Christ "took possession of me." Public domain, via Wikimedia.

ACKNOWLEDGMENTS

The section on George Herbert was first published in *Acumen*, edited by Patricia Oxley. Some of the material in this book first appeared in my *Love Burning in the Soul* (Shambhala, 2005). Even labors of love require support and encouragement, and I would like to thank Evie and Patrick for theirs. Also, many thanks to the staff of the Boole Library at University College, Cork, who were of great assistance. And, finally, I would like to thank Michael Dwyer of Hurst Publishers and give a special thank-you to Jan-Erik Guerth, who gave me so much wisdom and advice in the writing of this book.

PREFACE

The inspiration for this book occurred a few decades ago when, during a protracted period of physical debilitation, I was obliged to lie on my back in bed for long stretches of time. As a solace I started reading a range of spiritual works, from T. S. Eliot's *Four Quartets* and George Herbert's poems to Thomas à Kempis's *The Imitation of Christ* and the *Dhammapada*. At the same time, I began to pray and meditate—not in any structured way, but informally and intuitively. Over the weeks my meditations became more profound and peaceful, leaving me with a sense of calm and a new perspective on my anxieties. This process deepened and deepened until one morning I experienced an "implosion of light," which I have described in a poem like this:

> Then it happened –
> The splintering of mental membrane
> And flesh dissolving—a flash
> A wave, atomic blinding
> The ingress of obliteration
> No inside or outside
> A drowning in radiance
> As if a holy presence had descended
> And found an emptiness it had to flood,
> There was no me, no thought, no body
> Just new-born helplessness.[1]

In fact I did have one rogue, residual thought, lurking like the serpent in the Garden of Eden, whispering to me that I was either going to die or go mad—and this thought was enough to break the spell and haul me out of this blessed condition. But the sense of pervasive grace left me with an extraordinary residue of "love," a feeling of utter humility and compassion for people around me and

PREFACE

for the natural world. As someone who in his youth was typically selfish and self-interested, I was amazed to feel this love almost oozing out of me and all sense of my usual daily anxieties, resentment, jealousy, ambitiousness, and so on, removed. I remained in this "unity of being," to use W. B. Yeats's phrase, for about six months before my old self, my old self-centered life, reasserted itself. As a consequence of this I became avid to find out whether what had seemed to me to be a unique experience had been shared by others, and if so, how they had described it. I started reading compulsively about the lives and teachings of the Christian (and other) mystics in a quest to find kinship and even possibly a route back to the blissful at-one-ment I had experienced. This reading, reflecting and writing on the mystics also became the mainstay of my poetry and has never stopped.

This book, then, began as a highly-motivated personal quest rather than as an intellectual pursuit. It is not intended for professional theologians or academics but fellow pilgrims in search of "ultimate truth," curious to explore how the divine has manifested itself in the lives of certain individuals. I wanted to know what mystics had experienced, but also the sorts of lives they had lived that had brought them to the point when they enjoyed some sort of communion with the divine, or an extraordinary moment of transcendence, or, at the very least, a fascination with mystical experiences. In addition, I wanted to know something of the political and social conditions they lived in and whether these might have affected the way the mystics experienced and translated their transcendent moments into words. As Evelyn Underhill wrote:

> In reading the mystics ... we must be careful not to cut them out of their backgrounds and try to judge them by spiritual standards alone. They are human beings immersed in the stream of human history; children of their own time, their own Church, as well as children of Eternal Love. Like other human beings, that is to say, they have their social and their individual aspects; and we shall not obtain a true idea of them unless both be kept in mind.[2]

I have therefore broken the book up into short chapters relating approximately to different epochs. The brief historical introductions that preface each chapter are no more than simplified

PREFACE

scene setters, backdrops appearing as the curtain is raised on each new scene, before the players make their entrances. The players themselves, the Christian mystics, span two millennia, from the time of Christ to Thomas Merton and the Vietnam War era. I have concentrated on Western mystics but have included a chapter on the Orthodox tradition.

I have also included, in the Appendix, a small selection of poems I came to write about some of the mystics included in this book. My aim is to show how their lives and words can stimulate the imagination of anyone who takes the time to dwell on them. I wanted to show that their words are not simply to be read, appreciated, and moved on from, but are spiritually psychoactive with the potential for stimulating the imagination and possibly effecting personal transformation. Ignatius Loyola utilized the imagination in his *Spiritual Exercises*, in which he encouraged retreatants to imagine Gospel scenes vividly—the sights, sounds, and smells. Francis de Sales also advocated the use of the imagination in his meditative technique, advising meditators to conjure up Christ on the cross, for example, and trying to sense the actual sights and sounds of Golgotha. With a little time and intention, it is possible for anyone to imagine John of the Cross, say, incarcerated in a dark cell; or the anchoress Julian of Norwich waiting for the first needy visitor to arrive; or witnesses watching the death of Marguerite Porete at the stake; and every act of imagination helps to lodge a mystic and his or her words in a deep level of the psyche, with all the potential for spiritual change contained therein.

It goes without saying that in an introductory work of this scope and size, far too much has had to be omitted or simplified. My hope is that readers might become sufficiently intrigued to read (and imagine!) the writings of the mystics themselves, many of which provide fascinating insights into the soul's journey toward God (the autobiography of Teresa of Ávila and the journals of Thomas Merton spring to mind). If the book has been able to give enough of the flavor of the Christian mystical tradition to whet a greater appetite, it will have done its job.

INTRODUCTION

> The Lord is nigh unto all them that call upon him, to all that
> call upon him in truth.
>
> —Psalms 145:18

Reality can be explored, experienced, and described in different ways. The astrophysicist, for example, can approach the "reality" of the moon through empirical data, mathematics, and other scientific expertise. But astronauts such as Neil Armstrong and Buzz Aldrin, who actually walked on the moon in 1969, can describe firsthand what it feels like to be there, to participate in the experience emotionally. Similarly, when it comes to divine reality, Christian theologians (who may also be mystics) and mystics (who may be theologians) approach God in different ways. Theologians read, think, debate and write about such matters as the nature of God, say, or the relationship between God and Christ, or God and humanity, trying to express subtleties of distinction about ultimate reality in as precise a way as possible and building on a traditional corpus of knowledge. Mystics may do the same—for it is important to remember that until late medieval times the distinction between mystics and theologians was blurred; but what makes mystics unusual is that they claim to have had a direct, firsthand experience of God; and, like astronauts in the case of the moon, this gives them the authority to describe what it *feels* like to experience reality— which in their case is the ultimate reality: God.

The terms *mystic* and *mysticism* in the Christian tradition are difficult to define in a way that does justice to all the varied experiences of those who have been considered to be Christian mystics. The visionary, emotionally charged writings of the medieval English mystic Julian of Norwich, for instance, are very different from those of John of the Cross, with his rejection of visions and voices and his emphasis on the soul's purgation on its way toward union with the divine. However, it can be safely said that the experience of mystics has usually revolved around a *direct apprehension or awareness of God*— an experience that goes beyond the rational faculty of the mind and self-willed activity. It can also be said that it is an experience that has often required devoted and disciplined preparation (for example, through prayer and ascetic practices) and that it admits of degrees of profundity, from relatively mild spiritual illumination to union with God, a conjoining in which the will of the mystic is consumed, and which is often described as a spiritual marriage.

Modern commentators on mysticism have articulated their encapsulations of it along these lines. Evelyn Underhill said that mysticism "is the art of union with Reality" and that "the mystic is a person who has attained that union in a greater or lesser degree; or who aims at and believes in such attainment."[1] Bernard McGinn has said that mysticism is "the preparation for, the consciousness of, and the reaction to what can be described as the immediate or direct presence of God."[2] Joan M. Nuth says that mystical experience "involves an intense awareness of God's presence, accompanied by a knowledge and love of God that are recognized as extraordinary."[3]

As both McGinn and Nuth imply, the aftermath of the mystical experience is crucial to its definition: one of the traditional ways of distinguishing true from false mysticism has been to examine the fruits in question. Whereas false mysticism might result in a self-indulgent basking in spiritual delight, true mysticism has traditionally led to a profound transformation in the individual, who is blessed with a greater capacity for spiritual virtues, such as a heightened sense of compassion or greater humility or strength in performing charitable works. Francis of Assisi was tireless in his preaching and ministry to the poor; Teresa of Ávila combined profound contemplative prayer with a reforming zeal that resulted in the creation of a new Carmelite order; Catherine of Genoa brought succor to the sick in the challenging conditions of her local hospital.

Of course, there is bound to be a gray area as to who is or is not a mystic. For example, there is scholarly debate about the status of supernatural or suprasensual experiences such as visions, ecstasies, locutions (hearing what appears to be a divine voice), clairvoyance,

INTRODUCTION

and so on. Many mystics seem to have experienced these phenomena, but most have emphasized that they are ancillary and inessential to the direct awareness of the presence of God. Indeed, some mystics, such as John of the Cross, have been severely critical of suprasensual experiences, questioning their provenance. The consensus seems to be that the greater the pictorial content of a vision, the more the individual's personal experience and imagination is involved. Clearly, much hinges on what the content of the vision or locution is and what transformative effect, if any, it has on the life of the individual. The medieval German nun Hildegard of Bingen seems to have seen reality in an extraordinary luminous pictorial way denied to ordinary folk, but did she in her visions experience the actual presence of God?

Another area of debate concerns whether it is possible to be a mystic by writing about mysticism or contemplation without necessarily having had a "mystical experience." The question arises because there have been some persuasive mystical theologians (mystical theology being the science and study of the spiritual life), such as Meister Eckhart and Walter Hilton, who did not directly claim to have mystical experiences in the way that, say, Teresa of Ávila or Angela of Foligno did. Ultimately, it is impossible to assemble empirical evidence to "prove" whether someone has had a genuine mystical experience or not, and as Bernard McGinn has pointed out, it ends up being a fruitless exercise trying to sort out the experiential mystics from those who have only written about mysticism: "Theologically speaking, the issue is not, Was this person really a mystic because he or she claims to have had the experience I define as mystical? but, What is the significance of her or his writings, autobiographically mystical or not, in the history of Christian mysticism?"[4] In short, what matters in the end are the mystical texts themselves and the extent to which they shed light on the experience of becoming aware of the presence of God and its transformatory effect.

The use of the word *mystic* to describe someone who has had a direct experience of God did not come about until the later Middle Ages. Until that point, those whom we would now consider to be mystics were described by the word *contemplatives*—which is used more or less synonymously with *mystics* in this book. (On a historical point, *mysticism* comes from the Greek *mysterion*, meaning something "secret" or "hidden," and it was originally used in the context of ancient pagan "mystery religions," such as those connected with Orpheus and Mithras. In the early Christian era, the adjective *mystikos* was first used in conjunction with reading the Bible and referred to the "hidden" meaning of the text, the deeper spiritual level of interpretation inspired by God. The word was also used to describe sacramental rites, especially the Eucharist, and also broadly came to mean "spiritual" or "sacred.")

Contemplatives, usually monks, were those whose lives revolved around the practice of contemplation, which had, and has, a technical sense. First of all, it is usually differentiated from *meditation*, which involves concentrating and reflecting upon a biblical passage or a sacred image or a mystery of the faith in order to gain a greater spiritual understanding or depth of feeling. Contemplation or contemplative prayer differs from meditation in that it is nondiscursive: it moves beyond the use of thought, words, and reflections to a point where the contemplative reaches a simple, loving attention on God. Contemplation has also traditionally been divided into two types: "acquired contemplation" involves a degree of effort on the part of the individual, in the form of prayer, say, and mystical knowledge arrives via the senses. "Infused contemplation," by contrast, involves a direct and extraordinary contact with God, bypassing the senses.[5] Those attracted to contemplative prayer naturally needed solitude and time in which to reach a direct communing with God, so it is not surprising that the great seedbeds of Christian contemplation or mysticism up to the Reformation were the monasteries.

It is one thing to have a mystical experience, but it is quite another to describe it, since by definition it occurs beyond the temporal in a realm where time and space, and the words used to describe the content of those dimensions, are no longer relevant. So mystics down the ages have had to resort to metaphors, similes, and symbols to convey the inexpressible. The medieval English mystic Richard Rolle talks about being "enflamed with the fire of Christ's love." Bernard of Clairvaux refers to the ingress of the divine softening his "hard and stony" heart and that when the feeling of euphoria disappeared it was as if a flame had been removed from a "bubbling

INTRODUCTION

pot." Catherine of Genoa says that the serenity the soul finds in God is like being "immersed in an ocean of utmost peace."

For some mystics the ineffability of the experience of God led to an approach that was known as the negative, or "apophatic," way. This emphasizes the absolute transcendence of God, for whom, therefore, human concepts are ultimately inadequate: it is truer to express what he is *not* than what he is. So mystics in this tradition, such as Dionysius the Areopagite, Meister Eckhart, and Jan van Ruysbroeck, prefer to use terms such as "darkness," "nudity," "the void," and "the abyss" to convey the immeasurable and inexpressible divinity.

Many mystics not only described their own personal encounters with the divine but went on to reflect upon, analyze, and write about others' mystical experiences. This gave rise to mystical theology. One important development within this tradition was the idea that the soul's path to union with God had three parts to it. This tripartite journey, probably first formulated by Origen in the third century, became firmly established in the Middle Ages (and is referred to throughout this book). The three stages were known as purgative, illuminative, and unitive. The first one, the purgative, involves the soul purifying itself by getting rid of bad habits and vices (such as gluttony and laziness) and cultivating Christian virtues, for example, patience and charity. In short, it represents the conversion from the worldly to the spiritual life. The second, illuminative, stage carries on from the first: the soul is further weaned from its attachment to the world and increasingly becomes illuminated by spiritual virtues. The last, unitive, stage involves the final process of being united with God.

It should be pointed out, however, that the three stages do not necessarily constitute a straightforward progression—for example, aspects of purgation and illumination can recur even during the unitive stage. Also, the Christian mystic's union with God is a union with a transcendent, personal being, not an impersonal cosmic principle (as epitomized by the Neoplatonic philosopher Plotinus's "flight of the alone to the Alone"). And for Christians, union with God always means that the distinction between creator and created is maintained—it is a union of wills and not a complete absorption and loss of identity on the part of the individual.

This book, then, is an introduction to the written record of the mystics and mystical theologians of the last 2,000 years. It combines descriptions of the mystics' experiences of encountering the presence of God with their reflections on the whole phenomenon of contemplation. It also attempts to put the voices of the mystics into the contexts of their individual and historical circumstances. Although mystical experiences have a timeless quality that transcends the boundaries of different ages, the way they are expressed and the theology that surrounds them are influenced by the currents of history. The systematization of the mystical path outlined by Bonaventure is as indicative of the medieval Scholastic period in which he lived as the reasonableness of the writings of William Law is of the so-called Age of Enlightenment.

And if the way in which the mystics described the journey toward divine union was subject to time and place, so too was the way in which they prepared themselves for contemplation. For the fourteenth-century German mystic Henry Suso, mortification consisted of several years of severe, self-inflicted physical pain. More than 300 years later, at the start of the Age of Enlightenment, the French mystic François Fénelon considered mortification to be the ability to put up with people we find disagreeable and knuckling down to everyday duties.

It is difficult, however, to establish for certain what effect particular social or personal circumstances may or may not have had on the spirituality of different mystics. Is it significant (as some scholars have suggested) that Catherine of Siena was born with a twin sister who died at birth? That Julian of Norwich grew up at a time when the Black Death was raging over Europe? Were her well-known words "And all shall be well and shall be well, and all manner of things shall be well" a mantra of self-reassurance rather than an expression of hope? And is it significant that John of the Cross, famous for his description of "the dark night of the soul," was incarcerated in the "dark night" of an actual prison by his fellow Carmelites?

It was undoubtedly significant that the medieval beguine teacher and mystic Marguerite Porete lived at a time when irregular religious movements, especially those involving women, and writings and attitudes that challenged the authority of the church were being

INTRODUCTION

dealt with severely. If she had been born a few hundred years later, it is unlikely she would have been burned at the stake (as she was in 1307). And in the Romantic age in Britain, it is not surprising that individuals with mystical temperaments (for example, the poet William Blake) preferred to remain outside the established church, for which *mysticism* was still associated with the pejorative term *enthusiasm*. Nor is it surprising that the modern French mystic Pierre Teilhard de Chardin developed his idea of spiritual evolution at a time when the theories of Charles Darwin (who died in 1882, the year after Teilhard was born) were very much in the air. By locating mystics in the context of their political, social, and religious times, this book aims to shed light on the way in which they expressed the fruits of their encounters with ultimate reality, or the divine, or God.

1

FIRST SEEDS

The worth of love beams forth from light to light.
> —Clement of Alexandria

Christian mysticism would not exist at all without Jesus of Nazareth, whose followers believed and believe that he was the Christ (*christ* is the Greek form of the Hebrew *messiah*, meaning "anointed one"), the Son of God. They hold that he was executed by order of the Roman governor Pontius Pilate, and that he rose from the dead and ascended into heaven. By following Jesus's teachings, with their emphasis on selfless love and compassion, and the example of his life—which includes the darkness of Calvary as much as the glory of the Resurrection—Christians believe they can reach salvation.

But if Jesus is the cornerstone of Christian mysticism, it is not clear how much he himself was a dedicated "mystic"—at least in the popular conception, established in medieval times, of someone devoted to ascetic practices and contemplative prayer. In the Gospel accounts of Matthew, Mark, and Luke (known as the synoptic Gospels because they share a similar point of view), Jesus is portrayed more as a spiritual and ethical teacher and a healer than as a contemplative expounding a mystical theology. In the Gospel of John (known as the Fourth Gospel) there is a greater emphasis on Jesus's spiritual and mystical thoughts, especially in the Farewell Discourses (chapters 14–17), so called because they mark Jesus's final teaching to his disciples before his death. The difficulty here is that many scholars believe that John's Gospel records not so much the actual words of Jesus as reflections and meditations written by the author (traditionally identified with John the apostle, but more likely to have been a later Christian perhaps living in Asia Minor), inspired by Jesus's teachings. Scholars therefore refer to "Johannine spirituality"[1] (which also draws on the three New Testament letters attributed to John as well as the Book of Revelation), and this constitutes the main repository of New Testament mysticism along with what emerges from the life and teachings of Paul.

Paul never met Jesus during the latter's time on earth. But Paul's letters are infused with an acute sense of their author's knowing or experiencing a mystical communion with Christ "exalted" (that is, resurrected from the dead and sitting at the right hand of God). He also formulated the idea of the mystical body of Christ (the church) in which the faithful participated. During his life Paul (originally Saul) wrote that he experienced mystical, visionary, and ecstatic states. His most celebrated vision occurred when he encountered the full force of the presence of Christ during his journey to Damascus (Acts 9:1–19): "And as he journeyed, he came near Damascus: and suddenly there shined round about him a light from heaven: And he fell to the earth, and heard a voice saying unto him, Saul, Saul, why persecutest thou me?" But Paul also mentions having an ecstatic experience in 2 Corinthians 12:2–4, where he refers to himself in the third person: "I know a man in Christ who fourteen years ago was caught up to the third heaven."

Paul always claimed that his experience of Christ came directly as a living spiritual reality. In Galatians 2:20, for example, he says "I have been crucified with Christ and *I no longer live, but Christ lives in me*" (author's emphasis). Becoming like Christ is the goal of the spiritual journey, and it involves identification with Christ's passion and death before eternal life can be gained. Paul also refers to the "Spirit of Christ"—which he seems to use interchangeably with the "Spirit" and the "Spirit of God" (Romans 8:9)—as the divine vitalizing power that makes us "sons of God" (Romans 8:14), and he repeatedly uses the phrase "in Christ" to express union with him.

The Christ-mysticism in Paul's letters finds a different expression in John's Gospel, in which the essential nature and role of Jesus is described in terms of different concepts and images, for example, the Word, true vine, bread of life, and light. In the first chapter of his Gospel, John says that Jesus was the "light of men" and "the true light that gives light to every man," that is, a source of spiritual

FIRST SEEDS

illumination enabling those who welcomed and believed in him to become "children of God." Indeed, the idea and symbolism of light, with all its implications, is an important element in John and often reoccurs throughout the history of Christian mysticism (especially in the Eastern Orthodox tradition) as the expression of divine reality.

The New Testament world was dominated territorially and culturally by the Roman Empire. At the death of Augustus, the first emperor (27 BCE–14 CE), Roman-controlled lands stretched from the Atlantic Ocean to the Black Sea, from Egypt to the Rhine, and consisted of more than thirty provinces. The relatively stable conditions—the so-called Pax Romana—that the Romans established reached eastward to Asia Minor and Syria. Judea was the exception. The Jews had come under direct Roman rule in 6 CE, and despite being granted certain concessions (such as exemption from military service), their religious zeal and patriotism were constantly chafed by their pagan and often corrupt and ruthless masters. Resentment flickered away until in 66 CE it flared into the Great Rebellion. Four years later, after desperate Jewish resistance, the Romans put an end to the war, destroying Jerusalem in the process.

In fact, the Romans were generally tolerant of other peoples' traditions and culture so long as these did not threaten imperial security. The last centuries BCE saw an influx into Rome of various religious cults from abroad. By this time Rome's traditional state religion, centered on gods such as Jupiter and Mars, was failing to satisfy the needs of many of its citizens, who seem to have found it too cold and impersonal, devoid of an inner spirituality. They sought a more intimate and emotional style of worship—one that entailed greater personal involvement. Into this spiritual vacuum came a host of exotic cults and "mystery religions" from Greece and the Middle East. They included those of Dionysus, Orpheus, Cybele (the Great Mother), Isis and Osiris, and Mithras.[2]

Knowledge about these religions is relatively scarce, mainly because their adherents were bound to secrecy. Although they had their own sets of rituals and beliefs, they did share some common features, for example, worship of a savior deity, initiatory rites, private gatherings of members, shared sacramental meals, and the promise of personal salvation and life after death. Unsurprisingly, when Christianity began to spread, particularly in towns and cities, gaining converts from all levels of society, many pagans viewed it as just another mystery religion, and indeed Paul and later Clement of Alexandria are examples of Christians who used the language of the mysteries in their writings. Yet there were crucial differences. Christianity was not exclusive: unlike most of the mystery religions, it welcomed not only men but women into its ranks. Also, most importantly, Christianity stressed that its founder was not a mythical deity such as Cybele or Dionysus but a flesh-and-blood historical person.

From the time of the apostles until the reign of Constantine the Great in the early fourth century, the Christian way of life was at odds with the pagan culture in which it existed. The faithful were exhorted to live soberly, dress simply, and refrain from attending gladiatorial shows and serving in the army. More significantly, they refused to sacrifice to the Roman gods or participate in the cult of the deified emperor, even nominally. They kept to themselves and worshiped together in private houses. Inevitably, they came to be seen as outsiders, "atheists" (because they rejected the gods), and even, in the phrase of the Roman historian Tacitus in his *Annals* (44), "haters of the human race"; and there were rumors that they indulged in wild orgies, incest, and cannibalism (probably a misunderstanding of the Eucharistic feast).

There was little systematic state persecution of Christians until the third century, notably in 250 by Decius (r. 249–251), followed by Diocletian (r. 284–305) in 303. But Christians were always vulnerable to the whims of local pagan governors and mobs, especially when a calamity prompted the search for a scapegoat (the church father Tertullian [ca. 160–225] noted ironically that "if the Tiber rises too high or the Nile sinks too low, the cry is 'The Christians to the lion'"). Emperor Nero (r. 54–68) set an ominous precedent when he blamed and executed Christians for starting the great fire of Rome in 64 CE. But for Christians, martyrdom had the reward of a place in heaven among the blessed, and many actively sought it, provoking the authorities to achieve their end. Although many lives were lost in martyrdom, many more were attracted to the Christian cause. As Tertullian pointed out, the blood of the

FIRST SEEDS

martyrs is seed: the heroic way in which men and women met their deaths impressed onlookers and promoted the faith.

One such inspirational martyr was Perpetua (ca. 182–203), a Roman noblewoman living in Carthage (in modern Tunisia) who refused to abjure her Christian faith during the time of Emperor Severus and who seems to have had mystical, or at least visionary, tendencies. Incarcerated with five other Christians for refusing to worship the emperor, and awaiting death in the arena, Perpetua received a vision in which she saw a bronze ladder reaching up to heaven. Onto the sides of the ladder were affixed knives, swords, hooks, and spears, and at the bottom lay a great serpent. Perpetua was encouraged to ascend by her brother, Saturus, who was already at the top: trusting in Christ, Perpetua braved the serpent, who became docile, and climbed the ladder. At the top she

> saw a very great space of garden, and in the midst a man sitting, white-headed, in shepherd's clothing, tall, milking his sheep; and standing around in white were many thousands. And he raised his head and beheld me and said to me: "Welcome, child." And he cried to me, and from the curd he had from the milk he gave me as it were a morsel; and I took it with joined hands and ate it up; and all that stood around said "Amen." And at the sound of that word I awoke.[3]

Perpetua understood the vision to mean that martyrdom was nigh and prepared herself accordingly—she later died by the sword in the arena, but not before impressing the crowd with her courage and faith. (The image of the ladder reaching from earth to heaven is reminiscent of the ladder Jacob saw in a dream, in Genesis 28:12, on which angels were ascending and descending; and it also anticipates the cosmic ladder used figuratively by John Climacus, as we shall see, in his mystical treatise *Ladder of Divine Ascent*.)

There were other reasons why pagans converted to Christianity. Most evidently, perhaps, was the way Christians helped each other. Widows and orphans were cared for, prisoners visited, burials arranged for the poor, travelers given hospitality, and food made available during famines and war. "See how these Christians love each other!" exclaimed one pagan, according to Tertullian.[4]

As the church grew and established an organization based around local communities led by bishops, it also began to define its doctrine and establish its scriptures. One of the pressures to do so came from the threat of Gnosticism, a hybrid spiritual movement that became prominent in the second century. Gnosticism (from the Greek *gnosis*, "knowledge") was eclectic, mixing theological and philosophical ideas drawn from Judaism, Christianity, and Greek and Persian thought, mixed up with astrology, myth, and magic. In its Christian, and predominant, form, it stressed the central place of *gnosis*, or revealed knowledge, in bringing about salvation. Orthodox Christianity also recognized the place of revealed knowledge but viewed it more as something that had been given to the apostles and transmitted by the church to the faithful than as something directly receivable by the individual.[5]

Gnostics also distinguished between a supreme, transcendent, unknowable god and a lesser creator god, or demiurge, who had made the imperfect world, the human race, and matter. They were dualists, pitting spirit against matter, mind against body, light against dark, and they had a pessimistic view of the world, believing matter to be inherently evil. However, they did think some people could be saved by a gnosis that enabled them to liberate the divine spark within themselves from its prison of flesh so that it could return to its heavenly home. Most Gnostics considered Christ to be a redeemer figure, but they denied the Incarnation: how could the pure spirit of Christ have inhabited corrupt flesh? Gnostics believed Christ had merely assumed the appearance of a human being and therefore did not really die on the cross.

In a world of intellectual change and confusion, Gnosticism, with its esoteric timbre and bewildering variety of beliefs, proved attractive to many. For orthodox Christians, the silver lining to the Gnostic cloud was that in combating it they were forced to define and articulate their faith; for example, Christians came to believe that the soul, although capable of becoming divine, was not inherently so, as the Gnostics thought. One of the first Christian thinkers to enter the lists against Gnosticism was Clement of Alexandria, a city where the movement had put down strong roots. Clement also strove to make Christianity respectable to cultured pagans who doubted its intellectual sophistication; and he was important in mystical theology for bringing a Platonic vision to the Christian spiritual tradition. Following in the same mystical

FIRST SEEDS

tradition was Origen, reckoned to be the greatest theologian before the age of Constantine. Origen also happened to share the same Alexandrian teacher as the greatest pagan thinker of the time, the Neoplatonic philosopher Plotinus, whose mystical system of reality influenced the Christian contemplative tradition down the centuries.

Clement of Alexandria (d. ca. 215)

The first Christian writer to use the word *mystical* in his works, Clement of Alexandria is important for the way that he blends Christian theology with the philosophical tradition of Plato, with its stress on the reality of a spiritual realm, the transcendence of God or the One, and the soul's ascent and union with it. As would be the case with Plotinus and subsequent mystics, such as Dionysius the Areopagite, who drew on the Neoplatonist tradition, Clement emphasizes the mystery and ineffableness of God: What can be said, he asks, of something (i.e. God) that is "neither genus, nor difference, nor species, nor individual, nor number"?[6] He admits that in practice we do in fact use terms to describe God, such as the One, the Good, Father, and Creator, but these are really crutches for the mind: nothing can be predicated of him, for to do so would be to limit the illimitable. Our understanding of him, the great Unknown, must depend on divine grace and "the world alone that proceeds from him."[7]

Clement also stresses the importance to the spiritual lives of the Christians of "true gnosis," or revealed knowledge—as opposed to the false knowledge of the Gnostics, and he was important for developing the notion of "divinization," an influential idea summed up in the affirmation that God became man so that people could learn how to become like God. For Clement, the soul, although not originally divine, was capable of becoming divine.

Not much is known about Clement's life. He was born in the middle of the second century, probably in Athens, and was evidently well educated in the pagan classics. At some stage he embraced Christianity and set out abroad to find a suitable teacher. His travels took him to Italy, Palestine, Syria, and elsewhere, but to no avail. Finally he reached Alexandria in Egypt, where he found the right man: Pantaenus, probably a Sicilian, and a convert from paganism, who had become a Christian teacher.

Alexandria at this time was one of the great cultural centers of the Roman Empire, the home of a famous university, and a meeting place of people from many different ethnic and cultural backgrounds. In its liberal intellectual ethos, pagan Platonists could argue about the nature of God with Jews; and Christians could debate the importance of faith with Gnostics. It was in this tolerant atmosphere that a Christian catechetical school (one that gave religious instruction) came into being during the second century. Its aim was to teach theology to Christians, but interested pagans were also allowed to attend certain lectures. Pantaenus was the first known head of the school, and Clement, his pupil, succeeded him in 190, remaining at his post until 202, when a persecution in the city during the reign of Emperor Severus compelled him to flee. What happened to him next is obscure, but at some stage he seems to have arrived in Caesarea in Cappadocia (in modern Turkey), where he probably ended his days.

Clement wrote three principal works: *Exhortation to Conversion* (*Protrepticus*), an apologia for the faith and an attack on pagan worship; *The Tutor* (*Paedagogus*), a practical guide to Christian life and ethics; and, the most important, the unfinished *Miscellanies* (*Stromateis*), a work he compared to a field full of wildflowers because it was written in a consciously random, unsystematic way, engaging its readers more by poetic glimpses and variety than by a solid, methodical approach.

Clement's great challenge was to address himself to the needs of different groups in Alexandria. There were many Christians who had received little or no education and found pagan philosophy obscure and, since they associated it with the Gnostic heretics, suspect. Schooled in the classics himself, Clement was convinced that many a valuable truth could be found in pagan philosophy and poetry and that rejecting them wholesale was counterproductive. Instead he tried to make them at least palatable to his skeptical brethren by insisting that Plato had in fact received his inspiration from reading Moses and the prophets.

Conversely, Clement also wanted to make Christianity attractive to potential pagan converts and to show them that Christianity was not just for the underprivileged of society but capable of

FIRST SEEDS

sophisticated thought and expression. He was aware that many pagans were disdainful of the literary style of the scriptures, so he peppered his own writings with hundreds of allusions to classical authors; he also summarized Jesus's Sermon on the Mount in a manner the pagan intelligentsia would find congenial.

Clement also tried to show that far from underpinning Gnosticism, classical philosophy could be used to undermine it. Yet although he attacked Gnostic ideas, he did emphasize the need in the spiritual life for true gnosis, which was not, however, a prerequisite for salvation. Whereas for the Gnostics gnosis was a "skill in the manipulation of words and ideas in order to find a safe path through the cosmic maze,"[8] for Clement true gnosis was set firmly within church orthodoxy and was not just a matter of the intellect: "He who would enter the shrine must be pure, and purity is to think holy things. ... The more a man loves, the more deeply does he penetrate into God."[9] Gnosis makes possible the vision of God, the highest human attainment (he refers to the divine vision more than eighty times in his writings).[10] Clement does not ignore the importance of faith, by which we confess the existence of and worship God, but he maintains that "faith is perfected" by knowledge, which comes through the grace of God to those who have prepared themselves. And in the same way that knowledge is added to those who already have faith, so love is added to knowledge, and "the worth of love beams forth from light to light."[11]

Lying at the heart of the soul's mystical ascent to God, this knowledge or gnosis purifies and transforms us, transporting the soul to be with what is sacred and divine, as its own nature is. Knowledge, with its innate light, carries us along the mystical path:

> It removes [the soul] to what is akin to the soul, divine and holy, and by its own light conveys man through the mystic stages of advancement; till it restores the pure in heart to the crowning place of rest; teaching to gaze on God, face to face, with knowledge and comprehension.[12]

Origen (ca. 185–254)

In 203 the Christian catechetical school in Alexandria, which had been left rudderless by the departure of Clement during the

Severan persecution, was taken over by Origen, who was then only about eighteen years old. Origen was more critical of the pagan classical writers than Clement, but he followed his master in trying to reconcile the best of Greek thought with Christian teaching, especially as found in the holy scriptures; he, too, championed the faith against its Gnostic and pagan enemies. As a biblical commentator, theologian, preacher, and letter writer, he was enormously prolific and wrote hundreds of works, although relatively few of them have survived. After his death, some of his views, as passed down by his supporters, proved to be controversial, if not in error (for example, his idea that no one is ultimately barred from salvation, including the devil himself). But he was immensely influential on subsequent generations, including in the following century the Cappadocian Fathers—Basil the Great, Gregory of Nazianzus, and Gregory of Nyssa—the last of whom called Origen the "prince of Christian learning."

Origen's importance to mysticism lies in his Platonist-Christian vision of the one, transcendent God, as well as the essentially spiritual nature of the true reality, and the idea of the soul's return or ascent to God.[13] The soul, he says, is in existence before it inhabits its human body, and it will continue to exist after the death of its corporeal vehicle. When this happens, the soul faces the consequences of its sins and is purged by fire, which is not simply a divine punishment but a necessary means of purification. Origen is also important for his personal asceticism (which was to become influential in monastic spirituality) and the essentially Christian view that prayer, in the fullness of its experience, provides the means for the soul to ascend to contemplate God.

Most of what we know about Origen was written by the early church historian Eusebius (ca. 260–340) in book 6 of his *Ecclesiastical History*. Origen was born in about 185, probably in Alexandria, and brought up as a Christian by his parents. In 202, while he was in his teenage years, he suffered a personal tragedy when his father, Leonides, was thrown into prison and then put to death during the persecution of Emperor Severus. The young Origen tried to join his father in his fate, but his resourceful mother is said to have prevented him by the expedient of hiding his clothes. With his father dead, Origen supported his mother and six younger brothers by teaching,

FIRST SEEDS

and he was also helped financially by a local woman of means. After he took over the catechetical school in the absence of Clement, he was able to devote himself to teaching, reading the Bible, and studying pagan philosophy, receiving instruction from Ammonius Saccas, who was also the teacher of Plotinus. All the while Origen adopted an ascetic lifestyle, praying, fasting, and keeping vigils. He is even said by Eusebius to have taken literally Matthew 19:12 (the verse that alludes to "those who have made themselves eunuchs for the sake of the kingdom of heaven") and castrated himself, although in a later commentary on the verse he decried taking a literal approach to those words.

Origen continued to reside in Alexandria, writing his works, especially his various commentaries on the Old and New Testaments, until 230. In that year he was ordained a priest while staying in Caesarea in Palestine, an event that his local bishop of Alexandria, Demetrius, saw as a breach of his authority, to which he responded by banishing Origen. So Origen settled in Caesarea, where he founded a Christian school that quickly gained a reputation for excellence. For the next twenty years he continued to preach and write prolifically, occasionally making trips to Greece and Arabia. In 250, now in his sixties, he fell victim to the persecution instituted by Emperor Decius and was imprisoned and tortured. Although he survived the immediate ordeal, the experience took its toll, and he died in about 254.

Perhaps the most significant contribution Origen made to the tradition of Christian mysticism was his biblical exegesis, which he saw as a wholehearted spiritual endeavor, not just a scholarly pursuit, along with his view that the books of the Old and New Testaments had different strata of meaning and could be interpreted at a literal, a moral, and—the one he favored most—an allegorical level. For Origen, the Bible was a divinely inspired work, primarily a depository of spiritual truths, and its value as a historical record was less significant. This approach—that the biblical stories led to a deeper spiritual meaning—was in line with his belief in the Platonic notion that the things of the material world pointed toward an invisible, mystical realm accessible only to a spiritual elite by their ascent to Christ and God. This view, that the highest realms of spirituality were open only to the few, held the danger of creating

19

a two-tier system in the church, comprising a select group set over the community of believers as a whole.[14]

Origen's allegorical method is best known from his highly influential commentary on the Song of Songs in the Old Testament, a method that would later be developed by such greats of Christian mysticism as Bernard of Clairvaux, Teresa of Ávila, and John of the Cross. Origen interpreted the relationship between the lovers in this sensual book (it begins, "Let him kiss me with the kisses of his mouth") primarily in terms of the love between the Logos, or Christ, and the individual soul—Jews had traditionally viewed the relationship as being between God and Israel. For Origen, the soul's love for Christ, despite the sensual language, is intellectual, resulting in the soul's illumination. Another influential concept Origen explores in his commentary on the Song is the idea of the "senses of the soul," which are counterparts to the five bodily senses (so, the reference at the start of the Song to receiving a physical kiss actually refers, he thought, to the soul receiving the wisdom of the Logos). Together, the spiritual senses give the soul the sensitivity to "tune in" to God's will.

Origen was also influential in formulating the idea that the soul's journey to God has three progressive stages, which he characterized as: practice of the virtues; natural contemplation of the world and a realization that it is essentially ephemeral; and contemplation of God. This threefold division would later be developed by Gregory of Nyssa and Dionysius the Areopagite, the latter terming the stages purgative, illuminative, and unitive, the form in which they became famous in the later Middle Ages.

Another mystical theme Origen helped to establish was the superiority of the contemplative life over the active life (though both must work in tandem). He found support for this in Luke 10:38–42, the occasion when Jesus visits the sisters Mary and Martha (representing for Origen the ideals of contemplation and action, respectively) and defends Mary's "inaction" in the face of Martha's criticism. Some of Origen's insightful thoughts on contemplation can be found in his short treatise *On Prayer*, in which he talks about the mystical transference of the "eyes of the mind" from the objects of the sensible world to the contemplation of God alone—those eyes will then reflect the glory of God and be transformed into that

20

divine splendor. Origen describes the effect this divine radiance has on the individual soul:

> For when the eyes of thought are lifted up from dwelling on earthly things and being filled with the imagination of material objects, and are elevated to such a height as to look beyond begotten things and to be engaged solely in contemplation of God ... Surely those eyes themselves have already got the highest advantage in reflecting the glory of the Lord with face unveiled and being transformed into the same image from glory to glory, for they then partake of a certain divine perception shown by the words: "The light of your face, O Lord, hath been signalized upon us" [Psalm 4:6]. And indeed the soul being lifted up, and parting from body to follow spirit, and not only following the spirit but also merging in it, as is shown by the words "Unto you have I lifted my soul," is surely already putting off its existence as soul and becoming spiritual.[15]

For Origen, prayer is not just a matter of directing a petition or supplication or thanksgiving to God, but should be a way of life. At the heart of prayer is the practice of the commandments and virtues, so that it consists of a continuous round of holy actions, thoughts, and words. The life of the saint then becomes one extended ceaseless prayer.[16]

Plotinus (ca. 204–270)

Origen's teacher Ammonius Saccas was also the master of Plotinus, one of the great philosophers and mystics of history. Although Plotinus was not a Christian, it has been said that "no single man outside the Bible has exerted, directly or indirectly, so great an influence as Plotinus on the thought of Christian mystics."[17] Drawing on the works of Plato as well as later Platonic thinkers, Plotinus constructed a hierarchical system of reality that had circular rhythm: on the one hand, God, the ineffable, undifferentiated One, flowed out, or emanated, down through intermediary levels to the universe and the world of matter; on the other, individual souls sought to ascend and return to their divine home and unite with the One. His works, which are known as the *Enneads* (from the Greek for "nine," because they were arranged by Plotinus's pupil Porphyry into six groups of nine sections), deeply influenced Augustine and Dionysius the Areopagite and through them the Christian mystics of the Middle Ages. Plotinus himself experienced mystical ecstasies on a number of occasions, when he was lifted out of his body "into himself" and had the sense of "becoming external to all other things," witnessing "a wonderful beauty" and feeling that he was united with the divine, before eventually descending again to normal consciousness.[18]

According to Porphyry, Plotinus was born in about 204—he was probably an Egyptian with a Greek cultural background—and studied in Alexandria for eleven years. In 242 he apparently joined the military expedition led by the Roman emperor Gordian III against the Persians, although it is unclear in what capacity he went. He later moved to Rome, where he established himself as a teacher of philosophy, attracting pupils of different ethnic backgrounds and gender, with many of them drawn from among the intelligentsia, including politicians and doctors. He also became friendly with Emperor Gallienus (r. 253–268), through whom he hoped to fulfill his ambition to found a city in Campania near Naples that would be run according to the ideals of Plato (it was to be called Platonopolis), but his plans were never realized.

Plotinus taught in Rome for twenty-five years, living through a period of political turmoil. He gained a reputation for being gentle, kindly, good-humored, and an inspiring teacher; Porphyry said that when he spoke "his intellect lit up even his face."[19] He was greatly respected by one and all and was frequently entrusted with the care of orphaned children, a role he seems to have relished. Just before his death, suffering from a serious illness, he retired to Campania, where he passed away in 270. With his last words he declared that he was trying to return the divine in himself to the divine in the all, which succinctly articulates his aspiration for humankind.

In the *Enneads*, Plotinus sets out his vision of three descending levels or stages (often called hypostases) of reality, which are distinct from one another but also interpenetrating. At the top is the One, or the Good, sometimes referred to as God, although it is not a personal deity like the Christian God. The One is the first principle and is prior to all things that exist, and it is that to which all things aspire to reach. It is so transcendent that it is beyond all categories. Nothing at all can be predicated of it, not even terms such as *being*, *essence*, or *life*. Nor can it be described in words or thought of or understood in any way.

From the One comes the second hypostasis, known as Mind, or Intelligence (some refer to it by the original Greek word, *Nous*). Unlike the conscious act of creation of the Christian God, the One produces Mind through a timeless emanation or flowing-out, not through choice but because, Plotinus says, something good will naturally engender a reality that is less than itself. Plotinus compares this process of emanation to the way that a fire produces heat or the sun creates light.

So the One produces Mind, the second level of reality, and Mind is the timeless and spaceless realm of the archetypes, that is, Plato's Forms or Ideas. (For Plato, reality was divided into the material, sensible world of everyday objects and the immaterial, intelligible realm accessed by intellectual contemplation and consisting of the unchanging models, or Forms, of things, for example Beauty and Love. That which exists in the material world is only a copy or a shadow of a divine original in the realm of Forms. So a person's love for another is merely a copy of the Form of Love.) In Plotinus's scheme, the Forms exist in Mind individually, but each one also contains all the others in a system of mutual interpenetration.

From Mind there emanates the third and last hypostasis, Soul, which acts as a link between our everyday world and the suprasensible realm above it. (It might be added here that it was relatively easy for Christian Platonists to associate Plotinus's triad of the One, Mind, and Soul with the Trinity of Father, Logos [Son], and Spirit.) Soul, the third emanation, has two aspects: the higher one still participates in the realm of Mind, while the lower creates the things of our world—based on the archetypal models that it contemplates in Mind—and gives life and order to everything. Soul not only exists as a universal realm, or as the World Soul, but is also present, in whole, in all forms of life, including, of course, human beings. And just as the World Soul has a higher and lower aspect, so too does the human soul: the higher part can be united with Mind, which shines in and illumines it, whereas the lower part is conformed to sense perception and the external world.

At the furthest point from the One there is matter, which is described as nonbeing. While the One is the manifestation of the highest reality, matter is the embodiment of the lowest and is accounted evil, or rather, the deprivation of good. Although the soul can partake of the divine, it can also, through the encroachment of matter, which subjects the will, become subservient to the body and estranged from its higher nature: trapped in flesh, the soul forgets its true self and God. Yet Plotinus does not say that the material world is evil in itself (unlike the Gnostics, whose ideas he attacked): rather, it was created by Soul from immutable models and is full of beautiful things, which lead us to look beyond them to their divine causes and origins.

So the true vocation of the individual soul is to break free from the chains of flesh and rise to the realm of Mind and thence to God, the Good. The soul must practice detachment, leaving behind its attraction to physical beauty in the realization that it is merely a trace or shadow of something greater, and it must become purified of the corporeal accretions it has gained in the world. Plotinus likens this process to a sculptor of a statue who chips away and polishes a block of stone until he creates a beautiful face. So must we labor at our own inner statues, chiseling and honing, until the divine "splendour of virtue" shines out.[20] Through contemplation the soul can ascend to Mind and achieve union with it, a prelude to union with the One.

Drawing on his personal experience of union, Plotinus famously describes it as the "flight of the alone to the Alone."[21] He says that the One is always before us but that we do not fix our gaze on it because we are too distracted. We are like members of a choir who do not look at their conductor for direction: when they do, they are able to sing with great beauty. If we do receive a glimpse of the divine light, the temptation is to question whether it came from within or without, whereas all we can really say is that we saw it and now we do not. We cannot chase such an experience but only prepare ourselves for it and wait calmly, as we would wait for the sun to rise above the horizon. There is no quick shortcut to union; the cardinal virtues must be observed, and we must be patient in our contemplation. If we do so we might reach the state in which the observer is one with the observed; there is no movement, passion, and desire; mental activity, including self-consciousness, is in abeyance; and the soul, now "filled with God," resides in stillness and tranquility, having become restfulness itself.[22]

2

DESERTS AND MONASTERIES

Thou didst beat back the weakness of my sight, streaming forth Thy beams of light upon me most strongly, and I trembled with love and awe.

—Augustine of Hippo

After the Roman general Constantine became emperor of the Western Roman Empire in 312 (then emperor of the Eastern half in 324), the status of the church changed dramatically. It is said that before his decisive battle against his imperial rival Maxentius (r. 306–312), Constantine was encouraged by a vision he saw in the sky of the cross, which he attributed to the Christian faith; after his victory he showed his gratitude by making the faith the most favored in the empire. Clergy were excused taxes and municipal duties; the church was legally allowed to inherit property; financial penalties for celibacy were repealed; and Sunday was recognized as a holiday. The emperor ensured funds were made available for building churches, and in 330 he founded with Christian ceremonies his new eastern capital of Constantinople by remodeling the town of Byzantium on the Bosporus. He himself became involved in church affairs, presiding over the Council of Nicaea in 325. (The council condemned the Arian heresy, the view put forward by an Alexandrian presbyter named Arius that Jesus Christ was created by God the Father from nothing and was therefore a creature subject to change and not truly divine—against the orthodox view that Christ was both fully human and fully divine. The controversy rumbled on for most of the century until Arianism was finally vanquished at the Council of Constantinople in 381.)

After Constantine's death in 337, his successors continued to support the church—except for Emperor Julian the Apostate (r. 361–363), who tried in vain to reestablish paganism as the state religion. By the end of the fourth century Emperor Theodosius I (r. 379–395) had made heresies punishable offenses and had banned pagan sacrifices and destroyed temples, effectively making the empire an orthodox Christian state (although pockets of paganism did continue to survive). But even as the church became part of the establishment, enjoying its newfound status, many Christians rejected life in the world, with all its material distractions, and journeyed to desert places in Egypt and Syria to pursue ascetic lives dedicated to God. These "Desert Fathers," such as Antony of Egypt and Pachomius, and "Desert Mothers," including Syncletica of Alexandria and Mary of Egypt, thus started the monastic tradition that over the centuries became a great breeding ground of Christian mystics. The impulse behind the desert movement has been characterized as a desire for "white martyrdom," a dying to the world at a time when "red martyrdom"—death at the hands of the imperial authorities—was no longer an issue in the new Constantinian dispensation.[1] The modern theologian Karl Barth called it "a highly responsible and effective protest and opposition to the world, and not least to a worldly Church."[2]

Best known of these first monks (the word *monk* derives from the Greek for "alone") was Antony, who lived as a hermit on a mountain in Egypt, eventually attracting other solitaries to the area. In 305 he formed these hermits into a loosely knit group that was obedient to a rule but maintained the eremitical, or hermit-like, life. A contemporary of Antony's named Pachomius is said to have started the "cenobitical" tradition of monasticism (i.e. one based around a communal life) in about 320 near Thebes in Egypt. Pachomius founded a number of monasteries in the area for men and women and instituted a common rule for them. His cenobitical model was favored by Basil of Caesarea, one of the three so-called Cappadocian Fathers (along with his brother Gregory of Nyssa and Gregory of Nazianzus), who introduced it into the Eastern Roman Empire in the latter half of the fourth century.

The cenobitical form of monasticism also reached the West, through the likes of Martin of Tours, the patron saint of France, and

DESERTS AND MONASTERIES

John Cassian (ca. 360–435), a Scythian who had been a disciple of Evagrius Ponticus, a Cappadocian hermit and mystic who made his home in the deserts of Egypt. Cassian brought his desert experience to southern Gaul (France), where, in about 415, he founded two monasteries near Marseilles. By this time the cracks in the Roman Empire were beginning to widen; Rome itself had been sacked by the Visigoths in 410, an almost unimaginable event to contemporaries. It prompted the greatest theologian of the age, Augustine, to begin writing his magnum opus, *The City of God*, as an attempt to defend Christianity against its pagan enemies, who attributed the demise of the Eternal City to Christianity's usurpation of pagan worship.

The Desert Fathers and Mothers (ca. from the third to the fifth century)

Committed to the ideal of apostolic poverty and living in the deserts of Egypt, Palestine, Syria, and elsewhere, the male and female hermits and monks known as the Desert Fathers and Mothers attempted to live their lives as an embodiment of Jesus's words: "If you want to be perfect, go, sell your possessions and give to the poor, and you will have treasure in heaven. Then come, follow me" (Matthew 19.21). Setting up rudimentary dwellings in various wildernesses, these hardy, single-minded individuals strove to live in rugged landscapes of rock and sand, inhabited by wild animals and, they believed, angels and demons. By embracing humble, stripped-down lives—their possessions often amounted to little more than a reed mat for sleeping on, a lamp, a water jug, and a sheepskin—they created a model of simple living and hospitality that would remain the ideal of Christian asceticism for centuries. By the late fourth century, these hermits were being sought out by spiritual seekers who came to them to ask questions about the religious life. The short, sage answers given in response were remembered and written down to form the *Apophthegmata Patrum* (*Sayings of the Fathers*), which also included sayings of the Desert Mothers.

"Father of Monks" and the guiding spirit of the Desert Fathers, Antony (sometimes Anthony) of Egypt (ca. 251–356) inherited his Christian faith from his parents, who were Egyptian peasant farmers. In his mid-thirties Antony sought out a permanent spiritual retreat in an abandoned fort on a mountain near the Nile. Over the years

DAZZLING DARKNESS

(from about 285 to 305), followers established themselves in caves and huts near his retreat, imploring him to be their spiritual teacher. Eventually, in about 305, he emerged from his eyrie and organized these early monks into a community. After several years, however, he again sought the solace of isolation, this time on a mountain near the Red Sea. There he remained until his death, reputedly at the age of 105.

Stories about Antony's life, including his legendary battles with the devil, are known from the *Life of Antony* by Athanasius of Alexandria (296–373), as well as from the *Sayings*. According to the *Life*,

> [Antony] kept vigil to such an extent that he often continued the whole night without sleep; and this not once but often, to the marvel of others. He ate once a day, after sunset, sometimes once in two days, and often even in four. His food was bread and salt, his drink, water only. Of flesh and wine it is superfluous even to speak, since no such thing was found with the other earnest men.[3]

Antony is important in the history of Christian mysticism not only for being one of the most thorough practitioners of asceticism, the cornerstone of mystical endeavor down the centuries, but also for his reputation for visions, healings, and clairvoyance: "Some say of Saint Antony that he was 'Spirit-borne', that is, carried along by the Holy Spirit ... Such men see what is happening in the world, as well as knowing what is going to happen."[4] Many of his visions involved battles against the devil, who would apparently probe for Antony's weak spots, perhaps appearing as a seductive woman, or a monk offering him bread during a fast, or a wild animal. On one occasion, for example, the devil assailed him by means of desert hyenas. But in this situation, as in others, Antony was able to withstand the beasts by using the power of Christ as a shield: "If ye have received power against me I am ready to be devoured by you; but if ye were sent against me by demons, stay not, but depart, for I am a servant of Christ."[5]

Antony's visionary experiences were not always terrifying. On one occasion, when suffering from accidie, he prayed to God and shortly afterward saw nearby a man like himself plaiting a rope; this man then got up to pray and returned to his work, before again

DESERTS AND MONASTERIES

rising to pray. His "double" turned out to be an angel, setting him an example: prayer must be combined with practical work. Indeed, despite being a demanding ascetic, Antony was rooted in this world, quick to advocate charity and brotherly love: "Our life and our death is with our neighbor. If we gain our brother, we have gained God, but if we scandalize our brother, we have sinned against Christ."[6]

Next to Antony, the most influential of the Desert Fathers was Pachomius (292–348), an Egyptian born of pagan parents. Pachomius may have had direct mystical experiences—according to legend the monastic rule he formulated was dictated to him by an angel[7]—but his importance in the history of Christian mysticism is as the founder of the monastic *coenobium* (community), an environment that would be conducive to the contemplative life down the ages.

While serving as a conscript in the Roman army as a young man, Pachomius came into contact with Christians during military service at Thebes, on the Nile; he was impressed by the way local Christians gave help to those who needed it—even if they were strangers. On leaving the army in about 314 he decided to commit himself to the faith. He was baptized in the same year.

Over time, Pachomius developed a vision of the solitary life that was crucially different to that of Antony: whereas the latter favored a loose-knit arrangement of hermits, living separate lives in caves and stone dwellings, meeting only occasionally for worship or a meal, Pachomius believed the most effective and profound way of religious life lay in community. To this end, in about 320, he founded a monastic settlement at Tabennisi, on the banks of the Nile in Upper Egypt, instituting a cenobitic structure that emphasized cooperation and communality, lessons he had no doubt absorbed from army life.

Pachomius's monastic rule was designed to be kindly to those who struggled to conform to the strictest regimes; but it also gave support to those committed to more stringent practices. Monks would pray, work, and eat together (though provision was made for those who sought the silence of their cells at mealtime—water, salt, and bread were delivered to their cells). The rule was hierarchical, strict, and orderly, a state of affairs maintained by Pachomius's spiritual successors after his death. Everybody knew his place and

DAZZLING DARKNESS

what was expected of him. Monks had to seek permission from their superiors to do the most everyday of activities, such as shaving their heads or changing their clothes. Even taking out a splinter from one's flesh with tweezers needed permission.[8] In this way Pachomius began the communal monastic tradition that would become the seedbed of contemplative practice and reach its high point in the Middle Ages.

Down the centuries, monks and hermits in Egypt, Palestine, and Syria were able to retain their spiritual power and authority by demonstrating to their followers their commitment to austerity, a sine qua non in the fight against the devil and his wiles. At times, however, austere practices seemed like competitions in sheer physical endurance, as monks deprived themselves of sleep, food, or cleanliness. In Syria some ascetics began to show their determination to remove themselves from the world, literally, by living on top of stone columns. Most famous of these was Simeon Stylites (ca. 390–459)—his name comes from the Greek, *stylos*, a "pillar"—a Syrian shepherd who spent about forty years of his life living in a human bird's nest. According to the Syriac *Life*, his first column, topped by a balustraded platform, was a modest six feet high, but this was extended over time and eventually towered about sixty feet above the ground.[9] Food and water were brought to him by followers via a ladder. But Simeon's attempts to escape the world backfired: his column became a magnet for the faithful, who would crowd around it, seeking his blessings.

Simeon Stylites became a byword for ascetic excesses; but he was also a figure who captured the imagination with his gravity-defying feat. Lord Alfred Tennyson's poem, "St. Simeon Stylites," presented the saint's voice to a Victorian audience, and suggested the type of mind that corroborates spiritual progress with physical pain: "O Jesus, if thou wilt not save my soul, / Who may be saved? Who is it may be saved? / Who may be made a saint, if I fail here?" Simeon also captured the imagination of his contemporaries. During the centuries after his death, more than 100 solitaries took to living atop columns in Syria and Asia Minor. Like "living ladders to heaven … Stylites often became major players in Church politics, shouting down their theological pronouncements from their little elevated balconies to the expectant crowds below."[10]

30

DESERTS AND MONASTERIES

The early Christian hermits and monks of the deserts comprised not only men: significant numbers of women—popularly known as the Desert Mothers, or Ammas ("Holy Mothers")—also practiced asceticism in caves and shelters in Egypt, Palestine, and Syria. According to the Galatian monk and historian Palladius (ca. 364–420), there were almost 3,000 women living Christian lives in solitude in the deserts of Egypt, and many in time formed communities (sometimes in conjunction with male communities) under the supervision of a leader and with a set of rules for guidance, spending their days in worship, reading, praying, and household duties. This pattern of monastic life would eventually become established in Western Europe as well.[11] Knowledge of these women is relatively scant, compared to their male equivalents, whose lives were well documented in male monastic traditions. Three of them are referred to by name (Amma Sarah, Amma Theodora, and Amma Syncletica) in the *Sayings of the Desert Fathers*, and many are mentioned in Palladius's *Lausiac History*.

Why did so many women—often treated with hostility by male hermits, who saw them as agents of temptation and sin—fly from society to a barren, unforgiving world of sand and solitude? It has been suggested that a "love for Christ, the coercion of the family, and a fear of social disorder" were common reasons.[12] The *Lives* of the Mothers show certain typical patterns. Many, for example, fled to the desert to avoid an unwanted marriage; others wished to redeem a life of fornication. Once in the desert, the women would often dress in male clothing for security (women could easily be attacked by male hermits, convinced they were demons in disguise[13]) then establish themselves in a secluded place. Indeed, this outward adoption of maleness could be mirrored by an inward sense of masculinity, which might be used as a defense in the face of male hostility. Amma Sarah, for example, was once visited by two elderly anchorites, intent on making sure she knew her lowly status as a woman. Rather than asserting her femaleness, Sarah said to them: "According to nature I am a woman, *but not according to my thoughts*"[14] (author's emphasis).

Not much is known of Amma Sarah. She is thought to have lived in northern Egypt, possibly near the Nile, during the fifth century. There she lived a solitary ascetic life and "waged warfare against the demon of fornication" for thirteen years.[15] This spirit appeared to her on one occasion in a male human form and after trying to seduce her eventually admitted defeat, declaring that she had overcome him—to which Sarah retorted that it was not herself but Christ who had conquered him. Her few recorded sayings include: "I put out my foot to ascend the ladder, and I place death before my eyes before going up it." This sense of spiritual urgency is balanced by her worldly concern and the spiritual effect of giving: "It is good to give alms for men's sake. Even if it is only done to please men, through it one can begin to seek to please God."[16] That she wielded authority and charisma even in a world of male hermits is shown by the fact that a delegation of monks from the town of Scetis in northern Egypt came to visit her one day, bringing with them a basket of fruit. Inspecting the fruits they found some had gone rotten and ate these, leaving Sarah with the good ones—an action she duly commended them for.[17]

Amma Theodora is even more of a shadowy figure than Sarah, but it is reported in the *Sayings* that she addressed questions to Archbishop Theophilus of Alexandria (385–412), which places her life at the end of the fourth and beginning of the fifth century. Her pronouncements include an exhortation that we should not avoid challenges but use them to grow spiritually: "Just as the trees, if they have not stood before the winter's storms cannot bear fruit, so it is with us; this present age is a storm and it is only through many trials and temptations that we can obtain an inheritance in the kingdom of heaven."[18] She also warns of the perils of the solitary life. With peace and quiet comes the spiritual lethargy known as "accidie" and lack of courage and sinful thoughts. She cites the example of a monk who overcame illness by willpower and faith in prayer. Afflicted by fever, he reasoned "I am ill, and near to death; so now I will get up before I die and pray." By forcing himself to do this he managed to cure himself.[19] In other words, withdrawal from the world is only the start of the spiritual challenge, not an end in itself; one still has to use willpower and prayer.

She also emphasized that the only effective way to counter evil was humility—not vigils, suffering, or other ascetic practices. She gives the example of an anchorite who, after he had frightened off demons, was able to ask them what it was that gave him the power to

DESERTS AND MONASTERIES

vanquish them: "Is it fasting?" "We do not eat or drink," they replied. "Is it vigils?" "No, we do not sleep," came their rejoinder. "Is it the fact that I live away from the world?" "No, we too live in deserts." "So what power can banish you?" "Nothing except humility."[20]

Apart from Sarah and Theodora, the two most significant Ammas were arguably Mary of Egypt (d. 421?) and Syncletica of Alexandria (mid-fourth–mid-fifth century), both of whom became renowned for radically changing their lives and withdrawing from the world. Syncletica was a well-to-do Alexandrian woman whose pronouncements are recorded in *The Sayings of the Desert Fathers* and whose *Life* was written by Pseudo-Athanasius (an anonymous churchman claiming to be Athanasius), in the middle of the fifth century. According to her *Life* (which is really a collection of sayings attributed to her), she was born into a wealthy family and from an early age committed herself to a life of virtue and chastity, resisting pressure to take a husband. After her parents' death, she made a decisive break from the world: taking her blind sister with her, she withdrew to the site of a tomb beyond the city, cut off her hair, gave her possessions away, and began her life as a recluse.[21]

Residing at her tomb and removed from everyday society, Syncletica embraced asceticism, practicing poverty and prayer. As news of her renunciation spread, she began to attract dedicated followers, to whom she would give spiritual guidance, championing Christian virtues such as humility and chastity, and warning against vices such as anger, gossiping, perjury, and jealousy. In the *Sayings of the Fathers*, Syncletica suggests that she has engaged in the struggle toward mystical union with God and has experienced its reward of "ineffable joy." She describes this spiritual journey in terms of lighting a fire: at first we are choked by the smoke and our eyes stream, but then we obtain our end: thus, "we also must kindle the divine fire in ourselves through tears and hard work."[22]

Syncletica lived until her mid-eighties and died from a painful, heroically endured illness. It is said these last afflictions were caused by assaults by the devil, who took away her voice in order to prevent her "divine words" from reaching her companions, who were nevertheless strengthened in their faith by witnessing her patient suffering. As death approached, she experienced "visions and the power of angels, and exhortations of holy virgins to the ascension" and was "illuminated by ineffable light, and the land of paradise."[23]

If Syncletica embraced the ascetic life relatively young, Mary of Egypt came to it at a more mature age after living as a prostitute on the streets of Alexandria for about twenty years (her story is recounted in her *Life*, the authorship of which is ascribed to Sophronius [560–638], patriarch of Jerusalem).[24] Mary's years in the desert, living naked and subsisting mainly on a "diet of herbs," were as ascetic as those of any of the Fathers, and she became an iconic example of the holy penitent, appearing as such in Goethe's *Faust* (Part Two, Act V) and Mahler's Symphony No. 8. The modern British composer John Tavener also memorialized her in his opera *Mary of Egypt*, in which he emphasized the possibility of fundamental personal transformation.

At one point in her life, Mary left the seedy quarters of Alexandria to travel to Jerusalem on a pilgrim boat, not for the sake of piety, however, but to ply her trade with the sailors. Even being in the holiest city of Christendom did nothing to deter her from continuing her profession—until the Feast of the Exaltation of the Cross. When she tried to enter the Church of the Holy Sepulcher she found herself mysteriously repelled by an invisible force:

> Again my feet trod on the doorstep over which others were entering the church without encountering any obstacle. I alone seemed to remain unaccepted by the church. It was as if there was a detachment of soldiers standing there to oppose my entrance. Once again I was excluded by the same mighty force and again I stood in the porch. Having repeated my attempt three or four times, at last I felt exhausted and had no more strength to push and to be pushed, so I went aside and stood in a corner of the porch.[25]

It proved to be the catalyst for her profound remorse for her past life of degradation. At this moment of acute distress, she prayed to the Virgin Mary to be allowed to worship inside the church, pledging that she would give up her sensual life if her prayer were granted. The Virgin took mercy on her, allowed her in, and Mary remained true to her word. Shortly after her conversion it is said she heard a mysterious voice telling her that her salvation lay on the far side of the Jordan River. Mary obeyed this calling straightaway: she crossed

DESERTS AND MONASTERIES

the river and made her habitation in the desert, spending the next five decades living there.

The last year of her life, according to Sophronius, was marked by a chance encounter with a priest and monk named Zosima (also Zosimas), who had ventured forth into the desert to spend Lent there. When he stumbled across Mary, she fled from him, ashamed of her naked body. Only when he had given her his cloak to wear did she consent to talk to him. He was immediately struck by her spiritual insight and the way she had known his name and profession as a priest without ever having met him before. He also discovered she could quote from the scriptures, even though she had never read them or met anyone who might have taught them to her.

Mary told Zosima the story of her life and made him promise to return the following year, on Holy Thursday, and to give her the sacrament. He duly turned up, as arranged, and granted her request. She then asked him to meet her at a certain date during the course of the year at the same place where they had originally met. This, again, he did, but when he reached the rendezvous he found her dead body lying on the ground, her face turned toward the rising sun and her arms crossed; beside her was a written message asking him to bury her and indicating that she had in fact died on the very night she had received the sacrament from him. Zosima duly buried her and returned to his monastery, and kept alive the memory of their encounters and conversations, which formed the basis of her *Life*.

Gregory of Nyssa (ca. 335–395)

During the fourth century, the region of Cappadocia in what is now modern Turkey produced three outstanding churchmen, Basil the Great (ca. 329–79), his younger brother Gregory of Nyssa, and their friend Gregory of Nazianzus (ca. 325–89). Of the three, Basil was probably the most significant church figure for his work in establishing communal monasticism in Eastern Christendom, while his brother Gregory of Nyssa was the most mystical. Born in the mid-to-late 330s in Caesarea in Cappadocia, Gregory of Nyssa at first resisted a career in the church and married, becoming a teacher of rhetoric. But he was eventually drawn into the ecclesiastical

35

fold, and in 371 his brother Basil appointed him, against his will, bishop of Nyssa, a small town on the river Halys about ten miles from Caesarea. Eight years later, after Basil's death, Gregory took up the baton of leadership of the church in the East. In 381 he played a significant role at the Council of Constantinople, which the emperor Theodosius I had convened to end Arianism and establish orthodoxy for good. Not much is known of Gregory's subsequent life, except that it was one of prayer, contemplation, preaching, and writing.

Gregory's thoughts on mysticism are found in various works, including *On Virginity*, *Commentary on the Song of Songs*, and *Life of Moses*, in which Moses's ascent to God on Mount Sinai typifies the soul's climb to divine reality—Gregory may have been the first to use this image of spiritual ascent, which was later brought to fulfillment by Dante in his *Divine Comedy*. Gregory shows his debt to the Platonist tradition in *On Virginity*, his earliest work, in which he states that to reach the goal of absolute beauty—the desired end of Platonists—it is necessary to become detached from the things of this world, such as the desire for money, honor, and fame, and transient sensual pleasures.[26] All of these must be left behind as the soul rises on its spiritual quest. Our "powers of loving" must be cleansed from their attraction to base things, and as the soul ascends higher, it will come to realize the glory that exists above the heavens. It will become as beautiful and radiant as the Beauty and Light it has reached. Gregory then compares this process of spiritual illumination to the phenomenon of shooting stars. He refers to the contemporary theory that the gleams of light produced by shooting stars are caused by air around the earth being forced upward by blasts and irrupting into the ether (the upper regions of the sky), where it changes into the ether's luminous light. In a similar way the mind, under pressure from the spirit, enters the "true Purity" and takes on a radiant form. Gregory also compares illumination to a mirror or smooth expanse of water that can reflect light and shine when shone upon, but only if the surface is unstained and perfect: in other words, the soul must be pure and spotless if it is to be filled with and reflect back the divine light.[27]

Gregory eventually grew away from Platonism, as shown by his emphasis on the central place of feeling in the spiritual life and his

DESERTS AND MONASTERIES

stress that an unbridgeable divide separates the uncreated realm of the Trinity from the created world.[28] Therefore the soul, which is part of the created order—whereas for Platonists the soul was divine—cannot cross over into the uncreated sphere. Yet although the soul cannot know God directly, it can approach him, unknowable though he is, through the incarnate Christ.

Like Origen, Gregory sees the spiritual progress of the soul in three, sometimes overlapping, stages. In his eleventh homily on the Song of Songs, Gregory describes how the soul progresses through light, cloud, and darkness. The first stage (light) corresponds to the enlightenment that comes when our benighted views of God have been corrected. The second (cloud) involves a groping through the sensible world toward the realm of the invisible. The last (darkness) comes when the soul has progressed to the "secret chamber of divine darkness" and, with sense perception and reason now irrelevant, it can contemplate the divine mystery. As he says elsewhere: "The true vision and the true knowledge of what we seek consists precisely in not seeing, in an awareness that our goal transcends all knowledge and is everywhere cut off from us by the darkness of incomprehensibility."[29]

Gregory's speculation on the "divine darkness" and the incomprehensible nature of God is what is called negative theology, which, as we shall see, was more fully developed by Dionysius the Areopagite. In a similar "negative" way, Gregory described the soul's ascent to God as a never-ending journey—a correlative to the fact that God himself is boundless. This reaching out, or *epektasis*, for God is fulfilled only with a further desire to reach him. It is as if when having enjoyed the satisfaction of climbing to the top of a hill, we then see there is a higher peak beyond, which inspires us to continue our journey, until we see there is yet another higher peak, and so on ad infinitum.

Evagrius Ponticus (ca. 345–399)

One of the profoundest students of the Cappadocian Fathers, Evagrius Ponticus was a hermit, sage, and spiritual writer and "one of the first who made contemplative prayer the essence of monastic life and thus linked the forces of monasticism and mysticism in a powerful way."[30] For Evagrius, prayer in its highest form means contemplation of the Holy Trinity, a blessed state of being, devoid of mental images, that can occur only after the soul has been purified.[31] He was eloquent on mystical prayer, as his treatise *On Prayer* demonstrates, with aphoristic utterances such as: "Try to make your intellect deaf and dumb during prayer; you will then be able to pray;" and, "If you patiently accept what comes, you will always pray with joy."[32] He also made a contribution to negative theology with his idea of "infinite ignorance," which has echoes of Gregory of Nyssa's *epektasis*: whereas lack of knowledge of the created world is rectifiable by natural contemplation, ignorance of the immeasurably mysterious Holy Trinity must be infinite. In a similar vein, souls that reach the unitive state are paradoxically "always satisfied in their insatiability."[33]

Evagrius was born in Cappadocia in about 345. He was ordained a lector, or reader, by Basil the Great, then made a deacon by Gregory of Nazianzus. In 381 Evagrius moved to Constantinople, where he relished the city's intellectual atmosphere. But the entanglements of a love affair and an admonitory vision persuaded him to leave the metropolis of temptations for the more spiritual climate of Jerusalem. In 383 he embraced the eremitical life in the deserts of Egypt, first in Nitria, then Kellia. He lived as a solitary for sixteen years, until his death in 399, gaining a reputation for his asceticism and practical and speculative wisdom. However, his Origenist views on the preexistence of the soul and the idea of *apokatastasis*—that all things are finally restored in Christ at the end of time, so that even the devil will be saved—were eventually condemned at the Second Council of Constantinople in 553. His works were written in short, terse, gnomic chapters, a form that lends itself to meditation.

Influenced by Origen, Evagrius believed that reality consists of three stages (Evagrius is keen on tripartite divisions).[34] In the first, God created spiritual beings known as *logikoi*, who were originally united with the Holy Trinity but then fell from their beatific state through "negligence." The only unfallen *logikos* was Christ, and it is through him that the second creation was brought about. In this second stage, the *logikoi* became one of three entities, depending on their share of negligence: angelic beings, humans, and demons. Each *logikos* has a soul made up of three parts—a rational principle,

DESERTS AND MONASTERIES

desire, and a disposition toward anger, with the rational principle predominating in angels, desire in humans, and anger in demons.

In the third and final stage, the human soul returns to God on a journey that also has three parts to it.[35] The first part, *praktike*, or "active life," involves in effect combating temptation and controlling the passions to arrive at a state of *apatheia*, a term that plays an important part in Evagrius's spirituality and does not mean "apathy" but rather a state of imperturbable peacefulness, or dispassion. In the second part, *physike*, or "natural contemplation," the soul begins to gaze on the created world's underlying principles, which exist in God. In this way it comes to comprehend the workings of demonic powers and so is able to progress to the fulfillment of *apatheia*.

The third part is *theologia*, which is contemplation of God as the Holy Trinity, a unitive state in which the soul experiences no sense of separation from the object of its knowledge. Now it practices what Evagrius refers to as "true prayer," although it is more correct to say that this is not something you do so much as something you are: prayer is not so much a mental act—"For prayer means the shedding of thoughts"[36]—as a way of being.

Martin of Tours (316–397)

The monastic movement was not solely confined to the deserts of Egypt and other parts of the Middle East. Monks and hermits existed in the West, too, and during the fourth century, as happened with the Pachomian movement in Egypt, many of them began to congregate in monastic communities. The leading light of this movement was Martin of Tours—"father of Western monasticism" and patron saint of France—a bishop and missionary who was believed to have had extraordinary spiritual power and visions.

According to his *Life*, written by the chronicler Sulpicius Severus (ca. 363–425), Martin was born in Sabaria (modern Szombathely, in Hungary) and devoted himself to the Christian faith from boyhood (although he was not baptized). On becoming a young adult, he was compelled to enter the Roman army and soon found the prospect of active duty conflicting with his Christian conscience. It was during his time in the ranks that Martin had his legendary encounter with a beggar that prompted the vision that epitomized his charity

DAZZLING DARKNESS

and commitment to the faith. While stationed at Amiens in Gaul (northern France), he spotted at the gates of the city a beggar frozen from the cold. Martin took off his military cloak, tore it in two, and gave one half to the man. That night Martin saw a vision of Christ wearing the half-cloak he had given to the beggar and addressing an entourage of angels with the words: "Martin, who is still but a catechumen, clothed me with this robe." Immediately after this vision, Martin presented himself for baptism.[37]

Martin's stint in the army came to an end shortly after his refusal to fight in battle during a military crisis. Accused of cowardice, he rebutted this claim by declaring he would gladly stand in the front line with only a wooden cross for protection. When the crisis subsided, he exchanged his military career for a spiritual one and sought the spiritual direction of Bishop Hilary of Poitiers (310–368). For the next few years Martin became known as an evangelist, exorcist, and healer: various stories circulated about how he converted a cut-throat robber to the faith, fought the devil, restored to life a slave who had hanged himself, and confronted the followers of the Arian heresy. In about 361 he founded a hermitage at Ligugé, in a valley near Poitiers, and began to attract followers. Soon the hermitage grew into an abbey and became one of the earliest monasteries in Europe.

Martin's destiny as a spiritual organizer and leader took a decisive turn in 371 when, visiting Tours, he was proclaimed bishop of the vacant see by popular acclamation (despite complaints from some quarters about his filthy hair and ragged clothing). As bishop, he promptly founded the monastic settlement of Marmoutier, opposite Tours on the north bank of the Loire. For the rest of his life, using Marmoutier as his base, Martin continued to effect cures, cast out devils, establish monasteries throughout Gaul, and convert pagans, sometimes breaking their power by cutting down their sacred trees or destroying their temples. On one occasion, it seems that Martin voluntarily stood in the path of a falling pine then made it swerve past him by making the sign of the cross, much to the awe of the pagan onlookers. He died in 397 at Candes, about forty miles southwest of Tours.

Martin was more a man of action than a contemplative, but his *Life* suggests he was widely credited with visionary gifts and a

40

profound devotion to prayer: "In truth, just as it is the custom of blacksmiths, in the midst of their work to beat their own anvil as a sort of relief to the laborer, so Martin even when he appeared to be doing something else, was still engaged in prayer."[38] Apart from his vision of Christ wearing his cloak, Martin is also said to have had visions of angels: "It is also well known that angels were very often seen by him, so that they spoke in turns with him in set speech."[39] On one occasion, when failing to destroy a local pagan temple, he prayed for three days for divine aid from God.

> Then two angels, with spears and shields after the manner of heavenly warriors, suddenly presented themselves to him, saying that they were sent by the Lord to put to flight the rustic multitude, and to furnish protection to Martin, lest, while the temple was being destroyed, any one should offer resistance.[40]

Martin is then said to have returned to the village and completed his mission, watched by silent, impotent pagans. But this act of destruction seems to have belied his essentially peaceful nature. As Sulpicius Severus recorded: "No one ever saw him enraged, or excited, or lamenting, or laughing ... he seemed to have passed the ordinary limits of human nature. Never was there any word on his lips but Christ, and never was there a feeling in his heart except piety, peace, and tender mercy."[41]

Augustine of Hippo (354–430)

At about the time that Gregory of Nyssa died and Evagrius was in the last years of his sojourn in the Egyptian wilderness, over in the West a younger contemporary of theirs named Augustine was appointed bishop of Hippo Regius in northern Africa. One of the greatest of Christian churchmen, Augustine was a thinker, preacher, polemicist, and biblical commentator whose writings have had an incalculable effect on the history of the church. His best-known works are the *Confessions*—one of the great spiritual autobiographies, candidly describing his personal life and search for truth up to the point of his conversion to the Christian faith—and *The City of God*.

Augustine's place in the roll call of Christian mystics is still a matter of debate. He did not set out a systematic treatment of mystical theology in the manner of later medieval mystics, but then he lived at a time when there was no differentiation between mystical and dogmatic theology. It was his conviction that it was part of our nature to be restless until we find God, and that contemplation begins in this life but is perfected in the next: "Our hearts find no peace until they rest in you."[42] His high estimation of the contemplative life and his thoughts on the soul's ascent to God can be found in a number of works in his vast corpus—more than 500 sermons, some 200 letters, and 113 books have survived; and it seems from passages in the *Confessions* that he himself enjoyed mystical experiences.

A key element in Augustine's spirituality is the idea that a person's soul is the image of God, and since God consists of the Holy Trinity, this will also be the form of the divine image in human beings. Self-knowledge—another important aspect in Augustine's mysticism—makes the individual realize the need to reform (through divine grace) this interior image of God, which has been deformed by sin, a task which can be achieved by the mediation of Christ. Through the Incarnation, by which Christ partook of mortality, it is possible for man to partake of divinity.

Termed the "prince of mystics" by the modern Benedictine scholar Cuthbert Butler, Augustine was born in 354 in the Roman provincial town of Tagaste in what is now Algeria. His father, Patrick, was a pagan and his mother, Monica, a devout Christian, who brought him up in the faith. At the age of about seventeen Augustine went off to Carthage (in modern Tunisia) to study rhetoric at the university there. Living a somewhat dissipated lifestyle, he fathered an illegitimate son and was drawn toward Manichaeism (a dualistic religion positing a cosmic conflict between the forces of good and evil, light and darkness), which was to dominate his spiritual life for about a decade.

Augustine stayed in Carthage almost continuously until 383, when he moved to Rome to set up a school of rhetoric. A year later he accepted a professorship in Milan. By this time he was disenchanted with his Manichaeism and was becoming attracted to the teachings of the Neoplatonists. He also fell under the spell of Milan's charismatic bishop, Ambrose, whose sermons Augustine admired both for their content and for their elegant style. In 386

DESERTS AND MONASTERIES

he finally converted to Christianity and in the following year was baptized by Ambrose. Shortly after this he returned to Africa and set up a quasi-monastic community in his home town of Tagaste; but his secluded life there was to last only a few years. In 391 he was visiting the town of Hippo Regius on the coast when the townspeople pressed him, against his will, into becoming a priest. Augustine accepted ordination, and by 396 he had become bishop of Hippo, a position he held for the next thirty-four years, until his death. Apart from his considerable pastoral work as bishop, Augustine wrote his great works of theology and philosophy, his biblical exegeses, and his polemics against those groups who threatened the unity and doctrine of the church, namely the Donatists, Manichaeans, and Pelagians. In 413 he began his gargantuan *City of God*, which he continued writing until 426. Two years later the barbarian Vandals invaded northern Africa and by May 430 were laying siege to Hippo. Four months after that, Augustine died and was spared witnessing the fall of the city in the following year.

Although Augustine's mysticism has a pronounced intellectual element, he stressed that love for one's neighbor was a precondition for loving God,[43] and his descriptions of personal mystical experiences in the *Confessions* have infectious warmth and enthusiasm. In book 7, for example, he describes an experience he had in Milan in 386 after reading some Platonist works. He withdrew into himself and saw with the "eye of my soul" the unchangeable light, which lay above his soul not "as oil is above water" nor as "heaven is above earth" but "above to my soul, because It made me; and I below It, because I was made by It." From an almost scientific musing on the nature of the light, the passage becomes increasingly imbued with emotion as Augustine conveys the excitement of his spiritual insight:

> He that knows the Truth, knows what that Light is; and he that knows It, knows eternity. Love knoweth it. O Truth Who art Eternity! and Love Who art Truth! and Eternity Who art Love! Thou art my God, to Thee do I sigh night and day. Thee when I first knew, Thou liftedst me up, that I might see there was what I might see, and that I was not yet such as to see. And Thou didst beat back the weakness of my sight, streaming forth Thy beams of light upon me most strongly, and I trembled with love and awe.[44]

43

DAZZLING DARKNESS

This pattern of withdrawal from the world, turning inward, and seeing a revelatory light bears the stamp of Plotinus.[45] But though influenced by the Neoplatonist, Augustine differed from him crucially in his view of God, divine grace, and people's need for mediation. For Plotinus, the One is impersonal, and the soul, being inherently divine, is always able to ascend to it. For Augustine, God is personal (as one modern scholar has said, "Plotinus never *gossiped* with the One, as Augustine gossips in the *Confessions*"[46]); the soul is fallen and sinful and must rely for its ascent on the intervention of God through the incarnate Christ.

Perhaps the best and most quoted example of Augustine's personal encounters with the divine is the occasion in the *Confessions* when at the port of Ostia in Italy he shared with his mother, Monica—not long before her death in 387—a rapturous ascent of the spirit to the realm of ultimate truth. They were having a philosophical discussion when, Augustine says,

> we rose up with a more ardent affection toward [God] and by degrees passed through all material things, even through heaven from where the sun and moon and stars shine upon the earth; yes, we were soaring higher yet, by inward musing and discourse, and marvelling at Your works; and we came to our own minds, and went beyond them, that we might arrive at that region of never-failing plenty, where You feed Israel forever with the food of truth. ... And while we were discoursing and yearning for her, we for a moment touched on her with the whole effort of our heart; and we sighed, and there we left bound the first fruits of the spirit; and returned to verbal communication, where the spoken word has beginning and end.[47]

Again, the experience has a Neoplatonist feel to it, reminiscent of the idea of the soul's return to its divine home. Yet, as the modern scholar Andrew Louth has pointed out, unlike Plotinus's "flight of the alone to the Alone," Augustine's rapture is personal but not solitary and bears witness to that aspect of his thought that stresses the "social nature of final beatitude."[48]

One important aspect of Augustine's mystical thought that exerted a great influence on the Middle Ages was his analysis of visions. In book 12 of his treatise *Literal Commentary on Genesis*, he

DESERTS AND MONASTERIES

considers the nature of Paul's ecstatic experience, referred to in 2 Corinthians 12:2–4, when he was "caught up to the third heaven," unsure whether he was "in the body or apart from the body." Augustine goes on to categorize visions into three types: corporeal, spiritual (or imaginary), and intellectual. He illustrates these with an example. If we read a sentence that tells us to love our neighbor, our eyes see the physical words on the page as corporeal vision; our spirit or imagination then pictures our neighbor, although he or she is not present before us; and our intellectual vision can "see" the idea of love without the need of images—it, therefore, has the purest vision, the one that results in true knowledge. Spiritual/imaginary visions are not so pure and require divine help to distinguish them from ordinary dreams or the delirium of the sick.[49]

With regard to ecstasy, Augustine says that in this state the mind is withdrawn from sense experience. The person's eyes are open but sights and sounds cannot be seen or heard: the attention of the mind is directed either to the images of a spiritual vision or to the imageless things of an intellectual vision. The soul is "withdrawn from the senses more than is usual in sleep, but less than in death."[50] The highest form of ecstasy is that in which an intellectual vision occurs—as happened to Paul—when, in the words of the modern scholar Frank Tobin, "the soul is freed from carnality and confronts the intellectual object more intensely ... The light which enables the soul to see intellectually is God himself."[51]

Elsewhere, Augustine sets out his thoughts on contemplation in his commentary on Psalms 41 and his treatise *On the Greatness of the Soul*. In the latter, Augustine gives a systematic treatment of the soul's ascent to the divine, enumerating seven stages in the soul's operations, the last four of which correspond to what would become the three traditional divisions of the mystical quest: purgation, illumination, and union. In the first three stages the soul is said to be the principle of life, sensation, and intelligence. In the fourth and fifth the soul is purged and reformed before, in the sixth, it proceeds to the threshold of contemplation. The seventh and last stage is contemplation itself, through which the soul is able to gaze on truth.[52]

In his commentary on Psalms 41 he makes it clear that the starting point of mystical experience is eradicating personal vices,

45

DAZZLING DARKNESS

such as greed and sensuality, hatred and spite. He also outlines how the soul rises to the heights of the divine but then has to return to the realm of mortality and impermanence. More specifically, he describes the light of God as a "light that shall never be darkened," a light that may be seen only by the inward eye, if it has been prepared in the right way. The mind itself, which is subject to change, seeks God, or ultimate truth, which is immutable, but its attempt to find God in material things and in itself is fruitless. God's dwelling place is "above" the soul and is said to be full of angelic music, which "the ears of the heart" can hear as a mysterious and sweet melody—if it has not been drowned out by the sounds of the world. But although we may for a brief moment hear the sound of angelic music and glimpse the unchangeable God, the human condition is such that we must fall back from the heights of divine experience to our everyday condition, with its sorrows, and be filled again with worldly cares and an awareness of our separation from that place of delight. [53]

3

THE EARLY MIDDLE AGES

Holy angels, the citizens of the holy country, clad in white robes and flying with wonderful speed, began to stand around the saint while he prayed.

—Adamnán, describing Columba of Iona

Why the Western Roman Empire "declined" and "fell," to use the traditional terms, unable to resist the incursions of barbarian tribes in the fifth century, is still a matter of debate. Economic problems, societal weaknesses, and poor morale in the army (to which many barbarian soldiers had been recruited) all contributed. There was also a widespread, debilitating political ineptitude characterized by what the historian Peter Brown has called "amateurism, the victory of vested interests, [and] narrow horizons."[1] In any case, the beneficiaries of this situation were Germanic tribes such as the Goths, Franks, and Vandals who, pressured by the westward movement of central Asian peoples, sporadically crossed the imperial borders to little resistance. In 476 the last Western Roman emperor, Romulus Augustulus (r. 475–476), was deposed, and by the early sixth century Germanic tribes had carved out kingdoms within the empire. However, the early Middle Ages, often nicknamed the Dark Ages, which lasted from about the end of the fifth century to the eleventh century, was not without chinks of light. Although infrastructure, communications, and learning within the empire generally declined, barbarian elites did adopt and preserve some of the ways and customs of the conquered, and many were already Christians, albeit mostly of the heretical Arian variety. The exception was in Gaul, where Clovis, king of the Franks, was converted to orthodox Catholicism in 496.

DAZZLING DARKNESS

The church in the West retained a dominant role in this new society, centered on the papacy. Strengthened by Pope Leo I (d. 461), the see of Rome became widely regarded as the supreme authority in the Western church during the dynamic leadership of Gregory I, the Great (r. 590–604), the father of the medieval papacy. At a local level, bishops continued to nurture their communities, and new monasteries were founded that became self-sustaining havens of spirituality and scholarship. Monasticism in the West was consolidated by the Italian monk Benedict of Nursia (ca. 480–547) and his monastic Rule, which emphasized a balanced regime of prayer, study, and manual work. By the ninth century most monasteries in Europe would be following the Benedictine model. Perhaps the most spectacular example of early monastic growth occurred in Ireland, where, the century after the mission of Saint Patrick (ca. 390–460), monasteries were established at Bangor, Derry, Clonard, Clonmacnoise, and elsewhere. From them a stream of Irish monks and *peregrini* (from the Latin for "pilgrim"), such as Columba and Columbanus—with their English counterparts not far behind—made tracks to various parts of Europe to reinvigorate the faith, convert pagans, and found new monasteries.

By the 700s, the impetus of the Irish missions faltered as the Continental church became better organized, especially during the reign of the Frankish king Charlemagne (r. 768–814), who was crowned Holy Roman Emperor by Pope Leo III in 800. Charlemagne tightened ecclesiastical discipline and unified liturgical practices. He also stimulated learning, standardized laws, and expanded the Carolingian empire. Yet it was during Charlemagne's generally enlightened reign and his revival of culture and scholarship that Western Europe began to suffer from the depredations of the Vikings and, later, Muslim pirates in the Mediterranean and the Magyars from the Asian steppes. Only in the later tenth century was relative peace restored.

Although the Western Roman Empire had succumbed to the barbarian incursions, the Eastern empire (which became known as the Byzantine Empire) survived for another 1,000 years until its fall to the Ottoman Turks in 1453. Its capital, Constantinople, gained in prestige from being the home of the sole Roman emperor; and the city's bishop, the patriarch, acquired a status that was second only to

THE EARLY MIDDLE AGES

that of the pope. During the sixth century, Byzantine armies invaded Africa, Spain, and northern Italy to reclaim imperial territory, with some, albeit temporary, success.

In the seventh century, however, the map of the eastern Mediterranean and the security of the empire changed permanently with the rise of Islam. Founded by the Prophet Muhammad, who died in 632, the Muslim faith fanned out from Arabia, with its armies quickly conquering Persia, Palestine, Syria, and parts of Asia Minor in the East, and the coastal lands of northern Africa in the West. In 711 a Muslim Arab and Berber army invaded and conquered most of Spain, its advance into France checked in 732 at the battle of Poitiers. Constantinople itself remained unvanquished, but from now on its perennial concern would be with survival rather than expansion.

Columba (521–597) and the Irish peregrini

Situated on the western edge of the European continent, Ireland became Christianized from the fifth century onward, initially through the efforts of a certain Palladius, a Roman churchman sent by Pope Celestine to be the country's first bishop in 431. But it was Patrick (active in the fifth century), a native-born Briton, who is remembered as Ireland's greatest evangelist, diffusing the word of God throughout the country and laying the foundations for the growth of the faith. During the sixth century, significant monastic communities were founded and the country became renowned for its learned, zealous, and charismatic monks, many of whom took the Gospel abroad, braving desolate places and hostile pagans, and founding influential monasteries such as Bobbio in Italy, Ferrières and Luxeuil in France, and Saint Gall in Switzerland.

These adventurous pioneering monks were often called *peregrini*, a term that signified a particular type of pilgrim: not one with a predetermined destination in mind (such as Rome or Jerusalem), but one who was willing to set out into the unknown, putting faith in God to give direction, and being prepared never to see his homeland again. The *peregrinus* mentality is best exemplified in an incident described in the *Anglo-Saxon Chronicle* for the year 891: three Irishmen made landfall on the coast of Cornwall in a boat that

49

had no oars, the reason being that the men had trusted the wind to blow them wherever God desired them to go. They wished to "live in a state of pilgrimage, for the love of God, they cared not where."[2]

One of the first inspirational figures of these Irish *peregrini* was Columba (or Columkille), famous for making the Scottish island of Iona a monastic center for spirituality and evangelization. Born in Donegal in northwestern Ireland, Columba was descended from Niall of the Nine Hostages, high king of Ireland from 379 to 405. He imbibed the Christian faith wholeheartedly during his time at monastic schools and during his twenties he preached all around Ireland, founding churches and monasteries, including those of Durrow and Kells.

Why Columba settled on Iona and embarked on a mission to the Picts of Scotland is unclear. One tradition suggests that he was sent into exile by a church synod as a punishment for the part he played in an intertribal battle in Ireland. However, in his *Life*, written by the later Ionan monk Adamnán (ca. 628–704), Columba simply left Ireland of his own accord.[3] In any case, according to tradition, Columba set sail from his country with twelve companions in 563 and settled on Iona. These Columban *peregrini* soon established a community, constructing wood-and-wattle huts, an oaken church, and a perimeter fence; and from this base Columba and his monks set out to convert the Scottish mainland, at this time inhabited by a mixture of Picts, Britons, Angles, and Irish. Columba's first successful conversion was the powerful King Brude of the northern Picts, whose kingdom was based at Inverness in the northeast. In the following years, the Columban missionaries continued to convert pagans and found churches, gradually turning Scotland into a Christian nation.

Columba always returned to Iona for spiritual nourishment, praying, meditating, and copying manuscripts. He was also said to have had mystical encounters with the divine and to have performed miracles. On one occasion, for example, he was praying on a hillock named Cnoc an t-Sidhein, when he was visited by angels: "Holy angels, the citizens of the holy country, clad in white robes and flying with wonderful speed, began to stand around the saint while he prayed."[4] On another occasion, a monk named Colga was praying outside the monastic church when he suddenly saw it "filled

THE EARLY MIDDLE AGES

with heavenly light, which more quickly than he could tell, flashed like lightning from his gaze. He did not know that Columba was praying at that time in the church."[5] The association of divine light with Columba was attested by other witnesses. Brendan of Clonfert ("the Navigator"), for example, was visiting Hinba island, near Iona, where Columba was temporarily residing and watched him blessing the bread in chapel. As Columba did so a ball of fire, like a comet, hovered above his head and formed into a column of light, rising from the consecrated bread to heaven.[6]

Other important *peregrini* who were contemporaries of Columba included the aforementioned Brendan (ca. 486–578), and Columbanus (ca. 543–615). Brendan was reputed to have founded the influential monastery of Clonfert in central Ireland, of which he became abbot. But his fame rests on his legendary voyage to find the "Island Promised to the Saints," a story full of marvels and miracles, which became widely known in medieval Europe. The account can also be read as a mystical journey in which Brendan encounters different realms of reality until he reaches his final goal.

According to the story, Brendan and his seventeen fellow monks embarked on a seven-year quest to find their paradisal island, landing on various other islands along the way and encountering mysterious and surreal creatures and events. One island is the home of sheep the "size of bulls." On another one Brendan and his companions are settling in when the island starts moving: it transpires that they have landed on the back of a whale. On the "Paradise of Birds," they see a tree full of psalm-singing white birds, who turn out to be fallen angels. The *peregrini* continue their voyage, returning to the same islands, year after year, in a rhythmic repetition, until they are finally guided to the Island Promised to the Saints. There they are blessed by a mysterious young man and told they must return home. This they do, taking with them gems and fruit to show their brethren back in Clonfert.[7]

If Brendan represents the peregrinal sea-traveler, his terrestrial equivalent was Columbanus, "a man deeply self-conscious of his status as an exile, a *peregrinus*."[8] After training in the Irish monastery of Bangor, Columbanus left Ireland in about 590, determined to be an exile for the sake of the faith. He and his twelve companions landed in Brittany and began their mission to bring Christianity to the pagans of Gaul. Columbanus drove the mission forward with energy and zeal. He founded the monasteries of Annegray, Luxeuil, and Fontaine in Burgundy, created a monastic rule, and, according to the author of his *Life*, Jonas of Bobbio (600–659), performed healings and other miracles. As his following increased, the local bishops became hostile, resenting his popular acclaim and certain liturgical practices. Columbanus managed to overcome this opposition and, over the years, continued his travels through France and parts of Germany and Switzerland. In about 612 he journeyed to northern Italy and settled in the Apennine mountains at a place called Bobbio. The monastery he established there was his last foundation.

Like Columba, Columbanus combined great zeal, charisma, and organizational skills with, as Jonas maintains, mystical gifts. There were stories that he communed with animals, that he performed healings, and that he received visions. For example, at one point in his later missionary career, he was tempted to take the Gospel to the Slavs; but he then received a vision that caused him to proceed, instead, to nearby Italy:

> The angel of the Lord appeared to him in a vision, and showed him in a little circle the structure of the world, just as the circle of the universe is usually drawn with a pen in a book. "You perceive," the angel said, "how much remains set apart of the whole world. Go to the right or the left where you will, that you may enjoy the fruits of your labors."[9]

Columba and Columbanus were pioneers of the early *peregrini*, combining down-to-earth practicality with a mystical awareness of the divine. But many other Irishmen followed in their footsteps as "exiles for Christ." Fiachra (d. ca. 670), for example, established a hermitage in Breuil, east of Paris. Kilian (d. ca. 689) made his way to Bavaria in Germany, converted the local pagan ruler, Gozbert, and was later martyred in Würzburg (where his relics are now kept). And Fursey (ca. 597–650) left Ireland for Britain in about 633, founded a monastery in East Anglia, then, in the 640s, migrated to Gaul and established a monastery in Lagny-sur-Marne near Paris. He died around 650. Fursey was famous for receiving a vision of the afterlife that included a glimpse of hell, an experience that

THE EARLY MIDDLE AGES

was said to have left him with physical scorch marks, as well as the propensity to sweat even in the coldest of temperatures.[10]

Dionysius the Areopagite (active ca. 500)

The most significant—and mysterious—mystical writer of the early Middle Ages was arguably a man who called himself Dionysius the Areopagite (he is also known as Pseudo-Dionysius). For Christians used to conceiving of God in terms of love, light, goodness, and the like, Dionysius is like a gust of cold wind. For Dionysius is arguably the best-known exponent of negative (apophatic) theology. This approach to God is usually compared with affirmative (cataphatic or kataphatic) theology, by which God is given positive attributes that are normally used to describe humans (for example, "wise", "just", "good"), but extended to an infinite degree. Negative theology takes a different approach and involves "the stripping of attitudes, mental images and ideas which are considered to stand in the way of the active pursuit of relationship with God."[11] In other words, it maintains that it is truer to speak of what God is *not* than what he is. This is because God as the ultimate mystery exists beyond our understanding and so beyond all possible concepts or words. In short, nothing at all may be predicated of him. So in his *Mystical Theology*, Dionysius constantly resorts to symbolic or metaphorical language to refer to the ineffable divine—"darkness" being a favorite term. He refers, for example, to the "ray of divine darkness," "the darkness where lives the one which is beyond all things"; and in the opening chapter of the *Mystical Theology* he prays: "Lead us up beyond unknowing and light, up to the farthest, highest peak of mystic scripture, where the mysteries of God's Word lie simple, absolute and unchangeable, in the brilliant darkness of a hidden silence."[12]

Yet for one who lays such stress on the ultimate inadequacy of thought and language to describe the divine, Dionysius can still illuminate with words and images. For example, prayer is compared to the act of grabbing a shining cord hanging down from heaven to this world. As we tug at it, with our hands pulling alternately, we think we are drawing it down, but in fact we are being raised to the divine light. Or it is like being on a ship and pulling on ropes that

53

are tied to a rock to anchor the vessel: whereas we think we are drawing the rock toward our ship, we are in fact moving toward the rock.[13]

For centuries Dionysius the Areopagite was presumed to be the Dionysius whom Paul converted when he was preaching in Athens, as recorded in Acts 17:16–34. In the late nineteenth century, however, scholars showed that the Areopagite's writings were written much later than New Testament times. The consensus is that the author was in fact a Christian Syrian monk living in about 500 who adopted the name of Dionysius to give his writings authority, a practice that was common in the ancient world. Not much else is known about him apart from what can be inferred from his works. These show that he was indebted to Neoplatonic thought as well as to thinkers such as Gregory of Nyssa and Philo of Alexandria, and of course the scriptures. It is strangely fitting that the author who stressed the mystery and darkness of God should himself be shrouded in darkness. Yet his influence has been profound and crystal clear. Many important later mystics, such as Eckhart, Ruysbroeck, and John of the Cross, have dipped their pens into Dionysius's inkhorn of divine darkness, and his *Mystical Theology*, translated into Middle English by the anonymous author of *The Cloud of Unknowing*, was said by a medieval chronicler to have "run across England like deer."[14]

As well as the short *Mystical Theology*, Dionysius wrote three longer treatises: *The Divine Names*, *The Celestial Hierarchy*, and *The Ecclesiastical Hierarchy*. In these latter three works, Dionysius actually adopts an affirmative approach to God, for the affirmation and negation of God are really two sides of the same coin. Although correctly speaking it is false to speak of God as being Good, Just, and so on—because God is essentially unknowable—we may do so unstrictly because he is the cause of goodness or justice in the world.

Dionysius was also concerned, as the Neoplatonists were, with how God, who is beyond everything we know, can be connected with the world in any meaningful way. Taking his cue from the later Neoplatonist Proclus (412–485), Dionysius addresses this problem by asserting that reality consists of different gradations of beings in the form of threefold hierarchies (as for Evagrius Ponticus, triads loom large in Dionysius's thinking). At the peak is the triad of the Holy Trinity; below it is the celestial hierarchy of three groups of

THE EARLY MIDDLE AGES

three orders of angels (seraphim, cherubim, and thrones, followed by dominations, virtues, and powers, then principalities, archangels, and angels). Then comes the terrestrial hierarchy, with another three groups of three orders: the first rank are not people but sacramental rites (Eucharist, baptism, and anointing with oil); the second are bishops, priests, and deacons; and the third are monks, baptized Christians, and catechumens.

For Christians, the first step in their return to God is made through spiritual truths found in the symbolic reality of the liturgy and the Bible. The scheme follows the Neoplatonic pattern of a procession from the One, followed by a return to the source (which for Christians begins with spiritual truths found in the symbolic reality of the liturgy and the Bible). But there is a significant difference between the Neoplatonic system and Dionysius's model: "The Neoplatonic 'One' proceeds into multiplicity and participation as a matter of course; but the Dionysian God *desires* to share himself."[15] Dionysius also saw this graduated order not so much as a ladder of progression, with each group striving to move up a rung, but as a way in which each stratum could fulfill its spiritual potential proper to its place in the grand scheme, thereby becoming assimilated to God.

Yet for all his speculation on the affirmative approach to God and the use of symbols, it is Dionysius's apophaticism, set out in his short but highly influential *Mystical Theology*, for which he is best known. By ridding ourselves of ultimately futile attempts to describe God through his attributes, we draw nearer to the truth about his ineffable nature. Dionysius himself expresses this idea through the image (used by Plotinus) of a sculptor who must chip away at his block of marble before he is able to reveal, as it were, the statue hidden within.[16]

Dionysius advises that the senses and intellectual activity should be left behind and that with the understanding made quiet, we should strain toward union with God, who is beyond all being and understanding. By renouncing the self and all the things of the world, it is possible to be drawn upward to the "ray of divine darkness" that surpasses all existence.[17] He compares the mystic's journey to Moses's ascent of Mount Sinai in the book of Exodus 19–20. For Dionysius, as for Gregory of Nyssa, Moses represents the

DAZZLING DARKNESS

soul questing for God, and he uses the Moses story to illustrate the three stages in the soul's journey to God: the names he coined for these stages—purification, or purgation; illumination; and union—would become the classic formulation for later medieval mystics. First of all, Moses has to undergo purification before he hears the trumpet blast and sees flashes of lightning; he ascends the mountain but sees not God, who is invisible, but "the place where he dwells" (the stage of illumination). In a similar way, a person who perceives the "most high and divine things" must realize that these are merely symbolic of the God who transcends them. They may signify the divine presence "upon the heights of his holy places," but the divine presence then breaks away and plunges the "true initiate" into the darkness of unknowing (the stage of union). In this darkness, with the stilling of his rational mind, he is united to the unknowable God, and "by a rejection of knowledge he possesses a knowledge that exceeds his understanding."[18]

Dionysius ends the *Mystical Theology* with a list of what can be said, or rather what cannot be said, about God. Like his imaginary sculptor, he patiently chips away the excrescences that hinder the vision of ultimate reality and ends up with a triumphant affirmation of negation:

> Once more, ascending yet higher we maintain that It is not soul, or mind, or endowed with the faculty of imagination, conjecture, reason, or understanding; nor is It any act of reason or understanding; nor can It be described by the reason or perceived by the understanding, since It is not number, or order, or greatness, or littleness. ... Nor is It one, nor is It unity, nor is It Godhead or Goodness; nor is It a Spirit, as we understand the term, since It is not Sonship or Fatherhood; nor is It any other thing such as eye or any other being can have knowledge of.[19]

Pope Gregory the Great (ca. 540–604)

Although he did not have Dionysius's flair for speculative theology, Pope Gregory I, the Great, was nevertheless a highly influential figure in the history of Christian mysticism, especially in his role as one of the principal conduits through which patristic spirituality passed to the later Middle Ages and by his emphasis on the

THE EARLY MIDDLE AGES

importance of monastic life in contemplation. For Gregory, the life of contemplation was always an ideal, and he harbored regrets that his public duties prevented him from enjoying it. He was elected pope in 590 during a time of crisis. Rome's existence was being threatened by the barbarian Lombards, and its citizens were dying of plague and hunger. Gregory's heroic efforts in bringing relief to the suffering and organizing the affairs of church and state, as well as promoting monasticism and missions and writing numerous influential spiritual works, made him one of the greatest of popes and the father of the medieval papacy. Although he never wrote a systematic treatise on mysticism, his works, influenced by Dionysius and Augustine in particular, reveal a rich vein of thought about the subject: "The flame of Platonic mysticism, which had passed from Plotinus to Augustine, flared up again in the sermons of Gregory."[20]

Gregory was born in Rome in about 540 to a patrician family who owned a palatial residence on the city's Caelian Hill as well as extensive estates in Sicily. In about 573 he was appointed prefect of the city, the highest civic position Rome could offer. But within a year or so he stepped down from this position and embraced the life of a monk. In Rome he converted his family home into the monastery of Saint Andrew, which he himself joined, while over in Sicily he established six more monastic communities on his ancestral estates. His time in the cloister, however, was soon curtailed by Pope Pelagius II, who in 579 dispatched Gregory to Constantinople to be his ambassador at the court of the Byzantine emperor (who was governing Italy through a representative known as the exarch, based in Ravenna). Gregory stayed there for about six years before returning to Rome, where he became abbot of Saint Andrew's.

His life of contemplation abruptly came to a halt in 590 with the death of Pope Pelagius: Gregory was the overwhelming choice of the clergy and people of Rome to become the new pope, much to his personal distress that his monastic days would now be irretrievably snatched away from him. Rome was threatened by the Lombards and still feeling the effects of destructive floods the year before: buildings and granaries had been swept away, and famine and plague were taking their toll. Gregory set about tackling the various problems with skill and energy. He personally conducted negotiations with the Lombards; he spent vast amounts

DAZZLING DARKNESS

of church funds on relieving the plight of the sick and suffering; he reaffirmed the authority of the papacy both in the East and the West; and he strengthened the churches of Italy, Spain, and France and sent missionaries to England. For fourteen years he devoted himself to the spiritual and practical welfare of his flock, organizing, preaching, and writing commentaries and letters, of which more than 850 survive. All this was achieved despite poor health (possibly the result of constant fasting), which left him weak and in pain. He died in 604 and was canonized immediately by popular acclaim.

Gregory's thoughts on contemplation and mysticism have to be gleaned from a variety of works, including his *Dialogues*, *Homilies on Ezekiel*, *Pastoral Rule*, and *Moralia on Job*. He himself seems to have had three personal mystical experiences—for example he recorded that on one occasion in his monastery, his mind "rose above all that was transitory, and, though still in the body, went out in contemplation beyond the bars of flesh."[21] Gregory makes it clear that contemplation requires self-discipline, asceticism, and practicing the virtues of faith, hope, and charity. An attitude of humility is also crucial, as is the study of the scriptures. However, although all our efforts are necessary, they are not enough in themselves to bring about successful contemplation, which is ultimately a gift from God, an act of his loving-kindness.

Furthermore, the contemplative must have love, which is "an engine of the soul" (or "machine of the mind"), which draws the individual away from the distractions of the world.[22] The mind must rid itself of images and sense impressions before it starts the process of recollection, which involves gathering in scattered thoughts and turning inward to ascend to contemplation proper. This turning away from the world is crucial: "But you cannot recollect yourself unless you have learned to lock out the ghosts of images of earthly and heavenly things from the mind's eyes."[23] He refers to the "sweetness" of mystical experience and how it reveals spiritual truths and the baseness of earthly things.[24]

Gregory also speaks of the mind narrowing itself so that it might be enlarged, that is, keeping tightly focused on heavenly things and discarding temporal concerns in the hope that it may be filled with spiritual amplitude.[25] This idea of the soul being expanded emerges

THE EARLY MIDDLE AGES

in one of his anecdotes about Benedict of Nursia, the father of Western monasticism. (Benedict was born in Nursia in Umbria in central Italy and, as a young man, renounced the way of the world and became a hermit. Over time he founded small monasteries before establishing, in 529, a larger community at Monte Cassino in southern Italy. His monastic Rule, which emphasized a balance between manual labor and prayer, became integral to Western monastic communities.) According to Gregory, one night when Benedict was praying to God at the window of a tower, he looked out and saw that the darkness had been scattered by a celestial light that was brighter than daylight. Then "the whole world, gathered as it were under one ray of the sun, was brought before his eyes."[26] Gregory explains that the soul who sees the light of God, no matter how little, expands within to the extent that everything created, even the world itself, seems to shrink. In a similar vein, he uses the image of light streaming through "slanting" or "splayed" windows, which are narrow on the outside but wide on the inside, to convey the idea that our minds, although receiving a small glimpse of the divine light, are greatly enlarged within.[27]

The divine light is a recurrent image in Gregory's description of mystical experience (although Bernard McGinn has pointed out that beneath this affirmative approach there is also a strain of negative theology in Gregory's thought, for example that the limited human spirit cannot comprehend the unlimited spirit of God). He talks, for instance, of the mind overcoming its own dark ignorance and momentarily glimpsing boundless or unencompassed light before returning to its former self and the travails of everyday life.[28] And he refers to the boundless light being seen as a beam of sun pouring through a chink, an image that suggests we cannot see the sun directly, that is, God himself. The full vision of God—which was enjoyed by Adam before the fall—can be partially restored to the individual through Christ, but only fully enjoyed after death. Gregory maintains (not always consistently) that in this life "the mist of corruption darkens us from the incorruptible light"[29]—a reflection of Gregory's acknowledgment of the fallen world of sin and of human suffering.

DAZZLING DARKNESS

John Scotus Erigena (d. ca. 877)

For several centuries after the time of Gregory the Great, the recorded accounts of mystics or mystical theologians are scant. With the disintegration of the Roman Empire the tools of literacy and learning were confined largely to the monasteries, and there may have been any number of holy men and women living at this time, perhaps as hermits, whose mystical lives or experiences were not recorded. It is not until the ninth century that the next significant mystical writer emerges, in the shape of the Irishman John Scotus Erigena (or Eriugena), who is generally regarded as the one brilliant star in the intellectual firmament of the time. Influenced by Dionysius the Areopagite and the Greek monk and theologian Maximus the Confessor (ca. 580–662), John made translations from the works of both men and was an important link in transmitting their spiritual thought to the later Middle Ages. He himself was a philosopher and theologian whose speculative, sometimes difficult, works in the Neoplatonic and Dionysian traditions tried to reconcile mystical pagan philosophy with the Christian revelation.

John Scotus Erigena was born in the early 800s somewhere in Ireland. Very little is known about his life. At some point it seems he decided to seek his fortune abroad, and in about 845 he ended up in western Francia (the area that later became France) at the court of Charles the Bald, the grandson of Charlemagne. Charles appointed him head of his prestigious palace school, and in the following years, John taught and wrote, translating Dionysius (whose works had been presented to Charles by the Byzantine emperor) and Maximus the Confessor, and producing commentaries, homilies, and even poems. He died in about 877, probably in France, although a later tradition says he retired to England during the reign of Alfred the Great. In later centuries the church authorities came to believe that some of his ideas were in error—for example, by straying too close to pantheism—and they were condemned in 1210 and 1225. Modern scholars, however, tend to emphasize John's originality of thought and the depth of his learning—certainly his knowledge of Greek was a rarity in the West at the time.

John's greatest work was *On the Division of Nature* (or *Periphyseon*), with *nature* referring not just to the created world but to the whole

60

THE EARLY MIDDLE AGES

of reality, including God. Imbued with Neoplatonic mysticism, the book was written during the 860s and takes the form of a dialogue between a master and a student. In it John considers the relationship between the ineffable God and creation and the way in which all things flow out from God before returning to him. John divides his grand scheme of nature into four parts: (1) that which creates and is not created, (2) that which creates and is created, (3) that which is created but does not create, and (4) that which neither creates nor is created.[30]

The first division (that which creates and is not created) is God. He is the transcendent source of everything and exists beyond all categories. John describes him as being beyond human reason and as a "nothingness" and says that the correlative of his being infinite and incomprehensible is that he is unknowable even to himself. Yet John knew from the scriptures that God had appeared to people indirectly, so he made use of the idea of theophany, the manifestation on earth of the divine, notably seen in the case of the incarnate Christ. Yet in a way all parts of nature are theophanies inasmuch as everything partakes of the divine, the ultimate source of all being. So for John, the whole of creation is really "a graduated revelation of God."[31]

John's second division of nature (that which creates and is created) consists of the divine archetypes, or Platonic Ideas. God manifests himself timelessly as the Logos, or Word, which mediates between himself, the One, and the multiplicity of creation. And it is the Logos that contains or is the totality of the Platonic Ideas. The Ideas—for example Goodness, Power, and Wisdom—are created by God and constitute the patterns of the things of the visible universe, which they create in an eternal process through the power of the Holy Spirit.

The third division (that which is created but does not create) therefore consists of the phenomena of the universe, the created visible things, including human beings, brought forth by the Ideas as genera, species, and individuals. The created world, engendered by the Logos, is a manifestation of God and subsists in him.

John's fourth division (that which neither creates nor is created) is also God. But it is not God as creator but God in his aspect as the goal to which all things aspire to return. It is the nature of the cosmic cycle that it begins with God proceeding from himself and ends with all things returning to him, their source. Christ, the incarnate Word, is the means by which we journey back to God. And for the Christian elect, the final stage of the return is union with the divine. Employing images used by Maximus the Confessor, John says that the soul is united with God "as air is wholly illuminated by light, and the whole lump of iron is liquefied by the whole of the fire" (these comparisons would be frequently repeated in later medieval times).[32] But John did not envisage a complete merging of identity between God and the human soul, for God ultimately remains beyond all comprehension, known only through theophanies.

So in John's Christianized Neoplatonic vision, God stands at the beginning, as uncreated creator, and at the end of a process of creation that culminates with all things, not only man but also the rest of nature, returning to him. "Everything," as the modern scholar Gordon Leff notes, "is a participation in God's nature as expressed in creation; it is like the rays of light which reflect the sun. Because all creatures both derive from God as principle, and move toward Him as end, the whole of nature is a movement powered by love of God."[33]

4

THE TWELFTH CENTURY

> Then I saw an extremely bright light, and in the light the
> figure of a man the color of sapphire, and it was all burning
> in a delightful red fire.
>
> —Hildegard of Bingen

At the start of the eleventh century the Burgundian chronicler
Radulfus Glaber commented on the optimism and sense of spiritual
renewal at the start of the new millennium in Europe:

> So on the threshold of the aforesaid thousandth year, some two
> or three years after it, it befell almost throughout the world, but
> especially in Italy and Gaul, that the fabrics of churches were
> rebuilt, although many of these were still seemly and needed
> no such care; but every nation of Christendom rivaled with the
> other, which should worship in the seemliest buildings. So it was
> as though the very world had shaken herself and cast off her old
> age, and were clothing herself everywhere in a white garment
> of churches.[1]

Yet if it was true that at this time the fabric of sacred buildings was
being improved, it remained the case that the organization of the
Western church was suffering from a weak papacy and widespread
abuse, including simony and clerical marriage. Matters took a turn
for the better, however, with the election of the reforming popes
Leo IX (r. 1049–54) in 1049 and Gregory VII (r. 1073–85) in
1073, the latter famously clashing with the Holy Roman Emperor,
Henry IV (r. 1084–1105), over whether the church or the state
should make high-ranking clerical appointments (a struggle known

DAZZLING DARKNESS

as the "investiture contest"). The controversy continued until the Concordat of Worms in 1122, when a compromise solution helped to defuse, but not eradicate, the tension between pope and emperor.

The eleventh-century impulse for church reform also manifested itself in the founding of new monasteries. Western monasticism had suffered during the troubled times of the Viking age, but in the early tenth century there was a recovery, particularly through the influential Benedictine abbey of Cluny in Burgundy, founded in 910. By the eleventh century, many monastic houses had become large institutions with great estates, as well as patrons of art and centers of scholarship. As wealth and worldliness inevitably crept into them, a countermovement of reforming orders arose, seeking to return to the putative simplicity of the apostolic era, with a greater emphasis on poverty and discipline. Such an order was the Augustinian canons, who came into being in about the middle of the eleventh century, when small groups of clergy in southern France, northern Italy, and other parts of Europe formed themselves into communities dedicated to lives of poverty, celibacy, and obedience. In time they adopted the Rule of Saint Augustine, although this was modified locally. Some Augustinians were strict, stressing discipline, manual labor, and abstinence; others followed a more relaxed rule and became more involved in the world, running schools and hospitals. One of the best-known Augustinian establishments was the Abbey of Saint-Victor at Paris, founded in 1113, which produced a number of illustrious scholars and mystics, including the Scottish-born Richard of Saint-Victor.

The most significant reforming order at this time, however, was the Cistercians. The White Monks (so called for the color of their habits) were founded in 1098 by Abbot Robert of Molesme (1029–1111) at Cîteaux (Cistercium in Latin) in east-central France and sought to live their lives according to a stricter and more primitive version of Saint Benedict's Rule. In their quest for austerity, the Cistercians built their monasteries in wild, remote locations, often on the frontiers of civilization, where they cultivated large tracts of land, with the considerable help of *conversi*, or lay brothers; they emphasized the place of manual labor, strict diet, and silence, and their churches were grand but plain. The latter is demonstrated by the Cistercian statute (ca. 1145) which stated: *Vitreae albae fiant,*

THE TWELFTH CENTURY

et sine crucibus et picturis ("Let the windows be made of white glass without images or crosses").[2] Through good organization and inspiring leadership from the likes of Stephen Harding (d. 1134) and Bernard of Clairvaux and his friend and biographer, William of Saint-Thierry, the Cistercian houses expanded rapidly, with more than 500 houses founded by the end of the 1100s.

Something of the pioneer spirit and aggressive confidence of the Cistercians can also be discerned in the impulse behind the Crusades. The first of these momentous military expeditions—which also exhibited the piety and fervor of pilgrimage—occurred after the Seljuk Turks took control of Palestine, the Holy Land, in the late 1000s. Rallied by Pope Urban II, a vast army of Christian knights, foot soldiers, and hangers-on set out to recapture Jerusalem, which they took in 1099. Over the next two centuries the crusaders managed to maintain a fortified presence in Palestine, sporadically bolstered by a number of further Crusades (the first four being the most important), whose success was limited at best. By the end of the 1200s, however, the crusading movement had more or less fizzled out, and the last crusader stronghold of Acre fell to the Muslims in 1291.

Apart from the Crusades and monastic renewal, the twelfth century also saw the growth of Scholasticism, itself a product of the growth of towns and cities and cathedral schools at this time. In fact, urban society had begun to revive from the eleventh century onward, after the end of the Viking age. Political stability, the growth of trade, and improvement in food production all contributed to urban prosperity. Some towns, such as Cologne and Milan, were ancient foundations that now experienced a new lease of life. Some places grew up around castles or monasteries, or a holy shrine—Santiago de Compostela in northern Spain developed from being an important pilgrimage center. Other towns prospered from being centers of trade and manufacturing, such as the Flemish cloth towns of Ghent and Bruges.

Scholasticism itself was a method or approach to theology that emphasized the need for a systematic investigation of religious mysteries and the reconciliation of apparent contradictions in the scriptures. The main intellectual tools of the Scholastics were logic—which would be refined by an influx of Aristotle's work in new translations—and formal debates. Although traditional theologians were alarmed by this new approach, the Scholastics did not aim to undermine faith but to support it by reason and to map out an all-embracing view of truth. And the enthusiasm for system and order embraced by the Scholastics percolated through to spiritual writers of the time.

The spirit of mystical endeavor in the twelfth century was not confined to mainstream, high-status representatives of institutional Christianity, such as the likes of Bernard of Clairvaux, William of Saint-Thierry, and Hildegard of Bingen. All over Europe a sizable number of hermits or recluses (collectively known as anchorites and anchoresses), were living in wild remote places, relying on the patronage of local landowners or communities, and serving both with spiritual advice and prayer. In England, after the Normans conquered the country in 1066, the number of hermits may have been increased by the newly dispossessed Anglo-Saxons; these recluses did not fit easily into the new Norman religious dispensation and found succor among local people, many of whom preferred to receive spiritual blessings from their own countrymen and women. On the other hand, hermits needed patronage to survive, and that came to include the Norman aristocracy.

What was the motivation behind becoming a hermit? One primary motive seems to have been the aim of extirpating "sin" from oneself and also a community:[3] by rejecting the world, hermits made themselves ascetic models, spiritual athletes, imitating the poverty of the apostles, purging themselves of temptations of the flesh, and fighting the devil. One such medieval English recluse was Christina of Markyate, a woman who considered herself to be a "bride of Christ" and who received many visionary experiences.

Bernard of Clairvaux (1090–1153)

The most influential churchman of the twelfth century was probably Bernard of Clairvaux, a Cistercian monk, theologian, scholar, mystic, charismatic speaker, and tireless traveler who wrote, preached, and dispensed wisdom and warnings to kings, popes, and nobles alike. His personality and eloquence were so powerful that it is said that "mothers hid their sons, wives their

THE TWELFTH CENTURY

husbands, companions their friends"[4] in case they were led away pied-piper-like by his persuasive witness to the faith. His reputation for profound spirituality was canonized by Dante in *Paradiso* (canto 31), in which Bernard takes over from Beatrice as Dante's guide and directs the poet's gaze to the glory of the Virgin Mary. As a monk, Bernard did not shelter inside the cloister, nor did he flinch from weighing in when he thought he could make a difference to the affairs of the world. Despite the demands of the active life, Bernard was still able to practice contemplation and write passionately about it, albeit unsystematically, especially in his sermons on the Song of Songs. Indeed, it was his strongly held view that the active and contemplative lives are complementary—through contemplation the soul becomes zealous in its desire to serve God.

Bernard was born in 1090 of a noble Burgundian family and joined the Cistercian abbey at Cîteaux near Dijon when he was twenty-two years old. Three years later he left and established in a nearby Burgundian valley a Cistercian house that was named Clairvaux and with which he was associated for the rest of his life. There he maintained a severe, ascetic regime—detrimental to his own health—that attracted many new disciples, including his brothers and widowed father. Eventually the numbers proved too many for the monastery, so monks were sent off to found new houses (more than sixty were established directly from Clairvaux during Bernard's life).

Over the years, Bernard gained a reputation for honesty, piety, forcefulness, energy, and intolerance of corruption. He placed his considerable spiritual weight and rhetorical skill behind Innocent II in his struggle with Anacletus II for the throne of Saint Peter, and in 1140, at a church council in Sens, he presented the case against the controversial thinker and theologian Peter Abelard, who had been accused of heretical teachings. Six years later he again used his eloquence to devastating effect, when he preached the Second Crusade, galvanizing the French king and German emperor to launch an enormous expedition to reclaim the Holy Land for the faith. The crusade proved a dismal failure, however, and Bernard's reputation suffered as a result. In his last years he continued to involve himself in the affairs of the world, although his morale was lowered by the death of a number of friends, especially Pope

DAZZLING DARKNESS

Eugenius III, who had been his disciple. He himself died on August 20, 1153, at the age of sixty-three.

Bernard's mysticism emphasizes the supreme place of love, which is founded on humility.[5] In his short but influential treatise *On Loving God*, he outlines humanity's progressive journey from selfish to spiritual love, stating that there are four degrees of love. First there is our basic, selfish love for ourselves. Human nature is such that we are frail, enslaved to the flesh, and cannot love anything beyond ourselves. The second degree occurs when we realize that we cannot exist by ourselves without divine aid. God sends us trials and tribulations, and through them we turn to him for help. In this way, we come to love God not for his sake but for ours. When we have learned to honor and pray to God and to read the scriptures, we come to the third state, loving God for himself and not merely as a benefactor. The fourth degree, the love of self for the sake of God, is a state of blessed union in which happiness lies in acting in perfect conformity with the will of God—Bernard doubts whether it is possible to reach such a degree in this life, except, perhaps, for a fleeting moment, and he admits that he himself has not attained it.

Bernard's words on love and contemplation were based to some extent on personal experience. Although by later standards he was not forthcoming about his experience of mystical states, he does describe the effect of perceiving God as one of peacefulness: "The tranquil God tranquillizes all things, and to behold him is to rest."[6] He also speaks of frequent visits by Christ as the divine Word, who would enter his soul mysteriously: "There was no movement of his by which I could know his coming; none of my senses showed me that he had flooded the depths of my being."[7] Yet the Word could be known by the way he roused his "sleeping soul" and softened his "hard and stony" heart with an accompanying warmth. The withdrawal of the Word was equally mysterious: suddenly the sense of graceful euphoria would disappear, as if the flame had been removed from a "bubbling pot," leaving the soul deflated until the next visit.

Bernard's thoughts about the contemplative life are mostly scattered within his eighty-six sermons on the Song of Songs, which freely employ the biblical book's use of erotic imagery. Interpreting the Song allegorically, Bernard associates the bride primarily with the church or sometimes with the individual soul. The bridegroom

THE TWELFTH CENTURY

is Jesus Christ (when the church is the bride) or the divine Word (when the soul is the bride). The Holy Spirit is represented by the kiss given by the bridegroom to the bride at the start of the Song. The idea that the union of the Song's two lovers symbolizes the "spiritual marriage" of the soul with the divine Word had been used centuries before by Origen, and Gregory the Great had interpreted the lovers as Christ and the church, but in Bernard's work the spiritual marriage found its supreme formulation, continuing a tradition that later flowered in the writings of Jan Ruysbroeck, Teresa of Ávila, and others.

Bernard states that the contemplative life is open to everyone but is most likely to be fulfilled in the confines of the cloister. He also thought of the soul's journey to God as having three parts, along similar lines to the stages that Dionysius the Areopagite and others had formulated: purgation, illumination, and union. The mystic quest can only begin once the soul has conquered everyday vices such as anger and envy and is practicing virtues such as humility, justice, and gentleness, as well as good works.[8] The soul must then recollect itself (gather together its thoughts on God) and become detached from the sensory world.

Bernard also distinguishes between two types or ways of contemplation further along the mystic path: that of the heart and that of the intellect. The first way, which he favored, is to do with warmth of devotion and how the contemplative feels inside—in his sermons on the Song of Songs he talks about the soul's being embraced and how it is made to glow or has the sensation of a "sweetness" of love pouring into it. But Bernard did not ignore the vital contribution of knowledge and the intellect in the contemplative life. If the individual has been purified of sin, there may follow a sudden and extraordinary enlargement of the mind and a sense of the intellect's being illumined by an inpouring of light, enabling it to grasp the true meaning of the scriptures and sacred mysteries.[9] But such moments of sweetness in the heart and inner mental expansion are brief, and they are inevitably followed by the heightened pain of returning to the everyday world of suffering, the spiritual dryness that John of the Cross would be so eloquent about.

Bernard describes the union of the soul with God in *On Loving God* as deification.[10] This occurs when the will has been totally

69

purified and is conformed with the will of God: it is, he says, as if a drop of water had blended with wine, taking on its taste and color; or, using metaphors employed by John Scotus Erigena, he likens it to an iron that is glowing with fire, or air that has become the sunlight to which it has been exposed. But Bernard did not believe in a loss of identity between God and the soul, for the two are not of the same substance or nature. Rather, they are conjoined as one spirit (Bernard was fond of quoting 1 Corinthians 6:17, "But he who unites himself with the Lord is one with him in spirit"). In any case, such a union is reserved for the afterlife. In this life, Bernard suggests, the soul cannot see God face-to-face but dreams of him, as it were, in contemplation, able to see him only indirectly "through a mirror and in an enigma."[11] Our experience of God in this life can only be brief, and though this is more satisfying than any other earthly delight, it leaves us wanting more. Yet even in the afterlife, the soul continues to engage in a perpetual round of seeking and finding God—similar to the endless reaching out, or *epektasis*, of Gregory of Nyssa—"a searching never satisfied, yet without any restlessness ... that eternal, inexplicable longing that knows no dissatisfaction and want."[12]

William of Saint-Thierry (ca. 1080–1148)

A theologian and friend of Bernard of Clairvaux, William of Saint-Thierry was also a profound mystical writer and thinker in his own right. Thomas Merton has said that every line of his

> is a cry of love for God so full of light and joy and ardor that it lifts our hearts up to heaven on the wings of divine grace and desire, and we long for that perfect vision, the very thought of which was the daily bread on which this saint was nourished all his life.[13]

Not much is known of William's personal life. He was born in Liège (in modern Belgium) and in 1113 became a Benedictine monk at the abbey of Saint-Nicasius at Reims. About five years later, while traveling home from the south of France, he made a fateful visit to Clairvaux. There he met Bernard and immediately felt the latter's charismatic faith and the attractions of the Cistercian reform movement. From that moment William harbored a desire to join

THE TWELFTH CENTURY

the White Monks, a move that Bernard discouraged, believing that William's talents were better suited to the Benedictines.

William remained with the Benedictines for the time being, and in about 1119 he was elected abbot of the monastery of Saint-Thierry, situated on a hill above Reims. For sixteen years William resisted the promptings of his heart, and resigned himself to guiding his monastic brethren. But in 1135 he finally moved over to the Cistercians, joining the monastery of Signy in the Ardennes, about forty miles northeast of Reims. There, excused the hardship of manual labor because of his age and physical frailty, he wrote some of his most influential works, including *On the Holy Eucharist, On the Nature of the Soul and the Body*, and the so-called *Golden Epistle*. He remained at Signy for the rest of his life.

William wrote extensively and profoundly on the monastic life in a variety of treatises, polemics, letters, and other works. Many of his writings were designed to guide monks under his care, while others were addressed to private individuals. In the late 1130s, during his early years at Signy, he worked on his influential (and unfinished) commentary on the Song of Songs and also entered into a dispute with Peter Abelard, whose application of philosophical methods to theology was proving controversial. In the mid-1140s, a couple of years before his death, he embarked on a *Life* of his friend and mentor, Bernard, as well as, arguably, his most influential work, the *Golden Epistle*. Formally entitled *Epistola ad fratres de Monte Dei*, the *Golden Epistle* was addressed to the Carthusian monks of Mont-Dieu (a community about thirty miles southeast of Signy which William visited) and sets out his philosophy on the monastic life and the way of contemplation.

Throughout the *Epistle* William stresses the uncompromising commitment of the monastic: "It is for others to serve God, it is for you to cling to him."[14] With regard to reading, for example, William says that monastics should read specific texts at fixed times—otherwise variable, random reading will only undermine concentration and memory. Scriptures must be read and meditated on, with readers imaginatively identifying with the experiences of the biblical protagonists as best they can. Some daily readings should be systematically memorized and absorbed for subsequent rumination and as a salve for distraction. Reading should naturally

71

DAZZLING DARKNESS

lead to prayer, which in turn will purify the mind for understanding the texts even better.[15]

Concerning more directly mystical matters, William describes the monastic journey as a succession of three states by which monks can find their being in God. First there is the "animal" state, where the body is the main focus. Progress beyond bodily matters leads to the "rational" state and concern with the soul. Third comes the spiritually "perfect" state and finding rest in God. These three states are each divided into three stages (again showing the medieval fascination with triads), and each of these three stages denotes the monk's advancement in terms of beginning, progress, and perfection. The final category, the perfect state, leads to a direct vision of the glory of God—monks who have become "perfect" are transformed into the likeness of divine glory through the Holy Spirit.[16] And this state of perfected perfection is accompanied by a mystical experience or "divine sweetness" (achieved by suitable preparation and by the grace of God bestowed by the Holy Spirit).[17]

Love is central to this transformation, leading the soul to the *unitas spiritus*, union of spirit, a condition likened by William in his commentary on the Song of Songs to the union of bride and bridegroom.[18] William also believed that the faithful are united spiritually with Christ through partaking of the Lord's Supper, an idea that was to percolate through the monastic orders, as well as reaching, by the end of the 1100s, the Beguines, for whom the taking of Communion was deeply connected with the sacred marriage.

Richard of Saint-Victor (d. 1173)

During the twelfth century the Abbey of Saint-Victor in Paris, an Augustinian house of canons (the site of which is now commemorated by Rue Saint-Victor south of the Seine, near the Jardin des Plantes), was home to a number of distinguished theologians, mystics, and scholars and wielded great influence throughout France and beyond. Its two most important figures at this time were Hugh (ca. 1096–1141) and, a generation later, Richard, a Scot by birth, who eventually became prior of the abbey. It was Richard who showed the greater mystical bent, building on the work that Hugh had begun. Not much is known about Richard's life. His birth date is

72

THE TWELFTH CENTURY

unknown, and he died in 1173. Unlike Bernard, who combined monastic duties with affairs of the world, Richard's life seems to have been devoted almost entirely to the cloister and his theological and mystical works, among the most important of which were his studies on contemplation, particularly the *Benjamin Minor* and *Benjamin Major* and *The Four Degrees of Passionate Love*. Richard, in tune with the Scholastic zeitgeist, was a great systematizer, one who is important and influential for bringing orderliness to the experience of contemplation, presenting it in terms of different stages and qualities.

In the *Benjamin Minor* Richard uses the figures of the Hebrew patriarch Jacob and his family to represent the various stages that are required to prepare the soul for contemplation, which climaxes when "human reason succumbs to what it beholds of the divine light when it is lifted above itself and rapt in ecstasy."[19] Richard elaborated his thoughts on contemplation in the *Benjamin Major* (also called *The Mystical Ark*, referring to the Ark of the Covenant), a five-part work that influenced Dante. In it, Richard states that there are six stages through which the soul ascends until it finally "rejoices and dances when from the irradiation of the divine light it learns and considers those things which all human reason cries out."[20]

Richard also says that there are three qualities or modes of contemplation that the mind can attain.[21] The mind's vision can be "enlarged" through its own efforts; it can be elevated with the help of divine illumination and perceive things beyond the normal sphere of consciousness; and it can experience ecstasy, or "alienation of the mind," during which it loses its sense of self and time and gazes on divine truth without hindrance. With his love of analysis, Richard also states that this last, ecstatic experience has three "predisposing conditions" (in the modern Anglican churchman Dean Inge's phrase): first there is devotion, which Richard pictures in terms of the heat of love transforming the mind into smoke rising to God; then wonder, which Richard compares to the way a vessel of water receives sunlight and becomes so joined with it that when the water is still or expands, the light follows suit; and finally, exultation, joy, which points to "a new note of ecstatic rejoicing that was to find increasing favor among the mystics of the Middle Ages."[22]

Richard's thoughts on contemplation and his love of order are also shown in his short but influential treatise *The Four Degrees of Passionate Love*, written shortly before his death.[23] Richard sets out the different levels the soul can reach on the contemplative path. In the first degree, through meditation, the soul is visited by God and experiences a delicious sensation that is "sweeter than honey." Yet although it can feel God's presence, it cannot see God's form, which is still shrouded in darkness. The soul's desire for God is inflamed, and now, with much more effort on its part, it enters the second degree of love, receiving a vision of the divine light so powerful that it can neither forget it nor be distracted from it.

In the third degree, the soul is so caught up in the divine light that it loses all sense of itself and is filled with the glory of God. Those who have come this far abandon their desires and resign their will to God—their actions are now wholly determined by God's will. The soul is ready to be shaped, just as molten metal is shaped into different forms by molds.

The fourth and highest degree requires the soul to put on the humility of Christ, who, although divine, became a humble servant, obedient to God, even though it entailed the Crucifixion. So, having been glorified in the third degree, the soul must now "empty itself" and like Christ become a servant and return to the world to help its neighbors out of compassion.

Hildegard of Bingen (1098–1179)

Contemporary with Bernard and Richard, but very different from them both, was the extraordinary figure of Hildegard of Bingen. A medieval Renaissance woman, as it were, Hildegard was a visionary nun who corresponded with kings, emperors, and popes; a poet who composed choral songs for the liturgy and a play set to music; a writer who penned books not only on theology but also about the medicinal properties of plants and human physiology; and an artist who illustrated her texts with beautiful illuminations. A woman full of contraries—humble yet authoritative, diffident yet willful—she was widely recognized as a holy person during her lifetime, commonly referred to as Saint Hildegard, and in 2012 Pope Benedict XVI proclaimed her a Doctor of the Church. She

THE TWELFTH CENTURY

believed her mission, underpinned by her visions, was to "unlock the mysteries of Scripture, to proclaim the way of salvation, to admonish priests and prelates, to instruct the people of God."[24]

Hildegard was first and foremost a mystical seer, whose enigmatic visions, recorded in her *Scivias* and other works, continue to puzzle and fascinate. She writes with divine authority, founded on what she calls the illumination of "the shadow of the living light" and, within it, the "living light" itself, which made all her woes and sadness evaporate, so that she felt "like a simple maiden rather than an old woman."[25] The living light was a constant presence, revealing to her the inner meaning of visions: "And again I heard the living light speaking to me"[26]; "The living light says the paths of the scriptures lead directly to the high mountain."[27]

The "Sibyl of the Rhine" was born in 1098 into a noble German family in the Rhineland in western Germany, the tenth child of the family. From an early age she suffered from poor health and was aware of receiving visions. After her eighth birthday, her parents entrusted her to the care of a nun named Jutta, who lived as a recluse beside the Benedictine abbey at Disibodenberg in the diocese of Speyer. Hildegard received from Jutta a basic education, learning enough Latin to be able to read the Psalter and other texts. Over the years, as Jutta attracted more followers, a small community obedient to the Rule of Saint Benedict grew up around her. By the time Jutta died in 1136, Hildegard, now thirty-eight years old, was ready to step into her shoes as abbess of what was now a double monastery (one for both men and women).

Five years later in 1141 Hildegard began to write her visionary books, after a dramatic mystical experience: "Heaven was opened and a fiery light of exceeding brilliance came and permeated my whole brain, and inflamed my whole heart and my whole breast, not like a burning, but like a warming flame, as the sun warms everything its rays touch."[28] This celestial light illuminated her understanding of the holy scriptures; at the same time she also felt a divine call to write down the content of her visions, which she eventually showed to a monk named Volmar, her friend and confessor. The latter had no doubt about their divine provenance and was to provide support and encouragement to Hildegard until his death in 1173. Over time, Hildegard also sought and gained endorsement

75

for visions from various church authorities, including Bernard of Clairvaux, whose authority she held in the greatest esteem ("I run to you, I speak to you ... you are the eagle staring at the sun!"[29]). Her careful seeking for ecclesiastical approval "meant that, once her prophetic gift had been officially acknowledged as genuine ... her utterances were almost beyond challenge."[30] With church endorsement Hildegard set to work over the following decades, writing commentaries on her visions, which formed the basis for her renown and authority (in medieval times, the gift of receiving visions was one of the few means by which a woman's voice could be heard and respected: "Visions led women to the acquisition of power in the world ... Visions were a socially sanctioned activity that freed a woman from conventional female roles by identifying her as a genuine religious figure"[31]).

Before long, Hildegard's fame as a wise and holy person who could work miracle cures and perform exorcisms spread, and increasing numbers of women came to join her convent until, in 1147, Hildegard decided to found a new establishment at Rupertsberg, which lies across the Rhine opposite the town of Bingen. Nearly twenty years later she established a second, smaller convent at nearby Eibingen. For the rest of her life Hildegard supervised her nuns, wrote her books, and met and corresponded with people of all ranks of society—nearly 400 of her letters survive—including the likes of Henry II of England and Emperor Conrad III. Also, despite constant poor health and advancing age, she managed to travel throughout Germany and beyond, preaching the word of God, advocating church reforms, and attracting crowds wherever she went. She died in September 1179.

One interesting aspect of Hildegard's visions is that she emphasizes that they came to her not in sleep or dreams but "while awake and seeing with a pure mind."[32] She describes her soul as ascending "to the heights of the firmament" and spreading itself out "among various peoples ... in far away regions." And she describes an illuminating light that is brighter than a "sun-struck cloud" and in it "the scriptures, the virtues, and certain works of men" are reflected as water reflects the sun or moon."[33]

Hildegard typically experienced her visions in the form of luminous images, their spiritual significance usually being explained

THE TWELFTH CENTURY

to her, as we have seen, by a divine voice. She saw vivid symbolic representations of institutions and principles, such as the church and love. Ecclesia (church), for example, is dressed in pure white silk with a gem-studded cloak and onyx sandals; her clothing, though, is torn and muddied, apparently because of the sinful behavior of her priests.

On another occasion she saw a vision of the Trinity in the form of

> an extremely bright light [i.e. God], and in the light the figure of a man the color of sapphire [the Son], and it was all burning in a delightful red fire [the Holy Spirit]. And the bright light flooded through all the red fire, and the red fire through all the bright light, and the bright light and the red fire shone together through the whole figure of the man so that they were one light in one strength and power.[34]

Such were the vividness of these archetypal images that it has been said they were more real to her than the people she encountered on a daily basis and that she was a Platonist in "her most fundamental habits of thought and perception."[35]

The fruits of her visions are manifested in her trilogy of visionary works, *Scivias*, *The Book of Life's Merits*, and *The Book of Divine Works*. The best known of these, *Scivias* (short for *Scito vias Domini*, "Know the ways of the Lord"), took ten years to complete and is more prophetic than mystical, closer in tone to the book of Revelation than, say, the treatises of Bernard or Richard. The book is grandiose in its themes, covering the whole of creation, from Lucifer's fall to redemption through Christ and the day of Judgment. Arresting symbols and images abound; for example, Lucifer and his angels are depicted as shooting stars that are turned to cinders as they fall; and salvation is described as an edifice built on God's mountain, with the building's walls, cornerstones, and proportions having various allegorical meanings. There are frequent moments of awe and beauty, for example in this vision of a cosmic mountain:

> I saw a great mountain the color of iron, and enthroned on it One of such great glory that it blinded my sight. One each side of him there extended a soft shadow, like a wing of wondrous breadth and length. Before him, at the foot of the mountain, stood an image

full of eyes on all sides, in which, because of those eyes, I could discern no human form.[36]

The book ends with songs in praise of the Virgin Mary, angels, and saints, and a short morality play about the pilgrimage of the soul to heaven.

Throughout her works Hildegard emphasizes the dynamic power of the Holy Spirit, the conduit between God and Christ, and the animating force behind the universe. In her hymn "O ignis Spiritus" she describes the elemental motive power of the Spirit:

> Clouds stream from you, the ether flies,
> The stones conserve their moisture
> And water bubbles up in springs;
> The earth exudes green vigor.[37]

This "green vigor"—in Latin, *viriditas* ("greenness")—is given much emphasis by Hildegard, who saw it as a cosmic force with the added sense of fertility or a life-giving energy: for Hildegard it represents "not only verdure or foliage, but all the natural life as quickened by the Holy Spirit."[38] *Viriditas* is involved in the ability of plants to sprout flowers, fruit, and leaves, and, equally, the ability of human beings to "grow, give birth, and to heal."[39] At the start of her choral song, "O nobilissima viriditas," Hildegard alludes to the universal nature of *viriditas*:

> Most noble greening power,
> You're rooted in the sun
> As well as in a shining calm serenity—
> You blaze out from a wheel
> No worldly excellence can grasp.[40]

This cosmic aspect of *viriditas* can also be seen in one of her visions, recounted in the *Book of Divine Works,* in which she saw the radiant face of a female figure with wings, who tells Hildegard that she is the "supreme fire and energy" and describes her action in the universe as an animating force:

And I awaken all to life with every wind of the air, as with invisible life that sustains everything. For the air lives in greenness and fecundity. The waters flow as though they are alive. The sun also

THE TWELFTH CENTURY

lives in its own light, and when the moon has waned it is rekindled by the light of the sun and thus lives again; and the stars shine out in their own light as though they are alive.[41]

Despite Hildegard's constant experience of vision and prophecy, there is still debate among scholars as to whether she was technically a mystic.[42] It is clear that she was a visionary, but it is a question of whether or not in her visions she experienced the actual living presence of God—the core of mysticism—and also whether her writings shed light on the practice of contemplation. Certainly, some of her descriptions of her ecstasies suggest she did encounter the divine directly, such as the "fiery light" that entered her and illuminated her understanding of the scriptures; but her theological works are arguably more prophetic than mystical. Like William Blake, she is really *sui generis*, a seer of luminous, portentous visions that informed her writings, her musical compositions, and her holistic vision of the cosmos.

Christina of Markyate (ca. 1096–1160)

A hermit who was assiduous in her practice of meditation, contemplation, and prayer (the success of which was accompanied by her feeling there was a "fluttering bird" inside her chest, or the appearance of three celestial lights), Christina of Markyate was also a mystic who often felt the divine presence as a "sweetness" or warm ardor. Although she lacked the public persona and international presence that Hildegard enjoyed, many of her visions, the fruit of disciplined prayer, are rich in the sorts of vivid archetypal images Hildegard saw. In addition, "her sense of the immediate presence of God and her ability to visualize and experience him in human terms never left her."[43]

According to her anonymous and incomplete *Life* (probably the work of a contemporary monk of St Albans) Christina of Markyate was born in about 1096 in the town of Huntingdon, about twenty miles northwest of Cambridge in East Anglia, and grew up in a world in which Anglo-Saxon England was still feeling the devastating effect of its conquest by William, Duke of Normandy, thirty years previously.

DAZZLING DARKNESS

Christina showed signs of unusual piety from an early age—indeed, it is said that even while she was in her mother's womb, a pure white dove flew from the monastery in town and up her mother's sleeve, betokening the blessing of the Holy Spirit. Christina's first commitment to a life devoted to Christ, as his "bride," occurred when, still a teenager, she and her parents were on pilgrimage to the abbey of Saint Albans (about fifty miles south of Huntingdon), a place that by the mid-twelfth century "could claim to be at the center of a movement for cultural and religious renewal."[44] Christina was so impressed by the spiritual deportment of the abbey's Benedictine monks that she resolved to commit herself to the religious life there and then. (On leaving the abbey, she scratched the figure of a cross on a door with her fingernail as a token of her empathy with the place.) On the way home, at the town of Shillington, she went to Mass and pledged her allegiance to God and prayed for purity and her virginity.

That pledge was to be tested on more than one occasion. When still a young woman, Christina was nearly ravaged by the Norman bishop of Durham, Ranulf Flambard (who counted Christina's aunt as his lover), when he was visiting her parents' house. Christina managed to outwit him and escape his forceful advances, though Ranulph tried to gain his revenge by urging a local man named Beorhtred to marry the recalcitrant virgin. Christina resisted, asking her would-be-husband what he would do if someone else were to take her away and marry her. He replied that he would kill this man with his own hands if he could not have her as a bride. Christina answered: "Beware then of wanting to take yourself the Bride of Christ lest in his anger he slay you."[45] After this initial resistance, and with increasing pressure from her parents, Christina finally agreed to a betrothal with Beorhtred, but not a physical consummation, since she considered herself already married to Christ. In about 1115, however, unable to contemplate becoming a worldly bride, she ran away to the Saint Albans area, where she received shelter from local hermits, including a recluse named Alfwen at the village of Flamstead.

For two years Christina hid out at Flamstead before moving to Markyate, another local village, where she joined the hermitage of an elderly former Saint Albans monk named Roger. She lived there

80

THE TWELFTH CENTURY

in a cramped cell, fearful of being discovered and hauled back to a carnal marriage, until eventually Beorhtred released her from her vows. After Roger died in about 1121, Christina was forced to take stock of her life. Heeding the advice of the archbishop of York, she went to live with a certain local cleric (unnamed in the *Life*). Not impervious to sensual human emotions, Christina was so consumed with passion for this cleric that "she thought the clothes which clung to her body might be set on fire."[46] But she resisted the temptation and later, in about 1123, she returned to Markyate and became head of a small religious community of nuns that included her sister, Margaret.

A crucial figure who helped her at this period was Geoffrey de Gorran, the abbot of Saint Albans, who afforded her friendship and material support; Christina reciprocated by giving this sometimes headstrong and proud mentor spiritual guidance. In about 1131 she took formal vows to become a nun, and fourteen years later the Markyate community was officially recognized as a priory. When exactly Christina died is unknown: it is recorded that Henry II made a gift to her and her community in 1155, but after that the record goes blank.

Christina was devoted both to Christ (as his "bride") and the Virgin Mary and is said to have had visions of both. Indeed, she received different types of visionary experience, including clairvoyance, prophecy, as well as rapture, when she would surrender to "the contemplation of the countenance of her creator."[47] Perhaps most of all, Christina is credited with an ability to experience the divine reality as a living, immediate presence. For example, as a child she used to talk out loud to Christ "on her bed at night just as if she were speaking to a man she could see."[48] On another occasion Christ approached her in the form of a child: "he came to the arms of his sorely tested spouse and remained with her a whole day, not only being felt but also seen. The maiden took the child in her hands, gave thanks, and pressed him to her bosom."[49]

The basis for her ecstatic raptures, according to the *Life*, was the disciplined training given to her by Roger during her stay with him. Roger would take her to his chapel and show her how to pray by instruction and his personal example. Sometimes her mystical experiences were imageless, sometimes giving her direct insights;

DAZZLING DARKNESS

on other occasions they were filled with luminous images. At Shillington, for example, just after her visit to Saint Albans, when she decided to commit to a religious life, she began to meditate and imagined herself on her deathbed "as if the future were already present," and the thought came to her that after death "no one could foretell the abode of the freed spirit."[50] Also, during the time she was struggling with conjugal pressure from Beorhtred, she received a vision of the Virgin, assuring her she would overcome her betrothed, whom she then saw symbolically prostrate on the ground, dressed in black.[51] On other occasions she saw Christ (on the feast of the Annunciation) come toward her through a closed door, holding a gold cross; and the Virgin Mary sitting in heaven surrounded by shining angels.[52]

She received another powerful vision in 1131, while at her Markyate community, at a time when she was about to undergo a ceremony that would officially consecrate her as a virgin. She was praying to the Virgin Mary for a sign of her purity, when, on the seventh day of the feast of the Assumption, she stood by her bed and found all her fellow nuns asleep, unusually, and the world seemed to be plunged into a profound silence. Suddenly there appeared around her a host of beautiful divine-like youths, three of whom stood out. They greeted her as a "virgin of Christ" and presented her with a crown, whiter than snow and more gleaming than the sun, with two white fillets hanging down from it, like those on a bishop's miter; and they told her the crown would designate her as belonging to Christ.[53]

The motif of the crown that is reminiscent of a miter reappears in another vision Christina received, during a Christmas vigil, when she was mysteriously transported from her sick bed to the lectern of the church of Saint Albans just as the "Te Deum Laudamus" was being sung. As she surveyed the worshippers from the lectern she saw in the monks' choir the figure of an unknown pilgrim, who had appeared twice before in the church (the *Life* implies that he was Christ). This time, the pilgrim

> bore on his head a golden crown with shining gems set in it. Its appearance excelled whatever is fashioned by human skill. Also, on the top of the crown there was a cross of wondrous craft. It was

82

THE TWELFTH CENTURY

gold, made less by human means than divine. Two fillets ... were hanging from either side of his face. They were thin and attached to the crown. Pellucid sparkles, as if drops of dew, were seen from below on the tops of the gems.[54]

This crown, with its fillets, resembles the one Christina saw in her previous vision and associates her with the mysterious pilgrim-Christ figure, but also implies she had the authority of a mitered abbot.[55]

5

PREACHERS AND POETS
THE FRANCISCANS

Praise be to you my Lord for Brother Wind
And for the air, no matter if it's cloudy or fine,
And every kind of weather that sustains your creatures.

—Francis of Assisi

The rise of the Franciscans and their fellow friars—and sometimes rivals—the Dominicans in the early thirteenth century was partly due to the genius of their founders and partly because they were suited to the social conditions of the age. The friars added impetus to the reform movement inside the church at a time when the more recent monastic orders, such as the Cistercians and Augustinian canons, were losing their initial zeal. The friars were very much associated with universities and towns, and it has been said that "without the towns the friars would never have come into existence; without the universities they would never have become great."[1]

The friars needed the towns because they were mendicant, or "begging," orders that relied on charity to live. For the Franciscans, poverty was the central plank in their philosophy. Their founder, Francis of Assisi, distrusted the newfound mercantile prosperity he saw around him and held up as an ideal the spiritual wealth of owning nothing, an ideal espoused by his follower Clare of Assisi. But inspirational exemplar though he was, Francis's organizational skills left something to be desired, and after his death his ever-expanding order had to come to terms with how to survive. Begging for alms was feasible in the countryside only for small groups of mendicants. For large numbers a greater population density was needed, and towns supplied the answer. Whereas Cistercians had built at the frontiers of the known world, Franciscans and Dominicans sought out sites in the very centers of towns. There they set up houses of, say, twenty friars, who would receive alms and bequests for performing services such as burials and preaching the word of God to a populace often disenchanted by their local clergy. Needless to say, the latter often viewed the friars with suspicion and hostility, aggrieved that these zealous newcomers were often criticizing them explicitly or implicitly and competing with them for charitable gifts.

The friars were also active in the new universities. Until the twelfth century, the schools attached to cathedrals and monasteries had been the providers of education. But in the late twelfth and early thirteenth centuries, groups of professional teachers in certain cities and towns formed themselves into guilds or corporations (*universitas* is the late Latin for a guild or society of men) and taught small bands of students, who, if they stayed the course and paid the fees, came away with degrees, valid throughout the continent, that gave them license to lecture. Universities often specialized in subjects: Bologna was renowned for law, Paris for theology, a subject that Oxford also gained a reputation for. The friars needed training from theologians not only to preach and act as confessors but also to win the argument against heretics. Also, those who joined the mendicant orders were supported while they studied at universities in a way that others, reliant on family wealth, private patronage, or a church benefice, were not. So it is not surprising that many of the greatest theologians of the medieval period, including Albertus Magnus (ca. 1200–1280), Thomas Aquinas (1225–74), Bonaventure (ca. 1217–74), and William of Ockham (1287–1347), were either Dominicans or Franciscans.

Both orders expanded throughout the thirteenth century, and by the start of the next there were about 1,400 Franciscan houses, with nearly 30,000 friars spread across Europe.[2] Inevitably, the increase in numbers put a strain on the Franciscans' commitment to absolute poverty. Although they were allowed to use buildings, books, and other necessities that were kept in trust by custodians, a split occurred between the majority (the Conventuals), who wanted to adapt to changing times and requirements and to relax the rule of poverty, and a smaller group (the Spirituals), who insisted on maintaining the purity of their founder's vision. The latter's number

PREACHERS AND POETS: THE FRANCISCANS

included the mystical poet, Jacopone da Todi (see below). In the end the Spirituals' hardline adherence to poverty was condemned as heretical by Pope John XXII (r. 1316–34) and in 1318 four Spirituals were burned at the stake.

The condemnation of the Spirituals was testament to the fact that the demarcation between orthodoxy and heresy was not always clear cut. The Waldenses, for example, had similarities with the Franciscans—both movements grew out of the idea of imitating the apostolic life of the first Christians. The Waldenses were named for Peter Valdes, a prosperous French merchant of Lyons who in the mid-1170s gave up his possessions and became an itinerant preacher wedded to poverty. In 1179 Pope Alexander III approved Valdes and his followers but forbade them to preach without the permission of local bishops. But the Waldenses would not bite their tongues, and in 1184 Pope Lucius III declared them heretics. Despite this pronouncement, however, they continued to spread into various parts of Europe, drawing most of their followers from the rural lower classes.

Other heretical groups did not fare as well as the Waldenses. Also condemned with them in 1184 were the Albigenses, a branch of the Cathars, a group that originated in Bulgaria. The Cathars were dualists, believing that were two eternal principles: good and evil. They rejected the flesh and material things as being evil, and they thought that Christ did not become a flesh-and-blood man but remained an insubstantial phantom. Therefore he did not suffer and die on the cross, nor was he raised from the dead. The Albigenses (their name comes from the Cathar stronghold of Albi in Languedoc, southern France) could not be persuaded by orthodox preachers to see the error of their ways, so in 1208 Pope Innocent III launched a crusade against them. The crusaders came from the north of France and were motivated as much by winning land from the southerners as by extirpating heresy. A fierce, protracted war carried on until an uneasy peace was reached in 1229.

Francis of Assisi (ca. 1181–1226)

With his heartfelt and demonstrable love for his fellow human beings and the natural world, and his unrelenting emphasis on humility, poverty, and charity, Francis of Assisi is generally regarded as the saints' saint, the one great church figure who has come closest to Christ's example of how to live one's life on earth. The spiritual path Francis took was not outwardly predictable from his somewhat dissipated youth. By the end of his days, however, his followers were fanning out over Europe, spreading his ideals and injecting a new warmth and vitality into church practices. His life combined action and prayer, the one sustaining the other; his mysticism is evident not so much in what he wrote as how he lived, with his graceful and intuitive love of the world around him. His awareness of the presence of God in nature and everyday life was profound, and he also received more specifically dramatic spiritual experiences, as when he heard Christ speak to him from a crucifix and when, later on in his life, he received the stigmata, the five wounds of Christ.

Francis was born in the Umbrian town of Assisi in 1181 or 1182. His father was a wealthy cloth merchant, who must have hoped his son would follow in his footsteps. But Francis was guided in his career, his biographers tell us, by a divine voice. It was this that told him in a dream, after he had set out south to embark on the career of a soldier, to return to Assisi, reinforcing what was in fact a growing commitment to the spiritual life. There were other fateful moments strengthening his newfound direction, the most profound of which occurring when he was praying before a crucifix in the small Church of Saint Damian near Assisi. Suddenly he heard God speak to him with the words "Go and repair my house because it is falling into ruin." Taking the words literally, Francis sold some of his father's cloth and gave the proceeds to the priest of Saint Damian's. His father was enraged, but Francis had taken the plunge: he renounced his inheritance and embraced a life of absolute poverty, helping those in need and toiling by himself to restore Saint Damian's as well as another local church, Saint Mary of the Angels, at a place called the Portiuncula.

In 1208 his spiritual destiny was seemingly sealed when, while attending Mass, he heard a reading from Matthew 10:7–10 in which Christ exhorts his disciples to go out into the world and preach the gospel and heal the sick, adopting a life of absolute material poverty. Francis heard the words as a personal summons and immediately began to put them into action. Soon he was joined by a small

PREACHERS AND POETS: THE FRANCISCANS

number of followers, inspired by his example, and in this way the Friars Minor, or Little Friars, came into being. In 1210 Francis and his companions received the approval of Pope Innocent III, and in the following year they made their headquarters at the Portiuncula, where they built their wattle-and-daub huts. As the brothers went off into the countryside to preach the word of God, sleeping rough and working alongside the lowest in society, the movement grew in reputation and numbers. Among the new recruits was a young, well-to-do Assisi woman named Clare (see below), who ran away from home to join Francis. Struck by her religious enthusiasm, Francis founded in 1212 the Poor Clares for women who wished to follow the Franciscan ideals (although they differed from the friars in being an enclosed order), appointing Clare as its head.

In the following years, Francis's evangelical zeal prompted him to take his message abroad. Two expeditions to Syria and Morocco to convert the Muslims had to be aborted through shipwreck and illness, respectively. But in 1219 he arrived in Damietta in Egypt, during the Fifth Crusade, and managed to preach before the Egyptian sultan, Malik-al-Kamal, who politely listened to this brave spiritual warrior before returning him to the Christian camp. On his eventual return to Italy, Francis was confronted with various problems concerning his brethren. In short, the movement had grown so quickly that its commitment to simplicity and poverty was under threat. Consequently, at a grand assembly of about 5,000 friars at the Portiuncula in 1221, Francis decided it was time for him to step aside and let someone else take over the increasing administrative responsibilities the order required.

During his last years he continued his life of preaching and praying, and he also drew up a new rule for the order. In 1224 he received the most profound mystical experience of his life, when his imitation of Christ was acknowledged by the marks of Christ's crucified body on his own flesh. While praying during Lent on Mount La Verna, a local mountain in the Apennines, Francis saw "a Seraph having six wings, flaming and resplendent, coming down from the heights of heaven" with the figure of Christ's crucified body between its wings.[3] The vision left Francis with a "wondrous glow" in his heart, but he also found that he bore the stigmata, the five marks of Christ's wounds, on his hands and feet and the right side

89

of his body (these scars were noticed on his body after his death). For Francis's followers the stigmata, which can be seen as a type of union with God, were confirmation that Francis had imitated the life of Christ to the very last—that he had the "seal of the living God." However, by this time Francis's health, damaged by years of toil, asceticism, and illness, was beginning to deteriorate. He lived on for another two years, but eventually died at the Portiuncula on October 3, 1226, at the age of forty-four. He was canonized two years later.

Although Francis's life was guided by spiritual experiences, he did not write systematically about contemplation; indeed, it has been said that "the heart of Franciscan spirituality seems to be caught up in the mystery of the human person of Francis."[4] It is necessary to go to the saint's life and deeds, his wholehearted commitment to poverty and identification with the lepers, the poor, and the outcasts of society to find his deep spirituality. That he felt God was everywhere, revealed in his glorious revelation, comes out in the many stories told about Francis's love for nature, including the well-known occasion when he preached to the birds, which, as he spoke "began to stretch their necks, to spread their wings, to open their beaks, and to look intently on him."[5]

For Francis, everyone and everything is intimately related in Christ as brothers and sisters. This is memorably summarized in his "Canticle of the Sun,"[6] which he wrote a year before his death while staying with Clare and her nuns. In this short, sacred poem or hymn he praises God for all his works, listing various aspects of the natural world—"In beautiful things he saw Beauty itself," as Bonaventure wrote.[7] The hymn shows that Francis did not so much lose himself in creation as strike up a personal intimacy with its various elements, treating them as family members. There is Brother Sun, who fills the world with light, and Sister Moon and the stars, Brother Wind, Sister Water, and Sister Earth, who produces "grass and various fruits with coloured flowers." Francis even includes Sister Death, from whom no mortal can escape. The canticle ends with a verse that sums up the simplicity of Francis's spirituality: "Praise you and bless you my Lord, and give him thanks; / And serve him with great humility." Here is the canticle in its entirety:

PREACHERS AND POETS: THE FRANCISCANS

O highest, all-powerful, good Lord,
All benediction, glory, praise, and honor are yours.
For they belong to you alone, O highest one,
And there is no one worthy to speak your name.

Praise be to you, my Lord, through all your creatures,
Especially Brother Sun
Who lights the day and brings your brightness to us;
And he is beautiful and radiant with great splendor;
And shows us what you're like, O highest one.

Praise be to you my Lord, for Sister Moon and the stars
Whom you created in heaven as beautiful, precious and clear.

Praise be to you my Lord for Brother Wind
And for the air, no matter if it's cloudy or fine,
And every kind of weather that sustains your creatures.

Praise be to you my Lord for Sister Water,
Who is so useful, humble, precious and pure.

Praise be to you my Lord for Brother Fire,
Who is handsome, playful, strong, robust,
Through whom you illuminate the night.

Praise be to you my Lord for our sister, Mother Earth,
Who rules us and sustains us
Producing grass and various fruits with coloured flowers.

Praise be to you my Lord for those who are forgiving
For the sake of your love, and bear illness and tribulation.

Blessed are those who shall endure in peace,
For you, O highest one, shall crown them.

Praise be to you my Lord for our sister, Bodily Death,
From whom nobody can escape.
Woe to them who die in mortal sin;
Blessed are those who find themselves in your most holy will:
The second death shall bring no harm to them.

Praise you and bless you my Lord, and give him thanks;
And serve him with great humility.[8]

DAZZLING DARKNESS

Clare of Assisi (1194–1253)

Co-founder of the Order of Poor Ladies, or Poor Clares, Clare Offreduccio—known as the Seraphic Mother—was born at Assisi, the eldest daughter of wealthy aristocratic parents. As well as being a soulmate of Francis and founder of many Poor Clare monasteries, Clare also had a mystical side to her nature, centered on union with Christ, which was underpinned by a life of prayer.

The basic facts of Clare's life are set out in the *Acts of the Process*, the document that was drawn up for her canonization by Pope Innocent IV; other biographical information can be gleaned from a variety of sources, including Clare's own *Form of Life* and *Testament*. According to the *Acts*, Clare's spiritual destiny was foretold when her mother, Ortulana, about to give birth to her, heard a voice saying that she would bring forth a "a clear light that will illumine the world"[9] (Clare derives from the Latin for "bright one").

Committed to spirituality and prayer from early childhood, Clare was ready for a more intense relationship with God when, at the age of eighteen, she heard Francis preach at the church of San Giorgio at Assisi. Deeply moved by his words, she managed to see him in private and successfully persuaded him to help her live according to the Gospel. The decisive turning point came on Palm Sunday, March 18, 1212, when, after Mass, she slipped out of her parents' house and made her way to meet Francis at the Portiuncula chapel. This marked the beginning of her new life, based solely on Christ and holy poverty; in token of this, she cut off her hair, donned a plain brown tunic, and covered her face with a veil.

Despite pressure from Clare's father—who had set his heart on his daughter marrying well—Francis temporarily placed the spiritual runaway in two nearby convents, the first in Bastia Umbra, the second, Saint Angelo, at the base of Mount Subasio. As other women (including Clare's younger sister, Agnes) joined this community, Francis housed them next to the chapel of Saint Damian, which he himself had helped to renovate. This then became the first community of the "Poor Ladies of Saint Damian," or Poor Clares.

Clare and her nuns initially followed a modified Benedictine Rule until Clare objected that the Benedictine allowance of holding

PREACHERS AND POETS: THE FRANCISCANS

property in common contravened the Franciscan ideal of absolute poverty. Even when, after Francis's death, Pope Gregory IX pressurized Clare to accept some financial security for the convent, she refused. Gregory was moved by her integrity and granted her, in September 1228, the *Privilegium Paupertatis* ("Privilege of Poverty"), confirming that she and her nuns need not be constrained to receive any property.

From 1215, when Francis appointed her abbess of Saint Damian, until her death thirty-eight years later, Clare remained as the head of the Poor Clares, staying within the confines of the building and engaged in a life devoted to Christ, prayer, meditation, and manual labor. Over the years she was joined by other members of her family, namely her mother Ortolana, her aunt Bianca, and another sister Beatrix. At the same time, she continued to give encouragement and friendship to Francis. Shortly before his death, blind and feeble, he received sanctuary in a small hut Clare had built for him in an olive grove near Saint Damian (and where he composed his "Canticle of the Sun").

After Francis's death, Clare continued to uphold the Franciscan life in the manner of her mentor and to direct her nuns, becoming the first woman to draw up a Rule for women. Meanwhile, other Poor Clare monasteries were seeded all over Europe. Toward the end of her life, she suffered from painful illnesses, doubtless exacerbated by her austerities. Yet, undaunted, and even cheerful, she would sit up in bed and distract herself by spinning thread for corporals (cloths on which the holy sacrament was placed). She passed away on August 11, 1253.

As with Francis, the heart of Clare's spiritual life was a complete devotion to poverty: she believed that a person unburdened by possessions was free to enter a new dimension centered on God. This required, in turn, ultimate trust in God's providential care— an ideal ultimately derived from Matthew's gospel (6:25–34): if God feeds the birds and dresses the lilies of the field, what cause is there to worry about food and clothes? If a person's only concern is seeking the kingdom of God, then every practical need will be provided for. Clare brooked no compromise with this ideal. Material riches must be exchanged for spiritual riches. Christ, as Clare saw him, was born in humble surroundings, grew up poor in the world, and died naked on the cross. She and her nuns had to follow that example.

Clare's mysticism is not marked by the image-rich visions characteristic of Hildegard of Bingen and Christina Markyate. Yet according to the *Acts of the Process* she once received a vision in which she was ministering to Francis, bringing him a towel and hot water; the scene then changed, with Clare suckling on his breast— Francis is now her spiritual "mother," giving her intense, spiritual nourishment. She was also said to have been rapt, insensible, while in prayer for a whole day on a certain Good Friday.[10]

There were also stories of her having more dramatic mystical powers. When Emperor Frederick II, at war with the pope in 1234, was about to besiege Assisi, he and his men made an initial assault on Saint Damian. Facing the attackers, Clare raised the blessed sacrament up high as spiritual protection: the assailants were dazzled as if by a blinding light and fell back in disarray. On another occasion, when an even larger army tried to take Assisi, Clare and her nuns knelt in prayer and implored God to save the town. At once a storm arose and destroyed the encampment of the enemy, panicking them into flight.

Yet it is in a series of four letters Clare wrote to Agnes, daughter of the king of Bohemia, in Prague, that her mystical nature is best exemplified. In these she follows the tradition of nuptial love imagery and the idea that the Christian soul is the bride of Christ.[11] In her second letter, for example, Clare advised Agnes "to gaze on, weigh up, and contemplate your Spouse, even as you desire to imitate Him."[12] In her third letter Clare likened Christ to a mirror (a popular medieval image) in which one must gaze continually, studying one's face in it. She told Agnes to put her mind before "the mirror of eternity" and place her soul in the "brilliance of glory" and her heart "in the figure of the divine substance" so that through contemplation she might be transformed into the divine image itself and taste the "hidden sweetness" which God confers on those who are in love with him. As the Virgin Mary bore Christ in her body, so Agnes, too, must bear him spiritually in her own virgin's body.[13]

In the fourth letter Clare again refers to the mirror, bidding Agnes, as the bride of Jesus Christ, to gaze at her reflected face and, by a process of contemplation, thereby come to clothe herself,

94

PREACHERS AND POETS: THE FRANCISCANS

outwardly and internally, with a garment of many colors, composed of the flowers of virtues. In this mirror, too, she will see the three central virtues of poverty, humility, and charity. Clare prays that Agnes will be led, through contemplation and the practise of the virtues, to embrace Christ and receive the "most blissful kiss."

Bonaventure (ca. 1217–74)

The year that Francis died, Bonaventure, who was to become one of the great leaders and thinkers of the Franciscan order, was only five, and it is recounted that the young Bonaventure was healed of a life-threatening illness by invoking Francis.[14] Unlike the founder of the Friars Minor, Bonaventure was primarily a theological, philosophical, and mystical thinker who shaped and formalized the ideas and ideals of his Franciscan forebears. His writings, with their careful divisions, definitions, and erudition, show the influence of Scholasticism. But unlike many Scholastics, Bonaventure conveys great warmth in his works, and he declared that experiencing the "sweetness" of God was far better than intellectual research.[15]

Influenced by, among others, the Neoplatonists, Augustine, Dionysius the Areopagite, and Hugh and Richard of Saint-Victor, Bonaventure is an important mystical writer for the manner in which he brings order and system to the way of contemplation. Equally, he never loses sight of the vital necessity of love and devotion to Jesus Christ in the soul's progress to God. Despite his erudition, he stressed that a simple, unlearned person could experience God as much as a theologian. Whether or not he personally enjoyed mystical experiences is not entirely clear, although he does speak of once receiving a vision on Mount La Verna. He was also admired for being pious, kindly, humble, and without pretensions, qualities that earned him a place in Dante's *Paradiso* (canto 12). It is said that when he was created a cardinal bishop later on in his life, the papal envoys bearing his cardinal's hat found him busy washing up dishes and were told by him to hang the hat on a nearby tree until he had finished his work.

Bonaventure, called the Seraphic Doctor, was born in about 1217 (he was baptized Giovanni di Fidanza) near the town of Viterbo in Tuscany. He joined the Friars Minor in either the late 1230s or the early 1240s and proceeded to study at the University of Paris. Bonaventure went on to lecture at the university, continuing almost without interruption until 1257, when he was elected minister general of the Franciscan order. This appointment occurred at a time when there was a serious conflict between the Spirituals and the Conventuals, and Bonaventure played such a major role in resolving their differences that he was hailed as the order's second founder. His tact, intelligence, and leadership were qualities no pope could fail to wish to utilize, and in 1265 Clement IV asked him to become archbishop of York. Bonaventure modestly refused to accept what was a considerable honor, but he failed to resist Gregory X eight years later, when that pope insisted on creating him cardinal bishop of Albano. In the following year Bonaventure was a principal contributor to the Council of Lyons, at which the pope hoped to bring about union with the Greek church, but he died while the council was in progress.

Bonaventure's mystical teachings are found in a number of works, especially *The Journey of the Mind to God* and *The Threefold Way*. In the prologue to *Journey*, Bonaventure says that thirty-five years after Francis had received the stigmata on Mount La Verna, he himself climbed the same mountain to experience peace and meditate on the soul's ascent to God. He then witnessed the same vision that Francis had seen, namely the six-winged seraph with the figure of Christ's crucified body. The thought struck him—in a rather Scholastic way—that the number of the seraph's wings represented the six stages by which the soul passes into divine peace and wisdom, a journey achieved only through the "most ardent love of the crucified Christ."

So in *Journey* the spiritual quest involves three pairs of stages in a movement from the external and transient world to the interior realm of our souls and what is eternal and most spiritual. In the first pair of stages, we can discern God through and in his creation (Bonaventure's positive emphasis on creation echoes the joyful intimacy Francis had with it). From the world outside we pass into the interior of our souls, where, in the second pair of stages, we find that the soul's three powers of memory, intellect, and will are an image of the Triune God—the Father, Word, and Love. The soul, therefore, bearing the image of God, is close to him and can rise "as

PREACHERS AND POETS: THE FRANCISCANS

through a mirror" to contemplate the Trinity. Few of us, however, are able to see God within ourselves because of our fallen condition: suffering, distraction, and desires prevent any progress. Our only hope lies in Christ. No matter how intelligent or erudite we are, we must love and believe and hope in Christ to reach ultimate truth. And the divine image within our minds must be reformed or repaired through being purified, illuminated, and perfected.[16]

The final pair of the six stages involve the mind's contemplation of God through and in the divine light of eternal truth, since our minds are "immediately formed by truth itself" (as far as is possible in this life).[17] Bonaventure actually goes on to mention a further stage beyond the six he has set out; but this one comprises such a state of bliss that he is unable to describe it in rational terms. He says it is a stage when the mind leaves itself and the world of senses behind and passes over, through Christ, into an ecstatic state of mystical union (and he cites Francis as one who had experienced this). To indicate how this can be attained, Bonaventure resorts to the suggestive, riddling language of Dionysius: we must find out from "grace, not instruction; desire, not intellect; the cry of prayer, not pursuit of study; the spouse, not the teacher; God, not man; darkness, not clarity; not light, but the wholly flaming fire which will bear you aloft to God with the fullest unction and burning affection."[18]

Another contribution Bonaventure made to mystical theology was his elaboration, in his *The Threefold Way*, of the traditional divisions of purgation, illumination, and perfection, or union. Purgation, or purification, includes facing up to past sins and present temptations; with illumination we grasp the reality of God's mercy, begin to contemplate, and recover our "spiritual senses," so that the soul can once again experience God's sweetness. After illumination comes union with God, when we are raised up "above all that is sensible, imaginable, and intelligible."[19]

Jacopone da Todi (ca. 1230–1306)

Born into the noble Benedetti family in the Umbrian town of Todi, Jacopone became an ascetic and mystical poet who wrote powerful vernacular lyric poems about the spiritual life, including in all

DAZZLING DARKNESS

likelihood the *Stabat Mater*, a Latin hymn describing the sorrows of Mary, the mother of Jesus, during his crucifixion.

Much of what has been handed down about Jacopone's life has had to be inferred from his poems and gleaned from traditions that were established in the fifteenth century. It is thought that he initially studied law, probably at Bologna, before a sudden trauma brought on by his wife's death in about 1269 converted him to the religious life. It is said that during a great feast in Todi his wife was watching a spectacle high up in a stand that suddenly collapsed with the result that she was crushed to death. Jacopone rushed over to her lifeless body and found to his astonishment a hair shirt beneath her luxurious clothes. He came to believe that she was doing penance for his sins,[20] and on the basis of this seems to have experienced a spiritual conversion; he exchanged his expensive robes for rags, gave his wealth to the poor and became a wandering holy man:

> Now, whether because of this [his wife's] strange death, or whether because of the hidden life of virtue which she had led, Ser Jacomo [Jacopone] was by these things so stricken in mind, his heart so pierced, and so estranged from all his senses, that never again from that hour did he seem the same perfectly rational man that he was before; but as one witless and amazed he went to and fro amongst the people. And feeling himself so greatly moved both in body and in soul, he retreated within himself, and, being recollected within his own heart, there began in a marvellous manner, and helped by divine light, to open his eyes and consider his past life, how far it was from God's ways.[21]

Something of Jacopone's dramatic transformation from worldly lawyer to God-fearing ascetic and his rejection of luxury perhaps lies behind his poem, or *lauda*, "Quando t'alegri,"[22] which describes the vanity of riches and the disintegration of the human body at death. The poet graphically considers the degeneration of each body part, for example the head turning into a skull:

> Where is your head with that delightful hair?
> Did somebody assault you and tear it out?
> Did boiling water leave your skull so bare?
> You'll never need a comb again—no doubt![23]

98

PREACHERS AND POETS: THE FRANCISCANS

In 1278 Jacopone regularized his spiritual life by joining the Franciscan Order as a lay brother, preferring to side with the Spiritual Franciscans (those committed to absolute poverty) rather than joining their less-rigorous brethren. The uncompromising stance of the Spirituals drew the ire of various popes, including Boniface VIII, and Jacopone used his pen to promote their cause. But his loyalty to them and his scathing verse against Boniface eventually resulted in his excommunication and imprisonment (in 1298). However, with the election of Benedict XI in 1303 Jacopone was set free and found refuge in the monastery at Collazzone near the town of Perugia. He died there three years later.

Jacopone's reputation as a mystic rests on his intense, passionate poems, which describe the soul's relationship with God, as well as divine love and intimations of rapture. His poem "Fuggo la croce" ("I fly from the cross"),[24] for example, is "one of the greatest expressions in literature of the agony and surrender of love."[25] The poem comprises a conversation between two religious individuals, one a tormented soul who cannot bear the demands of the cross, with its "ardour and its power"; the other is mystified by his reaction and speaks from the point of view of someone who has surrendered to the cross and found peace and contentment in it:

> I once was blind, but now I see the light;
> Gazing upon the Cross I found my sight.
> Beneath the Cross my soul is glad and bright;
> Far from the Cross, I am in misery.

The poem is delicately balanced, with the reader swaying towards the perspective of both speakers as they state their experiences— tortured struggle and calm contentment respectively.

In another poem, "Amor de caritate" ("Love from charity")[26] Jacopone describes the all-consuming condition that comes with the ingress of divine love ("My heart is smote in two, / And burns with ardent love. / Glowing and flaming, refuge finding none, / My heart is fettered fast, it cannot flee; / It is consumed, like wax set in the sun"). Later in the poem he pronounces union with the divine through the agency of Jesus—a union in which nothing can divide the beloved from God:

99

Now are we one, we are not separate;
    Fire cannot part us, nor a sword divide;
Not pain nor death can reach these heights so great
    Where Love hath snatched and set me by His side:
Far, far below, I see the worlds gyrate,
Far, far above, my heart is satisfied:
My soul, who is thy Guide
    To this strange bliss?
    'Tis Jesu's kiss.
    All sweetness far above.

Finally, in the same poem, the poet turns from reasoned language to something more impetuous and passionate, part entreaty, part prayer, and part ecstatic surrender to the overwhelming force of love. In doing so he captures the turmoil and the breaking down of barriers that must happen for the mystic union to take place:

Love, Love, my heart is broken in its pride.
    Love, Thou hast hurt me, I am wounded sore:
Love, Love, Thy beauty draws me to Thy side,
    Love, Thou hast ravished me for evermore:
O Love, despised and scorned let me abide.
    Love, Love, my soul hath entered at Thy door;
    O Love, my Sea, my Shore!
      No more we part:
      Why bind my heart
In cords so ruthless, Love?

Jacopone was also influenced by the mystical apophatic tradition. In *Lauda* XCI, he writes about self-annihilation and how the soul is led to the sphere beyond knowledge and language. No words can express the indwelling of the divine light in the heart: "Love beyond all telling, / Goodness beyond imagining, / Light of infinite intensity / Glows in my heart."[27] The poem continues with the poet confessing he was wrong to have thought he could have been led to the reality of love through "reason" and "feeling." To find God is to experience the "spiritual faculties" becoming annihilated and "swept into infinity"—the reborn soul then gazes in wonderment at finding itself drowning in immensity and becomes speechless at the miraculous change: "Fused with God, it ventures forth / Onto a sea without a shore / And gazes on Beauty without color or hue."[28]

100

PREACHERS AND POETS: THE FRANCISCANS

Like other mystics before and after him, Jacopone placed divine love at the heart of his being and writings. In "O Amor, divino amore"[29] Jacopone relates how love penetrated his heart so softly, with "no stir, no sign!" Love outstrips thought and erudition: its essence is laughter and smiles, it is the key to "heaven's city," and it is the giver of light. It is also the agent of fundamental transformation in the human soul:

> Love, all things that have form are formed by Thee;
> And man, whose form is bent
> In vile disfigurement,
> Thou dost re-form in Thine own majesty.

Jacopone can change the tone of his verse from elegant discourse to ecstatic outpouring, and in this same poem his subject matter— the reality of divine love—finally elicits from him the exclamations of mystical rapture, complete with the paradox that divine love is inexpressible and yet there is a human need to express its ecstasy:[30]

> Heart and tongue must sing out
> "Love, love, O love!" to capture
> The sweetness of your rapture—
> The silent heart will crack apart.
>
> Those tasting your delight:
> Would feel their hearts break
> And they would suffocate
> If love could never speak.

Angela of Foligno (1248–1309)

If Bonaventure is a prime representative of the intellectual side of the Franciscan mystical tradition, the Blessed Angela of Foligno is, with her emphasis on poverty and humility, a more direct reminder of the fundamentals of Francis's teachings and the example of his life. Like the founder of the Friars Minor, Angela came from a well-to-do family and enjoyed a pleasure-ridden, somewhat wayward lifestyle until her spiritual conversion. From then on, she, like Francis, pursued a life of holy poverty, outwardly and inwardly, in the service of God and her fellow human beings. She

DAZZLING DARKNESS

also received visions and divine consolations, and her writings, in contrast to Bonaventure's, abound with what it is like to experience ineffable mystical states—her descriptions of them, if ultimately inadequate to the task (as she points out), nevertheless give insights into the highest reaches of mysticism and its effects. Angela could be dramatic and intense in her spiritual ardor and her devotion to Christ as "lover." On one occasion she felt compelled to disrobe in front of a cross and offer herself to Jesus. At other times she reached such a "blaze of love" that if she heard someone speaking of God, she screamed and could not have stopped even if "threatened with an axe."[31]

Angela was born in 1248 in the Umbrian town of Foligno, about ten miles south of Assisi. Her early life appears to have been conventional enough for the times: she got married, had several children, and enjoyed worldly pleasures. But looking back at these years after her spiritual conversion, she regarded her former self as dissolute, self-centered, and sinful. Her moment of transformation came during a personal crisis in about 1285, when she was in her late thirties. She ended up praying to Francis for help and shortly afterward was able to confess her sins to a Franciscan friar named Brother Arnold, who seems to have been a relative of hers. About three years later her entire family died, possibly as a result of plague, and in the aftermath Angela sold her home and possessions and embraced a life of poverty.

In 1291, at the age of forty-three, she became a Franciscan tertiary, or a member of the Franciscan Third Order, founded for laypeople. In the same year she made a pilgrimage to the tomb of Francis at Assisi, where she experienced the presence of God so profoundly that when it left her she began to scream and shout, to the consternation of those around her. During the remaining eighteen years of her life, Angela gained a reputation for holiness, and in Foligno she attracted around her a number of Franciscan tertiaries, who together formed a community committed to spiritual living and charitable works. She eventually died in Foligno on January 4, 1309, and was laid to rest in the local Church of Saint Francis.

Angela recorded her mystical experiences for posterity by dictating them to a scribe, probably Brother Arnold, who wrote them down in Latin. The visions form the basis of what became

102

PREACHERS AND POETS: THE FRANCISCANS

known as the *Memorial*, which, with her writings on the spiritual life, known as the *Instructions*, comprise her surviving works. Angela emphasizes the importance of the traditional Christian, and especially Franciscan, values and practices of prayer, humility, poverty, and love in the spiritual quest. The soul cannot rely on its own labors to come to know God but must receive the gift of divine grace, which is brought about by ardent prayer. She stresses that prayer is not simply a matter of uttering words but a holistic act that engages the mind and heart, soul and body, accompanied by constant meditation on the life of Christ.[32]

Prayer, which is in effect a way of life, leads to the experience of God, from which is born true humility. The establishment of humility allows divine grace to increase in the soul, and this in turn deepens humility—grace and humility work positively and reciprocally on each other.[33] For Angela, humility is the source from which the other virtues spring, and through it the soul appreciates its own nothingness and sinfulness as well as the vastness of God's goodness. In the soul's increased state of self-knowledge and yearning for God, the other virtues flourish, the most important being the love of God and humanity. Realizing that it is nothing, the soul is consumed with an ardent love of God that transforms it into God, enabling it to love all God's creatures, since it sees God's presence in them.[34]

Prayer, humility, grace, and love are essential to the soul's ascent to God, and it is Angela's own direct experiences of God that give rise to her most compelling writing, for example in her description of the presence of God in the world:

> The eyes of my soul were opened, and I beheld the plenitude of God, in which I did comprehend the whole world, both here and beyond the sea, and the abyss and ocean and all things. In all these things I beheld nothing except the divine power, in a totally indescribable way; so that through excess of marvelling the soul cried with a loud voice, saying "This whole world is pregnant with God!"[35]

When Brother Arnold once asked her to describe her vision of God, she told him that what she saw was a "fullness, a brightness," that filled her so much that she was unable to describe or compare

DAZZLING DARKNESS

it to anything. She did not see a "bodily form," as such, but an ineffable beauty that seemed to her to be the ultimate beauty and total goodness.[36]

The highest mystical experience, union with God, is described by Angela in different ways. She speaks of her will becoming one with God's and realizing that her love originates not from her but from him.[37] She also speaks of having encountered the divine darkness—echoing Dionysius the Areopagite—in which she simultaneously saw nothing and everything, as well as seeing the face of the "God-man" (that is, Christ). It is the vision of God in darkness that is for Angela the ultimate mystical experience: it goes beyond all the other expressions of the divine presence because the good that she saw in it was "the All," whereas everything else was simply a part. "All the countless and unspeakable favours God has done to me," she says, "all the words He has said to me ... are, I know, so far below the Good I see in that great darkness that I do not put in them my hope."[38] On her deathbed she was heard to cry out repeatedly, "O Unknown Nothingness! O Unknown Nothingness!"[39]

6

HOLY WOMEN

THE BEGUINES

But then she made me like hazel trees,
Which blossom early in the season of darkness,
And bear fruit slowly.

—Hadewijch of Brabant

The status of, and attitude toward, women in the Middle Ages was complex. In the songs of the Provençal troubadours and their German equivalents, the Minnesänger, the figure of the noble lady was central to the cult of courtly love, an idealized conception of love in which the woman was an object of unattainable desire and the cause of emotional pain to the frustrated suitor. In real life the honoring of women became part of the chivalric code of knights, and from the eleventh century this secular idealism was to some extent mirrored by the cult of the Virgin Mary. Indeed, the "Christianization" of courtly love can be seen in the writings of the beguines, an informal religious movement for women, for whom the figure of the "knightly suitor" represented the soul seeking the love of God.

There was also, however, an underlying misogynistic tradition in the church, going back to early times, which regarded women as daughters of Eve, the prime agent in the fall of man, and as sirens, ready to lure religiously inclined males onto the rocks of lust. The mastery of appetites and the prestige of sexual continence had become important in the church from the second century onward; celibacy and virginity were associated with spiritual potency, and for

Christian men "prolonged or lifelong abstinence ... made women seem strange, lurid, dangerous."[1] Fear of the effect of women on the male soul can be seen in the story of the third-century saint Martinian of Palestine, who exiled himself on a rock in the sea to escape the female sex:

> Through the wiles of the devil who wished to tempt him, a woman, Photina by name, managed to survive a shipwreck and was reluctantly saved from drowning by the recluse. However, so appalled was he by the thought of sharing his rock with a woman, that he immediately threw himself into the sea. Rescued by two dolphins, he continued his flight from women and travelled through 164 states before mercifully being released from the female scourge by death.[2]

This male wariness toward women continued down the centuries; for example, it was said that for Bernard of Clairvaux "every woman was a threat to his chastity,"[3] an attitude that can readily be imagined to be common in monasteries throughout Europe.

Although in medieval times there were convents that gave women a chance to escape the world and serve God, their numbers were relatively small, despite the monastic reforms of the eleventh and twelfth centuries. Cistercian convents did spring up, but these were barely recognized by the all-male General Chapter. The Franciscan Poor Clares also provided an outlet, but the nuns remained strictly cloistered, unlike their spiritual brothers. For women who wished to devote their lives to God but who found the strictures of the enclosed life too limiting, there were few, and sometimes not very orthodox, alternatives. The beguines were probably the most important of these groups; but there were others, such as the Franciscan and Dominican tertiaries, that is to say lay men and women who did not take strict religious vows but to some extent participated in the life of the order. And there were also other groups, such as the Waldenses, who were judged by the church to be tainted by heresy.

The beguines, who have been described as ranking "among the most creative innovations to late medieval religion,"[4] had taken root in the Low Countries by the end of the twelfth and beginning of the thirteenth century and were eventually viewed with suspicion and

HOLY WOMEN: THE BEGUINES

hostility by the church authorities (indeed, their name may derive from the heretical Albigenses, with whom their enemies associated them). The beguines were women who expressed their spirituality by living alone or together with other women in small convents or larger communities, dedicating their lives to God in prayer, worship, and good deeds. What was remarkable about them was that they fell between the categories of lay and religious. Unlike the religious orders, they did not have a formal structure, common rule, or supreme central authority. Also, they were free to leave their way of life and return to the everyday world (or join a formal religious order). They committed themselves to chastity, but only so long as they remained beguines. They were allowed to hold property and support themselves by, say, weaving, embroidering vestments, and teaching—indeed, this economic self-sufficiency was much praised by contemporaries. Also, they were unusual in being "basically a women's movement, not simply a feminine appendix to a movement that owed its impetus, direction, and main support to men."[5]

The attraction of the beguines, who were also referred to as *mulieres sanctae* (holy women), was that they answered the need of women who wanted to lead mutually supportive spiritual lives but did not feel ready to join an order. At the time, Western Europe had a surplus of unmarried women, owing in large measure to the Crusades and other wars, which had decimated the numbers of potential husbands. Some women became nuns, but not all wished to live a cloistered life. Whereas men were able to choose different ways of expressing their spirituality—for example, by way of the vigorous asceticism of the Cistercians: or the evangelical poverty of the Franciscan and Dominican friars—women had to choose between the home and the cloister. So the beguine way of life, more spiritual than family life, less constricting than convent life, was a tempting alternative.

Although the first communities arose in the Low Countries in places such as Liège and Nivelles in what is now Belgium, the movement spread to Germany, France, and other parts of Europe. In 1216 Pope Honorius III (r. 1216–27) gave a qualified endorsement to the movement, which also attracted powerful benefactors, such as Louis IX of France (r. 1226–70), who established a beguine presence in Paris in 1264. In time small discrete beguine communities were often superseded by larger complexes, or beguinages, which could comprise a number of convents, a church, hospital, cemetery, and other amenities (the beguinage of Ghent, for example, had its own brewery).[6] Beguines could form a significant percentage of a city's or town's population, as in Bruges, where the beguinage consisted of "walled-in rows of houses enclosing a central court where over a thousand beguines might live."[7] Writing in 1243, the English chronicler Matthew Paris (1200–1259) reported that in Cologne and neighboring towns there were 2,000 beguines and beghards (their male equivalents, who were less numerous and noteworthy).[8]

In their spirituality the beguines tended to emphasize the humanity and suffering of Jesus Christ and the central place of the Eucharist, as well as the spiritual marriage between the soul and God. Ascetic practices were common, as was the occurrence of supernatural phenomena such as visions, ecstasies, and prophecies. The movement produced some outstanding mystics and teachers, especially Marie of Oignies, Hadewijch of Brabant, Beatrice of Nazareth, Mechthild of Magdeburg, and Marguerite Porete, who was burned at the stake in Paris in 1310 for alleged heresy.

The church, however, was never entirely sanguine about the beguines, with their halfway-house status and their sometimes-untempered criticism of the clergy. With its ever-vigilant eyes watching for the slightest trace of heresy, the church from time to time focused its suspicions on the beguines, particularly their alleged association with the heresy of the Free Spirit, a group said to believe in the irrelevance of morality and the holy sacraments once a state of spiritual perfection had been reached. In 1299 the Synod of Béziers decreed that the beguines had "no approbation." Then in 1312 the Council of Vienne officially condemned them. Although ten years later Pope John XXII (r. 1316–34) softened the decision, the movement lost momentum and continued in decline until the Reformation, when many of their convents were suppressed. Those in Belgium fared better than most, even growing in number during the seventeenth century and surviving the religious turmoil of the French Revolution.

1. Plotinus, standing on the right, debates the finer points of philosophy with his pupil Porphyry in this 15th-century French illuminated manuscript.

2. Hirsute from her time as a solitary in the desert, Mary of Egypt accepts the gift of a cloak from Zosima the priest to cover her nakedness.

3. Martin of Tours, enlisted to fight in the Roman army, prepares to confront the enemy armed with only a wooden cross. This fresco is by the 14th-century Italian painter Simone Martini.

4. Gregory of Nyssa, shown in this 11th-century mosaic in St Sophia Cathedral in Kyiv, was, and still remains, a major mystical thinker in the Orthodox Church.

5. Dionysius the Areopagite is one of the first mystics to be associated with the approach to divine reality known as the *via negativa*, the negative way.

6. Bernard of Clairvaux looks suitably ascetic in this painting by the 16th-century Spanish artist, Juan Correa de Vivar.

7. With her scribe Volmar in attendance, Hildegard receives divine inspiration in her cell. From her work, *Scivias*.

8. Hildegard of Bingen's painting, from her *Book of Divine Works*, shows a schematic world divided into four simultaneously occurring seasons.

9. This fresco of Francis of Assisi at the abbey of Subiaco, near Rome, is the oldest known depiction of the saint, painted, perhaps, before his death in 1226.

10. Before her birth, Clare of Assisi was predicted to bring forth "a clear light that will illumine the world." Fresco by the 14th-century Italian painter Simone Martini.

11. Marguerite Porete's *Mirror of Simple Souls* includes dialogues involving the figures of Love, Soul, and Reason. The manuscript here shows text from Chapter 35 of the book.

12. Originally founded in 1245, the beguinage in Bruges no longer houses beguines but instead now functions as a Benedictine convent.

13. Meister Eckhart, shown in this fresco from Santa Maria Novella in Florence, said, "The eye with which I see God is exactly the same as the eye with which God sees me."

14. The Dominican Henry Suso turned from extreme austerities to a gentler form of mystical life, fully appreciative of the wonders of nature.

15. *The Book of Margery Kempe* relates the author's pilgrimages and mystical experiences. The first line shown here (from Chapter 18) reads "steadfastly believe that the Holy Ghost dwelleth in his soul. And …"

16. Bridget of Sweden was told by a divine voice that she would gather flowers from which people everywhere would "receive medicine."

17. Catherine of Siena believed a combination of humility, self-knowledge, faith, and perseverance would lead the soul to union with God.

18. John Climacus described the monk's path to God in terms of ascending a ladder on which he is assailed by demons and encouraged by angels. 12th-century icon from the Monastery of St Catherine, Mount Sinai.

HOLY WOMEN: THE BEGUINES

Marie of Oignies (ca. 1177–1213)

Although her biographer and confessor Jacques de Vitry (ca. 1170–1240), who wrote her *Life* or *Vita* in Latin,[9] referred to her simply as a *mulier religiosa*, a holy woman, Marie of Oignies is considered one of the first beguines. She was known throughout her life for her intense devotion to Christ and her psychic gifts: spiritual healing, ecstatic raptures, and prophetic and dream-like visions. In 1209, for example, she is said to have received a vision of a multitude of crosses falling from the heavens; from this troubling image she predicted the start of the Albigensian crusade.[10] She also had what was called the "gift of tears"—a gift, as we shall see, shared by the English mystic Margery Kempe—namely, the ability to weep with religious fervor, spontaneously, copiously, and uncontrollably. Jacques describes Marie crying so hard that her tears poured onto the ground as a *fluvium*, a river. Her holy demeanor affected those around her:

> She went meekly with a slow and easy pace, her head bowed and her face looking to the earth. In so much, truly, the grace of her soul shined in her face of the plenty of her heart, that many of those looking at her were spiritually refreshed and stirred to devotion.[11]

Marie, the "pearl of Christ," was born into a well-to-do Flemish family in Nivelles, near Liège in Belgium. Her parents married her off at the age of fourteen to a local man named John, but she, like the English hermit Christina Markyate, was already married—to Christ. She managed to convince her husband to abstain from carnal relations and pursue a virtuous life, tending to the poor and needy. This included working in a "leprosarium," or leper hospital, in Willambroux, near Nivelles.

Those who encountered Marie recognized that she had a spiritual aura and insight, and over time she gained a devoted following. Yet all she sought herself was a life withdrawn from the world and focused on God. In about 1207, aged thirty, she left her husband (with his permission) to go to live in a cell beside the Augustinian priory of Saint Nicholas at Oignies, about thirty miles southeast of Nivelles. There she spent the rest of her relatively short life as a recluse, devoting herself to prayer. She died at the age of about thirty-six.

109

DAZZLING DARKNESS

During her time at Oignies, Marie increased her reputation as a visionary, counselor, and spiritual healer. Although his account of Marie's life is colored by his great personal devotion to her, Jacques de Vitry says that Marie's mystical life went hand in hand with her round of religious devotions. She practiced extreme asceticism, bearing cold temperatures, welcoming pain, and sometimes going for a week without any food except the Eucharist, which was an object of extreme devotion for her. She yearned to be united with the Eucharist and, after Mass, would go up to the altar and spend hours gazing into the empty chalice. On at least one occasion her fascination with the Eucharist led her to see the host ablaze, more radiant than the sun. She was prone to seeing divine reality in terms of brilliant light. For example, one time when she was gazing on the relic of a splinter of the True Cross, kept in Oignies church, she saw it shine "*quasi caelestis claritatis*," as if with a divine radiance.[12]

Sometimes she would undergo a marathon vigil for about a month, "reposing with the Lord in a serene, holy silence," and the only words she would utter during this period were: "*Volo corpus domini nostri Jesu Christi*," ("I want the body of our Lord Jesus Christ"). And when she received the consecrated host she would remain silent for days at a time, sometimes having out-of-body experiences.[13] At other times, when the priest raised the host she might see the form of a "beautiful boy" between his hands and, simultaneously, a multitude of "celestial spirits" descending in glory. She was also apparently blessed to see Christ himself as a boy, these revelations being accompanied by the sweet scent of spices.

Jacques also said that God bestowed on Marie the seven traditional gifts of the Holy Spirit. These were: 1. The spirit of fear of the Lord—described by Jacques as the "custodian of all good things"—which is akin to a sense of awe at the glory of God.[14] 2. The spirit of piety: not so much religious conformity as a reliance on God and performing selfless deeds. (For example, Marie, whom Jacques calls the "pious maiden of Christ," was so affected by the image of people suffering in purgatory that she tried to help them with prayers and masses.)[15] 3. The spirit of knowledge: this gift helped Marie to see deep down into the core of the human personality; for example, at Mass she was able to discern, clairvoyantly, who was worthy of receiving the host, and who was not.[16] 4. Spirit of fortitude: Marie possessed

110

HOLY WOMEN: THE BEGUINES

great qualities of patient suffering and endurance; as Jacques put it, "she rejoiced in tribulations and welcomed the discipline of the Lord with great desire."[17] 5. The spirit of counsel: the gift of being able to guide with divinely-given insights all those who came to see her. Many who sought her advice "did not dare to tackle a big undertaking without her counsel."[18] 6. The spirit of understanding: a spiritual intuition that enabled Marie to see, for example, a divine corroboration of a human situation—such as witnessing holy angels rejoicing at Mass when priests were celebrating it in a devout and proper fashion.[19] 7. The spirit of wisdom: the highest gift of all, which brings illumination to the mind, a quality Marie embodied with a combination of her extreme devotion to God, her deep spiritual insights, and her wise counsel on the human condition.[20]

Hadewijch of Brabant (ca. first half of thirteenth century)

The Flemish beguine Hadewijch of Brabant is noted for her mysticism of love, which she expressed not only in letters and visions but also in poetry. Although she acknowledges the importance of the intellect, ultimately it is "love" alone that can reach God, abandoning itself to him, "plunging into the abyss ... where fruition is reached."[21] Little is known about Hadewijch's life apart from what can be inferred from her writings. She lived sometime during the first half of the 1200s, and allusions in her works to chivalric life may indicate that she came from a well-to-do family, possibly in or near Antwerp or Brussels. Judging from the fact that she knew Latin and French— although she wrote in medieval Dutch—and was knowledgeable about the scriptures, patristic writings, astronomy, music theory, and the art of writing poetry, she must have received a good education. It is likely that she was the head of a beguine convent, and it seems that for reasons unknown she was compelled to leave it against her will, although she kept in contact with some of her former associates, writing letters of advice and encouragement to them.

Hadewijch's existing works are thought to have been written during a twenty-year period after 1221. They consist of fourteen visions, thirty-one letters, and about sixty poems, some written in stanza form, others in couplets. During the late Middle Ages her

DAZZLING DARKNESS

writings disappeared from the record and were only rediscovered in the early nineteenth century. She did not systematically set out her spiritual teachings, which have to be patched together from her work. With regard to her own mystical experiences, she records in one of her visions that she encountered the living Christ in the Eucharist and felt that he was actually present in her body and that she was united with him.[22] In Letter 9 she again writes of mystical union, this time in reference to the spiritual lover and beloved: it is a state in which neither party can distinguish one from the other, with their mouths, hearts, bodies, and souls merged but with respective identities preserved: "sometimes one sweet divine nature transfuses them both, and they are one, each wholly in the other, and yet each one remains and will always remain himself."[23]

Central to Hadewijch's spirituality is the ideal of love. It is clear that she had absorbed the prevalent ethos of courtly love; and she used the literary conventions of the genre in her own spiritual works. So, the devoted lover becomes the ardent soul, and the beloved, the Lady, is now the divine love of God. Hadewijch is keen to stress that love involves suffering. She points out that, whereas everyone desires to live with God and partake of his glory, few are prepared to live after the model of his humanity and share his Passion. Suffering is not something to be avoided; rather, it is the means through which we reach the highest love, and it is this love that we must focus on single-mindedly, totally committed and trusting, before we can experience it. We must also practice virtuous works and be totally obedient to Lady Love if she is to penetrate us and take us out of ourselves into union with her.[24]

Obstacles to union, as Hadewijch explains in a letter, come from the fact that we are too self-centered and self-willed and too concerned with our rest and peace of mind, as well as being vulnerable to depression and dejection and attacks on our faith and honor. We care too much about gossip, socializing, nice clothes and food, beautiful objects, and entertainment, with which we try to escape from God (at the end of the letter she anticipates her reader's response to her strictures with the empathetic exclamation: "O Lord, how difficult it is!").[25] Hadewijch had no illusions about the travails of life, which she views in terms of being exiled from God. But we must desire to do what love asks us to do, no matter

112

HOLY WOMEN: THE BEGUINES

what the outcome may be.[26] We must also be aware that although love may bring us a "delightful sweetness," we should not measure it by this: the real fruits of love are found not in what we feel but what virtue it brings. Love can sustain qualities and virtues such as charity, mercy, humility, and reason—but *they* cannot sustain *her*: only her wholeness can do this.[27]

For Hadewijch, love is, ultimately, beguiling and mysterious. It is "beyond matter, immeasurable in God's great freedom, giving always from its superabundance."[28] In one poem, she describes love's paradoxical nature: to be imprisoned by her is to be free, her sweetest song is silence, her departing is her drawing near.[29] In another poem she beautifully evokes the mature effects of love on her: "But then she made me like hazel trees, / Which blossom early in the season of darkness, / And bear fruit slowly."[30]

Mechthild of Magdeburg (ca. 1210–82)

As is the case with Hadewijch and Beatrice of Nazareth (see below), nothing much is known about the life of Mechthild of Magdeburg apart from what can be gleaned from her writings. Her great work, *The Flowing Light of the Godhead*, is a masterpiece of visions, prayers, allegories, reflective pieces, and aphorisms, written in prose and verse. It established her as one of the greats of German mysticism as well as a lyric poet of the highest order. For Mechthild, again like Hadewijch, the central realities of the spiritual life were the experience of divine love and the celebration of the Eucharist. Allied to these was the practice of prayer, which, she says, enables God to reside in the heart and also propels the soul to God: it is, in short, the means of union between God and the soul, who together "converse long of love" in bliss.[31]

Born in Saxony in about 1210, probably of a noble family, Mechthild received her first visionary experiences at the age of twelve. As a young woman she felt the call to lead a more intense religious life, and in her early twenties, she left home to join the beguines at Magdeburg on the river Elbe. Here, for the next forty years or so, she lived an ascetic life devoted to prayer and continued to receive visions, which she began to write down. She eventually showed them to her friend the Dominican friar Henry of Halle, who collected them. Her psychic life did not, however, engross her to the extent that she was blind to the outside world: she was outspoken about the failings of the church and the local clergy.

Mechthild's time at Magdeburg came to an end in about 1270, when she was in her late fifties. For reasons that are unknown, she left the beguines and moved to the Cistercian convent at Helfta near the town of Eisleben. There she spent the last years of her life, dying sometime in the early 1280s. Earlier in her life she had confessed to God her fear about death and the passing of her soul from her body. God replied: "If that should happen, I shall draw you into my breath, so that you will follow me like you would a magnet."[32]

The visions Mechthild received were often powerful and sometimes cosmic. She describes how, when she was in rapture, her soul left her body and was elevated to a realm between earth and heaven where, in a state of bliss, she was able to see the shining figure of Jesus Christ and also the Holy Trinity.[33] In another vision she sees the world to come as a three-tiered realm consisting of hell, purgatory, and heaven, which also have subdivisions (some believe she may have influenced Dante in the writing of his *Divine Comedy*). She describes in some detail the horrors of hell, a structure that has three layers, with condemned Christians at the bottom, Jews in the middle, and pagans at the top. Lucifer himself lies chained in the deepest abyss, spewing pestilence, sin, and suffering from his mouth. The fate of those tormented in hell and purgatory exercised Mechthild, and she says that on one particular occasion she prayed for souls in purgatory and managed to free thousands of them from their bondage.[34]

Mechthild's major work, *The Flowing Light of the Godhead*, consists of seven books, six of them completed at Magdeburg between about 1250 and 1264, the last at Helfta. Mechthild wrote in a Low German dialect, but the two versions of her book that have survived are later translations into Middle High German and Latin. The book, which intersperses sections of prose with delicate verse, is full of imaginative and visionary power and exudes a sense of warmth and immediacy with its emphasis on love, frequently explored—as was the case with Hadewijch—through the literary conventions of courtly love. She often refers to the soul as the lover and Christ as the beloved in the sensual terms of the Song of Songs: "Many days

HOLY WOMEN: THE BEGUINES

have I wooed her / But never heard her voice. Now I am moved / I must go to meet her."[35] She also refers to love as "Lady love," who can bring "true safety" only through destroying a life attached to the world,[36] and to love "penetrating" the senses and capturing the soul, in which it grows with great desire for God until it expands and melts into the bodily senses, which then, like the soul, conform to love.[37] Elsewhere she compares the soul's drawing the senses along the path to God to a sighted person leading the blind,[38] and she says that the prolonged action of God's love on the soul has the effect of rendering it more pure, beautiful, and holy.[39] In a short, exquisite lyric she describes the way in which God descends on a soul: "I come to my beloved as the dew upon the flower."[40]

As well as focusing on the reality of divine love and its effects, Mechthild also emphasized the experience and necessity of suffering, which is bound up with identifying ourselves with the Passion of Christ. People experience the joy of God when they conform their will to his—so we must accept suffering with joy and consolations with fear; we must be one with him and rejoice in his will, remembering that "Enmity in our heart drives out the Holy Spirit."[41] She also stressed the reality of sin. She was all too aware of how deleterious our desires are, along with self-willed obstinacy, hatred, anger, false piety, which, if we fail to deal with them, will deprive us of paradise. Conversely, there is no substitute for practicing the virtues, especially humility, which is displayed in four ways: in our clothes and where we live, in our behavior toward others and the degree of loving-kindness we show to them, in our senses and how we "use and love all things rightly," and in the soul itself and the selflessness that raises us to heaven.[42]

Through the practice of virtue, through rigorous detachment from the world, and by inviting suffering we can reach the "true wilderness," a spiritual state of being emptied of false things and centered on love.[43] Virtues are essential to the harmonious spiritual life, a point Mechthild makes plain in an allegory that depicts a happily run convent staffed by various figures such as Charity, the abbess; Peace, the prioress; Meekness, the chaplain; and so on. In accordance with contemporary practice, all are subject to the male priest, Obedience. The virtues are not only good in themselves but are also, of course, the means of preparing

115

the soul for the journey that ends in union with God. Mechthild describes the flight of the soul toward God in another allegorical illustration. She says that if a bird remains on the ground for too long, its wings grow feeble and feathers heavy. But the longer it flies, "the more blissfully it soars, ... hardly alighting on the earth to rest. So it is with the soul: the wings of love have taken from it the desire for earthly things."[44]

Marguerite Porete (d. 1310)

For several hundred years from the end of the thirteenth century, an anonymous mystical text entitled *Mirror of Simple Souls* circulated around Europe, describing the various stages of the soul's journey to God. In 1946 it was finally established that the book's author was Marguerite Porete, who in 1310 had been burned to death in Paris as a heretic. Despite the actions of the inquisitors, however, the book lived on in various translations down the centuries, spreading far and wide her spiritual thought.

The only substantial biographical details that exist about Marguerite concern her trial and execution. It is thought she may have originated in Hainaut in Belgium; by the end of her life she seems to have become a wandering preacher, and this irregular lifestyle, along with biting criticism of the church and some dubiously orthodox statements in the *Mirror*, combined to antagonize the church authorities, who branded her as a beguine at a time when the name had become a term of abuse. Although Marguerite had secured the endorsement of three theologians for the *Mirror*, such support did not deter the bishop of Cambrai from warning her not to teach from or distribute her book, which he burned in public.

Heedless of his threats, and sublimely confident of her divinely revealed wisdom over theologians' book learning, Marguerite carried on her work as before and was duly arrested in 1308 and sent to jail in Paris. There she defied the Inquisition, refusing to disown her beliefs and teachings. Parts of her work, taken out of context, were then scrutinized by a team of theologians from the University of Paris, who found a number of alleged heretical statements. Still refusing to cooperate with the Inquisition, Marguerite was

HOLY WOMEN: THE BEGUINES

eventually condemned as a relapsed heretic and sentenced to be burned at the stake. She died, with dignity, on June 1, 1310.

Marguerite was unfortunate to have lived in an age when it was widely held by the church and other authorities that women should either be properly engaged in the religious life, that is, enclosed in a regular order, or committed to lay life as wives and mothers. There were other factors too. She made no friends, at least in clerical circles, by being an outspoken critic of the church, which she called, pejoratively, Holy Church the Less—as opposed to the ideal community of "free" or "simple" souls of Holy Church the Greater. She also emphasized the superiority of love over (and the "annihilated" soul's disregard for) the sacraments, the virtues, and reason, the latter being the mainstay of Scholasticism. There might also have been a political dimension to her death. The French king Philip IV had recently been engaged in suppressing the Knights Templar, who had had the backing of the pope. The king, it is suggested, might have been attempting to improve his standing with the pope by demonstrating his commitment to orthodoxy and the eradication of heresy in his kingdom.

Written in Old French, Marguerite's *Mirror of Simple Souls* is based around dialogues involving the figures of Love, Soul, Reason, and others, but it also includes poems and extended prose sections. A principal theme is the seven-stage journey of the soul that leads it to the point when it loses its will and reaches union with the Trinity. Marguerite summarizes these seven steps as follows. In the first stage, the soul, touched by grace, resolves to keep God's commandments "to love him with all her heart, and her neighbor also as herself." In the second stage, she, the soul, reaches a state where she scorns wealth, pleasure, and honors and does not fear material losses. The third stage involves the soul renouncing good works and abandoning her will to that of her Lover. In the fourth, she is exalted by Love through contemplation; and in the fifth, as a result of an influx of divine light she sees she has to abandon her will to allow the will of God to prevail in her: when this occurs, she is transformed into "Love's nature." Through divine knowledge she recognizes her nothingness, and yet she is everything and is drawn deep down into the abyss of her own evil, where she loses her pride. In the depths of herself, she can see divine goodness, which

117

makes her reexamine herself: she becomes "wholly at rest." In the sixth stage she does not see herself or God, but God sees himself in her, for there is nothing but him. So the soul is illumined, but not glorified. The final, seventh, stage is the state of glorification, about which we remain ignorant until death.[45]

Throughout her book, Marguerite is emphatic about how the human will is an obstacle to union. We lose our freedom when we will something—because the will strengthens the sense of "I." If we will nothing, then the soul can say: "I am alone in him, without myself, and wholly set free."[46] For those who no longer have any will, prosperity and adversity are of equal account: honor and shame, poverty and wealth, hell and paradise, are all esteemed at the same level.[47] She also describes those who operate by their own will as living by straw, stalks, and "coarse fodder," whereas those whose will has been replaced by God's live "by fine grain."[48]

The liberated soul is "completely dissolved, melted, drawn and joined and united in the exalted Trinity; and she can wish for nothing except the divine will through the divine operation of the whole Trinity. And a rapturous brilliance and light join her from ever closer at hand."[49] The soul has reached a level of spiritual transcendence at which it no longer seeks God through the sacraments, penitence, and thoughts, words, and deeds; nor does it seek or reject poverty and suffering, the Eucharist and sermons, fasting and praying. Also, without a will, it is prevented from sinning, since "without a will no one can sin."[50]

It is not surprising that the church authorities took exception to the idea of the soul jettisoning conventional religious observance and being incapable of sin. Similarly provocative is the moment when the liberated soul declares: "Virtues, I take my leave of you for evermore. ... There was a time I was your serf but now I break away."[51] Nor would Marguerite have helped herself by her negative theology in the Dionysian tradition, which could easily be misinterpreted. Yet Marguerite did not confine her poetic imagination to negative statements, and she is at her most attractive when evoking states of union and transcendence, as when she says that the liberated soul "swims in the sea of joy— that is, in the sea of delights flowing and streaming down from the godhead. She feels no joy, for she herself is joy, and swims and

HOLY WOMEN: THE BEGUINES

floats in joy without feeling any joy, for she inhabits joy and joy inhabits her."[52]

Beatrice of Nazareth (ca. 1200–1268)

Described as a "beguine-trained Cistercian nun,"[53] and influenced by the "love mysticism" and bridal imagery of Bernard of Clairvaux, as well as by the tradition of courtly love,[54] Beatrice (Dutch, Beatrijs) of Nazareth was born in the Belgian town of Tienen, about forty miles east of Brussels. Her parents, Bartholomew and Gertrud, were pious folk (Bartholomew, a merchant, helped to found three Cistercian abbeys during the course of his life) and raised their five children accordingly.[55] Beatrice was only seven years old when her mother died, after which she was sent to live with a beguine community in the town of Zoutleeuw (French, Léau), ten miles east of Tienen. A year later, her father transferred her to the Cistercian monastery of Bloemendaal (French, Florival) near Nivelles, some fifty miles southeast of her hometown. By the age of fifteen she was ready to become a Cistercian novice, and, after initial concerns about her age and health, she was accepted as a nun in 1216.

Beatrice was based mainly at Bloemendaal until 1236, when she moved to the newly founded Cistercian community of Nazareth at Lier, about forty miles northwest of Tienen. There she was soon elected prioress and remained leader of the community until her death in about 1268. During her life Beatrice kept a diary and this formed the basis of the anonymous thirteenth-century Latin *Vita Beatricis*.[56] But details are thin on the ground.

It seems that at various times Beatrice received rapturous experiences of being transported to angelic realms and was able to gaze on the face of Christ glorified.[57] She is also eloquent in describing the ingress of divine love into the soul, which feels "a great proximity to God, a spiritual radiance, a marvellous bliss, a noble freedom, and ecstatic sweetness, a great overpowering by the strength of love, and an overflowing abundance of immense delight." The soul feels that her will has been transformed into love, "and that she is so deeply immersed and so engulfed in the abyss of love that she herself has turned entirely into love."[58] In everyday life, she worked as a copyist (she studied manuscript writing at the abbey of

119

Rameya, or La Ramée, south of Brussels) and as a teacher. But her main contribution to the mystical tradition was a treatise called the *Seven Ways* (or *Manners* or *Degrees,* Dutch *Manieren*) *of Holy Love*—a text written in Middle Dutch that was not formally identified as being authored by Beatrice until 1926.[59] It has been described as the first known text written by a woman that can be called "essentially mystagogical," i.e. intended as a guide to help souls progress toward union with God.[60]

In this treatise Beatrice describes the seven stages in which the soul ascends to God.[61] (The way she speaks of love coming out of the highest source and then returning to it is reminiscent of the cosmic rhythm described by Plotinus and the Neoplatonists.) The seven stages begin with the soul's active desire (arising from love itself) to grow in love until reaching a union with God. Love, says Beatrice, is directed toward the purity and nobility of which the soul itself is composed. And its very striving toward these highest states of being inspires others devoted to love to do the same. In the second stage, the soul serves God unselfishly without thinking of any reward. Beatrice compares this attitude to that of a contemporary lady who "serves her lord for the sake of her love without any thought of reward, for whom simply to serve him is enough."[62] The third stage involves a painful yearning for God—the soul reaches a level of understanding by which it grasps that it is beyond its own power to comprehend God. Nevertheless, it does everything it can to obtain satisfaction.

In the fourth stage there occurs what Beatrice describes as a mystical visitation of love, a state of bliss in which the soul is consumed by love, plunging it into "nothingness." The heart feels close to God and experiences spiritual light and an ineffable bliss. (She compares her heart full of love to a barrel brimming with water that will overflow when stirred.) The fifth stage is in contrast with the fourth: the soul is engulfed with turbulence, confusion, pain—it is snatched from a state of bliss and feels the effects of burning love as a wound. For the more the soul allows love to enter, the more it desires it, and has to reside in a state of dissatisfaction.

When love has overcome "her inner resistance," the soul becomes stronger in the sixth stage. It gains a sense of self-mastery, inspired by the feeling that love has conquered it. Beatrice likens this state

HOLY WOMEN: THE BEGUINES

of unbridled freedom in the immensity of love to a fish swimming and resting in the depths of water, or a bird soaring into the expanse of sky. The soul "lives like an angel" on earth. Finally, in the seventh stage, the soul feels itself being drawn to a love that goes beyond human nature, beyond thinking and reason and affairs of the heart, toward eternal love, into the "vast abyss" of the Godhead; the world becomes a burden and a place of misery, but there it must live, in the hope of finally being enfolded by love, united with the Bridegroom.

7

MYSTICS OF THE RHINELAND

God illumines his true Friends, and shines within them with power, purity, and truth.

—John Tauler

The so-called Rhineland mystics were a group of fourteenth-century German and Flemish mystics who were among the most influential spiritual thinkers of the medieval period. Three of them, Meister Eckhart, John Tauler, and Henry Suso, belonged to the Dominican order, while Jan van Ruysbroeck founded a small community of Augustinian canons, an order to which Thomas à Kempis belonged. It is perhaps not surprising that such able mystical thinkers emerged from the Dominicans, because the Blackfriars (as they are also called on account of their black mantles) placed great emphasis on study and scholarship. Their founder, the Spaniard Dominic de Guzman (ca. 1170–1221), realized the importance of education and the ability to preach effectively when he was trying to convert the heretic Cathars of Languedoc during the Albigensian Crusade. He also wished to see a clergy that could outshine the most pious and worthy of the heretics through personal morality and poverty. The Dominican Order of Preachers that he founded adopted the rule of the Augustinian canons and followed the Franciscans in insisting on mendicancy (begging) and poverty. But more than the Franciscans, the Dominicans stressed the role of preaching and study, and they soon established friaries in university towns such as Paris, Bologna, and Oxford. Although never as numerous as the Franciscans, the order quickly spread; about a century after their foundation, there were approximately 600 houses established throughout Europe.

DAZZLING DARKNESS

The strong Dominican intellectual tradition peaked with the great Schoolmen Albertus Magnus (1200–1280) and his highly influential pupil Thomas Aquinas (1225–74), in whose encyclopedic *Summa Theologiae* medieval Scholasticism is said to have reached its peak. Born near Aquino in Italy in about 1225, Aquinas carried on the work of his master of trying to reconcile the thought of Aristotle with the Christian faith and the Augustinian intellectual tradition that had hitherto underpinned it. The works of Aristotle (384–322 BCE) had been known since early medieval times only in fragmentary form. But in the twelfth and thirteenth centuries, through increasing contact with Muslim scholars—who had accessed and absorbed more of Aristotle's works than their Christian counterparts—in Moorish Spain and Sicily, and as a result of the Crusades (especially the capture of Constantinople in 1204), Aristotelian texts began to flow into Europe.

In essence, Aquinas made an important distinction between the realms of faith and reason, which he saw as complementary, not mutually exclusive. On the one hand he used logic to substantiate Christian doctrine, but he recognized that there were spiritual mysteries, such as the resurrection of the body, that lay beyond reason. He did stress, however, that matters of divine revelation should at least not be *contrary* to reason. But although Aquinas's teachings came to hold a central place in Catholic theology after the Reformation, they did not command universal assent among his contemporaries, and in the fourteenth century they were challenged by the Franciscans Duns Scotus (1266–1308) and William of Ockham (1285–1347), the latter, with his emphasis on the gulf between faith and reason and the importance of empirical knowledge, marking the end of the Scholastic era.

The 1300s also saw the start of a turbulent period for the papacy and an increasing assertiveness of nation states such as England and France, as well as the continuing growth and influence of towns. Early in the century, the French king Philip IV (r. 1285–1314) clashed with Pope Boniface VIII (r. 1294–1303) on an issue involving the authority of the papacy, and the quarrel eventually ended with the pope having to be rescued from the clutches of the king's soldiers, but only after his dignity and health, and the status of the papacy, had been badly mauled. Then, in 1305 a Frenchman

124

MYSTICS OF THE RHINELAND

was elected pope as Clement V (r. 1305–14) and was pressured by Philip into moving the papal residency from Rome to Avignon in the south of France. For nearly seventy years successive French popes remained in what was ironically called the Babylonian Exile, a time when they were widely perceived to be susceptible to the bidding of the French monarchy.

The fourteenth century was also a time when the church sharpened its focus on irregular religious movements and individual heretics. At the Council of Vienne (1311–12) Clement finally suppressed the Knights Templar, after Philip, desirous of their wealth, had conducted his own violent assault against them. In 1318 Pope John XXII (r. 1316–34) had four Spiritual Franciscans burned as heretics and five years later officially pronounced their doctrine of poverty heretical. In 1327 John excommunicated Marsilius of Padua (1275–1342) for his work *Defensor Pacis*, which asserted that the church should be subordinate to the state. In the same year the German Dominican monk Meister Eckhart was summoned to Avignon to answer for alleged heretical statements in his works.

Meister Eckhart (ca. 1260–1328)

Known as the father of German mysticism, Meister Eckhart was a profound mystical thinker, a charismatic and controversial figure whose influence on mystics, theologians, and ordinary believers, as well as poets and artists, continues strongly to this day. His thoughts on the nature of God, the soul, and mystical consciousness are not methodically set out but scattered like sparks among the glowing prose of his sermons, treatises, and other writings, written in both German and Latin. His statements are often paradoxical, teasing, and provocative, and a number of them were officially condemned by the church as heretical after his death. Many of them have an authoritative tone and a proverbial neatness, such as: "As long as I am this or that, or have this or that, I am not all things and I do not have all things. Become pure till you neither are, nor have, either this or that; then you are omnipresent and, being neither this nor that, are all things."[1] And: "Why dost thou prate about God? Whatever thou sayest of Him is untrue."[2] And: "He who seeks God under settled form lays hold of the form, while missing the God

125

DAZZLING DARKNESS

concealed in it."[3] His sayings can also challenge the mind to make leaps of imagination to grasp the truth behind them. "The eye with which I see God is exactly the same as the eye with which God sees me"[4] is the sort of statement that challenges our logical thinking in the way that the riddling Zen koans do, such as the well-known "What is the sound of one hand clapping?" Indeed, the great modern Zen master D. T. Suzuki believed Eckhart to be the profoundest of Western thinkers.

Eckhart was born in about 1260 in the small village of Hochheim near the town of Gotha in the province of Thuringia in central Germany. Not much is known of his early years. His family seems to have been reasonably well off, and at the age of about sixteen he entered the Dominican order at Erfurt (the capital of modern Thuringia). There he underwent the usual scholastic training, learning grammar, rhetoric, mathematics, and other subjects, before embarking on a three-year course in theology. After that he was ordained a priest and began a distinguished career in the service of the Blackfriars. That he was valued for his leadership and administrative acumen is shown by a number of senior appointments in the years to come: by his mid-thirties he was prior of Erfurt and vicar of Thuringia; in the early 1300s, at about the same time that he had completed his studies at Paris and become a Master of Theology (whence the "Meister"), he was elected head of the new Dominican province of Saxony; and in 1307 he was made vicar of Bohemia.

Later, after spells of teaching and administering in Paris and Strasbourg, he ended up in Cologne in the early 1320s. There he fell foul of the local archbishop, Henry of Virneburg, who accused him of heretical teachings. Eckhart believed there was a personal animus behind Henry's attack and decided to appeal directly to Pope John XXII. In 1327, having publicly declared that he would gladly retract any statements found to be truly heretical, he made his way to the papal court at Avignon. But as the judicial proceedings rumbled on month after month, Eckhart suddenly died, possibly in early 1328. He therefore escaped the pope's declaration in the following year that seventeen of his statements were heretical. To take one example: Eckhart preached that it is wrong to talk of God's being "good." To anyone accustomed to the idea that God is the essence of goodness,

126

the statement would seem perverse. But Eckhart's intention was to stress that nothing whatsoever can be predicated of God: he is beyond being and lies so far from our understanding that it is meaningless to attribute to him any qualities, even positive ones.

The judgment against Eckhart came too late to damage him while alive, although the process may have hastened him to his grave. But it did immediately cast a shadow over his reputation, and it was left to his loyal, mainly Dominican, followers to keep his inspiration alive, with John Tauler and Henry Suso especially preserving the spirit of his teachings.

Although Eckhart exerted enormous influence on the Christian mystical tradition, there is little in his writings to indicate unambiguously that he himself enjoyed direct experience of the divine. Yet the confident authority of his works on mystical theology suggests that he probably did. His teachings were influenced by the Neoplatonists and the negative theology of Dionysius the Areopagite and include a number of important mystical themes, including the birth of God in the soul, the existence of a divine "spark" in the soul, and the necessity of detachment. He emphasizes that there is a distinction to be made between God and the Godhead (which he also sometimes, rather confusingly, refers to as God). The Godhead, like the Absolute of Plotinus, is the ultimate undifferentiated unity. Nothing can be predicated of it. It is beyond comprehension, beyond description, although Eckhart does refer to it as being "barren" and as a "desert," that is, a place where there are no forms or activity. So what is the relationship between the Godhead and God? According to Eckhart, the Godhead "reveals" or "manifests" itself as the Triune God—the Father, Son, and Holy Spirit.[5] So when he says rather startlingly, "Therefore let us pray to God that we may be free of God," he means that we need to get beyond the image or idea of God in his persons and back to the undifferentiated Godhead. Eckhart himself acknowledges the difficulty in comprehending the distinction between the Godhead and God:

> God and Godhead are as distinct as heaven and earth. Heaven stands a thousand miles above the earth, and even so is the Godhead above God. God becomes and disbecomes. Whoever understands this preaching, I wish him well. But even if nobody had been here, I must still have preached to the poor-box.[6]

DAZZLING DARKNESS

Eckhart also talks about the Father "ceaselessly generating the Son in eternity," while the Holy Spirit is the love that the Son reflects back to the Father. He goes on to say that not only does the Father beget the Son but he begets "me as his Son," that is, he transforms the individual into a being partaking of his divine nature. The birth of God in the soul, one of the Dominican's favorite images, comes about when the soul lays aside all its selfishness. Indeed, Eckhart says that the whole point of praying, fasting, performing devotions and good works, baptism, and the Incarnation is so that "God may be born in the soul and the soul born in God."[7] Elsewhere Eckhart talks about the birth in terms of God's pouring himself into the soul as light, which spills over into the body, making it radiant. Sinners, however, are deprived of this light because their sins block the channels of infusion. Eckhart therefore urges us to find the light by observing within ourselves the birth of God, which is something that God must do at all times, because it is part of his nature. We are blessed in the way we can passively receive God, and "the infinity of the soul's receiving matches the infinity of God's giving."[8]

Eckhart also stresses the importance of the divine image within the individual, which he calls variously the "spark," "crown," "light," and "ground of the soul." This image, which he equates with the intellect, lies beyond time and space and, like God, is one and simple. In fact, it is God's presence in the depth of the soul through which the latter can unite with God. By turning away from the created world, we can become "unified and sanctified in the soul's spark," which desires only God—not the Triune God but God beyond God, the "still desert" of the Godhead, where no distinction of person exists. "There, in that most inward place, where everyone is a stranger, the light is satisfied and there it is more inward than it is in itself, for this ground is a simple stillness which is immovable in itself."[9]

For Eckhart, the way of the mystic is founded on the individual's detachment from the world. This includes freedom not just from possessions but also from the images of objects that impede the mind. We need to strip away all images and to love God nonmentally in simplicity, without holding on to any idea of God as "spirit" or "person:" we must love him as he is, "One, pure, simple, and transparent."[10] In order to enable God to make his home in the soul, the will's attraction toward finite earthly things and the pleasures they hold must be overcome. We must embrace true poverty by renouncing the will totally—even the will to do God's will: "I tell you by the eternal truth that as long as you have the will to perform God's will, and a desire for eternity and for God, you are not yet poor. They alone are poor who will nothing and desire nothing."[11]

Eckhart believed the mystic's path and the goal of uniting the soul with God was not reserved for the elite. What is important is the transformation of the inner person, and for this to happen it is not necessary to seek solitude, to escape the world, or to practice special religious rituals. For "whoever truly possesses God in the right way, possesses him in all places, in any company, as well as in a church or a remote place or in their cell."[12] And to possess God requires bypassing the mental faculties: "Up then, noble soul! Put on thy jumping shoes which are intellect [i.e. intuition] and love, and overleap the worship of thy mental powers, overleap thine understanding and spring into God, into his hiddenness where thou art hidden from all creatures."[13]

John Tauler (ca. 1300–1361)

Eckhart's most significant followers were John (Johannes) Tauler and Henry Suso, the first of them renowned for his eloquent preaching and emphasis on practical spirituality, the second for the depth of his feeling about God. Tauler's sermons were hugely influential in Germany, being particularly dear to Martin Luther, who said that he had found "more true theology" in Tauler "than all the doctors of all the universities." Tauler was born in about 1300 in Strasbourg, the city with which he was associated for most of his life. He was educated at the local Dominican convent and subsequently spent most of the rest of his life in the city, preaching and acting as a spiritual director to Dominican nuns. His reputation as a good and holy man was enhanced during the Black Death in 1348, when he administered to the sick and dying. He died in Strasbourg in 1361.

Tauler's teachings are known primarily from his preaching, for which he became renowned (a contemporary said that he "set the world ablaze with his fiery tongue"[14]). Some eighty sermons have survived, and although they do not have Eckhart's originality and verve, they compensate with their vigor, lucidity, and warmth. Like the Meister, Tauler talks about the birth of God in the soul. In order to achieve this we must create the right conditions: "We should make inside ourselves a haven of quietness and peace, and live shut up inside it. We must make our spirit a refuge, a hiding-place, where we are protected against our senses, and make there a home of stillness and inward peace."[15] He also uses the image of the desert or wilderness to refer to where the ineffable God exists beyond all categories—a place of "unfathomable darkness" and yet, paradoxically, of "essential light." Here the soul may find the simple unity of God, where distinctions and multiplicity are absent.[16] In Dionysian mode, he speaks of love that is stripped of self, characterized by "non-Knowledge," dead to sensible images, and that constitutes a state in which "we are reformed in the form of God, clothed with his divinity."[17]

Tauler does not refer to Eckhart's "spark" of the soul, but he does speak of "the ground of the soul" and of God's image lying in the hidden depths of the spirit. He also outlines the mystic's ascent to God, which begins with self-control and discipline, spurred on by a fear of damnation. A key part of spiritual progress lies in personal preparation and making ourselves "empty" in order to receive the divine:

> We must abandon everything and even abandon our abandonment, and go out from ourselves utterly and completely. Henceforth we must hold everything as nothing, and lose ourselves in our own pure nothingness. Otherwise we shall certainly drive away the Holy Spirit and prevent His working in us in the highest way.

He then adds ruefully: "Nobody wants to follow this path of self-renunciation."[18] We then progress to contemplation of Christ and the letting go of "forms and images," which allows God to enter us: the irruption of the divine may be sudden and dramatic or happen gradually and quietly.[19]

Tauler describes union with God in different ways: for example, the individual, after the powers of his senses and reason have been unified, throws himself into the divine abyss, where the Godhead, descending into the soul, draws it up into union with its uncreated essence.[20] In Sermon 7, he talks about the blissful rapture

MYSTICS OF THE RHINELAND

experienced by the Blessed Virgin Mary, perhaps giving an insight into his conception as to what will happen to any devout Christian soul who manages to gain union with God:

> Her will was set alight with fervent heat, in silent love, passing beyond all created things. In this state of exaltation she was above all wisdom and all judgment. Here she received the outpouring of Divine Love, in silence, her spirit was steeped in the immaterial Spring, without any exercise of her own power. Here, above all things, she reposed in God, and, surrounded by Love unfathomable, she lost herself in the obscurity of the Godhead. She was united, without any intervention, and made one spirit with God, above all created gifts, graces and lights, in one single light that renewed itself unceasingly in the depths of her heart, in the highest exaltation of spirit.[21]

Whether Tauler himself experienced the mystical states he refers to is a moot point, but he did state that it was easier to experience the divine than describe it, which he often attempts to do in terms of light. He says that "God illumines his true Friends, and shines within them with power, purity, and truth;"[22] and he talks about the inner spirit of man being able to return to its divine origins, where it becomes the "light of lights," and when this shines into the soul, it is so dazzling that it appears as a darkness, in the same way, he says—in an echo of Plato—that the eyes see darkness when they "gaze at the disk of the sun."[23]

Tauler did not set the contemplative life against the active one, preferring to see them as complementary partners. People honor God in their various ways; it is not necessary to become a monk or a priest:

> One man can spin, another can make shoes, and all these are the gifts of the Holy Ghost. I tell you, if I were not a priest, I should esteem it a great gift that I was able to make shoes, and I would try to make them so well as to be a pattern of all.[24]

Henry Suso (ca. 1295–1366)

Of the three great German Dominican mystics, Henry Suso has the reputation of being the most passionate, colorful, and lyrical

DAZZLING DARKNESS

in his evocations of the mystical life. Subject for much of his life to ecstasies and visions, including one when the deceased Eckhart appeared to him, Suso was for a period one of the most ascetic of mystics, for many years following a regime of austerities that are not for the squeamish (for example, he wore a tailor-made nightshirt fitted with specially sharpened nails). The gory penances continued until one day he received an angelic message telling him that God did not require them of him anymore. From then on he realized that he should concentrate on detachment and abandonment of the self, and he advised others against severe penances.

Of aristocratic stock, Suso was born in about 1295 in or near Constance, where he joined the Dominican order at the age of thirteen. In the 1320s he went on to study in Cologne under the supervision of Eckhart, whose reputation he would later defend. For the rest of his life he wrote, preached, and gave spiritual guidance—especially to Dominican nuns—in Constance and various parts of Germany, Switzerland, and the Netherlands. The last years of his life were spent in the city of Ulm on the Danube in southwestern Germany, where he died in 1366. Centuries later, in 1831, he was beatified by Pope Gregory XVI.

Suso is particularly interesting for his insights into personal mystical experiences. For example, just after his inward conversion to the mystical life at the age of eighteen, he describes an ecstatic vision he had on the feast of Saint Agnes. He was sitting by himself in the choir of a convent church, burdened with angst, when suddenly

> his soul was caught up, in the body or out the body. There he saw and heard what all tongues cannot express. It was without form or definite manner of being, yet it contained within itself the joyous, delightful wealth of all forms and manners. His heart was full of desire, yet sated. His mind was cheerful and pleased. He had no further wishes and his desires had faded away. He did nothing but stare in the bright refulgence, which made him forget himself and all else. Was it day or night? He did not know. It was a bursting forth of the delight of eternal life, present to his awareness, motionless, calm. Then he said, "If this is not heaven, I do not know what heaven is."[25]

The ecstasy lasted for up to an hour-and-a-half, until he collapsed and came to. Afterward it seemed to him that he was "floating in the air" or that he was like a vessel from which some perfumed ointment had been taken but which had left behind its scent.[26] On another occasion an angel directed him to look at his body, and he saw "that his body over his heart was clear as crystal, and that in the centre of his heart was sitting tranquilly, in lovely form, the Eternal Wisdom."[27]

Despite his own mystical experiences, Suso believed that the aim of contemplation was not to receive visions and raptures for their own sake but to go beyond the realm of images, which are based on ideas of the created world. The ideal for the mystic is the imageless vision and the experience of God in his pure simplicity: "Say farewell to the creature and in future let your questions be. Simply hearken to what God says in you!"[28] Like Eckhart, Suso conceived of the ultimate divine reality in apophatic, or negative, terms. He describes the "place" where the soul dwells with the "eternal Son" as a "nameless existing nothingness."[29] He also refers to a "naked unity" which is a "dark stillness and restful calm that no one can understand but one into whom unity has shined with its essence." From this calm, true freedom shines and the spirit "is stripped of the murky light that, because of its being human, had followed it when these things were revealed. It is divested of this [murky] light because it finds itself in the manner of the previous light. As Paul says, 'I live, no longer I.'"[30]

Yet Suso's apophaticism is complemented by his enthusiasm and gift for lyric expression. His works were collected into a four-part volume called *The Exemplar*, which includes *The Little Book of Truth* and *The Little Book of Eternal Wisdom*, a devotional work on meditation that became a late-medieval classic. He writes in a vivid, sometimes florid, style, using anecdotes, poetic turns of phrase, and images to make his point. For example, he celebrates with genuine wonder God's creation and its creatures, which reflect the divine light of God. The myriad stars, the planets, the fruitfulness of the earth, woods and fields echoing with birdsong, and even the four elements of fire, earth, water and air—all of these praise and honor God:

DAZZLING DARKNESS

> Oh! when in summer time the beautiful sun bursts forth unclouded and serene, what fruitfulness and blessings it bestows unceasingly upon the earth! See how the leaves and grass shoot up, and the lovely flowers smile; how forest, heath, and meadow ring again with the sweet song of nightingales and other little birds; how all those little creatures, which stern winter had shut up, issue forth rejoicing, and pair together; and how men too, both young and old, entranced with joy, disport themselves right merrily. [31]

In *The Little Book of Truth* Suso is eloquent in his description of the individual's union with God as a result of the abandonment of the self. Using traditional metaphors, he compares the person who has entered the joy of God to a drunkard who has lost his sense of self, and to a drop of water added to an abundance of wine:

> Just as the drop of water loses itself, drawing the taste and color (of the wine) to and into itself, so it happens that those who are in full possession of blessedness lose all human desires in an inexpressible manner, and they ebb away from themselves and are immersed completely in the divine will. [32]

Yet Suso refrains from saying the union involves complete loss of identity: the individual's "being remains, though in a different form, in a different glory, and in a different power." [33]

Jan van Ruysbroeck (1293–1381)

Associated with Eckhart, Tauler, and Suso as one of the Rhineland mystics, Jan van Ruysbroeck (Dutch, Ruusbroec) is generally acknowledged to be the greatest Flemish contemplative. His books include *The Spiritual Espousals* (or *The Adornment of the Spiritual Marriage*), *The Sparkling Stone*, and *The Book of Supreme Truth*, which he wrote in the same Middle Dutch tongue as Hadewijch of Brabant. In them he describes and classifies the various stages of the contemplative life, using familiar Rhineland themes and motifs such as the divine darkness and the "abyss of namelessness," drawing, ultimately, on the influence of Dionysius the Areopagite. [34] God dwells in a place which is "wayless" and dark, but where "an incomprehensible light is born and shines forth: this is the Son of God, in whom a person becomes able to see and to contemplate

MYSTICS OF THE RHINELAND

eternal life."[35] Ruysbroeck also speaks of the birth of God in the soul and the soul's spark, and he emphasizes the place of Christ, the Trinity, and the sacraments. He was keen to stress the importance of both the contemplative and active lives, and he visualizes a spiritual rhythm whereby "the spirit of God blows us outside so that we may practice love and virtuous deeds;" then the spirit "draws us into itself as well so that we may give ourselves over to rest and enjoyment."[36] Ruysbroeck also had a reputation for being a humble, good-humored spiritual director, as well as an unflagging opponent of heresy. His saintliness is reflected in a pious tradition that later in his life he was once discovered sitting beneath a tree in a wood, where he used to write under the inspiration of the Holy Spirit, caught up in an ecstatic rapture and surrounded by a fiery glow of celestial light.

Ruysbroeck was born in 1293 in the small village near Brussels for which he was named. While still a child, he went to live with his uncle, Jan Hinckaert, who was a canon of the Collegial Church of Saint Gudule in Brussels. Hinckaert and a priest friend named Francis van Coudenberg brought up and educated Ruysbroeck, who, in 1317, entered the priesthood, becoming a prebend at the cathedral. He remained there for the next twenty-six years, living a simple, austere, pious life and, among other concerns, combating those believed to belong to the heretical Brethren of the Free Spirit, who were active in the area at this time.

In 1343 Ruysbroeck's life took a different turn. Now fifty years of age, he, along with his uncle and van Coudenberg, decided to leave the cathedral to pursue a more contemplative life in a country retreat. The spot they chose was a hermitage called Groenendaal (Green Valley) in the forest of Soignes near Brussels. There the three men, living their quiet, holy lives, soon attracted disciples, and within a few years they decided to formalize the arrangement by creating a community of Augustinian canons, with Coudenberg the provost and Ruysbroeck the prior. For the rest of his long life— he died in 1381 at the age of eighty-eight—Ruysbroeck, wrapped in the silence of the woods, continued to write his mystical works and counsel the many different visitors who came to the hermitage, drawn by its growing reputation as a spiritual center. Indeed, some of his writings were addressed not only to clerics but to a variety of

DAZZLING DARKNESS

people, including "a hermit, a church reformer, a converted banker and an impassioned priory cook."[37]

Ruysbroeck's best-known work is *The Spiritual Espousals,* or *The Adornment of the Spiritual Marriage,* which is divided into three parts. The first sets out the basis for the spiritual life. It deals with the "active life" and the need to develop virtues such as patience, gentleness, kindliness, compassion, generosity, temperance, and purity, as well as the importance of directing the will toward God in order to progress further on the contemplative path. When the moral foundations have been laid, a person may then feel "an unmeasured impulse" to see Christ himself, not just through his works on earth. Ruysbroeck compares this desire to the action of the tax collector Zacchaeus in Luke 19:1–10, who climbed a tree in order to see Jesus above the crowds in Jericho: the person who wishes to encounter Christ directly "must climb up into the tree of faith, which grows from above downwards, for its roots are in the Godhead."[38]

The second part concerns the interior life. Ruysbroeck begins by describing what is required to have spiritual "seeing" or insight. First "is the light of God's grace in a higher way than that which can be experienced in a life of exterior works without fervent interior zeal." Second is a stripping away of "all strange images and solicitude from the heart, so that a person may be free and imageless, delivered from attachments and empty of all creatures." Third is a voluntary turning of the will and "a gathering together of all the bodily and spiritual powers in such a way that the will, unencumbered by an inordinate affection might flow into the Unity of God and of the mind."[39]

Ruysbroeck also sets out how a person is transformed when divine grace, imagined as an inner living fountain, pours into the "higher powers" of the soul, that is, the memory, understanding, and will. He or she is then filled with love and compassion toward God and humanity. Later on Ruysbroeck says that the contemplative who has come this far can, through simple introspection, meet God without any intermediary. From the encounter with the divine unity, a spiritual light will shine into him and show him "darkness" (a state beyond intellectual comprehension), "nakedness" (losing the power of ordinary perception but being illuminated by a "simple

136

light"), and "nothingness" (complete loss of activity), through which he becomes "one spirit" with God. Now he feels a profound spiritual contentment flowing into his heart, and "in the deeps of his ground he knows and feels nothing, in soul or in body, but a singular radiance."[40]

Yet there is still a higher spiritual stage, which is described in the third part of *Spiritual Marriage*. It is what Ruysbroeck calls the "superessential" or "God-seeing" life, that is, the contemplative's union with God, or the Godhead, the undifferentiated unity about which nothing can rightfully be said. To achieve this a person must fulfill three conditions. First, his virtues must be "perfectly ordered" and he must be completely "empty" within, untroubled by any "images." Second, he must, through his love and intention, adhere inwardly to God.[41] Third, he must lose himself in the "divine darkness," where there is a brightness so powerful that the contemplative "sees and feels nothing but an incomprehensible Light; and through that Simple Nudity which enfolds all things, he finds himself, and feels himself, to be that same Light by which he sees, and nothing else."[42] He also refers to this ultimate goal of contemplation as "wayless" and "abysmal" and, in brilliant poetic phrases, as "the dark silence in which all lovers lose themselves" and "the wild Sea, whence no created thing can draw us back again."[43]

Thomas à Kempis (ca. 1380–1471)

A reclusive monastic figure, Thomas à Kempis is most notable for writing the *Imitation of Christ*, a manual of devotion (of which there were many in the fourteenth and fifteenth centuries) that became one of the most influential spiritual books in Christianity.[44] The *Imitation* has inspired a wide range of people down the ages, including Ignatius Loyola, founder of the Jesuits; John Wesley, founder of Methodism, who produced a translation of the book; Vincent van Gogh; the German theologian Dietrich Bonhoeffer; and Dag Hammarskjöld, secretary general of the United Nations.

> The reason [for the book's popularity] is to be found in two graces that Thomas had laboured for, in Purity and Simplicity, and in two that had come unsolicited, in Beauty and Dignity. He was simple,

DAZZLING DARKNESS

and he dipped his pen in simplicity. The character is not portrayed, but reveals itself. We see a white soul.[45]

Born Thomas Hemerken in Kempen near Cologne, and of humble origins, Thomas was educated at Deventer in east-central Netherlands, where he joined members of the Brethren (or Congregation) of the Common Life, a religious association founded by the Dutch theologian Geert de Groote (1340–80) to nurture a deeper sense of spirituality among its members. The community took no permanent vows and lived and worked together in chastity, poverty, and obedience, holding property in common. They also adopted a style of personal piety known as the *Devotio Moderna*, which emphasized the inner life and regular meditation, especially on the life of Christ. In 1386 the brethren founded the monastery of Agnietenberg just outside Windesheim near Zwolle (about twenty-five miles north of Deventer) and organized themselves as Augustinian Canons. In 1399 Thomas joined this monastery and was reunited with his brother John, who had become the prior. For almost the rest of his life he remained within these cloisters, becoming ordained as a priest in 1413, and leading a life of devotion and acting as a spiritual guide. He copied manuscripts and wrote many books on the religious life, but none as significant as *The Imitation*.

It is a moot point how much of a mystic Thomas was. One commentator has said that "Thomas à Kempis was a priest; he was a monk; he was also, in some sense, a mystic."[46] Another scholar has termed him a "mystical writer."[47] It is not known whether Thomas received raptures or ecstatic moments from contact with the divine, though occasionally the *Imitation*, while primarily a practical spiritual manual, does contain flights of highly-charged language consonant with mystical experience (for example in Book 2, Chapter 4, when Thomas says: "As iron cast into fire loses its rust and becomes glowing white, so it is that whoever turns completely to God is stripped of sluggishness and changed into a new man"[48]). Also, according to pious tradition, he had visionary dreams at least three times in his long life.[49] In one of them he was warned about the death of the Prior of Windesheim. In another, while he was still at Deventer, the Virgin Mary appeared and reproved him for

138

MYSTICS OF THE RHINELAND

neglecting her in his worship. In the vision Thomas saw himself and his fellow brethren gathered for devotions in a room in which the Virgin suddenly appeared in shining clothes. She embraced each of them until she came to Thomas, whom she rebuked for his lack of piety. He woke up vowing never to miss another devotion to her.[50] In the third dream he was lying in bed in a state between waking and sleeping, when he saw the Devil in a hideous form advancing toward his bed as if to snatch him away to hell. Thomas, terrified, cried out the name of Jesus Christ and the Devil flew away.[51]

The Imitation of Christ is divided into four books and is founded on the idea that the religious life should be based on Christ's life, especially his Passion, and that salvation comes through selflessness: the more a person dies to the self the more he or she lives in God (2.12). The first book ("Counsels on the spiritual life") describes the task of gaining self-knowledge and detaching oneself from worldly values. The second ("Counsels of the inner life") continues the task of deepening the inner life; the third ("On inward consolation") features a series of dialogues between a disciple and Christ; and the last book ("On the blessed sacrament") focuses on the Eucharist.

Thomas had a clear-eyed view of everyday reality and leaves his readers (primarily his monastic brethren) in no doubt as to the general misery of existence on earth and the demands of the cross, which cannot be avoided by anyone taking the Christian life seriously:

> The cross, therefore, is always ready; it awaits you everywhere. No matter where you may go, you cannot escape it, for wherever you go you take yourself with you and shall always find yourself. Turn where you will—above, below, without, or within—you will find a cross in everything, and everywhere you must have patience if you would have peace within and merit an eternal crown.[52]

Yet, while describing the formidable challenges of the imitation of Christ, Thomas balances the equation by setting out four ways to gain inner peace: 1) Doing the will of others rather than following your own; 2) Resolving to own fewer possessions rather than more; 3) Assuming the lowest place and considering yourself of less account than others; and 4) Praying that you will be able to let the will of God be manifest in you.[53]

DAZZLING DARKNESS

It is this balance in the *Imitation* that makes it so compelling. Thomas stresses the snares of the world and the actuality of what he calls our *misera vita*, wretched life, but then offers the prospect and consolation of hope and the saving power of love. In 1.23 he exhorts the reader to reflect on the chanciness of life and the need to galvanize oneself immediately to find salvation:

> You fool—why do you think you'll live for a long time when a day does not go past when you receive alarms? How many people have been deceived and suddenly snatched away? How often have you heard people say: "He has been killed by the sword; he has drowned: he fell from a height and broke his neck: he choked himself on his food, he died at the gaming table: one perished by fire, another by steel, another of the plague, another by robbers; and so death is the end of all: and our life suddenly passes like a shadow." Who will remember you when you are dead? And who will pray for you? Do now my beloved whatsoever you can do; for you know not when you shall die: nor yet what shall befall you after death.[54]

Yet Thomas offers hope through the transforming effect of divine love, which is an energy that cannot be tied to worldly values: "Love longs to soar: and will not be held down by things that are low. Love longs to be free, and estranged from all worldly affection: that its inner eye may not be dimmed; that it may not be caught by any temporal prosperity: or by any adversity cast down." Divine love is also immeasurable: "Nothing is sweeter than Love; nothing braver, nothing higher nothing wider: nothing sweeter nothing fuller nor better in Heaven and in earth; because Love is born of God: and can only rest in God above all created things."[55]

Thomas believed that the path to salvation included seeking truth directly and undistractedly in our reading of the Bible: "Truth, not eloquence, should be sought" (1.5). Yet reading by itself cannot achieve salvation: "It is certain that in the coming Judgement we will not be asked what books we have read but what we did: not how well we spoke, but how religiously we lived our lives" (1.3). Echoing Augustine of Hippo, he stresses the importance of detachment from the world and focusing on God: "There is no lasting home for you here. Wherever you are you will be a stranger and a pilgrim; nor

140

MYSTICS OF THE RHINELAND

will you find rest until you are completely united with Christ" (2.1). Thomas also says that our spiritual nature, shaped by our deeds and words, affects our vision of reality: "If your heart were right, then every created thing would be a mirror of life for you and a book of holy teaching ... for a pure heart penetrates to heaven and hell, and as a man is within, so he judges what is without" (2.4).[56]

In Book 3, in a more overtly mystical vein, Thomas equates light with divine truth and pours forth a rapturous prayer: "Enlighten me, good Jesus, with the brightness of internal light, and take away all darkness from the habitation of my heart ... Send forth Your light and Your truth to shine on the earth, for I am as earth, empty and formless until You illumine me."[57] Later in the same book he returns to the invocation of the divine light: "O Light eternal, surpassing all created brightness, flash forth the lightning from above and enlighten the inmost recesses of my heart."[58]

Although for Thomas it may be that his mystical yearnings were expressed more in entreaties than, say, in reflections on states of rapture (as was the case with Symeon the New Theologian), nevertheless his language—with its vividness, repetitions and urgency—has the spirit of the mystic, and the sensuousness of the Song of Songs. Here he delivers a prayer-paean on divine love, which, along with the divine light, provides the lodestar for the Christian pilgrim seeking home in heaven and not on this earth:

> Enlarge me in love; that with the inner mouth of my heart I may taste how sweet it is to love: and to be melted and bathed in love. Let me be held fast by Love: climbing above myself in ardent zeal and wonder. Let me sing the song of love, let me follow Thee my Beloved to the heights: let my soul spend itself in Thy praise exulting for love. Let me love Thee more than myself, and myself only for Thee, and in Thee all that love Thee truly: as the law of Love commandeth shining forth from Thee.[59]

8

THE FLAME OF ENGLISH MYSTICISM

They that begin to love Christ, afterward in great joy of love
and honey-sweet burning shall not cease to sing full lovely
songs to Jesu Christ.

—Richard Rolle

The English mystics of the fourteenth century—Richard Rolle, the
anonymous author of *The Cloud of Unknowing*, Walter Hilton, Julian
of Norwich, and Margery Kempe—stand out in an age that saw a
burgeoning of spiritual writings, including translations of the Bible
into English, sermons, practical manuals for priests, and poetry (for
example, the epic religious poem *Piers Plowman* by William Langland
[1332–86]).[1] Although the individual mystics differ from each other
in approach and temperament, they did share traits that were typical
of English spirituality of the time, for example, a preference for the
pragmatic over the speculative, a humane asceticism, and fidelity to
church teachings. They also expressed their wisdom and serenity
against the background of arguably the most turbulent century of
the Middle Ages, with its catalog of plague, war (particularly the
Hundred Years' War between England and France), and widespread
social unrest. From about 1347 to 1351 Europe suffered the horrors
of the Black Death, a plague that wiped out some twenty million
people, about one-third of Europe's population.

The devastation wrought by the plague had further social
consequences. Depopulation suddenly gave an economic advantage
to the peasants and laborers who had survived it and an impetus
for better pay and working conditions. When governments tried to
impose a freeze on wages and preserve the status quo, tensions rose

143

DAZZLING DARKNESS

and precipitated violent responses. In 1358 the so-called Jacquérie revolt in France, prompted by the aftermath of the plague and the disastrous effects of the Hundred Years' War, was savagely put down. In 1381 in England Wat Tyler (1341–81) and his peasant army tried to enforce radical reforms and were crushed.

The church, meanwhile, was continuing to lose its prestige and authority. At the start of the century the papacy had moved to Avignon, where it was widely believed to be under the sway of the French king. Toward the end of the century it returned to Rome, but there soon followed another calamity: the Western or Papal Schism in 1378, an unedifying struggle between two rival popes for the papal throne. Apart from difficulties at its head, the church was widely perceived as being too worldly and corrupt, as the satirical pens of the English poets Geoffrey Chaucer (ca. 1340–1400) and William Langland make clear. In *The Canterbury Tales* (VI) Chaucer satirized the trade in false relics through his portrait of a pardoner whose relic collection included a pillow case he claimed to be the Virgin Mary's veil. The Italian poet Boccaccio in his *Decameron* (6.10) also portrayed a corrupt pardoner, who paraded a parrot's feather said to have come from the wing of Angel Gabriel. These literary examples were written as amusing satire, but they suggest that spurious relics were commonplace. Although at the grassroots level parish priests were often hardworking pious souls, bishops and abbots and others higher up in the hierarchy were frequently indistinguishable from any other large landowners.

In England dissent toward the church emerged not only through writers such as Chaucer and Langland: another, more radical voice was that of John Wycliffe (1330–84), a theologian who became increasingly critical of church doctrine and practices. Wycliffe opposed the hierarchical structure of the church, emphasized the central place of the Bible, and attacked the use of the Eucharist. Condemned by the pope, he continued to write his anticlerical treatises in retirement, and after his death in 1384, his ideas were perpetuated by his supporters, known as the Lollards (thought to be a derogatory term meaning "mumblers"). With their own well-trained preachers, the Lollards were effective enough to provoke suppressive measures by the English government—in 1401 the first Lollard (William Sawtry) was burned. But after a failed

THE FLAME OF ENGLISH MYSTICISM

Lollard rebellion against King Henry V in 1414, the movement went underground, although its influence continued until the Reformation.

Richard Rolle (ca. 1300–1349)

The first of the great English mystics during these troubled times, Richard Rolle was a hermit and spiritual counselor who is important not so much for his mystical theology as for his witness to how it *feels* to experience the heights of mystical consciousness. In his best-known work, *The Fire of Love* (written in Latin as *Incendium Amoris*), Rolle writes with the enthusiasm of someone who is trying to convey what it is like to be filled with the deep, penetrating heat and "sweetness" that comes from the mystic's ardent love of God. For Rolle the mystical path was not confined to monks, priests, and other clerics but was open to anyone who would shun the vanities of the world and set his or her heart on loving God in utter humility.

Rolle was born in Thornton in Yorkshire, probably in about 1300. He studied at Oxford for a short while before leaving to pursue the life of a solitary dedicated to God. He returned north to Yorkshire but soon left his home and family for good, dressed in his idea of an authentic hermit's robe—a patchwork of two of his sister's tunics and his father's rain hood. Then with the help of the local squire, who provided him with clothes, food, and shelter, Rolle began his life as a solitary, living in places remote from towns and villages, writing his mystical works in both English and Latin, and providing spiritual counsel to anyone who sought him out.

Whether acting within the authority of the church or independently as "freelancers," hermits were part of the landscape of medieval life. They were sought out for their wise counsel, especially by those who cared little for the local priest. Certainly Rolle was as enthusiastic about the eremitical life as he was scathing about the representatives of the church. He chastises theologians for their bookishness and arguments—all for the purpose of getting good reputations and jobs—instead of concentrating on the love of Christ, the "sweetness" of which is dispersed by useless debates and "unbridled curiosity": an old woman, he declares, can know more about love than an erudite theologian.[2] Hermits, on the other

145

hand, base their lives around loving God and their fellow human beings: they scorn the approval of men, they shun laziness, they resist sensual pleasures, they yearn for spiritual things, they believe everyone to be more worthy than themselves, and they take delight in prayer.

Apart from the clergy, another object of his criticism was women. Perhaps fearing that his hermit's resolve might be fatally tested by the opposite sex, Rolle strongly warns against the company of women, who he claims have the power to befuddle a man's reason and distance his affections from God.[3] Elsewhere he complains of the latest fourteenth-century women's fashions—braided hair, makeup, and "wide-spreading horns on their heads, extremely horrible, made up of hair not their own."[4] Yet whether he was an out-and-out misogynist or simply conforming to the ascetic's dread of sensuality remains unclear. What is clear is that there were some women whom he met and admired, including a local anchoress named Margaret Kirkby. Also, toward the end of his life (he died in 1349, presumed to have been a victim of the Black Death), he moved to Hampole, near the town of Doncaster, where he gave spiritual direction to the nuns of the Cistercian convent there.

The turning point in Rolle's interior life occurred a couple of years after his commitment to the eremitical way. He was, it seems, praying in a certain chapel when, in the translation from the Latin by Richard Misyn (d. 1462), "suddenly I felt within me a merry and unknown heat. But first I wavered, for a long time doubting what it could be. I was expert that it was not from a creature but from my Maker, because I found it grow hotter and more glad."[5] Then, as he began to recite some psalms, he heard the sound of mysterious singing:

> [S]uddenly, I wot not in what manner, I felt in me the noise of song, and received the most liking heavenly melody which dwelt with me in my mind. For my thought was forsooth changed to continual song of mirth, and I had as it were praises in my meditation and in my prayers and psalm saying I uttered the same sound, and henceforth, for plenteousness of inward sweetness, I burst out singing what before I said, but forsooth privily, because alone before my Maker.[6]

THE FLAME OF ENGLISH MYSTICISM

The spiritual music that turned his thoughts and prayers into tuneful songs, accompanied by an "inward sweetness," caused him to sing, but only inwardly, for God. It proved to be an initial awakening that would take four more years until he was able to reach the "heights of loving Christ," and consolidate his spirituality.

Heat (*calor*), song (*canor*), and sweetness (*dulcor*) play a significant part in Rolle's mysticism. To love Christ truly involves these three experiences, which in turn require profound quietness (Rolle found that only by sitting still, as opposed to walking around or lying on the ground, could he maintain the requisite tranquility). More specifically, Rolle describes heat or fervor as a state of being when both mind and heart are ablaze—not metaphorically but as a physical sensation—with the fire of divine love. Song refers to the condition of the soul when it is brimming over with praise of God and thoughts have been transmuted into songs. From these two experiences, which are maintained only by committed devotion, comes a third: ineffable sweetness.

Rolle also distinguishes between two types of rapture. With the first, a person suddenly loses all bodily feeling (he cites the example of Paul being raised to the "third heaven" in 2 Corinthians 12:2–4) and may appear to others to be stricken. This type of rapture can even be experienced by sinners, who may see visions of the blessed and the damned. The second type, and for Rolle the more desirable one, comes when true lovers of God lift their minds up to him in the act of contemplation, when they are rapt by love, experiencing a seizure—but unlike in the first type of rapture, bodily feeling is never lost.[7]

Most important to Rolle, however, is the mystic's ardent love for God. Throughout *The Fire of Love* Rolle cannot emphasize enough the need for love, as well as its effects. To reach the point of burning love of Christ requires commitment and discipline, the rejection of the world and all its empty values. Then the ingress of the love will destroy lustful and other impure thoughts and compel complete attention to Christ:

> They that begin to love Christ, afterward in great joy of love and honey-sweet burning shall not cease to sing full lovely songs to Jesu Christ. Truly no earthly thing pleases him that truly loves

147

Christ, for by the greatness of love all passing things seem foul. With the bodily eyes fleshly things are seen, but the righteous behold heavenly things with a clean and meek heart: the which, enlightened by the flame of heavenly sight, feel themselves loosed from the burden of sin, and afterward they cease to sin in will; whose heart turned into fire halses [embraces] in desire nothing earthly but always is busy to thirl [penetrate] high things.[8]

Those who attain this love will then turn away from human consolation "as if it were reek [smoke] that hurts his eyes" and be utterly transformed. Just as "the air is stricken by the sunbeam, and by the shining of its light is altogether shining, so a devout mind, enflamed with the fire of Christ's love and fulfilled with desire for the joys of heaven, seems all love, because it is altogether turned into another likeness."[9] Rolle is optimistic that radical transformation can occur in the individual, from a world– and self-oriented perspective to one of loving God and one's neighbor; the groundwork for achieving this lies in humility: the "more that a man meeks himself the more he raises God's worship on high."[10]

The Cloud of Unknowing

After the warm, positive, spiritual exuberance of Richard Rolle, the anonymous author of the *Cloud of Unknowing*, which was written in the second half of the fourteenth century and is one of the great mystical treatises of medieval England, seems much more sober and measured in their apophatic approach. Yet *The Cloud of Unknowing* is equally rewarding, with its acute psychological insights and its insistence on the importance for the contemplative of "a naked intent directed unto God."[11]

Just who the *Cloud*'s author was remains a mystery. Most of those who have debated the issue believe he was a priest or a monk, possibly of the Carthusian order; it has also been suggested that the writer might have been a woman.[12] Whoever it was wrote in the same East Midlands dialect of English used by Chaucer and wrote a number of other works, including a translation of the *Mystical Theology* of Dionysius the Areopagite, whose negative theology is much in evidence in the *Cloud*. From his or her various writings, it can be inferred that the author was an experienced contemplative

THE FLAME OF ENGLISH MYSTICISM

as well as a confident and original thinker who possessed a keen satirical wit. Chapter 53 of the *Cloud*, for instance, wryly exposes false contemplatives and their affectations:

> Some set their eyes in their heads as they were sturdy sheep beaten in the head, and as they should die anon. Some hang their heads on one side as if a worm were in their ears. Some pipe when they should speak, as if there were no spirit in their bodies.[13]

The book's central theme is the practice and rewards of contemplative prayer and the idea of the "cloud of unknowing." The would-be contemplative must try to forget the things of the sensual world and develop a longing for God.[14] But having embarked upon the spiritual quest, he will soon encounter a sort of "darkness," which the author terms a "cloud of unknowing" (that is, a lack of knowledge). This cloud blocks the way to God. It prevents an understanding of God and the experience of the "sweetness" of his love. The contemplative's task is not to give up but to maintain desire for God. For the cloud is a fact of spiritual experience, and God can be felt, or seen, only in it.

To progress as far as the cloud of unknowing, which is, paradoxically, both a barrier and the means of access to God, it is first necessary to reject the world and the thoughts and memories it produces. This is done by putting what the author calls a "cloud of forgetting" between yourself and the things of the world.[15] For the very process of thinking about something causes the soul to focus on it—just as someone about to shoot stares at the intended target. So unless you forget the world and direct your thoughts solely at God, a barrier is created, preventing any sort of contact with him. Similarly, it is necessary to suppress the "sharp stirring" of your "understanding," or imagination, which presses upon you during contemplation: failure to suppress it means it will suppress you.[16] What is crucial is that you maintain "a blind stirring of love unto God for Himself," and keep secretly pressing on the cloud of unknowing: this is what is healthy for the soul, not pleasant visions of heaven with its angels, saints, and celestial music. You must direct your love to the cloud of unknowing or, rather, let it be drawn up by God.

There are other matters the apprentice contemplative must attend to in order to progress to the cloud and God, including

DAZZLING DARKNESS

reading, thinking, and praying. To read God's word (or hear it in a sermon) is like looking in a mirror. As a mirror reveals a speck of dirt on your face, so God's word enables the soul, otherwise blinded by sin, to see the dirt within its conscience. Prayer, for those who are some way along the contemplative path, consists of unpremeditated thoughts or words directed toward God. If words are used, then the fewer there are of them the better. In fact, a word of one syllable is best. For just as a man or woman frightened by a fire will simply yell out "Fire!" to attract attention directly and quickly, so a one-syllable word deeply felt "pierceth the ears of Almighty God" more effectively than "any long psalter unmindfully mumbled in the teeth."[17]

The mystic's path involves discipline, persistence, and hard work, as the author freely admits. Contemplatives must "beat upon" the cloud, toiling to eradicate memories of the sensual world, and subject themselves to the cloud of forgetting. But help may come in the form of divine grace. Operating within the soul, the action of grace can happen out of the blue, shooting out to God like a spark from a fire, causing the soul to forget in a flash the things of the world (although it can quickly backslide).[18] If the contemplative perseveres, God may sometimes reward him or her by sending out a beam of spiritual light that will pierce the cloud of unknowing that separates them. If this happens, the recipient will feel inflamed with the fire of God's love to an indescribable extent—the author of the *Cloud* will not dare to attempt to speak about it with his "blabbering fleshly tongue."[19]

In chapter 71 the author distinguishes between those who receive the grace of contemplation as an ecstasy only once in a while and those who are so spiritually attuned to God that they can experience his grace whenever they like (and in this state they are still able to participate fully in everyday life). Indeed, the author says that the practice of contemplation results in a number of benefits that enrich life in the world. Even plain-looking contemplatives will look attractive and be happy and cheerful company. They will feel comfortable with everyone they meet, whether they are sinners or not, and they will be able to discern people's personalities and needs and inspire others through their graceful nature to pursue the contemplative way. A self-portrait, perhaps, of the anonymous author?

THE FLAME OF ENGLISH MYSTICISM

Walter Hilton (ca. 1340–96)

The third peak of the mystical mountain range that rose in England in the fourteenth century was Walter Hilton, a man of great spiritual insight and practical wisdom. His greatest work was *The Ladder* (or *Scale*) *of Perfection*, which enjoyed great popularity up to the Reformation and was described as being "more precious than gold" in its first printed edition in 1494. Divided into two books, the first addressed specifically to an anchoress, the *Ladder*, with its implication of a progressive upward journey and its echo of Jacob's ladder connecting earth to heaven (the ladder image also appeared, as we have seen, in Perpetua's vision and was used by John Climacus), describes various aspects of the spiritual life. It gives the stages to be followed in order to reach contemplation of God, a journey that is centered on Christ (Hilton emphasizes the central role of Christ in the spiritual journey more than Rolle and the *Cloud* author do).

Not much is known about Hilton. It is thought he may have studied at Cambridge and that he may have been a hermit for a while. More certain is that he became an Augustinian canon at Thurgarton in Nottinghamshire. His date of birth is uncertain, but he is said to have died on March 24, 1396. What can be inferred about him was that he was a sensible, conscientious, humble, and devout soul who was extremely learned—his works indicate that he had studied Augustine and Bernard, among others. His temperament was such that he avoided the more speculative theology of the *Cloud* author and was wary of the highly experiential mysticism of Rolle. Yet, although he claims not to have had profound mystical experiences himself, his sensitivity toward and quiet enthusiasm for the contemplative life indicate that he was able, at the very least, to empathize strongly with such experiences.

The first of the *Ladder*'s two books gives sound guidance on how to develop the spiritual life. It talks of the merits of the active and contemplative lives, the former based around religious externals and good deeds, the latter concerned with the inner journey to God. The contemplative life has different stages. The first consists in getting to know God, through reason, teachings, and the scriptures, which, however, do not bring any direct "inward savour of God."[20] The second stage—more suited, he says, to uneducated, less

151

DAZZLING DARKNESS

sophisticated people—is simply loving God without the need for intellectual understanding. If blessed with divine grace, a person meditating on God may feel great love or a sense of trust or awe, and even an outpouring of emotion that can cleanse the heart of its sin.[21] The third and highest stage of contemplation involves both knowing and loving God, which happens when the soul, through perfecting the virtues, is "reformed" or restored to the "image of Jesus." This may result in the soul's being rapt and having such a perfect vision of ultimate truth—accompanied by a "soft, sweet, burning love"—that for a time it becomes one with God and bears the likeness of the Trinity.[22] Although the beginnings of this third stage can be experienced in this life, its fulfillment occurs only in heaven.

The second book of the *Ladder* begins by saying that the soul is the image of God, filled with love and light, and that it was corrupted by the sin of Adam, before God ensured the possibility of its being reformed by the atonement of Christ. The process of reforming can happen in two ways: by faith, through the sacraments of baptism and penance, which is enough for salvation, and, second, by faith and by feeling, which is rewarded by the bliss of heaven.[23] Suitable for contemplatives, this second way takes a long time and needs great effort, but it results in the destruction in the soul of sensuality and worldly desires and paves the way for the ingress of grace. The soul and its faculties are made new, and the reformed soul comes, bit by bit, to know and see God.[24]

In an extended passage, Hilton compares the reform of feeling in the soul to a pilgrimage to Jerusalem. In the same way that a pilgrim leaves behind his home and family, the spiritual pilgrim must leave behind his good and bad deeds and embrace poverty, setting his heart on the spiritual Jerusalem, which represents "contemplation in perfect love of God."[25] He also talks about the "night" that the pilgrim must travel through. The transition from the light of this world (that is, creaturely love of it) to the light of heaven, or love of God, does not happen suddenly—the night intervenes. Less daunting than John of the Cross's "dark night," Hilton's night represents the withdrawal of thoughts and affections from the world in order to focus on Jesus: it is a "good, glowing darkness" that excludes false, worldly love and leads to the light of truth. The

THE FLAME OF ENGLISH MYSTICISM

night may be a painful experience, but if pilgrims can get used to it, they will experience peace, gradual spiritual enlightenment, and the destruction of impure thoughts and desires. When this takes place, the goal is near at hand and they will glimpse Jerusalem far off "because of the twinkling rays of light shining from it."[26]

Julian of Norwich (ca. 1342–1420)

Perhaps the greatest of the medieval English mystics, Mother Julian of Norwich lived as an anchoress dedicated to a life of solitude and prayer in a cell attached to the city's Church of Saint Julian (from which she took her name). Her *Revelations of Divine Love*, which exists in shorter and longer versions, is a classic of the contemplative life. It continues to fascinate modern believers, many of them drawn by Julian's emphasis on humility, her view of God as being "homely and courteous," her devotion to the suffering Christ, and her espousal of the idea, articulated before by Anselm and others, of the motherhood of God—a view that stresses the tenderness and procreative power of the deity. Julian is also attractive for her optimism in the saving power of God, encapsulated by her oft-quoted words "And all shall be well and shall be well, and all manner of things shall be well" (lines made famous by T. S. Eliot in his poem "Little Gidding").[27]

Julian's life is mostly shrouded in mystery. She is thought to have been born in about 1342 and to have died in about 1420. The turning point in her life came in May 1373, when, at the age of thirty during a life-threatening illness, she experienced a series of sixteen "shewings" or revelations in the form of visions and spiritual truths and insights. In the first shewing she saw an image of Jesus during the Passion with blood trickling down from the crown of thorns. Over the course of one day, she experienced another fourteen visions, mostly of the Passion. Then, in the following night, she received the sixteenth and last one, when God reassured her that all the shewings she had received had come from him and were not hallucinations.

At some point after the revelations, Julian became an anchoress, that is to say a woman who withdrew from the world (the name "anchoress" comes from a Greek word meaning "withdraw") and lived in a cell close to a monastery or attached to a church to conduct a life of prayer and contemplation. Living as an anchoress was a recognized calling for women. Their life within a cell began ceremonially with a Mass for the dead, symbolizing their death to the world. The cell itself would typically have two windows, one that looked inwards to the church it was attached to so that the anchoress could hear Mass; the other looked outward and enabled contact with lay people. Recluses "gave advice, settled disputes, foretold events, and even pronounced on the fate of the dead."[28]

As an anchoress, Julian wrote down the essential substance of her mystical experiences. But she continued to ponder them over a period of twenty years and ended up writing a longer, more substantial account that includes her reflections on their meaning. She describes herself as being a "simple, unlettered creature"—she may in fact have dictated her thoughts to a secretary—but it is clear that she was well versed in the Bible and the thought of Paul and John. She could also write vividly. With an artist's eye she describes the moment during her first revelation when she watched blood falling like "pellets" in such number that it was like water dripping from "eaves after a great shower of rain" and that the drops of blood on Jesus's forehead were round "like scales from a herring."[29]

In her book, Julian is concerned with important theological issues such as the efficacy of prayer and the primacy of divine love. She is also preoccupied by the problem of sin. In a vision, Julian sees that God is present in everything, and she is certain that he can do no sin, which leads her to believe that sin has no substance: it is an absence of good, nothing. But in an age when sin and suffering abounded (indeed, many believed that the plague and other disasters were directly attributable to sin), Julian was not entirely happy about this concept of sin. She puzzles about it throughout the book, looking at it from different angles. She recognizes that sin is "behovable"—a necessary part of life—and asserts that people have a "beastly will" that chooses what is bad but also a "godly will" that can never assent to sin.[30] And God reassures her that because the Fall—the worst event ever to have happened to mankind—had been more than counteracted by Christ's atonement, any lesser sins could also be put right by him.[31] She comes to the conclusion that what people see as sin God sees from a different, eternal perspective, and that

THE FLAME OF ENGLISH MYSTICISM

through the atonement of Christ, "whenever God looks at any of us, even in our sin, God sees Christ."[32]

Julian is also instructive about prayer. In the fourteenth shewing, in response to her admission that she sometimes feels as dry and barren after prayer as before it, God tells her that he is the "ground of her beseeching"—the foundation of her prayer; it is his will that she should pray, and it is he who makes her will it and speak it. Prayer, she then goes on to say, is a "true, gracious, lasting will of the soul, united and fastened into the will of our Lord by the sweet inward work of the Holy Ghost." She also paints the attractive image of God taking prayer and sending it up above and placing it in the heavenly treasure, "where it shall never perish." So, despite any feelings of dryness, we must continue with our prayers—God will receive them with delight: our mood is irrelevant to their effectiveness since God accepts good intentions and work "howsoever we feel."[33]

Throughout her book Julian emphasizes the central place of the love of God for his creation—his "homely loving," as she calls it. She is granted a visual embodiment of this when God shows her in the palm of her hand a small object, as round as a ball and the "size of a hazel nut." She looks at it with "the eye of understanding" and wonders what it is. She receives the divine intuition that the object is "all that is made." It seems so small and fragile, however, that she wonders how it might last, but then receives the assurance that it will last and "last forever because God loves it." This little object teaches her three things—applicable to all creation and revealing the Triune God—namely that "God made it, God loves it, and God keeps it."[34]

The supremacy of God's love is reaffirmed at the end of the book. In response to Julian's long search for the meaning of her visions, God reveals the answer in unambiguous and memorable terms: "Would you learn your Lord's meaning in this thing? Learn it well; love was his meaning. Who showed it to you? Love. What did he show you? Love. Why did he show it? For love."[35]

Margery Kempe (ca. 1373–1438)

Born into a merchant family in Lynn, Norfolk, Margery Kempe was a mystic, pilgrim, and author of *The Book of Margery Kempe*, possibly

155

DAZZLING DARKNESS

the first spiritual memoir written in English. Apart from going on extensive, hazardous pilgrimages in Spain, Italy, Germany, and the Holy Land, she was known for a variety of mystical experiences, including visions of Christ and the "gift of tears."

Little is known of Margery's early life. Aged about twenty she married a respectable Lynn citizen named John Kempe, a union that would result in fourteen children. Evidence of her visionary gifts emerged after the birth of her first child, when, seriously ill, Margery is said to have heard the devil tell her she would be damned, and to have seen devils with fiery mouths. This ominous image was countered by a salutary vision of Christ, who came to her bedside and said: "My daughter: why do you reject me when I've never rejected you?" As he spoke, Margery saw the air become radiant and Christ slowly rose up before her eyes.[36]

Margery settled into the rhythm of being a dynamic medieval housewife, producing children, managing the family household, as well as becoming involved in local brewing and milling businesses. At the same time her mystical nature was continuing to develop. At one point in her life she heard a mysterious "melody" that was so harmonious she said it gave her an idea of what heaven was like.[37] This experience spurred her on to commit herself more wholeheartedly to the Christian faith and the practice of prayer, confession, and doing penance.

Over the following years Margery received visions of Christ and the Virgin Mary and began to long for freedom from her marriage and domestic responsibilities in order to devote herself to God. Her chosen way of withdrawing from the world was not a monastic cell, such as that of Julian of Norwich, but a life on the road, as a pilgrim. In 1413, with the consent of her husband (whom she had persuaded to agree to sexual abstinence) she made a pilgrimage to the Holy Land, via Venice, where she visited Jerusalem, Bethlehem, the Jordan River, and other holy places associated with Jesus. She returned home through Italy, stopping off at Assisi and Rome. Pilgrimage was a dangerous occupation in medieval times. Roads were rough, maps were non-existent, and brigands and outlaws haunted the woods, preying on unwary travelers. A woman journeying on her own, like Margery, had to rely on traveling companions for safety. But the Book suggests she was a difficult person to befriend. She often

THE FLAME OF ENGLISH MYSTICISM

seemed to live in a spiritual world of her own, prone to the "gift of tears," during which she would wail loudly in church and other public places, especially when she saw a mother holding a baby (which reminded her of the Christ child). When she tried to tag on to a group of English pilgrims in Venice, they apparently "forsook her and went away from her, leaving her alone. And some of them said that they would not go with her for a hundred pound."[38]

Whether protected by her faith in, and focus on, Christ, or perhaps simply by a thick skin, Margery was undeterred by reactions to her unusual behavior. In 1417 she again set out on a long pilgrimage, this time to Santiago de Compostela in northwest Spain. On her return journey, back in England, she was arrested in Leicester for suspected Lollardy, but she stood her ground against the church and civic authorities and escaped with three weeks in jail.

Margery continued her itinerant life up to the age of sixty. In 1433, after the death of one of her sons, she accompanied his German wife back to her home of Danzig in eastern Prussia. At the same time she took the opportunity of going to visit holy shrines at Wilsnack and Aachen. How she passed her final years is not clear, though it seems that she remained resident in Lynn.

Margery's life seems like a constant march of physical travel matched by spiritual or visionary flights. Not for her the stasis of Julian of Norwich, whom she once visited in her cell. Margery relates that she went to Julian on the command of the Lord and told the anchoress about "many wonderful revelations." She also complained to her that her usual confessor was "right sharp" with her and did not believe her feelings. Julian replied that God had appointed her confessor to be her "scourge" and that he was dealing with Margery in the same way that a smith uses a file to make rusty, dirty, iron gleam again. The sharper the confessor's words, the more Margery's soul would shine "in the sight of God."[39]

Although often rejected by human society, Margery found solace in God. She would talk and listen to him as if he were a present companion. For example, when she was sojourning in Rome, she said that God told her he would have her "wedded to my Godhead" and that she would live with him forever. She then received a vision of the marriage ceremony itself, at which saints and angels were present.[40]

The divine presence was not only a verbal phenomenon. Her tears were another manifestation of it—disturbing though they were to lay people and churchmen alike. Her book records that a friar of Lynn was highly critical of her weeping until he remembered that the beguine holy woman, Marie of Oignies, was also prone to tears. His change of attitude toward Margery was completed when, one time at Mass, on reading the Gospel, he himself broke down into copious and uncontrollable weeping, wetting his vestments and the altar.[41]

Apart from words and tears, Margery sometimes felt "the fire of love" burning inside her, reminiscent of the experience of Richard Rolle. At first she feared its effects, until God informed her it was the action of the Holy Spirit burning away her sins. Sometimes, again, she would hear sweet, divine melodies; or the sound of the Holy Spirit, which she compared to the sound of bellows being worked, or the song of a dove or a robin.[42] By these tokens she believed that God, or Jesus Christ, was reassuring her of his love for her, a feeling reinforced when Christ declared to her directly that she was obedient to his will and clung fast to him "as the skin of a boiled stockfish sticks to a hand." His commendation was followed by a promise that a soul like hers would never be parted from him.[43]

158

9

WOMEN MYSTICS OF ITALY AND SWEDEN

All that I have said is as nothing compared to what I feel within, the witnessed correspondence of love between God and the soul.

—Catherine of Genoa

The dominant concerns of the church in the late fourteenth century revolved around the return of the papacy to Rome from its exile in Avignon, which eventually occurred in 1377, and immediately following this homecoming, the Great Schism, when two popes, each with his own set of cardinals and bureaucratic machinery, claimed to be the rightful head of the church. The crisis gave momentum to what is called the conciliar movement, which asserted that the supreme authority of the church should reside not in the papacy but in a general council, which had the power to depose popes if necessary.

Although the Avignon popes were able to count a number of positives during their seventy years of office, such as the expansion and efficient running of the papal bureaucracy, and although faults such as nepotism could be found before and after their time, the papacy's very presence in the south of France and the vast preponderance of French cardinals led many in Europe to believe that its universalist aspirations were irretrievably compromised. Eventually, Pope Gregory XI, realizing acutely the need to return the papacy to the church's ancient spiritual center, and under pressure from influential individuals such as Catherine of Siena, made the momentous journey back to Rome in January 1377. However, his death in the following year created a worse crisis than

DAZZLING DARKNESS

the popes' exile. The newly elected Italian pope, Urban VI, formerly the archbishop of Bari, soon showed a despotic temperament, and the French cardinals, who made up the majority of the Sacred College and felt they had been pressured by the Roman mob to choose Urban, decided to elect another man, Robert of Geneva, as the antipope Clement VII, who duly returned to Avignon. So now there were two popes, with Europe split over its support for them: France, Spain, and Scotland backed Clement, while Urban could count on England, Germany, and Hungary.

To the despair of churchmen and theologians throughout Europe, the Great Schism lasted beyond the death of the two popes. Successors were chosen to fill their shoes, perpetuating the division. For many, the only hope seemed to lie in a general council that could depose the two rivals and elect a new pope who could unify the Western church. This nearly happened at the Council of Pisa in 1409; the problem was that after the election of the new pope, Alexander V, the Avignon and Roman popes refused to step down, so the church now had three pontiffs!

The schism was finally resolved at the Council of Constance in Germany (1414–18), when all three popes were replaced by a yet another new one, Martin V. The council also tried to settle the issue of papal authority, issuing a decree that stated its own authority came directly from Christ and that everyone, including the pope, "is bound to obey it in matters concerning the faith."[1] The council was also notable for the execution of the Czech reformer Jan Hus (1369–1415), a priest and university lecturer in Prague in Bohemia (modern Czech Republic). Hus, who was much influenced by John Wycliffe, emphasized the centrality of the Bible and condemned the lax morality of the clergy and practices such as the sale of indulgences, certificates that were believed to bring about a reduction or complete remission of the deceased's time in purgatory. Hus was summoned to Constance to defend his beliefs, and despite promises of a safe conduct by Emperor Sigismund, the ruler of Germany, Bohemia, and Hungary, he was condemned as a heretic and burned to death in 1415.

Although Constance seemed to vindicate supporters of the conciliar movement, the aftermath proved to be a disappointment to them. The principle that general councils were superior to popes

160

WOMEN MYSTICS OF ITALY AND SWEDEN

and that they should be held on a regular basis eventually foundered, despite the efforts of the Councils of Pavia (soon moved to Siena because of plague) in 1423 and Basel (1431–49). The latter was attended by the German Nicholas of Cusa (1401–64), a philosopher and churchman who also had mystical leanings. Nicholas initially supported the conciliar movement, believing that it represented the best opportunity for reform and unity in the church. But eventually he felt estranged by its radicalism and sided with the papal party. By the time Pope Pius II (r. 1458–64) described conciliarism as a "pestilent poison,"[2] the papacy had regained its preeminence, if not its prestige.

The Council of Constance may have healed the schism, but it was unable to implement much-needed church reforms. Wycliffe and Hus had been two militant figures voicing their disenchantment with the church establishment. But there were other, more mainstream voices at this time expressing their disquiet: the French churchman and theologian Jean de Gerson warned his sister not to expose herself to corruption by entering a convent, and the monk and scholar Ambrogio Traversari advised the Franciscan Bernardino of Siena not to compromise his evangelical spirit by becoming a bishop.[3]

Bridget (Birgitta) of Sweden (ca. 1303–73)

Those who did more than most to persuade Pope Gregory XI to move the papacy back to Rome included Catherine of Siena and Bridget (Birgitta) of Sweden, two women who combined deep mystical sensibilities with astute political acumen. Like Margery Kempe (who fervently admired her), Bridget of Sweden had two distinct phases in her life. The first was devoted to raising eight children with her devout husband, Ulf Gudmarsson. The second, after Ulf's death, involved a greater commitment to the religious and mystical life. In this second phase she not only continued to have powerful visions—experienced since childhood—but also took an active interest in church reform: she wrote letters to church and civic leaders and strove to persuade various popes to end the papacy's exile in Avignon and return to Rome. She also founded an order of nuns, known as the Bridgettines (Birgittines), and

161

DAZZLING DARKNESS

recorded her visions in her *Revelations*, which had a wide influence throughout Europe.

Born into Swedish aristocracy, Bridget was cousin to King Magnus II of Sweden and the daughter of the governor of Uppland, one of the wealthiest men in the country. Her life was recorded in Latin by Bridget's confessors and, according to their account, just before Bridget was born, a local parish priest saw a vision of a virgin sitting in a shining cloud in the night sky. The virgin proclaimed that a girl was about to be born whose voice would be heard throughout the world.[4]

Bridget was raised in a devout household (her father, grandfather, and great-grandfather had all made pilgrimages to Jerusalem), and from an early age was noted for her religious practices and determination. At the age of thirteen she was married off to a young nobleman, Ulf Gudmarsson, and over the years she bore him eight children, including a daughter who would become Saint Catherine of Sweden (1331–81). Meanwhile, she became renowned for her charitable nature and virtuous living.

In about 1341, now in her late thirties, Bridget embarked on a fateful pilgrimage to Santiago de Compostela in the company of her husband: on their return Ulf fell ill at Arras, near Flanders, and never recovered. His death in 1344 proved to be a turning point for Bridget. Responding to a vision in which she saw herself as the bride of Christ, she gave her possessions away and took to wearing plain garments. She immersed herself in spiritual practices and began to receive visions in greater number and luminosity. In one of these she was instructed by Christ to found a new religious order, the Bridgettines. With financial help from King Magnus, she established a new "double monastery" (for women and men, who lived together, but in separate houses) in the town of Vadstena in Östergötland in southern Sweden. Vadstena became the preeminent religious center in Sweden, and Bridgettine houses were subsequently founded throughout Europe.

In 1349, with her daughter Catherine by her side, Bridget set out on a pilgrimage to Rome, arriving there the following year in time for the Jubilee celebrations. Although Pope Clement VI was resident in Avignon at this time, he sent a cardinal to represent him at this huge Christian celebration in the Eternal City. At this point

WOMEN MYSTICS OF ITALY AND SWEDEN

in time, Bridget was concerned with two major issues: to obtain the pope's official endorsement for her new order's Rule (eventually confirmed by Urban V in 1370); and to agitate for the papacy to return from Avignon to its spiritual home. As it turned out, Bridget never returned to Sweden. Apart from making various pilgrimages in Europe and to the Holy Land, Bridget stayed in Rome until she died in 1373. After her death, her remains were taken to the Vadstena monastery.

Bridget is said to have had visions from an early age, often seeing Christ and the Virgin Mary (who on one occasion helped her during a difficult birth labor). Once, when she was seven, she saw in her bedroom a vision of an altar with a woman dressed in glowing clothes sitting above it, holding a crown. With Bridget's assent, the woman placed the crown on her head. About three years later, the night after she had listened to a sermon in church about the passion of Christ, Bridget saw the wounded Jesus, as if he had just been crucified. She asked him who had done this to him, and he told her it was those who "scorn me and neglect my love."[5]

From about 1345 onward Bridget received what became known specifically as her "revelations"—locutionary messages and visions. They began with Christ's personal commendation: "You shall be my bride and my channel, and you shall hear and see spiritual things, and my Spirit shall remain with you even until your death."[6] Over time she dictated about 700 visions to her confessors. Often stern and minatory, the revelations embody Bridget's intense piety and her concern for the renewal of society and the regeneration of the church. She often uses homely images—a dog off its leash, a dove seeing a hawk, a watermill, cloth twice-dyed in scarlet—to make moral or spiritual points. Some revelations celebrate the Incarnation of Christ or relate to worship of the Virgin Mary; others touch on Swedish politics and the papacy. Many have an otherworldly content, for example her detailed vision of purgatory in which souls burn in a furnace: "The darkness that appeared around the furnace is called limbo. It comes from the darkness that is in the furnace. Yet both make up one place and one hell. Anyone entering it will never dwell in God."[7]

Her biographers make it clear that Bridget "saw and heard spiritual things and felt them in spirit" when she was awake and

DAZZLING DARKNESS

fully in her senses.[8] Nor was it solely Bridget who received visions about her life and destiny. For example, when Bridget was visiting the Swedish monastery of Saint Mary in Alvastra on Lake Vättern, a lay brother named Gerekin fell into a rapture and was told by a divine voice that Bridget was God's friend and that she would gather flowers from which people everywhere would "receive medicine." After she had arrived, Bridget received a direct instruction from Christ himself to go to the Eternal City: "Go to Rome, where the streets are paved with gold and reddened with the blood of saints."[9] Her visions and intimacy with Christ continued to the end of her life. Shortly before her death he appeared to her in her bedroom and told her she had been tested and must now prepare herself to be "clothed and consecrated as a nun."[10] Five days later she passed away after attending Mass.

Catherine of Siena (1347–80)

The daughter of a Sienese dyer, Catherine of Siena, like Bridget of Sweden and Teresa of Ávila (she and Teresa were both honored by being declared doctors of the church in 1970), was one for whom the contemplative and active lives were mutually supportive. Joyful, determined, fearless, and charismatic, Catherine led a highly disciplined religious life, practicing austerities and enjoying profound visions and other religious experiences. Yet far from tempting her to remain in solitude, her inner spiritual world nourished her public mission to help the sick and poor, to heal the divisions of a fractured society, and to reform the church. It was as if she could not bear fragmentation at any level and that for her the ideal of the unity and wholeness of the church was like an outward reflection of the soul brought to perfection in union with God. Her spirituality was marked by her devotion to Christ, whom she described as a bridge between man and God, and to his Passion and all-encompassing love—she once said that "nails would not have held the God-man fast had not love held him there."[11] Her sympathetic understanding of Christ was dramatically expressed when, at the age of twenty-eight, she experienced the stigmata, the five wounds of Christ.

Catherine was born with her twin sister (who died shortly afterward) in Siena in 1347—her mother had already given birth to twenty-two children. Her father, Giacomo Benincasa, ran a cloth-dyeing business and seems to have been reasonably prosperous. From her early years Catherine showed signs of a religious temperament, and she received her first vision, of Jesus, at the age of six or seven, after which she took a vow of perpetual virginity. Her parents did not encourage her spiritual aspirations and wanted her to marry and live a conventional life. Catherine determined otherwise: at the age of sixteen she joined the Dominican order as a tertiary, or lay sister, adopting the habit and lifestyle of a nun but remaining in the world. In fact, she lived at home: for three years she confined herself to her room, except for excursions to Mass, and spoke to no one except her confessor. During this time she fasted, slept little, and prayed and recited the divine office.

This period of her life ended in about 1366 or 1367 after she received a vision of her mystic marriage to Christ: she saw the Virgin Mary take her right hand and hold it out to Christ, who placed a ring on her finger. The vision was also a summons to take up the active life, inspired by Christ's love, and Catherine responded by breaking her self-imposed seclusion and performing charitable works for the poor, lepers, and sick of Siena, doing the rounds of prisons and hospitals. She also attracted a number of followers, men and women from all sections of society, who formed a loyal and devoted "family," much to the derision of other Sienese townsfolk.

In 1370 Catherine received another powerful mystical experience during which Christ exchanged her heart for his and she was bidden to engage more widely in the world. Although illiterate until very late in her life, Catherine began dictating and sending letters—382 of them have survived—to people from all walks of life, including popes, kings, queens, and princes. In 1375 her devotion to Christ was confirmed by her receiving the stigmata. During Communion in a church in Pisa, she saw rays of light from the wounds of Christ stream toward her and pierce her hands, feet, and side, but in accordance with her prayer, the marks remained invisible while she was alive.

A year later, in 1376, Catherine became personally embroiled in the armed struggle that had broken out between Florence and the papacy and had led to the revolt of most of the papal states (territories, mostly in Italy, under the sovereign authority of the popes). At the same time she also found herself playing a pivotal part in ending the Babylonian Captivity. This occurred when she traveled to the papal court to negotiate with Pope Gregory XI on behalf of the Florentines. Although her mission was unsuccessful, she made a great impression on the pope and helped to persuade him to return the papacy to Rome, despite formidable pressure against this move by the king of France and most of the cardinals of the Sacred College. She carried on her crusade for church unity during the Great Schism. Despite having reservations about Urban VI, who was widely regarded as mentally unstable, Catherine recognized the legitimacy of his election and was prepared to fight his cause. At his request, she took up residence in Rome and sent letters across western Europe to drum up support for him. She stayed in Rome for the rest of her life, succumbing to a stroke on April 29, 1380. She was canonized in 1461.

Catherine's teachings are found principally in her work *The Dialogue*, completed in Siena in 1378 before her departure to Rome, as well as in her letters. Much of her spiritual thought came from divine inspiration received during mystical experiences. It is said that her ecstatic states would last for hours, during which she was unconscious to the world—to the extent that she did not respond to being pricked with a needle.[12] In *The Dialogue*, which takes the form of exchanges between God and Catherine herself, representing the human soul, she gives an insight into the nature of ecstasy. God explains to her that the soul unites with him through love, at which point the body loses its powers: the memory is filled only with God, the intellect rises up and gazes on the object of divine truth, and the affection loves and unites with the same object of truth. Because these powers are immersed in God, the body loses its ability to see, hear, and speak (except for divine utterance), and its members cannot move.[13]

Catherine emphasized the importance of self-knowledge in the spiritual quest. In a letter to a friend, she advises her to create within herself a spiritual abode, a "cell of true self-knowledge" that she can carry with her at all times. Self-knowledge, which leads to knowledge of God, is founded on humility.[14] Associated with humility is the need to get rid of self-will, which traps us in selfishness and prevents us from realizing the love of God. When the

WOMEN MYSTICS OF ITALY AND SWEDEN

soul feels this divine love within, it becomes emptied of ordinary desires and love, and it surrenders itself entirely to God. It becomes a vessel for God's goodness and extends the love received from God to all God's creatures.[15]

Anticipating "the dark night of the soul" of John of the Cross, Catherine says that on the road to union with God, the mystic must face the pain of God's withdrawing himself and the deprivation of his consolations. God does this to perfect the soul, to teach it humility and make it love him without any consciousness of self and attachment to sensuality. The soul, although acutely aware of God's withdrawal, must remain steadfast in its humble pursuit of self-knowledge, and it must wait in faith for the Holy Spirit to come to it.[16]

Humility, self-knowledge, faith, and perseverance lead to union with God, a state in which the soul no longer has its own will but is so ablaze with God that it is like a brand in a furnace that cannot be drawn out because it has turned into fire. Likewise, it is impossible to draw those united with God away from him—God tells Catherine in *The Dialogue* that he will stay in their souls both "by grace and feeling" so that whenever they want they can unite their spirits to him through love. Their union with God's love is so intimate that separation is impossible, and "every time and place for them is a time and place for prayer."[17]

Catherine of Genoa (1447–1510)

Like her Sienese namesake, Catherine of Genoa combined a life of asceticism, prayer, and mystical states with action in the world—in her case laboring for many years in her local municipal hospital. For the first twenty-six years of her life, however, there was little to suggest that she would reach the spiritual heights that enabled her to serve her fellow citizens with such compassion and energy. Marriage at the age of sixteen to a husband who proved to be faithless and neglectful seemed to be the lifelong cross she would have to bear. The extraordinary transformation that turned the chaff of her wretchedness into the gold of divine peacefulness and a new sense of purpose in life occurred in the form of a mystical experience when she was at her lowest ebb. From then on she became, in the

DAZZLING DARKNESS

words of Evelyn Underhill, "in fruition and activity, in rest and in work, not only a great active and a great ecstatic, but one of the deepest gazers into the secrets of Eternal Love that the history of Christian mysticism contains."[18]

Catherine was born in the great Italian maritime city of Genoa in 1447. Her parents were prominent members of Genoese society: her father's family, the Fieschi, boasted two popes, Innocent IV and Adrian V, among their forebears, and he himself became the viceroy of Naples. Catherine developed a religious sensibility from an early age, and by the time she was thirteen she was eager to enter a convent; her request was turned down because of her youth. Three years later she was married off to a certain Giuliano Adorno, a young Genoese nobleman, who quickly showed himself to be a dissolute philanderer.

For the first five years of marriage Catherine bore her misery with passive resignation; for the next five years she tried to adopt a more extravert lifestyle, seeking consolation, or at least distraction, in society—in vain. Then in March 1473 her life changed permanently when she underwent a sudden spiritual conversion. Her sister, who was a nun in a local convent, encouraged Catherine to make her confession to the nuns' confessor. As Catherine knelt before him, she felt in her heart "the wound of unmeasured love of God" and saw her faults and unhappiness beside God's goodness so clearly that she nearly collapsed. Now filled with boundless, ardent love, she vowed inwardly to cease from worldly desires and a sinful life.[19] Her ideal was to accept the will of God: "We must not wish other than what happens from moment to moment, all the while, however, exercising ourselves in goodness." [20]

This mystical experience was the spiritual foundation on which the rest of her life was built. That life was mainly devoted to sharing with the sick in the Pammatone, Genoa's hospital, the infinite divine love she had received. She was aided in her work, surprisingly, by none other than her husband, Giuliano, who had also felt the call of God and become a Franciscan tertiary. In 1479 the couple, who had agreed to live in continence, moved into the hospital to be nearer their charges. Catherine was eventually given a senior administrative position, and she continued to work tirelessly and selflessly, especially in 1493 when Genoa was ravaged by plague.

WOMEN MYSTICS OF ITALY AND SWEDEN

She herself caught the disease, but survived, as did Giuliano (although he died four years later). All this time Catherine had led a rather idiosyncratic religious life. She regularly fasted for long periods and received Communion on a daily basis, at a time when it was rare for laypeople to do so, but she did not have a spiritual director and rarely went to confession. Then in 1499 she found a congenial confessor in a priest named Cattaneo Marabotto, who for the rest of her life gave her spiritual guidance and listened to her innermost thoughts and concerns. She finally died, after a painful illness, in 1510.

Catherine's life and teachings were recorded in an anonymous work called *Vita e Dottrina* (Life and Teaching), which was published about forty years after her death and includes material on which her treatise on purgatory and her *Spiritual Dialogue* were based (in modern times Baron Friedrich von Hügel made a pioneering study of her in his *Mystical Element of Religion*, published in 1908). Scholars still debate the extent to which Catherine's works, which she did not write herself, record her actual thoughts, and the consensus seems to be that the important treatise on purgatory, at the very least, is an authentic reflection of her beliefs.

It is also clear that Catherine's postconversion life was underpinned by mystical experiences and an awareness of the divine presence. Her whole being appears to have been dominated by a sense of God, to the extent that nothing could distract her from him. Even when attending church she was oblivious to what was being spoken or done because she was absorbed in an inner divine light. Her attention to God made it difficult for her to converse with anyone, and she would become so enrapt that she would go off and find a secluded place. Sometimes she was discovered lying on the ground, face in hands, evidently caught up in a transport of indescribable joy and could not be disturbed by being shouted at. Equally, she could lie as still as a corpse for hours on end but then when called would immediately get up and go about her duties.

For Catherine such mystical consciousness and bliss is the result of a process directed by God, who "revivifies the soul with a special grace of His. In no other way could the soul renounce its self-centredness."[21] God finds the soul he calls to him to be initially full of sin, which is "the object of God's hatred, for it prevents his love from transforming us."[22] And so he inspires the soul with a sense of virtue and encourages it to reach a state of perfection; then, through his grace, he leads it to self-annihilation and transformation into a state of blessedness. At this point the soul does nothing of itself—whether it is speaking, willing, or feeling—because it is God who guides it directly. The soul itself is now in a state of blissful serenity, as if "immersed in an ocean of utmost peace."[23]

Throughout her life Catherine was only too well aware of suffering—mental, emotional, and physical—both in her own life and in the lives of those she tended. For her, spiritual suffering from an acute sense of sinfulness was a necessary condition of the soul, which begins the process of purification here on earth and continues it after death in purgatory—as she herself put it, the soul's "ardor in transforming itself into God is its purgatory."[24] It is a process that eventually ends with the soul's reaching the joyful state of being in God's presence without the impediment of sin. She compares the soul in purgatory encrusted with sin to an everyday object that has been covered up and cannot reflect sunlight. In the same way that the object reflects the sun in proportion to how much it is uncovered, so the soul will mirror the light of the true sun, God's love, as its sinful excretions are burned away by the purgatorial fire, and the more it is exposed to divine love, "the more the soul responds to that love and its joy increases."[25]

During her life Catherine felt this love firsthand—"All that I have said is as nothing compared to what I feel within, the witnessed correspondence of love between God and the soul"[26]—and she was able to channel it into selfless actions. She was fully aware of the constant struggle between self-will and God's will, the false self and the true self, and the way in which the individual could triumph only through the grace of pure love. This type of love is conditionless and selfless: "I will have nothing to do with a love which would be for God or in God. This is a love which pure love cannot abide; for pure love is God Himself."[27] And she was confident that her own experience of divine love was potentially open to everyone: "In this world, the rays of God's love," unbeknown to us, encircle us, "hungrily seeking" to penetrate us.[28]

10

EASTERN ORTHODOX MYSTICISM

He who sees in his heart a trace of hatred toward another
for some fault of his is a complete stranger to love of God,
for love of God can in no way tolerate hatred of man.

—Maximus the Confessor

The Orthodox Church emerged in the centuries after Emperor
Constantine I made Christianity the most favored religion in the
Roman Empire in the early fourth century (see Chapter Two) and
developed the small port of Byzantium into the imperial city of
Constantinople (today's Istanbul). From then on the empire had
two capitals, Rome in the west and Constantinople in the east, and
Christianity developed in these centers in different ways. After
the eclipse of the Western Roman empire in the fifth century, the
Eastern empire continued to thrive and gradually became known as
the Byzantine Empire.

At this point in time Rome and Constantinople were only two
among the five ancient patriarchal churches of Christendom (along
with Alexandria, Antioch, and Jerusalem). Rome, as the original
imperial capital and being the place where the two foremost
apostles, Peter and Paul, were buried, was accorded premier status.
But in the seventh century Muslim armies swept east and west from
Arabia and soon took Alexandria, Antioch, and Jerusalem, leaving
Rome and Constantinople as the two great remaining ecclesiastical
centers. At first, from about the middle of the seventh to the middle
of the eighth century, Greek influence at Rome was strong. Large
areas of Italy were under Byzantine control, and many popes were
of Greek stock. Eventually, however, the papacy realized that its

political security was better placed in a power that was closer to hand and more dependable than the Byzantines. So it was that in the mid-eighth century, under threat from the Lombards, Pope Stephen II turned to the West and formed a political alliance with the Frankish king Pépin. This distancing between the papacy and the Byzantine Empire was given further dramatic expression in 800, when Pope Leo III crowned Pépin's son, Charlemagne, Holy Roman Emperor, forging an alliance between the papacy and Western emperors that would last for centuries, although in time the relationship would prove difficult for both sides.

In addition to the political realignment between the East and the West, there were also differences between the Latin and Greek churches over doctrine and customs. Some of them seemed relatively slight: the Latins used unleavened bread during the Eucharist, the Greeks used leavened; the Greeks fasted on Saturdays, the Latins did not. The most important issue concerned the creed and what was known as the "procession of the Holy Spirit." In accordance with the ancient councils, the Greeks held that the Spirit "proceeded" only from the Father. The Latins, however, had gradually accepted the formula, possibly originating in Spain in the 600s, that the Spirit proceeded from both the Father *and the Son* (*Filioque*), which for the Greeks seemed to compromise the position of the Father as the only source of being. The discord between the two churches came to a head in 1054 during a meeting in Constantinople to discuss plans to counteract the threat of the Normans in southern Italy. The pope's representative Cardinal Humbert dramatically excommunicated the patriarch of Constantinople in the city's great church of Hagia Sophia, only to receive an anathema in return. The subsequent acts of mutual excommunication were formally revoked only in 1965.

The relationship between the two churches reached an all-time low during the Fourth Crusade (1202–04), when a formidable force of Western European crusaders (including French, Venetian and Flemish warriors) sacked Constantinople in 1204, leading to a profound bitterness and estrangement between the two churches that was not fully healed until the twenty-first century. Sir Stephen Runciman, the great historian of the Crusades, wrote that some of the crusaders "rushed in a howling mob down the streets and through the houses, snatching up everything that glittered and

EASTERN ORTHODOX MYSTICISM

destroying whatever they could not carry, pausing only to murder or to rape, or to break open the wine-cellars for their refreshment." The holiness of a building offered it no protection from looting:

> In St Sophia itself drunken soldiers could be seen tearing down the silken hangings and pulling the great silver iconostasis to pieces, while sacred books and icons were trampled under foot. While they drank merrily from the altar-vessels a prostitute set herself on the Patriarch's throne and began to sing a ribald French song. Nuns were ravished in their convents. Palaces and hovels alike were entered and wrecked. Wounded women and children lay dying in the streets. For three days the ghastly scenes of pillage and bloodshed continued, till the huge and beautiful city was a shambles.[1]

The crusaders duly installed one of their leaders, Baldwin, Count of Flanders, as the new Latin ruler of the Byzantine Empire, a regime that lasted for nearly sixty years. The remnants of the Byzantine government and the Orthodox Church were compelled to regroup in other parts of the empire, leaving their capital of Constantinople to the hated Latins. Pockets of Byzantine power were established in Trebizond on the Black Sea, in Epiros in western Greece, and in Nicaea, in Asia Minor. Eventually it was a Byzantine force from Nicaea that ended the Latin interregnum by recapturing Constantinople in 1261 and putting Michael Palaeologus on the imperial throne. The Orthodox Church then remained centered on the city until the Ottoman Turks captured it in 1453; after this, the city lost its spiritual authority: church buildings became dilapidated, the training of priests deteriorated, and clerical appointments were subject to corruption.

But if Byzantine Greece was the birthplace of Orthodox Christianity, it was Russia, after the fall of Constantinople to the Turks, that maintained Orthodox traditions most robustly into modern times. Christianity had penetrated Russia in the ninth and tenth centuries, mainly via the Byzantine Greeks. A turning point came in 988 when Vladimir of Kyiv (Kiev) (r. 980–1015), in the state modern historians call Kyivan Rus', was converted to the faith and married the Byzantine Emperor's sister, Anna, thenceforth making Orthodox Christianity the state religion. Initially the new official

173

DAZZLING DARKNESS

faith was confined to the cities. But over the years monasteries were founded, including the important Monastery of the Caves at Kyiv in 1051. During this period and for several centuries after, the Russian Church was subject to the Patriarch of Constantinople: Metropolitans of Russia tended to be Greek churchmen well into the thirteenth century.

In 1240 Russian Christianity was thrown into turmoil when the Mongols invaded and destroyed Kyiv. It was in the aftermath of this catastrophe that Sergius of Radonezh stepped onto the stage, the person who did more than anyone to strengthen the Russian Church, deepen its spirituality, and bring the Russian people together in the Christian faith. (Often associated with Sergius is his younger contemporary, the great icon painter Andrei Rublev [ca. 1370–1430], whose icon of the Holy Trinity, one of the finest icons ever painted, was created in honor of Sergius.)

Sergius helped to implant in the Russian religious psyche the importance of the spiritual figure known as the *starets,* a type of charismatic "religious elder" who gave spiritual counsel through wisdom of age and experience. However, the great age of the Russian *starets* was yet to come, in the nineteenth century, and the most significant of them at this time was Seraphim of Sarov (1759–1833).

* * *

The tradition of Orthodox mysticism goes back at least to the time of the Cappadocian Fathers and includes such notable spiritual figures as Dionysius the Areopagite and Maximus the Confessor. One important thread in the tradition is its mysticism of divine light, through which the faithful can become deified or divinized. This idea of a divine, transforming light is important in the works of the Orthodox mystics Symeon the New Theologian and Gregory Palamas and is rooted in the New Testament. Chapter 5 of Ephesians, for example, talks of true Christians being "light in the Lord" and "children of light." The Gospel of John describes Christ as "the true light that gives light to every man" (1:9); and the account of Christ's transfiguration on Mount Tabor before Peter, James, and John—"His face shone like the sun, and his clothes became as white as the light" (Matt. 17:2)—was a particularly significant text in

174

EASTERN ORTHODOX MYSTICISM

Orthodox spirituality. As the modern Orthodox scholar Vladimir Lossky has noted, "In the mystical theology of the Eastern Church, these expressions [of light] are not used as metaphors or as figures of speech, but as expressions for a real aspect of the Godhead."[2] Indeed, Lossky compared Western and Eastern approaches to spirituality to, respectively, the "solitude and abandonment of the night of Gethsemane" and "the light of the Transfiguration."[3]

Another distinctive feature of Orthodox spirituality was, and is, the practice of the mystical prayer known as "hesychasm," a word derived from the Greek *hesychia*, meaning "silence," "stillness," or "quietness." Beginning, it is thought, in about the fourth century, hesychasm developed through figures such as Gregory of Nyssa, Evagrius Ponticus, John Climacus, and Maximus the Confessor, and it especially thrived in monastic communities. Hesychasts attempted to rise to a level of prayer that went beyond sensuous imagery and the workings of the rational mind and resulted in a profound sense of inner peace. This, however, was not the ultimate aim, which was the reception of divine grace and deification. The prayer that became most favored in hesychast practice was known as the Jesus prayer, a constant repetition of a simple imprecation: "Jesus Christ, Son of God, have mercy on me" (sometimes "a sinner" was added at the end).

It was in the thirteenth and fourteenth centuries that hesychasm and the Jesus prayer became most influential, especially within the monastic community of Mount Athos in northern Greece, when it became part of a spiritual revival that penetrated other Orthodox countries such as Russia and Bulgaria. By this time the Jesus prayer was practiced in conjunction with a set of particular body postures and breathing techniques. There are some similarities with yoga, but it must be stressed that the prayer's physical aspects were not obligatory. Typically, hesychasts would bow their heads, with their chins on their chests, and focus their eyes on the place of the heart. They would then synchronize the words of the Jesus prayer with their breathing while attempting to sink the mind or intellect into the heart, which was seen as the integrating center of the total person and the "dwelling-place of God."[4] The emphasis on the "heart" was significant because it indicated that the prayer was not merely an intellectual activity but one that involved the spiritual,

175

DAZZLING DARKNESS

mental, emotional, and physical aspects of the individual. The merging of the intellect with the heart (which is why the prayer was also actually known as the "prayer of the heart") might eventually lead, God willing, to the vision of the divine uncreated light.

After the fall of Constantinople in 1453, hesychastic practice continued to hold an important place in the Orthodox tradition. In the late eighteenth century it was brought to much greater public notice after the appearance of a work named the *Philokalia*, published in 1782. Edited by Macarius of Corinth and an Athonite monk named Nicodemus, the *Philokalia* is a collection of writings by the great Eastern Christian teachers of the past, focusing on hesychasm, the Jesus prayer, and other aspects of mysticism. Soon after its publication, it was translated into Slavonic, and in the nineteenth century it had a great impact on the spirituality of Russia. Here the Jesus prayer became popular through teachers such as Seraphim of Sarov (see below), and especially after the publication in the late nineteenth century of a short spiritual work called *The Way of a Pilgrim*, which emphasizes the supreme value of the prayer.

The anonymous author of the *Way*, which became a classic, is a thirty-three-year-old widower who travels around the wilds of Russia and Siberia in search of someone who will enlighten him over the meaning of Paul's words "Pray without ceasing." At first his inquiries prove fruitless, but eventually he comes across a monk who teaches him the words of the Jesus prayer and encourages him to read the *Philokalia*; the pilgrim later obtains a copy of the book and becomes its ardent advocate.

The monk instructs his protégé to repeat the prayer first 3,000, then 6,000, and finally 12,000 times a day, which he finds induces a state of profound contentment. The pilgrim then continues his journey, living on water, bread, and salt, sleeping rough, taking on odd jobs, having memorable encounters with peasants, criminals, monks, and priests, and receiving in dreams spiritual guidance from his now-deceased mentor. He learns how to coordinate speaking the prayer with concentration on his heart, which brings about euphoric spiritual states: "My heart would feel as though it were bubbling with joy, such lightness, freedom, and consolation were in it." He also experiences a "burning love for Jesus Christ and for all God's creatures" as well as a profound spiritual understanding.[5]

176

EASTERN ORTHODOX MYSTICISM

John Climacus (ca. 579–649)

Also sometimes known as "the Scholastic," John Climacus is associated with the desolate mountainous region of Sinai and the monastery of Saint Catherine that nestles at the foot of Mount Sinai itself. He was called Climacus (from Greek *klimax*, "ladder") for his influential spiritual work, the *Ladder of Divine Ascent* (or *Ladder to Paradise*), which holds a special place in the Orthodox Church. It is regularly read during Lent and it inspired a much-copied icon of monks climbing a ladder stretching up to heaven and being greeted by Jesus at the top—while angels and devils help and hinder their ascent.

John was born in the late sixth century, but little is known about his life. A few biographical details have survived from a sketchy eulogistic *Life* written by a monk named Daniel of Raithou (modern El Tor on the gulf of Suez), himself apparently a contemporary of John, and some inferences about John's life can be made from the *Ladder* itself.[6]

According to Daniel, John came to Sinai at the age of sixteen and was given spiritual guidance by a certain Martyrius, who, four years later, initiated him as a monk. At the age of thirty-five John became a hermit in the region of Saint Catherine's. At some point it seems he decided to soften the rigors of his solitary existence and adopt a semi-eremitic life, associating himself with small groups of spiritual seekers. As a result of his contact with these like-minded souls, John gained a reputation as a spiritual guide and healer and was known to visit solitaries and monastic communities near Alexandria.

After about forty years of living in the desert, John was persuaded to become abbot of Saint Catherine's and proved to be a much-revered and popular leader. Eventually, however, the call of the desert proved too strong: he again adopted the eremitic life, leaving the abbacy to his brother George. Free from administrative cares, he lived out his remaining days in the wilderness he had sought as a teenager.

John wrote the *Ladder* sometime in his later years, at the request of an abbot named John of Raithou. Divided into thirty "rungs" or steps (thirty being the traditional age of Jesus at his baptism), the *Ladder* is addressed primarily to monks and describes the

DAZZLING DARKNESS

ways in which a monk might disengage with the world, practice virtues, attain *apatheia* (active dispassion), and gain union with God through the power of love. That John himself may have experienced mystical states of being is suggested by his Pauline description of encountering an angel while in the midst of a rapture:

> I implored him on the spot to lead me where my longings drew me, and he said: "The hour has not yet come, because the fire of incorruption does not yet burn sufficiently within you." Whether I was then with this earth, I know not; or out of it—I am quite unable to say.[7]

The first three steps of the *Ladder* concern withdrawal from the world. These are followed by the main section of the book, which considers the problem of "passions," such as physical appetites (e.g. lust and gluttony) and mental and emotional vices (e.g. anger, lying, maliciousness, despondency, and fear). John says that the passions can be overcome and replaced by virtues such as obedience, repentance, and fearing death, as well as "higher virtues" such as humility and simplicity. The last four steps, 27–30, show the true mystical nature of John's thought, focusing as they do on the contemplative life, stillness of mind, prayer, and, most of all, love.

Step 27 of the *Ladder*, for example, advocates the need to attain *hesychia*, or inner stillness, "holy quiet," an ideal that would remain central to the Eastern Church down the centuries. To gain *hesychia*, all "noise," outer and inner, must be cast off until the mind is inviolable, untouched by any disturbance. Only then can a person be "a house of love," not easily moved to anger. Other signs by which the hesychast will know he or she is on the right path include purity of thought, rapture toward God, constant desire to pray, wakeful vigilance, and detachment from the world. And the practice of hesychasm, John says, involves non-stop worship and waiting upon God. Although the hesychast aims to strip away "noise" and thoughts, he or she does so to be "filled with an all-embracing sense of the divine indwelling."[8]

In Step 28 John turns his focus to prayer and praying. He waxes lyrical about the nature and effects of prayer: it unites human beings with God, provides a bridge over temptations and a shield against adversity, which it destroys. Prayer is spiritual food and the fountain

178

EASTERN ORTHODOX MYSTICISM

of virtues; it enlightens the mind and eradicates despair; it is also "the mirror of progress ... a revelation of the future, a sign of glory."

Step 29 is mainly concerned with *apatheia*, or dispassion, a state of existential being when the soul is free from animal passions or selfish concerns and is filled with the spirit of God: "The firmament has the stars for its beauty, and dispassion has the virtues for its adornments; for by dispassion I mean no other than the interior heaven of the mind, which regards the tricks of the demons as mere toys."[9] Dispassion involves being in the presence of God and raising the mind above the sensual things of this world. It also means being immersed in the virtues to the same degree that those filled with passions are immersed in pleasure. Yet dispassion is not the final goal of the devout person. It prepares the way to a communion with God that is realized only by love, the subject of the last step of the ladder: "Blessed dispassion lifts the mind that is poor from earth to heaven, and raises the beggar from the dunghill of the passions. But love whose praise is above all makes him sit with the princes, with the holy angels, and with the princes of the people of God."[10]

The book ends with Step 30, in which John exalts the power of love as the greatest human quality or state of being. With the delicate flourishes of a poet, John tries to describe the ineffable. According to him, people experience love as "blessed rapture" and a "wound" or an "inebriation of the soul." Because love has a divine origin, measuring it is like trying to measure sand in the ocean. The presence of love in a soul banishes negative thoughts, and fear cannot survive in one who is filled with love: it is an abyss of patience and a sea of humility. Love is more than a means of eradicating contrary thoughts and behavior. It inspires prophecy and miracles and endless illumination: "Love is a fountain of fire— in the measure that it bubbles up, it inflames the thirsty soul. Love is the state of angels. Love is the progress of eternity."[11] John ends the thirtieth step with an invocation to love, asking it to guide him and quench his thirst: "Thou rulest over all. And now thou hast ravished my soul. I cannot contain thy flame. So I will go forward praising thee."[12]

DAZZLING DARKNESS

Maximus the Confessor (ca. 580–662)

A Greek monk and theologian, Maximus the Confessor was a mystical writer who also made a courageous stand against the Monothelite heresy (the belief that Christ has *two* natures but only *one* will), which resulted in his opponents harassing, exiling, and eventually mutilating him (his tongue and right hand were cut off to prevent him communicating his views). Maximus wrote paraphrases of Dionysius the Areopagite's work as well as many other texts, such as *The Ascetic Life* and *Four Hundred Chapters on Love*. These cover a variety of theological and devotional subjects, including the Incarnation of Christ, the liturgy, asceticism, and prayer. It is unclear whether he himself had direct personal mystical experiences, but his comment on the heights of contemplative prayer—that "the mind is ravished by the divine boundless light"—suggest that he might have done.[13]

Maximus was born in about 580 to a noble Constantinople family. After a thorough education he joined the court of Emperor Heraclius, working as his secretary. In about 614, however, he gave up life in the civil service and went off to join a monastery at Chrysopolis, across the straits from Constantinople. Twelve years later, with the community under threat from the invading Persians, he sought refuge on the island of Crete, before moving on to Africa. There he stayed for several years, first at Alexandria, then at Carthage.

During the 630s Maximus became increasingly involved in combating the Monothelite heresy, a struggle that would continue for the rest of his long life. The heresy, which was generally prevalent in the East and rejected in the West, was mixed up with politics as much as with theology. To preserve Christian unity in the face of external threats from the Persians and Arabs, the Monothelites wanted to reconcile two opposing Christian parties: the heretical Monophysites, who believed that the incarnate Christ had just one, single, divine nature; and orthodox Christians who believed that Christ had a double nature, human and divine (a doctrine that had been defined in the year 451 at the Council of Chalcedon).

To accommodate both sides, the Monothelites proposed a formula that Christ had two natures but only one, divine, will. For Maximus this was a compromise that was nonsensical and heretical: if Christ

EASTERN ORTHODOX MYSTICISM

had only a divine will, he could not be fully human, and this fatally undermined the Incarnation. Maximus argued that Christ had a free, human will that conformed to God's will in perfect obedience. Therefore, the "Christ who is known in two natures is able to be the model for our freedom and individuality, and for a mystical union in which man's separateness as a creature is respected."[14]

Maximus's opposition to the heresy, which was supported by Emperor Constans II (r. 641–668), drew the wrath of the Byzantine authorities. In 653 pressure was put on him to approve a reconciliatory document. When he refused, he was exiled to Thrace. In 662 he was again put on trial in Constantinople. This time his exile, to the Caucasus, was preceded by flogging and mutilation. Now an old man in his early eighties, he did not survive the year.

One of the major strands of Maximus's mystical thought was "deification," an idea that became especially influential in Eastern Christianity. The New Testament basis for deification is found primarily in the Second Letter of Peter 1:4, which speaks of Christians being able to "participate in the divine nature" and escaping worldly corruption. John's Gospel also refers to the mutual interpenetration of God, Christ, and human beings ("I have given them the glory that you gave me, that they may be one as we are one: I in them and you in me," 17:22). For Maximus, the goal of human beings, as God's creatures, is to share God's eternity so that, deified by his grace, they may become like him.[15]

The model for this spiritual end is the Incarnation, "which makes man god to the same degree as God Himself became man."[16] He also said that union with the divine being is effected by the energy of God and accompanied by ineffable joy.[17] Yet deification is not a self-indulgent flight to spiritual ecstasy, for Christ deifies us so that we might care for others more than we do ourselves.[18] At the heart of Maximus's mysticism is a solid core of compassionate love: "the lodestone of all his thought ... was the mystery of the Incarnation. This is for him the mystery of love."[19] He also considers the ultimate form of divine love in the *Four Hundred Chapters on Love*, in which he describes a mystical state of being: in its intense love of God, the mind leaves itself and, "illumined by the divine and infinite light, it remains insensible to anything that is made by him, just as the physical eye has no sensation when the sun has risen."[20]

DAZZLING DARKNESS

The greatest test for Christians is, perhaps, to love those who persecute them. Maximus considers this challenge in the *Ascetic Life*, and re-states the Gospel admonition that we should love our enemies and do good to those who hate us. The problem, he says, is that our love is usually directed toward material things and satisfying our own pleasure. This diverts us from selfless love.[21] For it is only selfless, God-directed love that can overcome hatred and bring people into communion with the divine: "He who sees in his heart a trace of hatred toward another for some fault of his is a complete stranger to love of God, for love of God can in no way tolerate hatred of man."[22] It is a triumphant affirmation from one who had to face such brutal verbal and physical violence during his life.

Symeon the New Theologian (949–1022)

"The greatest of the Byzantine mystics,"[23] Symeon the New Theologian described with great persuasiveness the experience of light mysticism, a dominant theme in Orthodox Christianity. He revels in trying to sum up the divine light, evoking it variously in terms of fire, the sun, the moon, or a shining pearl that grows in the heart.[24] He also makes it clear that the divine light is synonymous with God:

> God is Light, and those whom He makes worthy to see Him, see Him as Light. For the Light of His glory goes before His face, and it is impossible that He should appear otherwise than as light. Those who have not received this light, have not seen God: for God is Light.[25]

Symeon says that the divine light would often come to him, and that he would be desolate after its departure. When again he managed to achieve a state of complete humility, the light would return like the sun appearing dimly through a mist, growing brighter as a radiant orb, removing the inner darkness, insensitivity, passions, and sensuality.[26] Elsewhere he describes the light as a "flood of divine radiance" filling the room.[27]

Symeon placed great emphasis on experiencing the divine, which he felt all Christians had the potential to do, not just the select few.

EASTERN ORTHODOX MYSTICISM

Although he created as many enemies as he did admirers within the Orthodox Church by his outspoken criticism of moral laxity and by placing greater value on encountering God than on doctrine, he was careful to back up his teachings with scriptural authority. Also, he was solidly orthodox in placing Christ at the center of his spirituality and stressing the importance of the Eucharist. In one of his hymns he praises the union with Christ brought about by the Eucharist, which he depicts in terms of a divine fire: "I, who am but straw, receive the Fire, and—unheard of wonder!—am inflamed without being consumed, as of old the burning bush of Moses."[28] That Symeon was accorded the title "New Theologian" was a considerable honor, since it grouped him with only two other previous figures given the same appellation by the Orthodox Church, namely John the Evangelist and Gregory of Nazianzus.

The son of a minor Byzantine noble, Symeon was born in 949 in Paphlagonia in Asia Minor (modern Turkey). He studied locally until the age of eleven, when an uncle took him to Constantinople and the imperial court. There Symeon continued his studies and learned the niceties of the ways and protocol of the court. In 963 his life changed when he met a deeply spiritual monk named Symeon the Studite, so called because he belonged to the famous Studion Monastery near the Golden Horn in the west of the city. Inspired by the monk's aura of sanctity, Symeon yearned to join the Studion immediately; but the elder Symeon dissuaded him from doing so, feeling that his protégé needed to develop and test his spirituality further before contemplating such a move.

So in the following years Symeon spent his days in the service of the imperial court but devoted his nights to study and prayer. His spiritual commitment and awareness deepened over time, and when he was twenty he received a powerful mystical experience in which he saw or felt a divine light that was so pervasive it seemed to him as if he had turned into light. Seven years later, Symeon finally entered the Studion with the blessing of his mentor. But his launch into this new monastic world soon hit some unexpected rocks. Symeon's devout and uncompromising spirituality incurred the hostility of some of the Studion monks, and after a few months he left the community. He moved to the nearby monastery of Saint Mamas, where, within a few years, he was ordained a priest, then

183

DAZZLING DARKNESS

elected abbot. For more than twenty years Symeon devoted himself to transforming Saint Mamas into a model Christian community, but eventually his rigor and relentless emphasis on inner spiritual experience again aroused opposition from his fellow monks. In the end, in 1009, he was compelled by the church authorities to accept exile in a small village just across the Bosporus, where he founded a small monastery. Although the sentence of exile was soon quashed, Symeon decided to remain in his low-key locale, pursuing his spiritual path there until his death in 1022.

Symeon's sermons, hymns, and other works celebrate the glorious splendor of the divine light that can be experienced by all Christians, although he makes it clear that such an experience comes only when the right spiritual preparations have been made. He also says that raptures and ecstasies are really only experienced by beginners on the mystical path. He compares ecstasy to the experience of a man in prison who suddenly sees a vista of sunlit countryside through a crack in the prison wall. At first he is "ecstatic" because of his vision, but then his senses grow used to it. So, too, the soul that becomes accustomed to the spiritual life no longer holds ecstasies to be extraordinary.[29]

For Symeon, humility is one of the foundation stones of the contemplative life. We must be humble in heart and mind, taking care to carry out the precepts of the scriptures, ready to bear the trials and tribulations that may befall us.[30] Our model is Christ, who became incarnate and so swapped the glory of heaven for life on earth.[31] Through following the teachings of Jesus Christ, we will gradually become less subject to our passions, and our hearts will soften and embrace humility, which is deepened by tribulations and affliction, and our souls will eventually be cleansed.[32] Symeon insists that humility cannot simply be manufactured. Ascetic practices, such as fasting, sleeping on the ground, and wearing hair shirts, cannot replace a humble spirit and contrite heart, through which alone God can dwell in us.[33]

Although our efforts to practice virtues such as abstinence and controlling anger can take us only so far, God will grant us spiritual gifts to perfect our labors, so that by his grace our hearts will be in easeful conformity with our acts: the effort to tame anger will be rewarded with not just the desired control but a sense of

184

EASTERN ORTHODOX MYSTICISM

inner peacefulness.[34] Along with humility, repentance is another foundation stone, "the gate which leads from the realm of darkness into that of light."[35] The key to receiving the light is not to seek it directly but rather to repent and be humble, to follow God's commandment. By doing this we open a part of us that allows the light to enter: "The life of grace is an increasing progress in knowledge, a growing experience of the divine light."[36]

So when we are spiritually prepared we are rewarded with the experience of the divine light. Symeon attempts to describe the indescribable. He says God comes in a "definite form" but not with a particular appearance: simplicity is the keynote, along with a sense of "formless light." Symeon is acutely conscious of the paradox that God is invisible but in a sense can be seen, and that he speaks to those "whom by grace He has begotten as gods."[37] Symeon also says that the divine light brings great joy and peace, and that the light is a glimpse of the eternal light, a reflection of the light of "everlasting blessedness." The soul, as if looking in a mirror, sees its tiniest flaws and is drawn into the depths of humility, and it is then awestruck by the divine glory and filled with ecstatic joy. In this way a person is transformed—knowing God and being known by him.[38]

Gregory Palamas (1296–1359)

If the divine light is crucial to the mysticism of Symeon, it also has a central place in the teachings of Gregory Palamas, one of the towering figures of Orthodox spirituality, who championed hesychasm and the distinction between God's essence and his energies, which, as we shall see, became an issue of great controversy in the Orthodox Church. For Gregory, too, God is light and is experienced in increasing intensity according to the spiritual worthiness of the individual. However, Gregory was clear that we cannot experience God directly in his *essence*, only in his *energies*. Those who participate in the divine energies become united to them and transcend both sensual and intellectual knowledge, and God, as light, dwells in those who love him.

Gregory was born in 1296, probably in Constantinople, to a noble family. He was drawn to the idea of becoming a monk from an early age and later managed to persuade his siblings, widowed mother, and various family servants to embrace the monastic life. He himself, in his early twenties, traveled to Mount Athos, where he was introduced to the practice of hesychasm and the Jesus prayer. After his ordination as a priest in 1326, he lived as a hermit in Beroea in Greece for several years before returning to the monks of Athos in 1331. Eight years later he became embroiled in a dispute over hesychasm with a monk named Barlaam (ca. 1290–1348) from Calabria in southwestern Italy, who, whether he had been baptized into the Orthodox Church in his local community or had converted from Catholicism, spoke with authority on Orthodox doctrine. The controversy lasted more than ten years and drew in the highest echelons of church and government. In the end, Gregory was vindicated by an Orthodox Church council in 1351 and was able to enjoy the fruits of this success for another eight years before he died in Thessalonica in 1359. Nine years later he was canonized and became an Orthodox saint.

Barlaam, Gregory's principal theological opponent, was an exceptionally learned man who had been invited to teach in the university at Constantinople. Although he was at first critical of Latin Christianity, he was sympathetic toward the humanistic outlook of the nascent Italian Renaissance. He laid great stress on the apophatic tradition, reaching back to Dionysius the Areopagite, that God was totally transcendent and therefore unknowable: he could only be experienced indirectly. Therefore, those who claimed to see the uncreated light of God through hesychastic practices were deluding themselves, for it was possible to see God only in the life to come. What they actually saw was a light that was natural and created.

Gregory rose to Barlaam's challenge, writing in defense of the hesychasts his important three-part *Triads*, a work enthusiastically supported by the Athonite monks. Gregory agreed with Barlaam about God's transcendence. In his essence, God is totally unknowable: "No single thing of all that is created has or ever will have even the slightest communion with the supreme nature, or nearness to it."[39] But Gregory emphasized an important distinction (found in the early church fathers) between God's essence and God's energies. God, in his essence, may be unknowable; but his uncreated energies, in which he is wholly present, can be known by

186

EASTERN ORTHODOX MYSTICISM

divine grace. As Basil the Great said: "It is by His energies that we say we know our God; we do not assert that we can come near to the essence itself, for His energies descend to us, but His essence remains unapproachable."[40] It is as if God in his essence were the sun, which cannot be looked at directly, and his energies the visible rays streaming out. According to Gregory it was precisely God's energies that the three disciples saw as a dazzling radiance during the Transfiguration, when Jesus was transformed into glorious light on Mount Tabor. And it was this same light that it was possible for hesychasts to see through prayer. Gregory described it as "that Light which is the Glory of God, without end, and the splendour of Divinity, divine and eternal, uncreated, being itself the Majesty of God."[41]

The Transfiguration was a key event for Gregory, for whom it displayed the effect of divine grace and its transformational power on human beings. As Christ appeared to Peter, James, and John, so does he continue to manifest himself to true Christians: "He is not experienced in his essence, ... but in a most mysterious manner, he shines upon them the radiance of his proper nature and grants them to participate in it."[42]

Barlaam, in common with other antihesychasts (many of them in sympathy with the ideas of the Scholastic thinkers of the West), asserted that God was a simple unity and could not be divided into essence and energies, which smacked of ditheism, the doctrine that there are two Gods. He also made fun of the idea that hesychasts prayed while directing their eyes to their own bodies, referring to them as "omphalopsyches" (that is, those with souls in their navels).

While not viewing the physical practices of hesychasm as indispensable, Gregory defended them by affirming that a human being was a unified combination of body and soul. He stressed the importance given to the physical body in the Bible, especially with the Incarnation. When the Bible states that people were made in God's image, this refers to the entire psychosomatic entity. And by assuming human form, Christ made the body "an inexhaustible source of sanctification."[43] So the hesychasts were not guilty of materialism, as their opponents claimed, but were staying true to the biblical tradition that gave due honor to the flesh. The body

DAZZLING DARKNESS

had its part to play in hesychasm and receiving divine illumination, and those praying could meet God halfway in an ecstasy of union: "Our mind, then, comes out of itself and becomes united with God after it has transcended itself. God also comes out of himself and becomes united with our mind by condescension."[44]

The hesychast controversy came to a head in 1341 at the first of a series of councils held to settle it. Convened in the church Hagia Sophia in Constantinople on June 10, the council was a resounding success for the hesychasts, who trounced Barlaam and his supporters. Barlaam himself was compelled to retract his accusations and soon departed for Calabria, where he changed his religious allegiance and became a Roman Catholic. But the disagreement rumbled on. Barlaam's place was taken by other able opponents, and the matter was complicated by the fact that it took on a political dimension, with leading members of the Byzantine government and the church split between the two sides. Gregory himself suffered a downturn in his fortunes when he was arrested in 1343 and imprisoned for four years—the virtue from this necessity was that he was able to continue writing. Matters improved for him in 1347 when the prohesychast John Cantacuzenus came to power and Gregory was consecrated archbishop of Thessalonica. Then in 1351 the sixth and last council was held to debate the hesychast issue, and the Palamite side won a decisive and enduring victory, with hesychasm declared the official teaching of the Orthodox Church.

Sergius (Sergei) of Radonezh (ca. 1314–92)

While Gregory of Palamas was busy dueling with Baarlam and dealing with the hesychast controversy, over in Russia, Sergius of Radonezh, the best-loved of his country's saints, was following his own spiritual path and gaining a reputation for his simple, honest, and gentle nature as well as for his selfless kindness. Over time he became known as a wise spiritual elder, or *starets*, and attracted a number of followers, who shared his communal forest life. Living in the wild, it is said that he smelled of "fresh fir wood" and wore, despite his well-to-do background, old peasant clothes "saturated with sweat, and heavily patched."[45] Sergius also had a mystical side

188

EASTERN ORTHODOX MYSTICISM

to his character and was said to have received visions of the Virgin Mary and, on occasion, to have glowed with spiritual light. Indeed, he is a hugely important figure in the Russian mystical tradition if only for reviving monasticism through his leadership, authority, and charisma. He was founder of Russia's greatest monastery (or *lavra*), the Holy Trinity, at a place that was later named for him: Sergiev-Posad, near the town of Radonezh, about forty miles northeast of Moscow.[46] After his death he became patron saint of Moscow and Russia.

Sergius was born to a noble family in the town Rostov (about 100 miles northeast of Moscow) only a century after the Mongols, or Tartars, had invaded Russia. Before the invasions Russian monasteries had been based in cities; afterward, there was a trend for spiritual solitaries to seek out forests and remote caves in order to live ascetic lives. Sergius was part of this general movement of "Slavic desert fathers."

At about the age of twenty, after the death of his parents, Sergius, along with his brother Stephen, became a hermit in a forest near Radonezh and was later joined by others seeking the spiritual life. According to his *Life*, written by a fifteenth-century Serbian monk named Pachomius, Sergius constructed a wooden cell and chapel and would commune with wild animals, in way reminiscent of Francis of Assisi, even sharing his food on a daily basis with a local bear.[47]

In time, Sergius's followers persuaded him to take on a more formal spiritual role and become their abbot. Sergius now ordered his and the lives of his followers on a stricter, more regulated basis— he himself took on various jobs to keep the nascent community going, including cooking, mending clothes, and doing woodwork. In about 1355 the community, which comprised a group of wooden cells and refectory and a stone chapel, was formally established as the monastery of the Holy Trinity, with Sergius at its head. Over time, however, his strong emphasis on the importance of the common life and asceticism caused dissension among some of his monks. Rather than involve himself in conflict, Sergius simply left to found another monastery in the forest (he was to found some forty monasteries during his life, spiritual "colonies" around which towns grew).

DAZZLING DARKNESS

Four years later he rejoined the Holy Trinity and resumed his role as leader. He continued to administer his community, dispensing help and advice to all who sought it, including the great political rulers of the day. In 1378 he was asked to become metropolitan of Moscow, but refused to take the position. Two years later he gave crucial encouragement and blessings to Prince Dmitry Donskoy of Moscow before the battle of Kulikovo, fought successfully against the Mongols.

Sergius's mysticism is manifested more in his person than in any recorded writings. The example of his life, for instance, inspired a tradition of mystically-minded "forest hermits," or wandering charismatic holy men. He emphasized the importance of the practice of hesychasm,[48] and he himself, according to his biographer, experienced clairvoyance (he "saw" that the Russians would defeat the Mongols at Kulikovo). It is said that during prayer he would receive visions of the divine uncreated light, and that often when he was conducting the liturgy, light would glow around the consecrated host on the altar. On one occasion Sergius and two priests were conducting a service when a witness saw a fourth figure standing with them, dressed in dazzling robes: Sergius explained afterward that it was an angel of the Lord.[49] On another occasion, a witness stated that when Sergius was about to receive communion, "the divine fire moved up from the altar, curled up as a kind of cloth, and entering the holy chalice."[50]

Sergius was also credited with spiritual gifts such as exorcising evil spirits and healing, as well as receiving visions. He is even said to have received a vision of the Virgin Mary herself (a rare occurrence in Russia at this time), who was in the company of the apostles Peter and John. The Virgin shone brighter than the sun and promised Sergius his monastery would continue to be influential after his death. Afterward, Sergius remained in a state of ecstasy, glowing with light and trembling all over.[51]

Seraphim of Sarov (1759–1833)

Baptized Prokhor Moshnin, Seraphim of Sarov was born into a merchant family in the Russian city of Kursk and became one of Russia's most influential mystics and spiritual elders, or *starets*, of

EASTERN ORTHODOX MYSTICISM

modern times. The visions he received helped to convince him that the central purpose of the spiritual life was to allow the Holy Spirit to enter the soul and be guided by it in all things.

Seraphim's religious journey began in earnest in 1778, when, at the age of nineteen, he entered the monastery of Sarov (about 250 miles east of Moscow) and as a novice embarked on a strict regime of prayer, manual work, and study. During this period he fell ill for three years and only recovered, it is said, after receiving a vision of the Virgin Mary. In 1786 he was tonsured as a monk, and seven years later he was ordained a priest. Seraphim seemed to be set on a lifelong vocation inside the monastery. But in 1794 he decided to withdraw from community life and live as a recluse. He took himself off to a nearby forest, cut trees, built a wooden hut, grew his own vegetables, and began a life of prayer and reading the Bible. On Sundays he would walk to Sarov to attend Mass. Like Sergius before him, he seems to have communed with wild animals, including wolves, foxes, and bears.

For ten years Seraphim enjoyed this solitary life, deepening his spirituality. But in 1804 he was set upon by a group of robbers, who beat him almost to death. He managed to drag himself back to the Sarov monastery, where he recuperated for five months, helped by a vision of the Virgin Mary. Shaken and left with a permanent stoop, he returned to his hermitage in the forest and remained there for five years.

In 1810, increasingly frail and still suffering from injuries received from his attackers, Seraphim rejoined his old monastery, living as a strict recluse in a cell. After several years of total solitude, he was persuaded by a vision of the Virgin Mary to give up his seclusion and receive visitors, who duly arrived in their thousands to seek his counsel. Although infirm himself and living according to a strict, ascetic regime, he encouraged his followers to be cheerful and embrace life. He also became the spiritual director of the nuns of the neighboring Diveyevo convent. In 1825 he returned to his hermitage to practice hesychasm, while still receiving visits from followers. He died in 1833 and was found facing an icon of the Virgin Mary in a prayerful position.

Seraphim is said not only to have received visions of the Virgin Mary and the apostles during his life but also to have had prophetic

DAZZLING DARKNESS

insight and the power to heal. One of those to benefit from his healing was a young Russian nobleman named Nicolas Motovilov, who had suffered from chronic rheumatism. During a famous meeting with Seraphim out of doors in November 1831, Motovilov made a note of their conversation about the Holy Spirit. It is a remarkable account of a direct mystical experience and summarizes Seraphim's belief that the ingress of the Holy Spirit is the ultimate goal of the faithful: everything else is a means to obtaining it, and all gifts of grace flow from it.[52]

Motovilov records that their meeting took place on a cold, gloomy winter's day with snow thick on the ground and snowflakes falling from the sky. He was sitting on a tree stump in a field, with Seraphim squatting opposite him. Immediately, Seraphim revealed his clairvoyance, claiming, correctly, that Motovilov had been anxious to know the aim of the Christian life since childhood.

Seraphim soon got to the point: the true aim of Christians was to acquire the Holy Spirit of God. Practices such as fasting, praying, holding vigils, were only a means to an end. The Holy Spirit quickened every soul. Prayer was indispensable to preparing the way for the ingress of the Spirit, but when the latter descended and made its presence felt, the devout must maintain silence, to hear the words of eternal life. If a person was not in the Spirit, then he or she must go on searching. When blessed with the Spirit, a person must distribute its gifts of grace, like a candle that lights other candles without its own light being diminished. Seraphim emphasized the image of light in regard to the Spirit: quoting Psalm 118:105, he likened the Spirit to the word of God as "a lamp to my feet, and a light to my path." Seraphim also reminded Motovilov of how the Spirit made Moses shine with an extraordinary light after his encounter with God on Mount Sinai, to the extent that no one could look at him. Likewise, when Jesus was transfigured on Mount Tabor, his form shone with great brilliance.

Motovilov asked Seraphim how he himself could know whether he was in the grace of the Holy Spirit. Seraphim took him by the shoulders and told him that at that very moment both of them were in the Holy Spirit and asked Motovilov why he was not looking at him. The nobleman replied that he could not look Seraphim in the face because his eyes were flashing like lightning and his face was

EASTERN ORTHODOX MYSTICISM

brighter than the sun. Seraphim reassured him that he, Motovilov, was also radiating divine light, just like himself. His words capture a sense of divine communion and illumination and the presence of the Spirit: "Fear not, my son, you too have become as bright as I. You too are now in the fullness of God's Spirit, otherwise you would not be able to look on me as I am."[53]

11

MYSTICS OF SPAIN

If a man wishes to be sure of the road he travels on, he must close his eyes and walk in the dark.

—John of the Cross

Although the Protestant Reformation gave impetus to the Catholic Church to bring about internal change, currents of reform had been felt within the church before and during the ructions caused by Luther's protest. At the end of the fifteenth century, for example, the puritanical Dominican friar Savonarola in Florence denounced the corruption and laxity of the clergy and papacy with a careless fanaticism that brought him excommunication and later death at the stake. In Spain, Cardinal Jiménez de Cisneros (1436–1517), impressive in his personal asceticism and piety, presided over important reforms and patronized learning, founding the University of Alcalá. Yet it is clear that the revival of the church known as the Counter-Reformation, or Catholic Reformation, was made more urgent by the Protestant movements. One response to the latter was the formation of new religious orders, such as the Theatines, established in Rome in 1524, and the Capuchins, a branch of the Franciscans, in the late 1520s. In 1534 a former Spanish soldier named Ignatius Loyola founded the Society of Jesus, or Jesuits. Formally approved by Pope Paul III in 1540, the Jesuits became renowned for their superb organization and flair for teaching and missionary work, which they carried abroad to the New World and the Far East.

The principal doctrinal conduit for the renewal of the church was the Council of Trent (a city in northern Italy that was part

DAZZLING DARKNESS

of the Holy Roman Empire), at which, intermittently from 1545 to 1563, Catholic prelates and theologians attempted to define doctrine, correct abuses, and implement reforms. The council had far-reaching effects on the life of the church. Protestant teachings were repudiated and traditional doctrines, such as on the validity of the seven sacraments, relics, and purgatory, affirmed; the position of the pope as the supreme head of the church was confirmed; extra provision was made for the education of the clergy; and the Latin Vulgate Bible was endorsed as the authoritative text, with the church preserving the sole right to interpret it.

In tandem with reforms, however, the church developed more aggressive and intimidating ways of maintaining order and discipline within its ranks. The Index of Prohibited Books, first issued in 1557 (and finally abolished in 1966), forbade the reading of certain books deemed inimical to the faith. More serious was the role of the Inquisition, which was first established in the 1200s and gained added notoriety during Renaissance times with the founding of the Spanish Inquisition at the end of the fifteenth century. Initially aimed at rooting out baptized Jews and Muslims who were believed to have reverted to their original faiths, the Spanish Inquisition later included Protestants in its web of violence. Then in 1542 Pope Paul III founded in Rome another version of the Inquisition, officially known as the Holy Office and mainly restricted to the confines of Italy.

The combination of reforms and discipline (and targeted persecution) did much to bolster and revitalize the Catholic Church in the face of rival denominations. At a practical level, Catholicism was able to reclaim from the Protestants Poland, southern Germany, and other parts of Europe, as well as stake claims in North and South America. Yet the Counter-Reformation also had its interior spiritual side, notably in Spain, a country that had been recently unified by the marriage of Ferdinand of Aragon and Isabella of Castile and had become the dominant European power under Emperor Charles V (r. 1516–56).

Confident and aggressive in its colonial adventures in the New World, Spain was a faithful supporter of the pope and wielded significant influence at the Council of Trent. Spanish spirituality bubbled up in the Alumbrado (Illuminated) movement—small

196

MYSTICS OF SPAIN

informal groups of individuals whose devotion toward mystical prayer and emphasis on the interior, as opposed to the externals of piety, brought some of them into conflict with the Inquisition. But the greatest flowering of Spanish spirituality was seen in the writings and lives of the Carmelite reformers Teresa of Ávila and John of the Cross, two of the church's greatest mystics, as well as those of Ignatius of Loyola, founder of the Society of Jesus, or the Jesuit order.

Ignatius of Loyola (ca. 1491–1556)

Soldier, reformer, spiritual guide, and mystical writer, Ignatius was born in the castle of Loyola in the province of Guipúzcoa in northeastern Spain, the youngest son of a wealthy Basque nobleman. Just over five feet tall, dynamic, and musical, Ignatius seemed set for a life at court or in the army. Indeed, at the age of twenty-six he became a soldier and, in 1521, found himself defending the town of Pamplona against a French army. Wounded by a cannonball, he was forced to rest in order to convalesce and spent the time studying the lives of saints. Through his reading he came to see the act of serving God as a spiritual equivalent of chivalry; he also became acutely conscious of his sins and resolved to do penance for them.

In February 1522 Ignatius embarked on a new, spiritual life, dedicated to God. He journeyed first to the pilgrimage center of Montserrat, near Barcelona, where for three days he confessed his sins and ritually abandoned his sword and dagger. He then made his way to nearby Manresa, where, for a year, he practiced austerities, lived like a beggar, and prayed for seven hours a day. It was a period of spiritual struggle, doubt and temptation, but also punctuated with moments of joy and visionary, mystical experiences. While staying at the hospital in Manresa, he would often see in the courtyard on moonlit nights "an indistinct shape" that appeared so "symmetrical and beautiful" he was filled with profound pleasure. This strange shape resembled a "serpent with glittering eyes, and yet they were not eyes" and when he gazed on it he "felt an indescribable joy steal over him."[1]

On another occasion, while praying to the Virgin Mary, he seemed to see "the Blessed Trinity in the form of a lyre or harp,"

197

DAZZLING DARKNESS

a vision that brought him to tears. Another time he had a vision of how God had created this world. He saw "a white object" emitting rays of divine light. At first he was unable to account for this vision; but shortly afterward, when he was at Mass and the host was being elevated, he saw white rays descending from above and he made the connection with his vision.[2]

Perhaps the most influential mystical experience he had was when he was sitting by the side of a stream, gazing at the water.

> While seated there, the eyes of his soul were opened. He did not have any special vision, but his mind was enlightened on many subjects, spiritual and intellectual. So clear was this knowledge that from that day everything appeared to him in a new light ... From that day he seemed to be quite another man, and possessed of a new intellect. This illumination lasted a long time.[3]

After his life-changing stay at Manresa, Ignatius went on pilgrimage to Jerusalem, where he made the decision to devote the next part of his life to study—in order to help others find the spiritual path he had taken himself.[4] From 1524 to 1534 he spent his time in the world of books, ending up with a degree from the University of Paris. It was in Paris, too, that he became leader of a group of religiously-minded companions who committed themselves to poverty, chastity, and obedience, a group who would offer their services to the pope and become founders of the Society of Jesus, the Jesuits.

In 1537 Ignatius was ordained a priest, and three years later Pope Paul III formally endorsed the Society of Jesus. From this time on, Ignatius spent most of his time in and around Rome. Under his leadership the Jesuits became famous for their discipline, spiritual fervor, loyalty to the pope, and their emphasis on education. They were mobile and adaptable, unconfined to any cloister, and prepared to live anywhere in the world. Before long they had spread out over Europe and were organized into administrative areas, or provinces. While presiding as the "general" of the order, Loyola suffered increasingly from illness. In 1551 he became so sick that he tried, unsuccessfully, to resign the leadership of the order. He soldiered on, in good Jesuit style, writing letters, sending out Jesuit missionaries, and deepening his own spirituality. He died in Rome in July 1556.

MYSTICS OF SPAIN

Apart from his visions, Ignatius's mystical temperament found expression in his *Spiritual Exercises*, one of the most influential of all spiritual works. He first began to formulate ideas for the book during his stay at Manresa in 1522, but it was not until 1548 that it was published. The *Exercises* was intended as an instruction manual on retreat programs, aiming to deepen the religious sympathy, imagination, and piety of the retreatants.

The exercises, which are still used, normally take thirty days to complete and are divided into four "weeks," or sections. The first week is concerned with contemplation of personal sins and the divine mercy. The second involves a series of meditative exercises on Christ's life up to the passion. The third focuses on the passion and salvation through Christ's love. The fourth and final part brings the retreatant to an experience of joy through Christ's resurrection.

The essence of Ignatius's method is to describe a way of imagining the Gospel events to make them more immediate and real, thereby enabling the retreatant to empathize with them more fully. He says that we must utilize our five senses. First, we must see the Gospel characters "with the sight of the imagination," and meditate and contemplate details about them. Then we must try to "hear" what they are talking about, and smell and taste the "fragrance and sweetness of the Divinity," reflecting on oneself and drawing profit from it. Last, we must "touch" the places where the apostles walked and sat.[5] When this method is applied to envisaging the nature of hell, for example, Ignatius says we would see eternal fires and burning souls; hear howlings, cries, and blasphemies against Christ; smell "smoke, sulphur, dregs and putrid things"; taste tears, sadness, and the "worm of conscience"; and feel "how the fires touch and burn the souls."[6]

In this way, Ignatius aimed to take biblical stories from the written page and relocate them as three-dimensional realities in the mind and soul of the retreatant. The exercises are existential, rather than merely descriptive: they are practical instructions to enter into a new sympathetic relationship with Christ's life by means of a disciplined, heightened awareness.

DAZZLING DARKNESS

Teresa of Ávila (1515–82)

Ebullient, courageous, patient, humble, and humorous, Teresa of Ávila was remarkable for being able to combine practice of the most profound mystical prayer with a dynamic involvement in the world, seen particularly in her reform of her own Carmelite order and the foundation of seventeen new convents. In her writings she gives an insider's guide to contemplation, which she saw as a journey of the soul from the outside world to its innermost depths and union with God. More a describer than an analyzer, unlike her more intellectual friend and fellow Carmelite John of the Cross, she was eloquent about the various supernatural concomitants of mysticism, such as ecstasies, visions, locutions, and raptures, which she described as a "powerful eagle rising and bearing you upon its wings."[7] "Let everyone understand that real love of God does not consist in tear-shedding, nor in that sweetness and tenderness for which usually we long, just because they console us, but in serving God in justice, fortitude of soul, and humility."[8]

The daughter of a well-to-do merchant named Alonso de Cepeda, Teresa was born in 1515 in the town of Ávila in central Spain. She grew up to be a sociable and confident girl with an adventurous, romantic streak—the story is told that at the age of seven she set out from home with an elder brother in order to seek martyrdom at the hands of the Moors (their efforts were thwarted at the city gates by an uncle).

Sometime after her mother died in 1529, Teresa was sent to be educated at an Augustinian convent in Ávila. The onset of poor health, however, forced her to return home after eighteen months. During her convalescence she read the letters of Jerome, which consolidated her desire to become a religious. But the opposition of her father prompted her to run away and join the Carmelite's Convent of the Incarnation in Ávila in November 1535. Faced with this *fait accompli*, Alonso relented and dropped his objections. A year later Teresa's convent life was disrupted by a serious illness that continued for years, despite the best efforts of doctors. In 1539 her health deteriorated and she fell into a coma for four days; when she regained consciousness, she found herself partially paralyzed, a condition she endured for the next three

MYSTICS OF SPAIN

years, until finally her health improved through, she believed, the intercession of Joseph.

During the following years, Teresa practiced mental (that is, not vocalized) prayer and occasionally enjoyed supernatural experiences, but this was generally an unexceptionable period of spirituality for her. In 1555 her contemplative life deepened after she experienced a "second conversion" while praying in her oratory before a small statue of Christ being scourged at the pillar. From this time the number of visions, locutions, and other divine favors she received increased—causing alarm to some of her confessors, who believed they were inspired by the devil. Any doubts Teresa may have had were dispelled by an inner consolation from God, culminating in 1559 with the dramatic experience of the "transverberation," when she felt an angel piercing her heart with a red-hot spear. She was also supported by a number of friends and close associates, especially Peter of Alcántara.

In the early 1560s Teresa turned her attention to reforming the Carmelite order. For some time she had been less than happy with the relatively relaxed lifestyle at the Convent of the Incarnation. Finally, on August 24, 1562, despite opposition from her own convent and the townspeople of Ávila, she founded a new house of Discalced (Shoeless, or Barefoot) Carmelites, dedicated to Joseph and obedient to a stricter ascetic rule. Four years later, the general of the Carmelite order visited the new convent and was so impressed by what he saw that he gave the go-ahead for the foundation of more Discalced houses for both nuns and friars, a process recounted in her *Book of Foundations*, written in the 1570s. During this time she also began to write her greatest work, *The Interior Castle*, an account of the different stages of mystical prayer. Opposition to the expansion of the Discalced Carmelites continued, however, until in 1580, with the backing of the Spanish king Philip II, they were finally granted the right to have a distinct province of their own. By this time Teresa was frail but still able to found houses at Palencia, Soria, and Burgos. She eventually died in Alba de Tormes in October 1582. She was beatified in 1614 and canonized eight years later.

Teresa's great contribution to mysticism is the intimacy, honesty, and vividness that she brings to her descriptions of the different stages of spiritual growth and contemplation, including the highest

DAZZLING DARKNESS

state, of "spiritual marriage." In her autobiographical *Life of the Mother Teresa of Jesus*, for example, she compares the four stages of mystical prayer to four ways in which a garden may be watered, an image used by Augustine and others. These four ways proceed with decreasing personal (and increasing divine) involvement: (1) by drawing water from the well by hand, (2) by drawing water from the well with the help of a waterwheel and a windlass, or winch, (3) by watering the land by means of a stream or spring, and (4)—best of all—letting the land be watered by heavy rain.

She then explains the analogy. Irrigating the garden with water laboriously drawn from a well corresponds to beginners in prayer who strain to recollect their senses while trying not to succumb to distracting sights and sounds. There may come a period when they feel "dryness" and lose heart. But they must remember that their work is not for their own sake but for the Lord and that their labors will be rewarded.[9]

The second way (well water drawn with the help of a windlass, or winch) results in a greater abundance of water with less effort and is like the soul when it is more advanced in recollection and receives some mystical experiences. It still has to make some effort, but because it feels divine grace to a greater degree, the labor is less intense. Also, the soul loses its appetite for sensual and worldly things and enjoys a sense of peace and contentment.[10]

The third way, involving the use of a stream or spring, requires much less labor than the first two methods, although a degree of effort is needed to channel the water to the right place. This represents the soul that has reached a point when, with its faculties dormant, it enjoys considerably more sweetness and delight than before. At this stage it is not only immersed in contemplation but can also participate in the active life, for example, doing charitable works.[11]

The fourth and final way, which involves downpours of heavy rain and therefore no human effort, corresponds to the soul that has progressed to a state in which it feels nothing but delight—a delight that has no object. This is the condition of divine union, which Teresa does not attempt to analyze, saying that she cannot differentiate between "mind," "soul," and "spirit" (although she does liken the soul to a flame that sometimes leaps out of a fire, the

MYSTICS OF SPAIN

substance of which it shares). Yet although she does not analyze union, she does describe its effects, for example, the way the soul feels it is fainting with peacefulness and joy, its faculties being in suspension and the body almost catatonic. She also says that on one occasion, when experiencing this state, she was wondering what was happening to the soul when she heard God say to her that it "dissolves utterly, my daughter, to rest more and more in Me. It is no longer itself that lives; it is I."[12]

Teresa's most sustained work on contemplation is *The Interior Castle*, which she wrote at top speed in 1577 after she had received a vision. In the book she depicts the stages of the soul's inner spiritual quest for divine union in terms of a journey through seven sets of rooms, or "mansions," located within a castle made of crystal or diamond. The soul's destination is the innermost room, where it will find ultimate union with God.

From the castle's outer courtyard, the soul passes through the castle gate, representing prayer and meditation, to the first three sets of rooms, where it learns the importance of virtues such as humility, prayer, and perseverance. It then moves on to the fourth lot of rooms, where it begins to learn the prayer of recollection and of quiet. The fifth rooms concern the prayer of union and spiritual betrothal. At this point, Teresa introduces the memorable image of the soul as a silkworm that eats mulberry leaves until, when it is fully grown, it spins a silk cocoon from which it emerges as a white butterfly. Similarly, the soul feeds on outer nourishment provided by the church, such as sermons, confessions, and holy books, until it, too, becomes fully grown. It then begins to spin its cocoon—that is, Christ—in which it can hide itself. And just as the silkworm has to die to become a butterfly, so the soul must die to its attachment to the world and emerge transformed by its proximity to God.[13]

In the sixth set of rooms, the soul, seeking to progress from betrothal to marriage, has to undergo further physical and spiritual suffering. But when it finally arrives at the seventh rooms it experiences union with God and receives a wondrous vision of the Trinity. The very last room—the center of the soul itself—is the locus of the spiritual marriage between the soul and God. Teresa clearly distinguishes between permanent spiritual marriage and betrothal, in which separation may occur. She compares spiritual

DAZZLING DARKNESS

betrothal to two candles that have been joined near the tops so that their wicks combine to give a single flame but that can be pulled apart into two separate objects. Conversely, spiritual marriage is like rain falling into a river, when the river's water is impossible to distinguish from the rain; or it is like a stream entering the sea or a room in which light pours in through two large windows—"it enters in different places but it all becomes one."[14]

John of the Cross (1542–91)

Teresa's cofounder of the Discalced Carmelites and one of the great analysts of contemplation, John of the Cross once wrote that "if a man wishes to be sure of the road he travels on, he must close his eyes and walk in the dark."[15] "Darkness" and "night" are words popularly associated with John, particularly through his famous description of the "dark night of the soul," during which the soul is gruelingly purged so that its will can be united with God's. For John, the soul's attachment to the world and to spiritual practices has to be completely broken: "The worth of love does not consist in high feelings, but in detachment, in patience under all trials for the sake of God whom we love."[16] He compares existential attachment to the plight of a bird that cannot fly away to freedom until the cord that grounds it has been cut. To do this, we must always seek the road less easy: "In order to arrive at having pleasure in everything, / Desire to have pleasure in nothing."[17]

But although his teachings can seem daunting, John was no cheerless pessimist. A diminutive man, just over five feet tall, he was warm and saintly, and he himself emphasized that at the end of the night came the reward—the glorious light of God. In *The Living Flame of Love*, he describes how the soul, when it is on fire with love, feels as if an angel has struck it with a burning brand, and how at the moment of contact it suffers a wound that is "unimaginably delicious" and enjoys the sense of diffusion of heat through its "spiritual veins" until it feels like an "immense sea of fire."[18]

John was born in 1542 at Fontiveros near Ávila. The following year his father, a nobleman who had been disinherited by his family for marrying a poor weaver, died, leaving John and his two brothers to be brought up in poverty by their mother. At the age of seventeen

MYSTICS OF SPAIN

he studied at a Jesuit college in Medina del Campo; then, convinced he had a religious vocation, he joined the Carmelite order, taking the habit in 1563. But he still continued with his education, embarking on a three-year course at the University of Salamanca, during which time he was reckoned sufficiently proficient to teach students himself. In 1567 he was ordained a priest, and in the same year, at Medina, he fatefully met Teresa, who persuaded him to help her reform the Carmelite order and set up a Discalced monastery. Next year John and two other Carmelite friars established such a house in Duruelo, the first of fifteen he was to found.

For the next four years John was involved in various administrative duties for the reform movement before becoming confessor to the nuns of Teresa's original Convent of the Incarnation in Ávila, staying there until 1577. In the same year he was imprisoned by the mainstream Carmelites, who were hostile to the radical reforms that he and Teresa had been implementing. Interrogated and flogged, John was kept prisoner in a tiny windowless cell in the Carmelite priory at Toledo. Thrown back on his spiritual resources and faith in God, he responded by writing some of his finest poetry, including part of the "Spiritual Canticle," which became the wellspring of his mystical treatises. After eight months' incarceration he managed to escape, taking with him his precious writings. From then on he continued to administer Discalced monasteries, act as a spiritual director, and write his mystical works. He died in 1591, and his last words were reputed to be "Tonight I shall sing matins in heaven." He was beatified in 1675, canonized in 1726, and declared a doctor of the church in 1926.

John plumbed great depths of mystical experience and wrote about them in a carefully considered, meticulous way. But he is also one of the greats of Spanish lyric poetry, and his mystical poems form the basis for longer prose commentaries. In the "Spiritual Canticle" he draws on the bridal mysticism of the Song of Songs, interpreting the love between man and God in terms of that between bride and bridegroom, with the stages of the relationship representing the stages of the mystical path. His lines are often simple in diction but haunting in resonance, both sensual and spiritual at the same time:

DAZZLING DARKNESS

> My loved one is the mountains
> The lonely wooded valleys
> The strange islands
> The rushing streams
> The hushing of the amorous winds.[19]

John is best known, however, for his description of the soul's "dark night"—a painful but inevitable stage of its journey toward union with God—which he elaborates fully in *The Ascent of Mount Carmel* and *The Dark Night of the Soul*. These two unfinished treatises, based on two poems, really form one continuous work and were designed to be read by monks. John says that to reach union with God, the soul has to undergo purgation by passing through two states of darkness, or "nights"—John's terminology ultimately goes back to Dionysius the Areopagite, but he expands and enriches it. (It should be noted that John's "nights" are not necessarily sequential since different aspects of the journey may be experienced at different times.)

In the night of the senses, the soul is purged of its desire for things of the world as well as emotional attachments. The second, more painful state, the night of the spirit, relates to those who are further along the contemplative path and involves purgation of any residual spiritual consolations, whereby the soul feels itself agonizingly abandoned by God before its final union with him. (With regard to this union, John says that God is "substantially present" in every soul, whether that of a sinner or a saint. But John distinguishes between this divine presence, naturally occurring in every creature, and the union of the soul with God through love, when the soul's will and God's will are in perfect consonance.)

John also says that both nights have their active and passive phases. The active one involves the soul's making efforts to effect the necessary purgation. So, in the active night of the senses, the soul must try to imitate the life of Christ and reject anything that does not glorify God. The emotions of joy, hope, fear, and grief must be mortified and the soul should try to pursue the most difficult, despised, and unpleasant things in life. The active night of the spirit concerns the higher part of the soul. The use of the imagination and meditation, for example, picturing Christ on the cross, must come to an end, since the soul must stay in darkness, emptied of sensual images. Also, the memory must be stripped of its knowledge of sense objects, and the soul must not reflect upon supernatural experiences, such as visions and inner voices (of which John, unlike Teresa, was extremely wary). It must simply focus on God in loving affection.

The passive stages of the two nights require the soul to do nothing but allow God to work on it. John says that there are three indicators that the soul is going through the passive night of the senses: it derives no comfort in divine or created things, it feels "dryness" owing to God's transferring "to the spirit the good things and the strength of the senses,"[20] and it is unable to meditate or stimulate the imagination. It also feels forsaken by God and is tempted to revert to its old habit of meditation—which it may lapse into, unless guided by a spiritual director. The soul should remain quiet, letting its faculties remain inoperative, and so allow God to do his work in it, "for by not hindering the operation of infused contemplation, to which God is now admitting it, the soul is refreshed in peaceful abundance, and set on fire with the spirit of love."[21]

Finally, the more-demanding and painful passive night of the spirit, in which the soul keenly feels the lack of spiritual consolation, ultimately leads to loving union with God. This last phase of the dark night involves the soul's doing nothing except attending to God in love and allowing his light to enter it. The divine light is like a "ray of darkness" because it leaves the soul in a darkness that comes from nonunderstanding and a sense of its own impurity. This light overcomes the light of natural reason and is so radiant and pure that the soul it enters recognizes its wretched state and suffers greatly, thinking it has been removed from God's grace. But the darkness, which can last for years, is in fact purifying the soul "as fire consumes the rust and mouldiness of metal,"[22] and the soul must allow itself to be refined so that it can become united with God in love. God, in short, makes "the soul die to all that is not God" so that being "denuded and stripped" it may become renewed. "This is nothing else," John says, "but the supernatural light giving light to the understanding, so that the human understanding becomes divine, made one with the divine."[23] In *The Living Flame of Love*, John states that the substance of the soul cannot be changed into the

DAZZLING DARKNESS

substance of God. Nevertheless, the soul can be "united in Him and absorbed in Him, and is thus God, which comes to pass in this perfect state of the spiritual life, although not so perfectly as in the next life."[24]

12

PROTESTANT MYSTICS OF THE
SEVENTEENTH CENTURY

I knew nothing but pureness, and innocency, and righteousness; being renewed into the image of God by Christ Jesus, to the state of Adam, which he was in before he fell.

—George Fox

Scholars still debate the various and complex causes of the Protestant Reformation in the sixteenth century, which should probably be seen not as a sudden eruption but as the culmination of a reform movement whose tremors can be traced back to the likes of Hus, Wycliffe, and others before them. But in the early 1500s the forces of reform surfaced with even greater vehemence and tenacity, most notably through the protest of the German monk Martin Luther (1483–1546)—who in fact had not intended to break away from the church, only to correct its abuses—and then through Huldrych Zwingli (1484–1531) and John Calvin (1509–64). The Protestants' attack on, and eventual split from, the church ushered in a new chapter in its history. The effects were felt at all levels of the ecclesiastical structure. Reformers debated, challenged, and often modified or rejected church doctrine and practices, such as the theological basis of the Mass, and in the process they did much to undermine popular piety, including pilgrimages, the cult of holy relics, and recitation of prayers for the dead.

The Reformation affected the tradition of mysticism in various ways. For example, the reformers' bias against what they spurned as "superstitions" could easily extend to other nonrational aspects of

DAZZLING DARKNESS

religion, and such a climate was generally unconducive to those who claimed to hear divine voices or to see the face of Christ or to feel the presence of God. In a more practical way, the decline in Protestant countries of the religious orders and their monasteries—the great seedbeds of mysticism—destroyed or at least reduced some of the most favorable habitats for contemplatives. Nevertheless, despite the fact the Protestant churches had removed themselves from the mainstream tradition of contemplative prayer, mystics still appeared in Protestant lands—but they were as likely to be shoemakers (for example, Jacob Boehme and George Fox) or poets as they were members of the clergy.

One of the main instigators of the Reformation, Martin Luther was born in Saxony in 1483 and became an Augustinian monk and, later, a professor at the University of Wittenberg. He was profoundly influenced by Paul's Letter to the Romans, which convinced him that people were justified by faith in God and not by good works (a tenet that implied that priests and the church were unnecessary as mediators between people and God). At the time this seemed, as the church historian Diarmaid MacCulloch has noted, "an exhilarating, liberating idea, because it ended the tyranny of religious observance and of external demands on the human soul."[1] Luther also became increasingly critical about clerical morality and practices, particularly the sale of indulgences and with it the implication that human effort could affect a soul's destiny in the afterlife. Eventually he was moved to nail to the door of Wittenberg's castle church his Ninety-five Theses, a document that included the excoriation of the practice of indulgences, and invited a debate about them.

The church was slow to react to this challenge to its authority, but finally, in 1521, the pope excommunicated Luther. With the help of the newly developed printing presses, however, the "new opinion" of Luther and his followers, with its emphasis on the central place of the Bible as against the traditional authority of the church and papacy, leaped across Europe, causing debate, division, and violence. Politics further complicated the religious turmoil: in Germany, for example, the local princes were often guided in their decisions whether or not to support Luther by a need to make prudent political alliances as much as from a concern for doctrine.

PROTESTANT MYSTICS OF THE SEVENTEENTH CENTURY

The hostility between the Lutheran and Catholic sides was partially resolved by the Peace of Augsburg in 1555, when it was established that people should adopt their particular ruler's faith, whether it be Catholic or Lutheran.

Elsewhere in Europe, the momentum of reform was continued in Switzerland by Huldrych Zwingli in Zurich and, especially, John Calvin in Geneva. Calvin, who more than Luther stressed the idea of absolute predestination (the belief that God, before creation, had predestined people to either salvation or damnation), established in Geneva a theocratic and puritanical regime that was fearless in using severe punishment to ensure "good moral behavior." Calvinism later spread to France, the Netherlands, England, and Scotland (under the charismatic leadership of John Knox), and parts of Germany, although it was excluded from the terms of the Peace of Augsburg.

Meanwhile, in England, Henry VIII (r. 1509–47), in conflict with Rome over his desired divorce from his childless wife, Catherine of Aragon, declared himself the head of the Church of England. In 1536, as part of Henry's reforms, English monasteries began to be "dissolved," their pews torn out and roofs stripped of lead. In fact, Henry, whose previous enthusiasm for the papacy had been rewarded by the title Defender of the Faith, was conservative in doctrinal matters. But reform ideas took root during the reigns of his Protestant successors Edward VI (r. 1547–53) and—after the rule of the reactionary Catholic Mary (r. 1553–58)—Elizabeth I (r. 1558–1603), when the Anglican Church stabilized liturgically on a compromise position between the extremes of Puritan Calvinism and Catholicism. This position was formalized in 1563 by the Thirty-Nine Articles, a set of dogmatic tenets that aimed to settle religious controversies. Elizabeth herself was pushed into an aggressive anti-Catholic stance when Pope Pius V excommunicated her in 1570 and released her subjects from allegiance to her. And because Catholic Spain had become a national threat, a shadow of suspicion was cast over English Catholics, who could now be viewed as potential fifth columnists.

The subsequent defeat of the Spanish armada in 1588 unified the country around their Protestant queen, and anti-Catholic sentiment increased. One of those who fell foul of the zeitgeist, for example, was the mystical writer Augustine (born David) Baker (1575–1641), an Oxford-educated Welshman, who, at the age of twenty-five, after a near fatal accident, searched for the meaning of life and found it through his wide reading in the doctrines of the Roman Catholicism. He was received into the Catholic faith in 1603 and spent much of his subsequent life abroad, away from the perils of being a practicing Catholic in his native country.[2] He joined the Benedictine order in Padua and was later ordained a priest in Rheims in 1613. In 1624 he was sent to Cambrai in northern France to be spiritual director of a convent of English nuns, then transferred to another Benedictine community in nearby Douai in 1633. He died in London in 1641. Baker was a prolific writer and his best-known work was the two-volume posthumous *Sancta Sophia*, or *Holy Wisdom*, published 1657. In this thorough, detailed, erudite, and methodical work he outlines the way of the inner life, including the need for self-mortification, prayer, meditation, and contemplation.

By the middle of the seventeenth century the Calvinist party within the Church of England had become the dominant religious force in the country after the Puritan Parliamentarians under Oliver Cromwell defeated King Charles I (r. 1625–49) and his Royalist armies during the English Civil War (1642–51). But their victory was temporary, lasting for only about a decade of rigorous religious morality that impacted on national festive occasions: "The de facto ruler throughout most of the 1650s, Oliver Cromwell ... eventually authorized the abolition of Christmas and tore down maypoles around which the English had danced on their spring holidays."[3] When Charles II restored the monarchy in 1660, he reestablished Anglicanism and at a stroke those with die-hard Puritan principles suffered for their beliefs. In 1662 the Act of Uniformity established the primacy of the Anglican Book of Common Prayer in public worship and ministers were obliged to assent to it. Those who refused this and other stipulations were deprived of their livings, including some 2,000 Presbyterians. One of those who suffered from the Royalist Restoration was John Bunyan (1628–88), who drew on his conflict with the Royalist authorities, as well as his own personal spiritual crises, to create his great devotional work, *Pilgrim's Progress*.

The period during and after the civil war, therefore, was something of a spiritual melting pot in England. On the one hand

PROTESTANT MYSTICS OF THE SEVENTEENTH CENTURY

the fractious zeitgeist led some to turn towards introverted personal devotion, such as Bishop Joseph Hall, who in the preface to his book *The Devout Soul*, wrote:

> That in a time when we heare no noise but of Drums and Trumpets, and talk of nothing but arms, and sieges, & battels, I should write of Devotion, may seem to some of you strange & unseasonable; to me, contrarily, it seems most fit and opportune; For when can it be more proper to direct our address to the throne of grace, then when we are in the very jawes of Death? or when should we goe to seek the face of our God, rather, then in the needful time of trouble?[4]

Perhaps it was also as an escape from the troubles of the times, as was the case with Bishop Hall, that the "religious life of the century flowered into the devotional and philosophical mysticism" of English Metaphysical poets such as George Herbert (1593–1633), Henry Vaughan (1621–95), and Thomas Traherne (1637–74).[5]

At the same time, however, the seventeenth century saw more extrovert and public expressions of spirituality through a range of religious and quasi-religious movements, although some of them vanished before too long. Apart from bigger groups such as the Presbyterians, Independents, Baptists, and Unitarians, there were smaller, more radical sects such as the Ranters, Diggers, and the exotically named Fifth Monarchy Men and Muggletonians. There were also the Seekers, many of whom became absorbed into the Quaker movement.

Apart from attaching great importance to the Bible, these movements along with the main Protestant faiths emphasized the idea, found in medieval spirituality (especially in Rhineland mysticism), that the divine can only truly be found within: the kingdom of heaven—often described as the "inner light" or "true light" or the "spark"—lies within us, in the innermost recesses of the soul. This stress on the divine within was central to two of the greatest Protestant mystics, the German Jacob Boehme and the Englishman George Fox.

DAZZLING DARKNESS

Jacob Boehme (1575–1624)

The offspring of German peasants, Jacob Boehme lived at a time when the Lutheran Church was becoming doctrinaire and authoritarian, a tendency against which he revolted, conducting his life according to the divine illumination he claimed to receive. His inclination toward mysticism, however, did not make him withdraw from the world. On the contrary, in 1599, at the age of twenty-four, having completed his training as a shoemaker, he set up shop in his local town of Görlitz and married Katharina Kuntzschmann, the daughter of a local butcher, by whom he was to have four sons. Conversely, his conventional lifestyle did not seem to block his ability to receive mystical experiences, on which he drew for his teachings. Not that what he wrote was always pure inspiration: many of his concepts and terms were drawn from astrology, the Rhineland mystics, and the writings of alchemists, especially those of the Swiss physician Paracelsus (1493–1541), and they often make his books complex and obscure.

Yet Boehme's self-conviction and vivid, colorful, and authoritative style won him many contemporary admirers as well as influencing a number of later mystics and thinkers, including William Law, William Blake, and Hegel. One of his best-known concepts is the *Ungrund* (literally "unground"), which is sometimes translated as "abyss" and bears resemblance to Eckhart's unknowable "Godhead." The *Ungrund* refers to the primal, undifferentiated state, devoid of dualities such as good and evil, from which God is eternally becoming self-aware, manifesting himself in the light and wisdom of the Son.

Boehme was born in 1575 in the village of Alt Seidenberg near the town of Görlitz. He learned enough at school to be able to read and write well, but he never enjoyed a formal higher education, remaining an autodidact for the whole of his life. After school he became an apprentice shoemaker, learning his trade for three years. It was during this time that he had a striking encounter with a stranger who came to buy shoes at the shop where Boehme worked. Having bought his shoes, the man left the premises, then stopped and called Boehme outside. The apprentice did what he was told, and the man gripped his hand and told him he would

PROTESTANT MYSTICS OF THE SEVENTEENTH CENTURY

astonish the world and should study the scriptures. For Boehme it was a fateful encounter, a call to the spiritual life. His vocation was later confirmed during his time as a journeyman cobbler (the grade up from apprentice), when, after a period of intense prayer, he received an infusion of divine light and joy, the effects of which lasted for seven days.[6]

In 1600, the year after his marriage, Boehme received his most profound illumination to date. It seems to have been triggered by reflected light. One day he was staring at a pewter bowl when the sunlight flashing off its surface induced in him an ecstatic state during which he formed the impression that he could see into the inner workings of nature, the fundamental principle of things. Thinking that it might only be his fancy, he went outside to snap out of his rapture. But as he stared at the town green, he found he was able to see into the essential nature of "grass and herbs." Many years later he recalled that this sensation was accompanied by a feeling of God's love and of being reborn.[7]

Over the next decade Boehme began to record his spiritual experiences, thoughts, and reflections, which coalesced into his first book, *Aurora*, completed in 1612 when he was thirty-seven. A dense, difficult work, *Aurora* explores fundamental spiritual themes such as the relationship between God and creation and the nature of good and evil. Unfortunately for Boehme, the local Lutheran pastor, Gregorius Richter, took violent exception to its content and pressurized the town council to take action: Boehme only just avoided being banished from Görlitz, but he was ordered to cease writing. He obeyed this command for several years, but by 1618 he was writing a number of treatises (collected and published in 1623 as *The Way to Christ*), and over the next few years these were followed by several other weighty works, including *The Signature of Things* and *Mysterium Magnum*.

In early 1624, however, his old foe Richter became outraged when he read *The Way to Christ* and splenetically denounced Boehme from the pulpit and in a pamphlet. At the instigation of the town council, Boehme left Görlitz and took refuge in Dresden at the court of the elector prince of Saxony, where he was well received. By the time he returned to Görlitz a few months later, Richter had died. But Boehme enjoyed only a short triumph before he, too,

215

DAZZLING DARKNESS

passed away, in November 1624. His last words were reported to be "Now I am going into Paradise."[8]

Boehme's writings can try the patience of even the most dedicated reader, especially when he is yoking alchemical and astrological lore to his spiritual teachings (the eighteenth-century English bishop William Warburton said they would "disgrace Bedlam at full moon"[9]). But he can also be admirably clear, for example in the two dialogues that comprise his short work *Of the Supersensual Life*, in which a scholar questions his master as to how he may see and hear God.

During the course of the first dialogue in this work, Boehme emphasizes the need for stillness and complete surrender in order to experience the divine: when the intellect and will are quiet and the soul has risen above the sensual world, then the human spirit, being now the organ of God's spirit, will hear the divine voice. What prevents the encounter with God is self-will and a concern for the things of the world, which trap the soul in its self-created jail. The scholar asks how, since human nature leads to this self-imprisonment, it is possible to rise above nature without destroying it. The master replies that there are three things a person must do: resign the will to God, resist the dictates of the will, and bow the soul to the way of the cross in order to overcome the temptations of the flesh. This entails a rejection of the world and its values, a course the scholar despairs of achieving: success lies in surrendering constantly and totally to the mercy of God and to the sufferings of Christ and his intercessory power. Only then will the soul receive the strength to conquer death and be impervious to temptation. Belief in Christ and self-surrender bring their reward. If the will could "plunge itself into that where no creature is, or can be; presently it would be penetrated and clothed upon with the supreme splendour of the divine glory."[10]

As a soul receives the gifts of God, it finds paradoxically that it both loves and hates itself simultaneously. It loves the divine wisdom, goodness, and beauty that have become part of it but hates the self that is still wrapped up in the world and its snares. Love and hate, the master explains, are a necessary duality, since they define themselves through each other. The master then launches into a paean in praise of love, whose power "supports the heavens

216

PROTESTANT MYSTICS OF THE SEVENTEENTH CENTURY

and upholds the earth." Love is higher than the highest, greater than the greatest, and whoever "finds it, finds nothing and all things"—"nothing" because love is so incomprehensible and so much deeper than everything that nothing can be compared to it: it is an ineffable mystery. Yet the discoverer of love also finds "all things" because love is the beginning and the end of everything—"all things" are "from it, and in it, and by it."[11]

In the second dialogue, the scholar complains that his ability to receive the divine light is blocked by an inner wall. The master replies that the wall is the "creaturely will," which can be broken only by the "grace of self-denial." This cannot happen through the soul's own effort—it must passively obey God's divine light, which penetrates the darkness of its "creaturely being." Boehme distinguishes between the superior light of God and the inferior light of nature or reason and insists that the first must inform the second to bring about true enlightenment and harmony in the soul. We must seek "the fountain of light," and wait in the "deep ground" of the soul for the "sun of righteousness" to rise, increasing the light of nature sevenfold, since it "shall receive the stamp, image, and impression of the supersensual and supernatural."[12]

Later in the second dialogue, Boehme again emphasizes the role of the will in encountering God and his love. When the will desires something, it enters that object, which then takes it over and fills it with darkness. But if the will desires nothing, then it enters nothing, whereby it can receive God's will and reside in the light.[13]

The total surrender of the will means that the love of God becomes part of human nature. Giving up self-will is a sort of death—to the world—but in doing so people allow God to live within them. Few reach this state, because they seek love in *something*, an *object*, in which they find only that object. Finally, the soul arrives at that nothing "out of which all things may be made" and says to itself, "I have nothing ... I can do nothing ... I am nothing ... and so sitting down in my nothingness, I give glory to the Eternal Being, and will nothing of myself, that so God may will all in me, being unto me my God and all things."[14] By embracing nothing, the soul allows the entry of divine love, which needs a place that is still before it can make its home there. When it does so, it rejoices with its "love-fire," which burns up the center of selfishness—the "I"—and increases in

217

heat until it has accomplished its task within the soul, which cannot bear to be separated from it.

George Herbert (1593–1633)

Encountering the divine love that Boehme described was something the Anglican priest and poet George Herbert tried to do for most of his life. His work is an inner pilgrimage full of the troughs of failure, but with glimpses of divine light and love along the way— he himself described his poems as "a picture of the many spiritual conflicts that have passed betwixt God and my soul."[15] Although it is doubtful that Herbert underwent direct mystical experiences, it can be argued that there is enough profound spiritual engagement in his poetry to consider him, at the very least, a mystical writer. In poem after poem he returns to the conundrum of companionship and intimacy with Christ or God, seeking atonement, yet always conscious of the gap that he, as a representative of fallen humanity, had to close.

Born in Montgomery, Wales, Herbert grew up in a distinguished and learned household. His father died when he was three and his mother, a bright, kind, witty woman, moved home several times, eventually ending up in London, where Herbert went to school. After school he won a scholarship to Cambridge University, where he began to write poetry, stating in a letter to his mother that his verses would be dedicated to the glory of God. In 1620, at the age of twenty-seven, he was appointed the university's Public Orator (which involved delivering Latin orations to the university and liaising with members of the royal court).

Herbert seemed destined for public life, and in 1624 he was elected as a Member of Parliament; however, he relinquished the post almost immediately and swapped politics for religion, becoming ordained as a deacon. In 1628 he moved down to Wiltshire in the west of England, and in the following year he married a woman named Jane Danvers. In 1830, he became rector of Saint Andrew's Church, Bemerton, a village near Salisbury, where he would live for the final three years of his short life.

Herbert set about repairing Bemerton church at his own expense and was known for his kindliness, generosity, and devotion

PROTESTANT MYSTICS OF THE SEVENTEENTH CENTURY

to duties, visiting the sick, teaching, and conducting services. His parishioners nicknamed him "holy Mr. Herbert," and it is said that on one occasion a friend of Herbert's looked in through the church window and saw him lying prostrate on the ground before the altar.

While administering to his local flock, Herbert had time to write an influential prose work called *A Priest to the Temple: or the Country Parson* (published posthumously in 1652), and he was also able to write and revise poems and hymns. But having often suffered from ill health in the past, Herbert now succumbed to tuberculosis and parted from the world on March 1, 1633. On his deathbed he gave instructions for his poetry to be burnt, unless "it could turn to the advantage of any dejected poor soul." His work was duly saved.

Herbert's quiet, orderly spirituality and inward approach to God pervade his poems. Some were put to music (Herbert himself played the lute and viol) and are still sung as hymns in the Anglican faith. Scholars still debate how much and in what way Herbert was a mystic, or even if he was one at all. Some have seen him as a mystic-poet of the *via affirmativa*, others of the *via negativa*.[16] One scholar has suggested that his poetry is full of mystical content and traces the traditional mystic stages of awakening, purgation, and illumination (but not unification with the divine),[17] while the modern poet and critic John F. Deane has said that Herbert "is a man whose very thought focuses on his God, whose every mood is examined in the light of God's love, God's presence or seeming absence."[18]

What is compelling about Herbert's work is the directness and simplicity of his language, which make readers trust they are privy to the poet's innermost thoughts. These almost always concern God, Christ, the human condition, and the poet's struggle to feel a living connection with ultimate reality. If Herbert aspired toward the *via negativa* with his heart, his mind constantly celebrated the world—in the joy of language, ideas, and musicality of words, and the intricacies of poetic form. He rejoiced in finding connections between this world and the spiritual dimension, often using homely images to make plain and concrete what might otherwise feel beyond the ken of human nature. In this regard he resembles the Dutch painter Vermeer (1632–75), whose orderly, domestic scenes are full of radiant light and otherworldly suggestiveness. In "Prayer," for example, Herbert's heart seeks a vital conduit to God while his

219

DAZZLING DARKNESS

mind revels in metaphor, piling up image after image to illustrate the nature and effect of prayer. Prayer, he says, is our heart going on a pilgrimage, it is a type of song, it is thunder in reverse, or a person wearing his Sunday best; it is "The milky way, the bird of Paradise, / Church-bells beyond the stars heard, the soul's blood, / The land of spices; something understood." The fecundity of imagery seems to pour out, like an ecstatic prayer itself, marrying the mystical and the sensual.[19]

Yet when prayer is absent, or when God does not seem to hear it, Herbert was all too conscious of the fallen human condition. In "Grace," he writes: "Death is still working like a mole / And digs my grave at each remove ... Sin is still hammering my heart / Unto a hardness, void of love." The only response is to implore grace to "Drop from above." In "Affliction (I)," Herbert laments that books cannot lead him to God: "I read, and sigh, and wish I were a tree; / For sure then I should grow / To fruit or shade: at least some bird would trust / Her household to me, and I should be just." By becoming a tree there is nothing else for us to do but wait, then grace, like a bird building a nest, will make us its home. And home on earth, transformed by grace, becomes a heavenly abode.

Home is important to Herbert as a place of graceful ease both in this world and the world to come. In "Home" he voices his frustration at his absence from it in a poetic voice akin to that of the Psalms: "Come Lord, my head doth burn, my heart is sick, / While thou dost ever, ever stay: / Thy long deferrings wound me to the quick, / My spirit gaspeth night and day. / O show thy self to me, / Or take me up to thee!" God's "long deferrings" would feel that much more acute to one who had suffered from ill health for most of his years on earth; and this sense of urgency in Herbert's life surfaces elsewhere, such as in "Denial": "O cheer and tune my heartless breast, / Defer no time; / That so thy favors granting my request, / They and my mind may chime, / And mend my rhyme."

Herbert consistently captures the mystic's erratic search for God with searing honesty; at the heart of the search is love, the subject of arguably Herbert's most celebrated poem, "Love (III)" (which made such an impression on the French-Jewish mystic Simone Weil that it encouraged her to convert to Christianity). In the poem, Love is envisaged as a host, inviting the human soul to a

220

PROTESTANT MYSTICS OF THE SEVENTEENTH CENTURY

meal, with echoes of a homely supper, such as might be enjoyed in a rectory, as well as the Eucharistic feast and the biblical idea of the heavenly banquet, promised to the faithful in the afterlife. The soul is tortured with a sense of its own sin and unworthiness, the result of the Fall; but Love keeps insisting, gently, tenderly, that the soul should eat "meat," (i.e. "food") reminding it that Christ has borne the blame for the Fall.

> Love bade me welcome: yet my soul drew back,
>   Guilty of dust and sin.
> But quick-eyed Love, observing me grow slack
>   From my first entrance in,
> Drew nearer to me, sweetly questioning,
>   If I lacked any thing.
>
> A guest, I answered, worthy to be here:
>   Love said, You shall be he.
> I the unkind, ungrateful? Ah my dear,
>   I cannot look on thee.
> Love took my hand, and smiling did reply,
>   Who made the eyes but I?
>
> Truth Lord, but I have marred them: let my shame
>   Go where it doth deserve.
> And know you not, says Love, who bore the blame?
>   My dear, then I will serve.
> You must sit down, says Love, and taste my meat:
>   So I did sit and eat.

In "Denial" the poet asked God to tune his "heartless breast" so that his divine favors "and my mind may chime, / And mend my rhyme." The ending of "Love," with the perfect rhyme of "meat" and "eat" suggests that the poet's breast has been tuned and his rhyme has been truly mended: the poet is at one with himself, and one with God.

Henry Vaughan 1621–95

"The greatest of the nature mystics of the seventeenth century,"[20] Henry Vaughan expressed his mystical instincts within the context of

221

DAZZLING DARKNESS

the Anglican Church and its worship and liturgy, although his thought and spiritual aspirations were "fused equally with Platonism."[21] He was deeply influenced by George Herbert and penned his verses with a similar ingenuity, wit, and passion. His greatest poetic work, *Silex Scintillans* ("The Flashing Flint"),[22] emerged in two parts in 1650 and 1655. He also wrote devotional prose works, including *The Mount of Olives* (1652) and *Flores Fortitudinis* (1654). Although lacking Herbert's consistent ability to craft and bring a poem to its completion, Vaughan was master of the striking phrase, the daring thought, and able to evoke the glory of the world and the cosmos, with its stars and constellations, in memorable poetic phrases; his poetry is suffused with traditional mystical images of fire and, especially, light, which he employs as a symbol for the inner light that draws us to the glory of God. Although often making references to his native Welsh countryside, his poetry is better known for its celebration of transcendence, for example in the visionary opening of "The World," with its echo of Plato's idea that time is "the moving image of eternity":

> I saw Eternity the other night
> Like a great Ring of pure and endless light,
> All calm, as it was bright;
> And round beneath it, Time in hours, days, years,
> Driv'n by the spheres
> Like a vast shadow mov'd; in which the world
> And all her train were hurl'd.

The plangent opening of his poem "They are all gone into the world of light!" also shows Vaughan's tangible sense of a realm lying beyond the earthly one:

> They are all gone into the world of light!
> And I alone sit lingering here;
> Their very memory is fair and bright,
> And my sad thoughts doth clear.

As with many other mystics or mystical writers, it is unclear to what extent if at all Vaughan experienced a rapture or encounter with the divine or profound sense of grace. However, his poem "Mount of Olives" does suggest he was familiar with a serenity and spiritual

PROTESTANT MYSTICS OF THE SEVENTEENTH CENTURY

contentment associated with the presence of the divine as well as a subsequent disenchantment with the falseness of the outer material world that "did only paint and lie."

Descended from an old established Welsh family, Vaughan was born in 1621 in Newton-by-Usk, in Brecknockshire, in south-central Wales, along with his twin brother Thomas, who became a philosopher and alchemist. He was educated for a while at Jesus College, Oxford (but did not take his degree), before going on to London to study Law. With the outbreak of the Civil War he returned home to Wales and acted as secretary to a Royalist judge, and he, as an ardent Royalist himself, may have fought for the king.

The 1640s was a dark, grim era of political struggle, religious division, and what Vaughan called the "juggling fate of soldiery," especially for Vaughan himself, who not only found himself on the losing Royalist side and had to witness his Anglican clergy friends losing their livings, but also suffered a serious physical illness. Nor was he immune from spiritual darkness—as he expresses in his confessional poem "The Eclipse," in which he asks God plaintively: "Whither, whither didst thou fly / When I did grieve thine holy Eye?" Yet he was also aware that within the darkness—national and personal—there is hope of a divine revelation lurking, as he expresses in "They are all gone into the world of light!": "If a star were confined into a tomb, / Her captive flames must needs burn there; / But when the hand that locked her up, gives room, / She'll shine through all the sphere." But darkness as a symbol also had a positive aspect for him: in his poem "The Night" he distinguishes between the darkness of spiritual benightedness and the divine radiant darkness in words reminiscent of the apophatic language of Dionysius the Areopagite and *The Cloud of Unknowing*:

> There is in God, some say,
> A deep but dazzling darkness, as men here
> Say it is late and dusky, because they
> > See not all clear.
> O for that night! where I in Him
> Might live invisible and dim!

In 1646 Vaughan married a woman named Catherine Wise and was still writing mainly secular poems; there then came a marked

223

DAZZLING DARKNESS

change in his poetic direction, with spiritual themes coming to the fore. The urgency of these poems has prompted some to speculate that he had a life-transforming spiritual experience or conversion ("God had drawn him secretly to Him in divine light, and this brought about a sudden conversion."[23]); but the reality might have been a more gradual easing away from his secular material, perhaps accelerated by the death of his brother William in 1648, as well as by an intense reading of Herbert's poetry. At the very least, as he wrote in the preface to *Silex Scintillans*, he became conscious of himself as a sinner whose "follies" would never "be expiated without special sorrows."

However it was that Vaughan turned up the pressure on his poetry and changed its focus, it is interesting to note that he himself reported a story told to him about the sudden "conversion" of a shepherd boy to being a poet. This boy was tending sheep in the summertime in Wales when he

> fell into a deep sleep in which he dreamt that he saw a beautifull young man with a garland of green leafs upon his head, & an hawk upon his fist: with a quiver full of Arrows att his back, coming towards him (whistling several measures or tunes all the way) att last lett the hawk fly att him, which (he dreamt) gott into his mouth & inward parts, & suddenly awaked in a great fear & consternation: butt possessed with such a vein, or gift of poetrie, that he left the sheep & went about the Countrey, making songs upon all occasions, and came to be the most famous Bard in all the Countrey in his time.[24]

It is unlikely that Vaughan swallowed, metaphorically, the equivalent of a hawk and experienced a spiritual conversion overnight, but the publication of *Silex Scintillans* in 1650 established him as an important spiritual poet, one who was a questing soul seeking the *fons et origo* of the true Christian life, his restlessness fueled by the distractions of the world as well as the biblical idea, articulated by Augustine and Thomas à Kempis and others, that we are pilgrims in this life, searching for our heavenly home. As he says in his poem "Man":

> Man hath still either toys, or care,
> He hath no root, nor to one place is tied,

224

PROTESTANT MYSTICS OF THE SEVENTEENTH CENTURY

> But ever restless and irregular
>   About this Earth doth run and ride,
> He knows he hath a home, but scarce knows where,
>   He says it is so far
> That he hath quite forgot how to go there.

For the devout Christian, the spiritual journey is a single-minded and life-long venture—as T. S. Eliot says in "Little Gidding," "We shall not cease from exploration." For Vaughan "home" was an important rooting element in his life, especially at a time of national turmoil and division: he gave himself the nickname of the Silurist, in recognition of the ancient local Silures tribe; and he adopted the sobriquet "Swan of the Usk" after the river that flowed through the memories of his childhood. From these secure foundations he was able to set forth on his pilgrimage of spiritual imagination toward ultimate truth:

> … all night have I
> Spent in a roving ecstasy
> To find my Saviour; I have been
> As far as Bethlehem, and have seen
> His inn and cradle; being there
> I met the wise men, ask'd them where
> He might be found, or what star can
> Now point Him out, grown up a man? ["The Night," p. 33]

For Vaughan nature was a manifestation of God's creation, a locus where the divine sphere and the human world can meet; and God he sometimes describes, in imitation of Herbert, as an intimate, a divine being he can confide in, as in his poem "Religion": "My God, when I walk in those groves / And leaves Thy Spirit doth still fan, / I see in each shade that there grows / An angel talking with a man." Nature comprised not only the countryside around him— the River Usk, the woods and copses—but the vast cosmos and the majestic order of the stars ("hosts of spies"), which he evokes in "The Constellation": "With what exact obedience do you move / Now beneath, and now above, / And in your vast progressions overlook / The darkest night, and closest nook!"

For all his love of his natural surroundings, however, Vaughan shared Plato's idea that the world was a copy of an eternal

DAZZLING DARKNESS

imperishable dimension of Forms and that what we see on earth is merely a copy of this transcendent sphere of archetypes. For Vaughan there was a constant longing to achieve the spiritual vision that was being obscured by the slings and arrows of daily living. So, for example, in "Distraction" he prays to God to: "come and relieve, / And tame, and keep down with Thy light / Dust that would rise and dim my sight!" Elsewhere, in "The World," in an echo of Plato's parable of the Cave and the prisoner's journey from darkness to light, he emphasizes the way a person's inner spiritual light can illuminate "The way which from this dead and dark abode / Leads up to God, / A way where you might tread the Sun, / and be More bright than he." And in "The Search" the inner voice of the mystic advises him to eschew exterior sight in favor of interior vision; any mind distracted by externals will end up perceiving nothing spiritual:

> Leave, leave thy gadding thoughts;
>   Who pores
>   And spies
> Still out of doors
>   Descries
> Within them nought.

Rejecting "gadding thoughts" and embarking on a life of spiritual reflection and worship leads to the possibility of the transcendent vision of eternity that appears like "a great ring of pure and endless light"; or, as he says in his beautifully realized poem "Peace," a "country / Far beyond the stars" where beyond the din of the world and the strife of war "Sweet Peace sits, crown'd with smiles":

> My soul, there is a country
> Far beyond the stars,
> Where stands a winged sentry
> All skilful in the wars:
> There, above noise and danger
> Sweet Peace sits, crown'd with smiles,
> And One born in a manger
> Commands the beauteous files.
> He is thy gracious friend
> And—O my soul awake!—

226

PROTESTANT MYSTICS OF THE SEVENTEENTH CENTURY

Did in pure love descend,
To die here for thy sake.
If thou canst get but thither,
There grows the flower of Peace,
The Rose that cannot wither,
Thy fortress, and thy ease.
Leave then thy foolish ranges;
For none can thee secure,
But One, who never changes,
Thy God, thy life, thy cure.

George Fox (1624–91)

The year that Jacob Boehme died, 1624, saw the birth of George Fox, the English visionary, mystic, and founder of the Quakers, or Society of Friends, who are still known for their tolerant spirit, pacifism, and acts of charity. There were parallels between the two men. Like Boehme, Fox received only a basic school education and was apprenticed to a shoemaker. Fox, too, experienced mystical visions of reality, including one in which, like Boehme, he was able to see into the heart of nature:

> Now I was come up in spirit through the flaming sword, into the paradise of God. All things were new; and all the creation gave unto me another smell than before, beyond what words can utter. I knew nothing but pureness, and innocency, and righteousness; being renewed into the image of God by Christ Jesus, to the state of Adam, which he was in before he fell. The creation was opened to me; and it was showed me how all things had their names given them according to their nature and virtue.[25]

Boehme's writings were in fact beginning to circulate in England at about the period when Fox had started his itinerant spiritual mission, and it is said that the German's works were studied by Fox's followers.

Central to Fox's spiritual vision was the Bible, and in common with other fringe religious groups of the civil war period, he saw the world in dualistic terms, as a cosmic struggle between light and dark, love and death, God and Satan. Underpinning his spirituality, however, was "an earthy wisdom and salt entirely his

227

own, and an insistence on the love and light of Christ which is centrally Christian."[26]

Fox was born in the village of Fenny Drayton in Leicestershire. His father, Christopher, was a weaver and a devout Christian (his neighbors called him "Righteous Christer"), while his mother could claim as an ancestor a Protestant martyr who had died during the reign of the Catholic queen Mary I (r. 1553–58). George felt a strong religious instinct from childhood, and at one point his family considered making him train as a priest. Instead, he worked for a shoemaker and wool trader until, in 1643, at the age of nineteen, he experienced a direct call from God, who said to him: "Thou seest how young people go together into vanity, and old people into the earth; thou must forsake all, young and old, keep out of all, and be a stranger unto all."[27] Impelled to leave home, Fox felt the great weight of spiritual despair on his shoulders, and he set out to find an answer to it. For the next three years he wandered around the Midlands and the north of England, seeking out priests who he hoped might remedy his depression and sense of sin. None could offer him any comfort. One of them, Fox says, told him "to take tobacco and sing psalms"; another man seemed to him to be "like an empty, hollow cask"; another suggested Fox should undergo some blood-letting.[28]

During this time of seeking, however, Fox experienced what he called "openings" or revelations—divinely revealed knowledge of the truth of which he was inwardly certain. It was "opened" to him, for example, that all believers, whether Protestants or Catholics, were born of God; that attendance at the universities of Oxford and Cambridge was not a sufficient training for the priesthood; and that God did not dwell in man-made temples or churches. Meanwhile, Fox continued his travels, fasting, reading his Bible, and reflecting upon life in "hollow trees and lonesome places," or pitching up at some town, where he would take a room for a time. Having given up on the priests of the established Anglican Church, he sought out those of the dissenting faiths, such as the Baptists and Congregationalists. But even though he found some of them to be "tender" (one of his most positive adjectives), they could not help his wretched condition. This only strengthened his desire for God without the mediation of any person or book.

228

PROTESTANT MYSTICS OF THE SEVENTEENTH CENTURY

Then on one occasion, after a period of solitude, he received a mystical revelation accompanied by a profound experience of divine love.

> One day, when I had been walking solitarily abroad, and was come home, I was taken up in the love of God, so that I could not but admire the greatness of His love; and while l was in that condition, it was opened unto me by the eternal light and power, and I therein clearly saw that all was done and to be done in and by Christ, and how He conquers and destroys this tempter the devil, and all his works, and is atop of him; and that all these troubles were good for me, and temptations for the trial of my faith, which Christ had given me.[29]

The experience gave him a solidity of faith, "as an anchor in the bottom of the sea," but the divine light also served to intensify his awareness of the darkness in his life, with all its trials and temptations. From then on, however, he began to draw large numbers of followers, especially among craftsmen and yeomen. His new recruits were borne along by their leader's glowing spirituality, self-conviction, keen sense of justice, charity, and bravery in the face of persecution. For Fox inevitably made enemies wherever he went. Apart from taking constant issue with priests, judges, schoolteachers, and other establishment figures, he refused to doff his hat to his social superiors, and he showed a puritanical streak in his attitude toward those activities, which he considered made people "vain" and "loose," including "feasts, May-games [an assortment of games to celebrate the coming of spring], sports, plays, and shows." (In a similar vein he referred to the days of the week by numbers, not by their names, because the latter reflected the names of pagan gods.) He was rewarded for his advice and warnings to all and sundry with beatings, stonings, whippings, the stocks, and jail. But nothing could prevent him from his aim to declare "the Word of life and reconciliation freely, that all might come to Christ."[30]

In 1652 Fox's mission became firmly established after he took residence at Swarthmoor in northwest England. There he got to know the aristocratic judge Thomas Fell, who gave valuable support to the nascent movement. In the following years Fox began to give the Quakers organizational shape, instituting regular monthly,

229

DAZZLING DARKNESS

quarterly, and yearly meetings between members. Later, in 1669—the year he married Thomas Fell's widow—Fox took his message abroad to the people of Ireland, then to the West Indies and America in 1671–72, and to the Netherlands in 1677 and again in 1684. For the rest of his life he continued preaching and overseeing the organization of the movement. He died on January 13, 1691, and his *Journal*, which became a spiritual classic, was published three years later.

For Fox the central spiritual reality of existence was the divine inner light, which is received directly from God and which transforms and guides a person through life. This meant that churches and priests were unnecessary and the scriptures secondary (for the light precedes the scriptures) to what was a God-given inner certainty. He sums up the essence of this teaching in his *Journal*, in which he says it was revealed to him by God that everyone was "enlightened by the divine Light of Christ," and that those who believed in it "came out of condemnation to the Light of life, and became the children of it; but they that hated it, and did not believe in it were condemned by it, though they made a profession of Christ."[31]

Fox echoes the sentiments of the first chapter of John's Gospel, but he stresses that his insights were revealed to him, not learned from holy writ:

> For I saw, in that Light and Spirit which was before the Scriptures were given forth, and which led the holy men of God to give them forth, that all, if they would know God or Christ, or the Scriptures aright, must come to that Spirit by which they that gave them forth were led and taught.[32]

There is, then, a divine principle that is found in every soul and manifested outwardly in righteous actions. It is our disobedience to the calling of this inner spirit of God that causes disharmony. But heeding it brings enlightened self-knowledge; for example, we see that by harming our neighbor we really are harming ourselves. It was Fox's mission to restore people to their spiritual selves, which in turn would bring about true religious devotion, charity, and justice.

So, inspired by Fox's writings and example, the Quaker movement was founded on spiritual and radical egalitarian

230

PROTESTANT MYSTICS OF THE SEVENTEENTH CENTURY

principles on the basis that the divine light and spirit reside with everyone, not just "qualified" priests. Quakers abandoned the rigid structures of the established churches, preferring to emphasize the need for each individual to acclimatize and tune in to his or her own inner, divine voice.

John Bunyan (1628–88)

A Puritan preacher and writer, John Bunyan was author of *The Pilgrim's Progress*, one of the most influential spiritual works ever written. Bunyan himself seems to have received at different times in his life powerful dreams and auditory experiences, as well as visions or at least powerful eruptions of the imagination. For example, in his autobiography, *Grace Abounding to the Chief of Sinners*, he says that "in a kind of a vision presented to me," he saw the poor people of Bedford (in the county of Bedfordshire in the English midlands) on the sunny side of a mountain, while, on the other side of a forbidding wall, he was shivering in the cold. He eventually found a little doorway in the wall and with a great struggle he made his way through and "sat down in the midst of them, and so was comforted with the light and heat of their sun."[33] *Pilgrim's Progress* itself has both a visionary atmosphere and the narrative trajectory of a mystical path with a series of stages: an initial calling, a commitment to be in the presence of God (the "Celestial City"), the journey itself, and the eventual arrival.

Bunyan was born in Bedfordshire, the son of a tinker or brazier (an itinerant mender of pots and pans). Knowledge of his outward life is sketchy, though Bunyan does supply some details in *Grace Abounding*. He learned the basics of reading and writing at school, but appears to have educated himself later through reading the Bible, John Foxe's *Book of Martyrs* (a 1563 work that detailed Protestant victims of Catholic persecution and which became a favorite among Puritans), and other spiritual books. He was not one of those spiritual greats who were pious from an early age: he tells us that he swore, told lies, and blasphemed. But he does seem to have possessed something of a visionary nature in the way he was prone to "fearful" dreams and visions while asleep at night, involving images of "devils and wicked spirits, who still, as I then

DAZZLING DARKNESS

thought, laboured to draw me away with them, of which I could never be rid."[34]

There was also a time when he was playing a game called "Cat" on the local village green, when

> a voice did suddenly dart from heaven into my soul, which said, Wilt thou leave thy sins and go to heaven, or have thy sins and go to hell? ... I looked up to heaven, and was, as if I had, with the eyes of my understanding, seen the Lord Jesus looking down upon me, as being very hotly displeased with me, and as if He did severely threaten me with some grievous punishment for these and other ungodly practices.[35]

Bunyan's early adulthood showed few signs of his becoming a visionary writer. He was often depressed and dejected, and reveled in "all manner of vice and ungodliness." In 1644, when the civil war was raging, he joined the Parliamentary army and served for three years, probably seeing little action. His experience did, however, give him an insight into spiritual action: by mixing with rank-and-file soldiers he encountered members of radical sects such as the Quakers, Seekers, and Ranters. He came to realize that religion was not to do with outward forms of worship but with a matter of conscience; it was a personal search for God, reliant on the bestowal of grace.

Bunyan was discharged from the army in 1647 and married soon afterward; his wife was as poor as himself (he said they had not "a dish or spoon betwixt us"), but she did have two books of evangelical spirituality that inserted a seed of religion in him. Yet it took years for him to become fully converted to the Puritan form of Christianity he became known for. At first, following his marriage, he began to take more interest in the Anglican church, gradually forsaking worldly pleasures such as dancing and sports for what he believed was a life more pleasing to God. But for years he struggled to find spiritual peacefulness, beset by temptations and obsessive thoughts: "I could neither eat my food, stoop for a pin, chop a stick, or cast mine eye to look on this or that, but still the temptation would come, *Sell Christ for this, or sell Christ for that; sell Him, sell Him.*"[36]

In about 1655 he joined the Baptist church in Bedford and embraced this form of worship, soon being appointed a lay

PROTESTANT MYSTICS OF THE SEVENTEENTH CENTURY

preacher. Five years later, with the Restoration of Charles II, the various Christian sects that had flourished under the republicans were banned. In November 1660 Bunyan was charged with holding a service contrary to Anglican practices and imprisoned for twelve years, though he was allowed out on parole at various times. On his release in 1672—the year that penal laws concerning Nonconformist churches were relaxed—Bunyan rejoined his Bedford community and became their pastor. He also began to publish his influential books, including *The Pilgrim's Progress* (1678), *The Holy War* (1682), and *The Pilgrim's Progress, Second Part* (1684). He died in London in 1688.

Pilgrim's Progress became, after the Bible, the most popular devotional book in the English-speaking world until modern times. Written in a plain, direct, lucid style, this allegorical story involves the journey of the lead character Christian from the City of Destruction (a place that burns with fire and brimstone) to the Celestial City, a pilgrimage based on Bunyan's own inner progress from spiritual dejection to salvation. The book begins with Bunyan setting the scene, attributing the events of the story to a dream, thereby giving it a mystical timbre: "As I walked through the wilderness of this world, I lighted on a certain place where was a den, and laid me down in that place to sleep; and as I slept, I dreamed a dream."[37]

The narrator sees Christian, weighed down by his burden of sin and seeking deliverance from it. Guided by a character called Evangelist, Christian leaves his home to find salvation in the Celestial City atop Mount Zion. On the way he encounters various obstacles and a range of helping and hindering characters, such as Simple, Sloth, and Presumption. He also visits places such as the Hill of Difficulty; the House of the Palace Beautiful; the Valley of Humiliation, where he successfully battles against the monstrous dragon, Apollyon; the gloomy and terrifying Valley of the Shadow of Death; and Vanity Fair, a fair that displays the vanity and seediness of the world, with its "jugglings, cheats, games, plays, fools, apes, knaves, and rogues, and ... thefts, murders, adulteries."[38] Farther along the way, Christian, with his companion Hopeful, is captured by Giant Despair, who takes them to Doubting Castle, from which they eventually escape.

DAZZLING DARKNESS

Finally they cross the River of Death and reach the Celestial City, where they are greeted with jubilation:

> Now, just as the gates were opened to let in the men, I looked in after them, and behold the city shone like the sun; the streets also were paved with gold; and in them walked many men, with crowns on their heads, palms in their hands, and golden harps, to sing praises withal.[39]

The Celestial City is like the New Jerusalem, dazzling with gold, and Christian receives confirmation of his blessed state when he hears the words, "Enter ye into the joy of your Lord." It is the crowning moment of the pilgrimage. Having taken his readers through the landscape of his soul, Bunyan leaves them with a vision of reflected light and glorious, continual sound: "There were also of them that had wings, and they answered one another without intermission, saying, Holy, holy, holy is the Lord."[40]

Thomas Traherne (ca. 1636–74)

Twelve years younger than his fellow mystical poet Henry Vaughan, and dying of an illness before he was forty years of age, Traherne was a cleric, devotional writer, and poet whose lyrical verse was discovered only in 1903, more than 200 years after his death. A devout Anglican (a contemporary by the name of Thomas Good said he was "one of the most pious ingenious men that ever I was acquainted with"[41]), who, according to a modern scholar, "enjoyed the vision of God,"[42] Traherne wrote consistently about the interior spiritual life and in particular the state of what he termed "Felicity," which might be best understood as a state of beatitude.[43]

He also seemingly enjoyed intimations of the presence of God: in his *Select Meditations* (4.3) he said that he once had such a powerful spiritual experience "that for a fortnight after I could Scarsly Think or speak or write of any other Thing."[44] Elsewhere he wrote "Sometimes I should be alone, and without employment, when suddenly my Soul would return to itself, and forgetting all things in the whole world which mine eyes had seen, would be carried away to the ends of the earth."[45] And in his poem "Rapture," his sequence of short exclamatory phrases are reminiscent of Blaise

PROTESTANT MYSTICS OF THE SEVENTEENTH CENTURY

Pascal's description (see Chapter 13) of being filled with holy fire: "Sweet Infancy! / O fire of heaven! / O sacred Light! ... // O Heavenly joy! / O great and sacred blessedness / Which I possess! / So great a joy / Who did into my arms convey!"[46]

Traherne also wrote in his great prose work *Centuries of Meditations* (3.60) about ultimate happiness as a beatific gift that "transforms the Soul and makes it Heavenly—it powerfully calls us to communion with God, and weans us from the customs of this world. It puts a lustre upon God and all His creatures and makes us to see them in a Divine and Eternal Light." In this state of profound contentment, Traherne says, "you will not believe, how I was withdrawn from all endeavours of altering and mending outward things. They lay so well, methought, they could not be mended: but I must be mended to enjoy them."

Traherne was born in 1636 or 1637 in the royalist city of Hereford (his father John, who was a shoemaker, fought on the side of Charles I against the Parliamentarians). Traherne went up to study at Oxford in 1652 and five years later became rector of Credenhill near his home city, staying there for most of the rest of his time on earth, enjoying the life of a country cleric. In 1674 he began working as private chaplain to Sir Oliver Bridgeman, the Lord Keeper of the Great Seal to Charles II (who had been restored to the throne in 1660), and Traherne must have conducted private services for his family and servants. But Bridgeman died in his villa in Teddington in Middlesex in June 1674 and Traherne followed him to the grave (the cause of his death is uncertain) in late September. He was laid to rest in St Mary's Church in Teddington "under the reading Desk in the church, just entering into the Chancell he had no stone laid over him."[47]

Two important themes that emerge in Traherne's spiritual thinking are the image of God and the holy innocence of childhood. The image of God is implanted in us from birth, guiding us so that we can enjoy our lives and the "treasures of God in the similitude of God" (*Centuries* 3.59). God is part of us and thereby confers on us a happiness that "transforms the Soul and makes it Heavenly ... and weans us from the customs of this world. It puts a lustre upon God and all His creatures and makes us to see them in a Divine and Eternal Light." On realizing this state of being, Traherne says he

235

found that the external world revealed a pattern and harmony and that only he was out of kilter:

> All things were well in their proper places, I alone was out of frame and had need to be mended. For all things were God's treasures in their proper places, and I was to be restored to God's Image. Whereupon you will not believe how I was withdrawn from all endeavours of altering and mending outward things. They lay so well, methought, they could not be mended: but I must be mended to enjoy them.[48]

For Traherne, throughout his work (for example in the poems "Wonder," "Eden," and "Innocence"), the state of infancy "is not only an intimation of the soul's state in glory but also a type of the mind which has found felicity in this world through meditation."[49] His thoughts were attuned to the divine early in his life. Even at the age of four, as he later recalled, he was "sitting in a little obscure room in my father's poor house" and thinking "If there be a God certainly He must be Infinite in Goodness" and that he was prompted into thinking this via what he calls "a real whispering instinct of nature."[50] At the start of his apparently autobiographical poem "Wonder" he describes the light and revelation experienced when he was (or as if he were) a new-born baby:

> How like an Angel came I down!
>   How bright are all things here!
> When first among His works I did appear
>   O how their Glory me did crown!
> The world resembled His Eternity,
>   In which my soul did walk;
> And every thing that I did see
>   Did with me talk.

The poem evokes Traherne's sense of at-one-ment with himself and his surroundings, and he goes on to say that his inner being was flowing "With seas of life, like wine; / I nothing in the world did know / But 'twas divine." The verses, with their simple diction and emphatic rhymes (reminiscent of the early style of William Blake), convey certainty and a visionary quality:

19. Saint Gregory of Palamas was a leading proponent of hesychasm, the Orthodox tradition of mystical prayer.

20. Sergius of Radonezh – shown here surrounded by depictions of his life in this 17th-century icon from Yaroslavl – was a mystical forest hermit who became the patron saint of Russia.

21. Teresa of Ávila receives inspiration from the Holy Spirit in the form of a dove. A copy of a painting by the Baroque Spanish artist Jusepe de Ribera.

22. John of the Cross is associated with the "dark night of the soul" – an austere conception belying his reputation as a warm, cheerful man.

23. Jacob Boehme believed that the "creaturely will" could be overcome only by the "grace of self-denial."

24. For George Fox, founder of the Quakers, the divine inner light was the central spiritual reality of existence.

25. The title page from John Bunyan's *The Pilgrim's Progress*. Bunyan is shown asleep and dreaming while his hero Christian is making his way to the Celestial City.

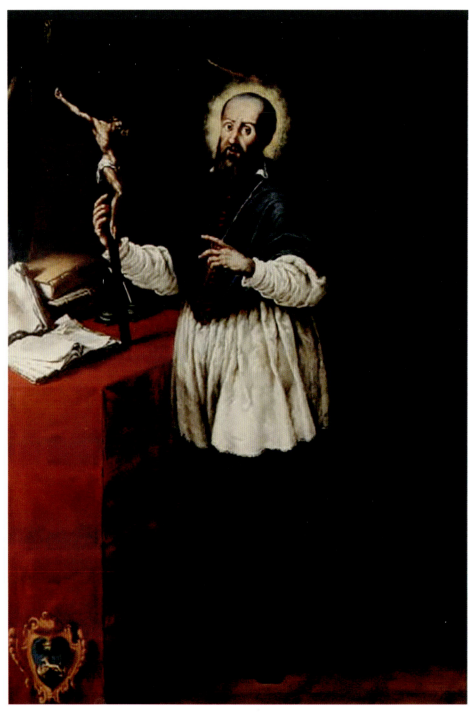

26. Francis de Sales described contemplation as "simply the mind's loving, unmixed, permanent attention to the things of God."

27. Blaise Pascal ended his account of the mystical experience he had on November 23, 1654, with the words "Joy, joy, joy, tears of joy."

28. François Fénelon advocated a state of "holy indifference" in which grace enables the soul to desire only what God desires for it.

29. The founder of Methodism, John Wesley said that all his strength "lay in keeping my eye fixed upon Him and my soul waiting on Him continually."

30. William Blake's typically visionary painting shows "Jacob's Ladder," with angels ascending and descending to and from heaven.

31. William Blake said that on one occasion in his youth, he was watching haymakers in the fields when he suddenly saw angels walking among them.

32. Ralph Waldo Emerson, the American Transcendentalist, believed the "inner light" worked "to bring the universe into the possession of a single soul."

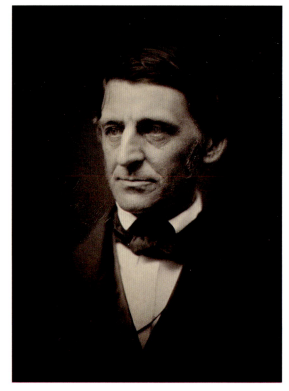

33. Thérèse of Lisieux's memoir *The Story of a Soul* became a spiritual classic. For her, "the most beautiful thoughts are nothing without good works."

34. Charles de Foucauld's hermitage can still be seen near the Hoggar Mountains in the stark landscape of southern Algeria.

35. On one occasion when Simone Weil was reciting George Herbert's poem "Love (III)," she said that Christ "took possession of me."

PROTESTANT MYSTICS OF THE SEVENTEENTH CENTURY

> The streets were paved with golden stones,
> The boys and girls were mine,
> Oh how did all their lovely faces shine!
> The sons of men were holy ones,
> In joy and beauty they appeared to me,
> And every thing which here I found,
> While like an angel I did see,
> Adorned the ground.

However, perhaps his most luminous paean to childhood as a state of paradisal innocence occurs not in his poetry but in his prose *Centuries of Meditations*. Here, in one of his best-known passages, Traherne evokes a sacramental vision of reality worthy of the Book of Revelation, in which particular material forms disclose their divine origins or, as he says, "something infinite behind everything appeared":

> The corn was orient and immortal wheat, which never should be reaped, nor was ever sown. I thought it had stood from everlasting to everlasting. The dust and stones of the street were as precious as gold: the gates were at first the end of the world. The green trees when I saw them first through one of the gates transported and ravished me, their sweetness and unusual beauty made my heart to leap, and almost mad with ecstasy, they were such strange and wonderful things: The Men! O what venerable and reverend creatures did the aged seem! Immortal Cherubims! And young men glittering and sparkling Angels, and maids strange seraphic pieces of life and beauty! Boys and girls tumbling in the street, and playing, were moving jewels. I knew not that they were born or should die; But all things abided eternally as they were in their proper places. Eternity was manifest in the Light of the Day, and something infinite behind everything appeared which talked with my expectation and moved my desire. The city seemed to stand in Eden, or to be built in Heaven. The streets were mine, the temple was mine, the people were mine, their clothes and gold and silver were mine, as much as their sparkling eyes, fair skins and ruddy faces. The skies were mine, and so were the sun and moon and stars, and all the World was mine; and I the only spectator and enjoyer of it. I knew no churlish proprieties, nor bounds, nor divisions: but all proprieties and divisions were mine: all treasures and the possessors of them. So that with much ado I

DAZZLING DARKNESS

was corrupted, and made to learn the dirty devices of this world.
Which now I unlearn, and become, as it were, a little child again
that I may enter into the Kingdom of God.[51]

Traherne suggests that if we are blessed and touched with holy
vision the world around us is transformed (thus, in the passage above
old men become "reverend creatures," and boys and girls become
"moving jewels"). In a similar vein, his poem "The Preparative"
proposes that it is our quality of perception, not the external world
itself, that leads to blessedness, or, to use his favorite word, Felicity:

> 'Tis not the object, but the light
> That maketh Heaven: 'tis a purer sight.
> Felicity
> Appears to none but them that purely see.

For Traherne the outer world is instrumental in leading to a
condition of inner illumination: "The Heavens and the Earth serve
you, not only in shewing unto you your Father's Glory, as all things
without you are your riches and enjoyments, but as within you also,
they magnify, beautify and illuminate your soul."[52] In his poem "The
Vision" the world is again transformed by a heavenly way of seeing
that is "deep and infinite," so that "Even trades themselves seen in
celestial light, / And cares and sins and woes are bright."

As with other mystics, Traherne grappled with the challenge of
expressing the ineffable in words, for example in his poem "My
Spirit" in which he painstakingly, sometimes falteringly, traces in
detail a state of profound inner joy that had suffused his entire being
and connected him with God:

> A strange extended orb of Joy,
> > Proceeding from within,
> > Which did on every side, convey
> > Itself, and being nigh of kin
> > To God did every way
> Dilate itself even in an instant, and
> Like an indivisible centre stand,
> At once surrounding all eternity.
> > 'Twas not a sphere,
> > Yet did appear,

PROTESTANT MYSTICS OF THE SEVENTEENTH CENTURY

One infinite. 'Twas somewhat everywhere,
  And tho' it had a power to see
    Far more, yet still it shin'd
      And was a mind
Exerted for it saw Infinity.
  'Twas not a sphere, but 'twas a might
    Invisible, and yet gave light.

Yet, if he was capable of careful, reasoned descriptions of ultimate states of reality, he was also unafraid to let loose his emotional response to them and being in a state of Felicity, or Love, as he calls the rapturous experience in this poem of the same name:

  O nectar! O delicious stream!
O ravishing and only pleasure! Where
    Shall such another theme
Inspire my tongue with joys or please mine ear!
      Abridgment of delights!
        And queen of sights!
O mine of rarities! O Kingdom wide!
O more! O cause of all! O glorious Bride!
    O God! O Bride of God! O King!
    O soul and crown of everything!

13

EARLY MODERN FRENCH MYSTICS

In the noise and clutter of my kitchen, while several persons are at the same time calling for different things, I possess God in as great tranquility as if I were upon my knees at the Blessed Sacrament.

—Brother Lawrence

During the course of the seventeenth century, France became the dominant European state. The country gained a reputation not only for the cultural brilliance of the court of its "Sun King," Louis XIV (r. 1643–1715), whose absolutist ambitions impacted all levels of society, including the life of the church, but also for its influential thinkers, churchmen, and mystics, including René Descartes, Blaise Pascal, and Francis de Sales. Yet France's national confidence and preeminent status had come only after many years of civil war, known as the Wars of Religion, in the second half of the sixteenth century, as well as its involvement in the bitter conflict of the pan-European Thirty Years' War in the early 1600s.

The tension that existed between Catholicism and the newly formed Protestant churches had added a distinctly religious dynamic to a number of conflicts in post-Reformation Europe—struggles that also involved territorial ambitions, political power-broking, and dynastic disputes. This was certainly true of the Wars of Religion, fought intermittently from 1562 to 1598 between France's Catholic majority and its Protestant minority, who were Calvinists known as Huguenots. The war finally drew to a close only when the Huguenot Henry of Navarre, who had ascended the French throne as Henry IV (r. 1589–1610) in 1589, converted to

DAZZLING DARKNESS

Catholicism in 1593 and, five years later, proclaimed the Edict of Nantes. This granted the Huguenots civic rights and the freedom to worship in certain cities within the country. (Almost a century later, in 1685, Louis XIV revoked the edict, precipitating the migration of some 300,000 Huguenots to Prussia, Holland, England, and other parts of Europe, as well as to South Africa and America.)

At the start of the seventeenth century, France also became involved, along with most of the other European countries, in the immensely complex Thirty Years' War (1618–48), in which politics and religious convictions again combined to produce widespread brutality, death, and destruction, particularly in Germany. Hostilities eventually came to an end with the Peace of Westphalia in 1648, which realigned territorial boundaries and reaffirmed the principle that a state's ruler should determine his people's faith. The war had other effects: Germany lay in ruins, exhausted by the effects of the fighting; the Holy Roman Empire was now virtually impotent; and France emerged as the most powerful European state.

French spirituality during the latter half of the seventeenth century was marked by the attempt by Louis XIV to draw the French church away from the orbit of Rome and more into his own gravitational field. Also, his reign saw the rise of significant religious controversies, especially over Quietism and Jansenism, a spiritual doctrine named for Cornelius Jansen (1585–1638), a theology professor who became bishop of Ypres. Jansen and his followers were deeply influenced by Augustine and, like the Calvinists, emphasized predestination and the idea that only a small group of Christians—the "elect"—will be saved from damnation.

The Jansenists were pessimistic about the human condition and the all-too-numerous travails of life, and they advocated strict moral discipline and asceticism. They were also hostile to the Jesuits, who were influential at court and therefore dangerous enemies. One of the notable champions of the Jansenist cause was the French mathematician and spiritual thinker Blaise Pascal, whose sister attended the Jansenist-dominated convent at Port-Royal near Paris. In his *Provincial Letters*, which sold in their thousands, he attacked the Jesuits and what he saw as their worldliness and argued for a return to more austere forms of worship. The conflict between the Jansenists and the Jesuits—as well as the French king and the

242

EARLY MODERN FRENCH MYSTICS

papacy—continued for the rest of the century. (In 1713 Jansenist teachings were condemned by a papal bull and the tide was turned decisively against them.)

When Louis XIV's government clamped down on Port-Royal in the 1660s, it "signalled the anti-mysticism which characterized the latter part of the seventeenth century," and from then on there was a "subtle restraint on open discussion of the interior life, an attitude which endured [in France] until well into the twentieth century."[1] It was, therefore, an unpropitious time for the appearance of the Quietists, who believed that people should abandon themselves totally to God through complete self-abnegation, passivity, and annihilation of the will. Quietists thought that any mental or emotional activity that involved self-awareness, including meditation and petitionary prayer, was counterproductive to attaining the desired state of perfection: the aim was simply to surrender oneself into God's hands in an act of pure, careless faith.

The best-known proponent of Quietism at this time was a Spanish priest named Miguel de Molinos (1628–97), who was eventually found guilty of error and spent his last years in jail. However, the Quietist tradition was continued in France in a moderated form by Madame Guyon and François Fénelon. All the aforementioned were involved in bitter disputes with the church authorities, who objected to the way Quietists seemed to elevate themselves above ecclesiastical authority and the norms of external worship. They also feared that Quietist teachings could lead people to believe that having reached enlightenment through passivity, they were incapable of committing further sins and were therefore free to lead immoral lives.

Benet Canfield (1562–1610)

One who had a profound effect on French spirituality and mysticism in the late sixteenth and early seventeenth centuries was actually an Englishman named William Fitch, or Benet Canfield, as he became known by his religious name. Born in Little Canfield in Essex, Benet came to renounce his Anglican faith and convert to Catholicism, thereby making him an enemy of the Elizabethan English state. His sanctuary in France drew him into the circle of

243

DAZZLING DARKNESS

Madame Acarie, Pierre de Bérulle, and Vincent de Paul (ca. 1580–1660, founder of the Lazirists and the Sisters of Charity), all of whom he influenced with his mystical writings. The modern French spiritual writer, Henri Brémond, has called him "the master of the masters themselves."[2]

Not much is known of Benet's early life, apart from the fact that he was the third of four sons of his father's second marriage. In about 1580 he went to the Middle Temple in London to study law. There his life changed when he read a devotional book called *The First Book of the Christian Exercise Appertaining to Resolution* written by a Jesuit named Robert Persons. It was enough to deflect him into Catholicism. In 1585 he formally converted and soon afterward studied at the English Catholic College at Douai in Belgium. In 1587 he joined the Capuchin order as a novice at their house in Rue Saint-Honoré in Paris, where he adopted his new name, Benet (also, Benedict and Benoît). During this initial period he had mystical experiences in the form of raptures and ecstasies that troubled his Capuchin superiors. Eventually they accepted his religiosity as genuine and he was ordained in about 1591.[3]

After a stay in Italy, where he finished his theological studies, Benet eventually returned to England in 1599. But the country was still unsafe for Catholics, and he was imprisoned, being released only when Henry IV of France lodged an appeal against his incarceration. In 1603 the English authorities sent him back to France, where he joined the Capuchin convent in Rouen.

In 1609 Benet published his *Rule of Perfection*, for which he is best known (even though eighty years later the church authorities took exception to some of its content, believing it showed signs of Quietism, and placed the book on the Index of Forbidden Books, i.e. publications deemed heretical by the Roman Catholic Church). The following year Benet died, in Paris.

Influenced by the *via negativa* tradition of Dionysius the Areopagite, Benet referred to God "annihilating" a person's will and stressed the importance of the passion of Christ in a God-centered universe. He also upheld the Capuchin emphasis on mental prayer, advising four types of prayer: vocal prayer for beginners; mental prayer, which has more "spiritual light" than vocal prayer; short prayers, or "aspirations," that come sometimes from the heart and sometimes from the mouth and have "less speculation" about them; and finally prayer made according to the will of God, appropriate for those who have had their minds purged of images.[4]

The *Rule* is divided into three parts and the core of its teaching is reflected in Matthew 6:10: "Thy kingdom come. Thy will be done in earth, as it is in heaven." This is the only thing we have to do in our lives: surrender actively to the will of God in all things. A person, Benet says, might have different motives for certain actions, such as trying to eliminate vices or gain virtue to avoid hell or reach heaven or to imitate Christ; but "to do his work only for the will of God, and only to please him, is an intention far excelling them all." We should never embark on any enterprise or action until "we have first addressed our intention to God, saying by word and thought, or at least by thought from the bottom of our heart: 'O Lord, I will do this or I will suffer, I will resist or will pursue etc. this thing only for thy will and pleasure.'"[5]

The *Rule*'s three sections each relate to the three different ways by which we receive or relate to God's will. Canfield calls these: 1. The external (active) will of God; 2. The internal (contemplative) will of God; 3. The "supereminent" will of God. The external will refers to the moral and religious codes, laws, and commandments found in society and the church. The internal will is more personal and involves the guidance of the Holy Spirit through "inspirations and illuminations" and by listening to our thoughts and feelings. Finally, the supereminent will is also internal but at a greater depth; it is a condition in which we are so in harmony with God's will that his will seems to us to be ours. It is the "knowledge of God arising intuitively from the love of God."[6]

Madame Acarie (1566–1618) and Pierre de Bérulle (1575–1629)

Two of the leading figures in French spiritual history at the end of the sixteenth and beginning of the seventeenth century, Madame Acarie and her cousin and follower, Pierre de Bérulle, both combined an intense mystical inner life with a capacity for organization and performing public works of charity.

Madame Acarie is probably best known for introducing the order of Discalced Carmelites into France (at her death there were

DAZZLING DARKNESS

seventeen convents), but she also helped to reform Benedictine monasteries and strengthen the Ursulines. Known as the "conscience of Paris" for her godliness, she was subject to apparitions and raptures. As a spiritual guide, with the gift of "discernment of spirits," she influenced many of the leading French religious of the time.

Born in Paris of well-to-do parents, and baptized Barbe Avrillot, Acarie was sent to the convent of the Poor Clares in Longchamp, Paris, as a young girl. Although her time at the convent deepened her desire to become a nun, at the age of sixteen she obeyed her parents' wishes and married a devout, affluent man named Pierre Acarie. Thenceforth she resigned herself to domestic life and bore her husband six children. Yet throughout this period she was still developing her spirituality and becoming prone to receiving ecstatic experiences (one time after the end of Mass she failed to return home and was later found in an ecstasy "like one dead"[7]). Apart from uncontrollable ecstasies, she is also said to have received the stigmata, the wounds of Christ, in her feet and hands.

However, life in her family household was thrown into disarray by the country's political and religious struggles. Pierre Acarie was a leading light in the so-called Catholic League, which was fiercely opposed to the Protestant faction led by the Huguenot Henry of Navarre (when Henry laid siege to Paris in 1590 Madame Acarie did much to help the starving citizens). When Henry acceded to the French throne (for which he abjured the Protestant faith in 1593), the league was defeated and Pierre exiled from Paris (though he was allowed to return five years later).

Without her husband as a support, Madame Acarie remained in Paris, looking after their children and dealing with Pierre's chaotic business affairs. Her predicament was made worse by a fall from a horse that left her permanently invalided. But she managed to overcome her difficulties and became known for her kindness and charity toward the sick and the poor. Her reputation for godliness drew a succession of devout souls to her residence in the Rue des Juifs, including Pierre de Bérulle and Benet of Canfield. Also, for a short period, Francis de Sales became her spiritual director. Acarie's salon of souls became the spiritual center of the city, radiating ideas of spiritual reform.

246

EARLY MODERN FRENCH MYSTICS

Toward the end of 1601, Acarie studied a new translation of the life of Teresa of Ávila that brought home to her the power of prayer. Soon after this, she received apparitions of Teresa herself. The third one she experienced when she was praying in the church of St Nicholas in the town of Saint-Nicholas-de-Port in northeast France:

> The monks were chanting Matins in their choir, and while Madame Acarie was kneeling, absorbed in prayer and in the Office which she so devoutly loved, St. Teresa was made apparent to her for the third time, not as before, by an interior vision only, but clearly visible to the eye, and speaking audibly to the outward ear.[8]

Teresa told her that God wanted her to help found reformed Carmelite convents in France and that she herself would join such an order. Acarie obeyed this calling, and with the help of Henry IV and his wife, Marie de Médicis, she was instrumental in setting up, in 1604, the Discalced Carmelites, with nuns brought over from Spain.

Acarie's religious vocation did not end with the Carmelites. She also helped to establish Ursuline convents in France, and she supported Pierre de Bérulle to found the Oratory of Jesus Christ (see below). When her husband died in 1613, Acarie made the decision to join the Carmelite convent at Amiens, taking her vows in 1615 (and taking the name of Marie of the Incarnation). In the following year she transferred to the convent of Pontoise, twenty miles northwest of Paris, where she ended her days.

One of those who became Madame Acarie's most influential protégés was Pierre de Bérulle, a reformer, spiritual writer, and cardinal, who helped to instigate spiritual renewal and clerical reform in France. He is credited with co-founding what has been known historically as the "French school of spirituality."

Unlike Acarie, Bérulle was not the recipient of countless visions, though he does occasionally seem to have had intimations of the divine. In 1607, for example, Bérulle received a "mystical grace" after he was asked to tutor the Dauphin and refused to do so. He suddenly saw his vocation in a new light, which left him in no doubt: he was not destined to serve in the court of Henry IV, but the court of Jesus Christ. He later said that this grace was one of the most memorable events that he had had in his life. From now on the

247

DAZZLING DARKNESS

Incarnate Word would be at the heart of his life and thinking. He would become, as Pope Urban VIII called him, "the apostle of the Incarnate Word."[9]

Bérulle was born into an aristocratic family near Troyes in the province of Champagne and educated by the Jesuits before attending the Sorbonne. By the mid-1590s, barely out of his teenage years, he was part of Madame Acarie's spiritual salon, soaking up the ideas and enthusiasm of the leading religious figures of the day. In 1599 he was ordained a priest, and five years later he was helping Acarie establish the Discalced Carmelites in Paris. Then in 1611 Bérulle founded the Oratory of Jesus Christ, a congregation of lay priests living together in a community, without vows. Bérulle based this organization on the model established by the Italian Philip Neri (1513–95), but preferred a centralized organization and put more emphasis on training priests in seminaries.

Bérulle, like Acarie, had an extravert side to his personality and excelled as a diplomat. No stranger to the court of Henry IV, he negotiated the marriage between the king's daughter, Henrietta Maria, and Charles I of England in 1625. Two years later, as a reward for his diplomacy, he was made a cardinal. He died in 1629, in Paris, while officiating at Mass.

Influenced by a number of mystics and theologians, including Ruysbroek, Ignatius of Loyola, and Teresa of Ávila, Bérulle's spiritual and mystical thought has several strands, which emerge in his numerous writings. The most important of these are *L'Estat et les grandeurs de Jésus* (1623) and *Vie de Jésus* (1629), which explore the need to: adore God for his grandeur and perfection; hold a Christocentric view of reality; and be devoted to the Virgin Mary (Bérulle made a vow to serve both Jesus and Mary). Bérulle also wrote letters to clerics and nuns, giving them spiritual encouragement and sharing his conviction in the saving light of the divine. In a letter to a Carmelite prioress, for example, he wrote: "I pray to the same Holy Spirit that he give you his light and his love, for he is light and love. Quite often what we consider to be light, in the ways of God, is not. However, the Holy Spirit gives us the true light, which causes us to progress in the ways of the Son of God, in the ways of humiliation, strength, justice, penance, submission, patience and poverty. For since the Son of God and the Holy Spirit

248

are but one essence, they accomplish the same work. Jesus Christ begins it, and the Holy Spirit finishes it."[10]

Behind Bérulle's thought lie the Neoplatonist ideas of Dionysius the Areopagite and the idea of a cosmic spiritual circuit: we, God's creatures, come from Him and to Him we will return (by means of Jesus Christ): "So God who is unity leads everyone to unity, and through distinct degrees of unity comes and descends toward man that he might ascend toward God."[11] This "instinct" or "reflex" toward God is woven into us by God himself; that is, the fact of being human is to be part of this universal movement, which will endure eternally.[12]

Francis de Sales (1567–1622)

Francis de Sales, who grew up during the Wars of Religion and lived to see the start of the Thirty Years' War, once wrote that "it is an error—no, a heresy—to wish to banish the devout life from the army, from the workshop, from the courts of princes, from the households of the married folk."[13] An aristocrat by birth, a prominent churchman, and eventually a doctor of the church and the patron saint of writers, Francis was especially concerned to help ordinary people, not just the ecclesiastical professionals, to achieve a profound intimacy with God. His spiritual approach to the divine may lack the intensity and soul-searching of other mystics, but in his writings, especially his classic *Introduction to the Devout Life*, he unfolds a sane, achievable, and attractive way by which the soul may be led into the fulfillment of the spiritual life.

The eldest of six boys, Francis was born in 1567 in the small duchy of Savoy, which lay between France and Italy. He was educated by the Jesuits at Clermont College in Paris, where he experienced an inner conversion. For some time he had been filled with despondency about the church's debate on predestination and the likelihood that he would fail to be one of the elect saved from damnation. One day, exhausted with anguish, he prayed on his knees before the statue of the Virgin Mary in a local church and afterward felt a profound sense of liberation and healing. He subsequently vowed himself to chastity and to the service of the Virgin. It remained his deep conviction that everyone had the ability

249

to receive God's abundant grace and be saved, and this became the basis of his spirituality.[14]

After Clermont, Francis went to Padua to study law, completing his studies there in 1592. In the following year, against the wishes of his father—at least initially—he entered the church and embarked on a mission to convert the region of Chablais, on the southern side of Lake Geneva, which had become a Calvinist stronghold after the Reformation. Despite the danger to his life, he traveled throughout the area, preaching, teaching, and above all impressing people with his personal sanctity, eventually leading many back to the Catholic fold. Over the following years he gained a reputation for his diligence and spirituality, and in 1602 he was appointed bishop of Geneva, administering his diocese from Annecy in Savoy, since Geneva itself was still solidly Calvinist. Two years later, while he was in Dijon, he had a momentous meeting with a woman named Jeanne de Chantal (1572–1642), an aristocratic widow who was later beatified for her sanctity: he became her spiritual director, and, bound by a deep friendship and love of God, they together founded in 1610 the new contemplative Visitation order, intended for women who were unable to bear the asceticism of the traditional orders. For the remaining twelve years of his life, Francis continued his preaching, spiritual direction, pastoral care, and writing. He eventually died in 1622, at the age of fifty-six, while visiting Lyons.

Francis's teachings are found in a number of works, including his letters and sermons and in particular his two spiritual classics, *Introduction to the Devout Life* and *Treatise on the Love of God*, which were published in 1609 and 1616 respectively. He developed his *Devout Life* from a spiritual manual intended originally for the private use of a relative. Its commonsense practicality, full of encouragement to reflect fruitfully on life and to practice meditational exercises, shines through as it attempts to show how religious devotion is possible amid the everyday concerns of the world.

Devout Life is addressed to "Philothea" (that is, the "God-loving" soul) and consists of five parts, which deal with (1) purging the self, (2) the importance of the sacraments and prayer, (3) practicing the virtues, (4) remedies against temptations, and (5) exercises for the soul's spiritual renewal. Francis emphasizes throughout the importance of being aware of the ubiquitous presence of God and

EARLY MODERN FRENCH MYSTICS

the need to develop devotion, which bursts forth from charity as "flame from a fire."[15]

Francis's style and approach can be gleaned from his method of meditation in the second part of the book, a section that concerns prayer and the use of the sacraments. The meditation is divided into four parts. The first begins with the soul's preparation, which entails being aware of the presence of God and asking him for help. To become truly conscious of God, it is important to realize that "just as wherever birds fly they always encounter the air, so also wherever we go or wherever we are, we find God present."[16] We should also try to imagine Christ literally standing by our side, like a friend. Then, having become aware of God and of our own unworthiness, we must ask him for grace to serve and worship him. We should also conjure up in our minds a particular gospel scene or spiritual truth to meditate upon; for example, we might picture Christ on the cross and try to sense the actual sights and sounds of Golgotha, or meditate, perhaps, on death or hell. Beginners should stick with subjects that can be pictured in some way, rather than abstractions, which are more suitable for those further along the contemplative path.

The second part is to reflect meditatively on such biblical scenes as the Crucifixion in order to understand them better. Francis makes the point that meditation differs from reading a book or from ordinary thinking in that it entails spiritual growth and an increasing love of God. So we should not only picture something but also consider its deeper import: "Imitate the bees, who do not leave a flower as long as they can extract any honey out of it."[17]

The third part concerns exercising our affections and resolutions. Meditation rouses our emotions: through it we feel love of God and of our neighbors or a general sense of compassion or shame for our past sinful life—and we should allow ourselves to feel these feelings as much as possible. Yet it is not enough just to be aware of them. We must use them to achieve practical ends, to correct some personal failing, such as getting annoyed by "the disagreeable words" uttered by "some man or woman who is my neighbor, a manservant, or maid."[18]

The meditation concludes with the fourth part. We should thank God for his help in the meditation process, offer him our affections

251

and resolutions, and ask him for his blessing, so that our meditation will bear fruit. Francis ends by suggesting that we should gather "a little devotional bouquet," that is, pick out a couple of points from the meditation and savor them, just as a person can enjoy throughout the day a handful of flowers plucked from a beautiful garden.[19]

Further along the spiritual path is contemplation, which Francis considers in his *Treatise on the Love of God*. Contemplation, Francis says, is born from the marriage of meditation with love. Love rises from meditation and enables us to contemplate, and this in turn inspires us with a more ardent love.[20] He also describes contemplation as "simply the mind's loving, unmixed, permanent attention to the things of God." Through contemplation, the soul enters a grace-given state of tranquility in which it and its faculties are in abeyance—memory and imagination are not needed, and only the will remains, drawing upon the presence of the divine.[21]

Brother Lawrence (ca. 1605–91)

One of those who fought in the Thirty Years' War was a certain Nicholas Herman, a young Frenchman who would later metamorphose as Brother Lawrence of the Resurrection, a lay brother and mystic of the Carmelite order. Working in a monastic kitchen for some thirty years, he was able to practice being in the presence of God to such an extent that his inner peacefulness and radiance gained him a reputation for holiness that spread way beyond the confines of the monastery. He spoke of his ability to remain constantly aware of the divine presence in terms of "an habitual, silent, and secret conversation of the soul with God, which often causes in me joys and raptures inwardly, and sometimes also outwardly, so great that I am forced to use means to moderate them, and prevent their appearance to others."[22]

Herman was born in about 1605, in Lorraine, in eastern France. His career in the army was cut short by a leg wound, and then for a short time he became a footman to the treasurer of the king of France, a post he remembered primarily for his clumsiness and propensity to break things. He then decided to commit his life to God, having already had in his late teens a profound conversion experience: one day in winter while he was reflecting upon a

EARLY MODERN FRENCH MYSTICS

stripped tree and realizing that soon in the coming spring its leaves, blossoms, and fruits would appear again, he "received a high view of the providence and power of God, which has never since been effaced from his soul."[23]

After this experience he first became a hermit, then in 1649 he joined the Carmelite monastery in Paris. Now adopting the name Brother Lawrence, he worked in the kitchen for most of the rest of his life, developing over time the saintly demeanor and cheerfulness for which he became famous. Among those who met him was a priest named Joseph de Beaufort, who recorded four conversations with Lawrence, later publishing them along with some of the latter's sayings and letters shortly after his death in 1691. Although Lawrence's posthumous reputation in France suffered from his being quoted by François Fénelon, bishop of Cambrai, who was condemned for his association with the Quietist movement, his writings were influential elsewhere, particularly in England, where de Beaufort's book was translated in the early eighteenth century as *The Practice of the Presence of God*.

One of the most significant points of Lawrence's teaching is that there is for those who practice God's presence no separation between the different activities of life. It is not a case of doing mundane tasks without the awareness of God, then going off to chapel to reconnect with him. Life, when lived in true faith and commitment to God, is not compartmentalized: a person's relationship with the divine continues uninterrupted whether he or she is peeling potatoes, gardening, or kneeling down and praying. There are parallels with Zen Buddhism, in which the sacred is not so much searched for beyond the self as realized in the total awareness of the present moment.

The divine peacefulness that Lawrence found by not looking or thinking beyond anything that was not God allowed him to retain his composure and inner joy, day in, day out. All tasks, great and small, he said, must be dedicated to God and done out of love for him. In fact, he claimed that he felt closer to God when occupied with his daily duties than when he withdrew to pray. Even when the kitchen was at its most hectic, he is said to have kept calm, with his focus on heaven. He neither dallied nor rushed around but did the right jobs at the right time, professing that "in the noise and clutter of my kitchen, while several persons are at the same time calling for different things, I possess God in as great tranquility as if I were upon my knees at the Blessed Sacrament."[24]

Brother Lawrence also emphasized that he did not arrive at his awareness of God through books but through simple faith and love. Love is the key and the bedrock of all activities: acts of penance and mortification and other exercises that are performed without love are of no use. His philosophy can be summed up by his words, "Our only business is to love and delight ourselves in God."[25]

Blaise Pascal (1623–62)

A mathematician, scientist, inventor, and spiritual writer, Blaise Pascal is also considered to be a mystic if only because of an intense revelation of divine reality that he received on the evening of November 23, 1654. This two-hour (yet timeless) experience had such a profound effect on him that he wrote it down on a piece of parchment that was found sewn into his clothing after his death. Referred to as the "memorial," the event was responsible for what Pascal called his "second conversion." The memorial states:

> From about half past ten in the evening until half past midnight. Fire. "God of Abraham, God of Isaac, God of Jacob," not of philosophers and scholars. Certainty, certainty, heartfelt, joy, peace. God of Jesus Christ. God of Jesus Christ. My God and your God. "Thy God shall be my God." The world forgotten, and everything except God. He can only be found by the ways taught in the Gospels. Greatness of the human soul. "O righteous Father, the world has not known thee, but I have known thee." Joy, joy, joy, tears of joy.[26]

The son of a taxation official and mathematician, Pascal grew up mainly in Paris and Rouen. Schooled by his father, he soon showed signs of prowess in mathematics (even gaining the attention of the great French philosopher René Descartes). In the 1640s, alongside his scientific work, Pascal began to take religion more seriously and question the orthodox Catholicism in which he had been raised. In 1646 he became drawn to the Jansenist view of life and persuaded his family to follow him in this direction. At the same time, he did not abandon his scientific interests. He conducted various experiments,

EARLY MODERN FRENCH MYSTICS

including on atmospheric pressure, invented a type of syringe, and wrote various research papers (for example on vacuums).

However, the balance of his life dramatically altered in 1654 when he had his mystical experience. In the following year he went on retreat at the Jansenist convent of Port-Royal, where his sister Jacqueline was a nun, and spent the time in prayer and reconfiguring his life. From there on he abandoned science and increasingly explored religion and the spiritual life, formulating ways of defending Jansensism and gathering his thoughts for two works that would become spiritual classics: the *Provincial Letters* and the *Pensées* ("Thoughts"). The *Letters* consist of eighteen letters written to defend the Jansenists against the Jesuits and other enemies, and to attack what Pascal believed was the Jesuits' lack of strict morality and spiritual earnestness. The *Letters* emphasize a return to a more spiritual, inner, approach to religion. But celebrated though they became, they failed to save the Jansenists from royal disapproval and harassment.

After completing the *Letters*, Pascal still felt he had unfinished business with the Christian faith and began a work called *Apology for the Christian Religion*, jotting down notes of his thoughts. At the time of his death in 1662, however, he had not finished his projected tome, and his provisional notes were later edited and published as the *Pensées*.

Presented as a series of aphorisms, the *Pensées* mix philosophy with spirituality and mystical thinking. They investigate, explore, and ruminate on the religious life and the nature of the human condition. Some make a direct appeal to reason. For example in one of them, he posits what has become known as "Pascal's Wager": people should live their lives as though God exists because, if it turns out that he does not, they will have lost relatively little (such as foregoing certain pleasures); but if God does exist then they stand to gain the rewards of heaven. Other thoughts have the air of timeless sagacity: "Rivers are roads which move, and which carry us whither we desire to go."[27] And: "One must know oneself. If this does not serve to discover truth, it at least serves as a rule of life, and there is nothing better."[28]

One recurring theme through the work is Pascal's meditation on the human condition and our existential place in the universe:

255

DAZZLING DARKNESS

When I consider the short duration of my life, swallowed up in the eternity before and after, the little space which I fill ... I am frightened, and am astonished at being here rather than there; for there is no reason why here rather than there, why now rather than then. Who has put me here?[29]

He speaks as a scientist, aware enough of the dimensionless universe, but also as an ordinary believer beset with anxiety: "The eternal silence of these infinite spaces frightens me."[30] Another important thread is the emphasis he puts on what he sees as the fundamental task in life, namely the investigation of the immortality of the soul "which is of so great consequence to us, and which touches us so profoundly, that we must have lost all feeling to be indifferent as to knowing what it is."[31] Yet another important subject is the limitations of reasons and knowledge. Religion, at its core, is a matter of feelings, of personal experience: "It is the heart which experiences God, and not the reason. This, then, is faith: God felt by the heart, not by the reason."[32]

In the section called "The Mystery of Jesus," Pascal affirms through an exchange between his inner voice and the imagined voice of Jesus, the reconciliation between sinner, trapped in spiritual servitude, and the savior. Jesus assures him: "Physicians will not heal thee, for thou wilt die at last. But it is I who heal thee, and make the body immortal."[33] Pascal, whose last years were marked by a grueling illness (probably cancer), identifies himself with the rejected, wounded Christ, and takes due comfort: "But He has healed Himself, and still more so will He heal me. I must add my wounds to His, and join myself to Him; and He will save me in saving Himself."[34] And Pascal, who at times seems to terrify himself with his speculations on how insignificant human beings are in the scheme of the universe, arrives at an accommodation with the divine that provides a practical and loving *modus vivendi*: "Do little things as though they were great, because of the majesty of Jesus Christ who does them in us, and who lives our life; and do the greatest things as though they were little and easy, because of His omnipotence."[35]

EARLY MODERN FRENCH MYSTICS

Madame Guyon (1648–1717)

One of those influenced by the Quietist movement—as well as by Francis de Sales—was a Frenchwoman named Madame Guyon, who also taught that people should renounce their self-centered lives and abandon themselves totally to the will of God. By doing this they will enter a state of complete passivity and be indifferent about what the future might hold. Like the Quietist Miguel de Molinos, she suffered for her views, being imprisoned for several years in the Bastille in Paris. Yet despite the hostility she encountered, she remained, in her own eyes, a devout Catholic until her dying days. After her death her ideas, although largely neglected at home, were taken up by Protestants in England, Germany, Switzerland, and elsewhere.

Madame Guyon was born Jeanne-Marie Bouvier de la Motte in 1648 in the town of Montargis about fifty miles south of Paris. She was a delicate, religiously inclined child whose education was interrupted by her parents' constantly moving (nine times in ten years). In 1664, at the age of sixteen, she married a thirty-eight-year-old invalid named Jacques Guyon. The union, which lasted twelve years, was a miserable experience for Jeanne, who produced five children, two of whom died. But thrown back on her own inner resources, she did find time to explore and deepen her mystical bent through books and the spiritual direction of a priest named François Lacombe.

After her husband passed away in 1676, Madame Guyon was able to devote herself fully to her religious life and felt called to make public the fruits of her spiritual experiences. In 1685 she published her influential *Short and Easy Method of Prayer*, and in the following year, accompanied by Père Lacombe, she moved to Paris. But her attempts to promulgate her ideas were ill-timed. It was only a year since Molinos had been imprisoned for his Quietism, and in Paris Louis XIV was eager to clamp down on those who held similar views. Lacombe and Madame Guyon were duly sent to jail, in 1687 and 1688, respectively: Lacombe remained incarcerated for the next twelve years, while Madame Guyon was released several months later through the influence of the king's second wife, Madame de Maintenon.

On her release, Madame Guyon managed to establish herself in the royal circle and through it came into contact with François Fénelon, who was to become her most illustrious supporter. Yet the opposition to her teachings did not diminish, and in an effort to clear her name she asked for her writings to be examined by an ecclesiastical commission. Her request was granted, but at the Conference of Issy in 1695 she was condemned and again imprisoned, despite a signed retraction. She was released in 1703 and allowed to live with her son in Blois, where, until her death in 1717, she spent the time in seclusion, receiving occasional visits from those interested in her ideas and devoting herself to writing religious verse and letters to her friends.

Madame Guyon's teachings spring from personal experience, the most significant moment of which was her spiritual conversion when she was nineteen years of age. Throughout the first years of her unhappy marriage, she had tried to find solace in God, but in vain. The turning point came when she went to see a visiting Franciscan friar, who told her that she was "seeking without that which you hold within" and that she would find God in her heart. His words had an almost instant effect: "They were to me like the stroke of a dart, which penetrated through my heart. I felt a very deep wound, a wound so delightful that I desired not to be cured."[36]

From this time on her practice of contemplation was devoid of sensual imagery—indeed, she taught that prayer should be one of simple abstraction, empty of visual meditation, even on God's attributes and the person of Christ. The soul, she believed, passes through three stages on the journey toward union with God: first there is the withdrawal of the senses and the will from the external world and an apprehension of the divine presence. The soul then realizes that its pleasure in the divine is in danger of becoming a substitute for God himself. This results in a stage of spiritual desolation in which the loss of God's favors is felt, like John of the Cross's "dark night." The last stage is an "apostolic state" in which the emptied soul is possessed by God, its will replaced by his. The soul now feels joy and a "holy indifference," a complete detachment from what might befall it, including even the prospect of being saved from damnation.[37]

EARLY MODERN FRENCH MYSTICS

Francois Fénelon (1651–1715)

Appointed archbishop of Cambrai in 1695, François Fénelon was a great admirer of Madame Guyon's personal spirituality and the ideas set out in her works (but not always of the way she expressed them), and he defended her in writing. In doing so he incurred the wrath of his former friend, the formidable Jacques-Bénigne Bossuet, bishop of Meaux, which led to a protracted and bitter controversy about Quietism.

Fénelon's mysticism, like that of Francis de Sales, was eminently temperate. It was not a matter of having supernatural experiences. He did not deny that saints in the past had had these experiences, but they did not by themselves constitute holiness. For him "faith working by love" was the guiding principle, which led the soul to a profound sense of inner peace:

> It would be a mistake to suppose, that the highest state of inward experience is characterized by great excitements, by raptures and ecstasies. ... One of the remarkable results in a soul of which faith is the sole governing principle, is, that it is entirely peaceful. Nothing disturbs it. And being thus peaceful, it reflects distinctly and clearly the image of Christ; like the placid lake, which shows, in its own clear and beautiful bosom, the exact forms of the objects around and above it. [38]

Fénelon does address the mystics' concern with the union with God, but he equates it with being in the state of "pure love." We must strive after it and "not be discouraged by the difficulties we meet with; remembering that the obligation to be holy is always binding upon us, and that God will help those who put their trust in Him." [39]

Fénelon was born in 1651 in Périgord in the Dordogne into an old aristocratic family that had fallen on hard times. In about 1672 he entered the celebrated seminary of Saint-Sulpice in Paris, and after his three-year course, he was ordained. Then in 1678 he was appointed head of the "New Catholics," a community designed to educate recent Protestant women converts. Fénelon soon became renowned as a spiritual director, educator, and preacher, and in 1681 his reputation led to his being appointed tutor to the

DAZZLING DARKNESS

young Duke of Burgundy, grandson of Louis XIV. Of much greater significance to him was his meeting Madame Guyon in 1688, for his personal admiration of her and his warm espousal of her teachings would now shape the course of his life. In 1697 he published a defense of her position in his *Explanation of the Maxims of the Saints*, in which he attempted to show that her ideas were part of the Catholic mainstream mystical tradition. Immediately attacked by Bossuet, the book was finally condemned by Rome two years later. Fénelon, who accepted the judgment, was ordered to remain in his diocese of Cambrai for the rest of his life. After his death in 1715, his reputation, damaged at home, blossomed abroad, especially in Britain, where the Anglican writer Alexander Knox (1757–1831) proclaimed that "no Catholic was more popular in Protestant countries than Fénelon."[40]

Fénelon taught that it was possible to experience a love of God that was completely pure, untainted by any desire for future bliss or dread of damnation: God should be loved simply for himself, without any other motive. Having reached this unitive state, the soul practices "holy indifference" and insofar as it allows God's grace to work within it, it desires only what God desires for it. Fénelon stresses that holy indifference is not the same as inactivity: "It is the furthest possible from it. It is indifference to anything and everything out of God's will; but it is the highest life and activity to anything and everything in that will.[41]

The trials and temptations encountered in life are the way in which our love of God is purified; it is the means by which we lose our selfish desires. Love is sought not for any personal happiness but because God desires it of us; sins are confessed not for personal salvation but because it is something God wants us to do for his sake. With regard to worship, Fénelon believed that souls that had progressed far along the way toward disinterested love do not have the same need for organized church services as others, since their love is strong enough for them to be united with God inwardly at any time and in any place. This, however, does not mean that they should disregard outward observances, if only because it would set a bad example to beginners.[42]

As our love becomes purified of self-interest, so the soul is led through states of detachment and self-abnegation: "We are to follow

EARLY MODERN FRENCH MYSTICS

God's grace, and not to go before it. To the higher state of pure love we are to advance step by step; watching carefully God's inward and outward providence; and receiving increased grace by improving the grace we have, till the dawning light becomes the perfect day."[43]

The soul eventually reaches a state of passivity in which its will is replaced by God's: there is no further motive for actions beyond what God desires. Fénelon likens this transformed soul to a ball on a flat surface. The ball can be "moved with equal ease in any direction. The soul, in this state, having no preferences of itself, has but one principle of movement, namely, that which God gives it. In this state the soul can say with the Apostle Paul, 'I live; yet not I, but Christ liveth in me.'"[44]

14

LIGHT AND REASON

Begin to search and dig in thine own field for this pearl of
eternity that lies hidden in it ...and when thou hast found it
thou wilt know that all which thou hast sold or given away
for it is as mere a nothing as a bubble upon the water.

—William Law

The period known as the Age of Enlightenment, or the Age of Reason,
lasting approximately from the late seventeenth century to the end of
the eighteenth, embraced a wide variety of cultural, psychological,
and spiritual attitudes and interests that generally emphasized the
central place of reason and empiricism as well as a commitment to
greater tolerance and justice. The foundations for the Enlightenment
had been laid by the scientific and philosophical revolution begun
by the likes of Galileo (1564–1642), Descartes (1596–1650), and
Newton (1643–1727), and it was carried forward particularly
in France, at this time the most sophisticated state in Europe, by
thinkers known as the *philosophes*, men such as the writer and satirist
Voltaire (1694–1778) and the encyclopedist Denis Diderot (1713–
84), who explored a variety of intellectual pursuits, spurred on,
at least initially, by their optimism and faith in the idea of progress
through rationalism. This was an era when nature had begun to give
up its secrets to scientific instruments, such as the telescope and
microscope; and "new technologies such as steam engines pumped
water out of mines, physicians inoculated against smallpox, and hot-
air balloons lifted people to a place where no human had ever been."[1]

The Catholic and Protestant churches, some of them bound
closely to their national, often absolutist, governments, differed

from place to place in their response to the new rationalist zeitgeist, which found much greater acceptance in the salons and coffeehouses of the intelligentsia than with the masses, for whom the nonrational mysteries of traditional religion still remained strong. Those who subscribed to the latest philosophical thinking but did not want to jettison God completely could turn to Deism (see below) or pantheism (the doctrine that God does not exist as a transcendent anthropomorphic reality but rather as a divine immanence within the created world); others who were less sanguine about Enlightenment ideals and found mainstream religion too tepid took refuge in revivalist movements such as Pietism and Methodism, which should be seen within a "pan-European and transatlantic context of religious revivals which stressed a 'religion of the heart' or affective piety."[2]

The Deists, who included among their number the U.S. Founding Fathers Thomas Jefferson and Benjamin Franklin, advocated "natural religion," that is, they believed that knowledge about God was discoverable by human reason without the need for divine revelation. For Deists, God was like a divine inventor who had fashioned the universe like a machine, then left it to carry on without his intervention. They challenged the nonrational aspects of Christianity, such as mystical experiences, prayer, and miracles, which seemed to contradict the idea of a noninterventionist god, and although their religion seemed to many to be devoid of warmth and intimacy, it did have the positive effect of promoting tolerance (for example, its anti-supernatural bias helped to end the persecution of witches). Deism was relatively small in England, where it was made known by writers such as John Toland, author of the influential *Christianity Not Mysterious* (1696). But the movement proved to be more popular in France, where it was championed by Voltaire, and also in Prussia during the reign of Frederick the Great (1740–86).

If Deism appealed to the rationalist instincts of believers, Pietism, founded by the Lutheran minister Philipp Jakob Spener (1635–1705), aimed at their hearts. At a time when the Lutheran Church had for many become dry and rigid in its dogmatic teachings, Spener attempted to introduce more warmth and life into religion through an emphasis on personal conversion as

LIGHT AND REASON

well as by prayer meetings and Bible groups, and he also sought to get more laypeople involved in the church. Spener's revivalist movement quickly spread throughout Germany—although it varied from place to place—especially through Spener's follower August Francke, whose Pietist ideals translated into the founding of an orphanage and a home for vagrants in Halle in northeastern Germany; and also through Spener's godson, Count von Zinzendorf (1700–1760), who gave spiritual care and leadership to a group of Protestants known as the Bohemian, or Moravian, brethren, whom he had allowed to take refuge on his estate of Herrnhut in Saxony in 1722 (John Wesley was to visit them in 1738). During the rest of the century Moravian missionaries founded missions in different parts of the globe, including in Africa and the New World, where, for example, in 1741 they set up in Pennsylvania a mission that became the town of Bethlehem.

Pietism and Calvinism also fed into the movement known as the Great Awakening, an evangelical revival of the Christian faith that gained momentum in New England during the 1730s and 1740s. Spearheaded by the charismatic preachers George Whitefield (1714–70) and Jonathan Edwards (1703–58), the movement emphasized the importance of visible signs of conversion, the effects of which should be evident in the individual, for example by a noticeable increase in love of God and neighbor, and a greater interest in the scriptures and religious practices. Religion was to be felt and lived, and not just thought or assented to.

The Enlightenment affected the tradition of mysticism by asserting values that were inimical to the nonrational, suprasensual basis on which it was founded. The idea of "enthusiasm," defined by Dr. Samuel Johnson as "a vain confidence of Divine favour or communication," was repellent to many orthodox churchmen, as in the case of the Anglican bishop Joseph Butler (1692–1752), who told John Wesley, the founder of Methodism, that "pretending to extraordinary revelations and gifts of the Holy Spirit is a horrid thing; a very horrid thing!"[3] In fact Wesley himself was wary of supernatural visions and voices, and it would be interesting to know what Butler would have made of a Hildegard or Teresa. Visions and voices are not of course synonymous with the direct apprehension of the presence of God, but it is easy to believe that even profound

265

DAZZLING DARKNESS

mystical experiences without the visionary pyrotechnics would have elicited considerable skepticism at this time. In truth, the eighteenth, like the seventeenth, century was not a fruitful period for mysticism, especially in its more dramatic manifestations: the mystical outlooks of the French Jesuit Jean-Pierre de Caussade and the English writer William Law were serious but understated, unlikely to outrage any rationalist.

Jean-Pierre de Caussade (1675–1751)

Greatly influenced by his fellow countryman Francis de Sales, Jean-Pierre de Caussade can be seen as a sort of epilogue to the controversy over Quietism, of which he was critical. De Caussade was little concerned with the more extreme approaches to contemplative prayer, and although he refers in a letter to the experience in prayer of "sweet tranquility" and an "intense sweetness" that has "a charm that draws almost all the soul's attention to the heart,"[4] the focus of his mysticism was on the idea that divine grace was freely available to all Christians who surrendered or abandoned themselves to God's will. Like Brother Lawrence, he tried to convey the importance of living in the present, and he coined the memorable phrase "the sacrament of the present moment" to suggest the religious import of concentrating exclusively on the here and now, a practice that leads to a radical spiritual liberation: "It is necessary to be disengaged from all we feel and do in order to walk with God in the duty of the present moment. All other avenues are closed. We must confine ourselves to the present moment without taking thought for the one before or the one to come."[5]

Not much is known about the details of de Caussades's life. He was born in France in 1675 and at the age of eighteen joined the Jesuit order in Toulouse as a novice. In 1705 he was ordained a priest, and three years later he took his final Jesuit vows. Over the following years he excelled as a teacher, confessor, and preacher in Toulouse and elsewhere; then in 1729, at the age of fifty-four, he moved to Lorraine in eastern France, where, in Nancy, he became spiritual director to some of the nuns of the Visitation (the order founded by Francis de Sales and Jeanne de Chantal). His conversations with the sisters were sometimes noted down, and these, along with letters to nuns imparting spiritual advice, were later published, in 1860, by a priest named Henri Ramière as *Abandonment to Divine Providence*. The book established de Caussade's reputation as a deeply perceptive spiritual writer with marked mystical leanings.

De Caussade himself published just one book during his lifetime, *Spiritual Instructions*, in 1741. This work took the form of a series of imaginary dialogues with Jacques-Bénigne Bossuet, the formidable bishop of Meaux, who had died in 1704 but who still remained an influential spiritual figure in France. De Caussade tried to show that true contemplative prayer, the reputation of which had suffered in France during the Quietist saga, was actually supported by the traditional teaching of the church, and he quoted from Bossuet to substantiate his point. For the last decade of his life he resided at Perpignan, Albi, and Toulouse, where he died in 1751.

The keystone of de Caussade's mysticism, as suggested by the title of his posthumous book, is the idea of abandoning the self to divine providence. We must surrender ourselves totally and unconditionally to God and accept as the right thing any situation we are in at any moment, even if it is fraught with hardship or danger. He urges that we give up the pleasures of our senses and withdraw from a self-oriented outlook on life, with its illusions, pretenses, and vanity, and commit ourselves to God's will. This commitment is not to be a long-thought-out act of determination but a spontaneous and instant commitment to the present moment, to the flotsam and jetsam of life's everyday dealings, big and small, that come our way. For it is not our external circumstances that affect our relationship with God but the way in which we accept them: "The divine will is a deep abyss of which the present moment is the entrance. If you plunge into the abyss you will find it infinitely more vast than your desires."[6]

God uses the events and people we encounter every day to draw us closer to him. The challenge is for us not to filter out those things that we do not enjoy or think will not help us to grow spiritually: we must accept whatever comes our way in the knowledge that it has a divine provenance and is moving us toward union with God. "Every moment of our lives may be a kind of communion with the divine love,"[7] and may be, he says, as spiritually efficacious as receiving the Eucharist—de Caussade does not seek to denigrate the latter and

DAZZLING DARKNESS

lower the spiritual to the realm of the mundane but, rather, to raise the mundane, the quotidian, to the sphere of the spiritual.

Underlying our abandonment to the will of God is faith. Lacking faith "we wander like madmen in a labyrinth of darkness and illusion."[8] But with the benefit of faith we can see reality in a different way: the veil of illusion is ripped away and eternal truth is revealed. The key to faith and abandonment does not lie in books, history, or the saintly exemplars of the past. De Caussade emphasizes that it is a pointless exercise harking back to the age of the saints for inspiration. Instead, "we must listen to God from moment to moment" and reach out to discover "the fountain of living waters" that flows at hand. The divine commandments are declared by the present moment, which is the "ambassador of God." With total attentiveness to the divinity of the now, there is no need to choose or distinguish between alternative states of being. Categories such as health and sickness, solitude and society, verbal prayer and silence, become irrelevant.[9] Whatever is encountered comes from God and must be surrendered to. "Thus, the present moment is like a desert in which simple souls see and rejoice only in God, being solely concerned to do what he asks of them. All the rest is left behind, forgotten and surrendered to him."[10]

De Caussade's mysticism is simple in outline but difficult in practice. Abandonment to the present requires a mind that is empty of the past and the future—a mind that can ignore the events leading up to the present and can resist speculating about the future. Filled with the inspiration of grace, we must obey the impulse that comes to us at any given moment—whether it is to read a book, for example, or speak or listen to someone—without chewing it over or making an effort or steeling ourselves if something unpleasant is involved: "Give yourself up to these things for as long as God wishes without doing so through any self-will." For those who can surrender, the soul is "as light as a feather, liquid as water, simple as a child" in the way it receives and follows the dictates of grace. It is like molten metal, which can be shaped by different molds, or a blank canvas on which God can create beautiful patterns, or a stone being sculpted into a statue. As work proceeds, the soul can only feel the blows of the chisel and, blind to what it is to become, can only trust its master, the sculptor, enduring the work with

LIGHT AND REASON

resignation. We must cooperate "with all these divine operations by a constant submission, a forgetfulness of self, and an assiduous application to duty."[11]

Constant submission is not easy, especially during times of physical and spiritual trial. De Caussade compares the soul's journey to that of a traveler who, when passing through trackless fields at night in a foreign country, has no option but to trust his guide: "If one is convinced that he is a good guide one must have faith in him, and abandon oneself to his care."[12] Yet given this trust, the soul, liberated from expectations built up from study and secondhand experience, can experience the renewing vitality of the unknown, because the "divine action is ever fresh, it never retraces steps, but always marks out new ways."[13]

William Law (1686–1761)

In "an age of religion without mystery, of a theoretical God and a mechanical universe, of Christianity, not as something to be lived, but as something to be proved,"[14] William Law and his younger contemporary John Wesley attempted, each in his own way, to bring new meaning, depth, and fervor to the Anglican faith. Opposed to the cold impersonality of Deism, William Law was at pains to emphasize that the riches of the spiritual life could only be found within. He points out the dangers of a life alienated from God, a state of being which compels the individual into an endless train of self-destruction:

> When, therefore, this natural Life is deprived of, or fallen from God, it can be nothing else in itself but an Extremity of Want, continually desiring, and an Extremity of Desire, continually wanting. And hence it is, that its whole Life can be nothing else but a Plague and Torment of Covetousness, Envy, Pride, and Wrath, all which is precisely Nature, Self, or Hell.[15]

The point of life is to seek Christ, the eternal Word of God, who lies hidden in the soul "as a spark of the divine nature," able to conquer sin and regenerate the "life of heaven." Against those who were content to find God in books, debates, and church structures, Law proclaimed: "Seek for Him in thy heart, and thou wilt never

DAZZLING DARKNESS

seek in vain, for there He dwells, there is the seat of His Light and Holy Spirit."[16] Law did not deny the value of the scriptures, but he saw them primarily as a signpost to the divinity within. The word was overshadowed by the Word—that is to say, Christ, "the light, life, and salvation of fallen man," and the Bible was an "outward, verbal direction" pointing toward him.[17]

Law received his mystical understanding from the writings of, among others, Dionysius the Areopagite, Ruysbroeck, Tauler, Fénelon, and when he was in his forties, Jacob Boehme. His best-known work, *A Serious Call to a Devout and Holy Life*, attempts to stir people to commit themselves to the Christian way *wholeheartedly*, and to cultivate ascetic living, meditation, and virtues such as humility and temperance, dedicating all their activities to the glory of God. The book's directness, spiritual warmth, and clear, elegant style all contributed to its success. John Wesley praised its "beauty of expression" and "depth of thought." Even the pragmatic Dr. Samuel Johnson recalled that the first time he thought in earnest about religion was after reading Law's book as an undergraduate at Oxford.

The son of a tradesman, William Law was born in 1686 in King's Cliffe, near Stamford in Northamptonshire. In 1705 he went up to study at Emmanuel College, Cambridge, becoming a fellow of the college in 1711, the same year that he was ordained a deacon. In 1714, however, he refused to swear the oath of allegiance to the new Hanoverian king of England, George I, and so became a Nonjuror, one who pledged loyalty to the Stuart dynasty, whose last representative, James II, had been deposed in 1688. Because of his stance, Law was deprived of his fellowship and had to earn his living by other means. One way was by teaching, and in 1727 he became tutor to the father of the great historian Edward Gibbon, living in the family home in Putney in London. His post lasted for ten years and allowed him time to publish, in 1728, *A Serious Call*, which soon became a spiritual classic.

In 1740 Law's life took a radical change of direction: along with two middle-aged women, an affluent widow named Mrs. Hutcheson and Hester Gibbon, sister of his former pupil, he retired to King's Cliffe, where they established a small religious community devoted to pious living and good works. They founded schools and

270

LIGHT AND REASON

almshouses and gave out clothes, food, and money to the poor to such an extent that vagrants from all around were beating a path to their door, much to the dismay of the local inhabitants and the parish priest. For more than twenty years Law remained in his home village, studying, writing, and performing good works. He died in 1761.

Law's mysticism is most apparent in his later Boehme-influenced treatises, *The Spirit of Prayer* (1749) and *The Spirit of Love* (1752). In *The Spirit of Prayer* he taught that the only way of discovering God is by reverting to the divine light he believed everyone possessed; for although God is omnipresent, he is only present to the individual in the depths of the soul. The bodily senses are helpless in trying to effect union with God, as are the faculties of understanding, will, and memory: these can grasp at God but cannot provide a dwelling place for him.

There is, however, a place at the "bottom of the soul" from which the mental faculties spring ("as lines from a centre or as branches from the body of a tree") which is the "unity, the eternity," and this cannot be satisfied except by the "infinity of God." The treasure of this inner sanctum should be the object of our desire, to be won at any price:

> Begin to search and dig in thine own field for this pearl of eternity that lies hidden in it; it cannot cost thee too much, nor canst thou buy it too dear, for it is all; and when thou hast found it thou wilt know that all which thou hast sold or given away for it is as mere a nothing as a bubble upon the water.[18]

Like other Protestant mystics, Law suggests that everyone has a spark of divine light and spirit, given to the soul by God so that it can regenerate the paradisiacal life that was lost with the fall of man. This inner spark has an innate and almost infinite disposal to seek and return to God's eternal light and spirit, from where it originally came and in whose divine nature it partakes. Our inner light and spirit, therefore, are always tending toward God, who has the endless and immutable desire to fill our soul with his riches, "just as the spirit of air without man unites and communicates its riches and virtues to the spirit of the air that is within man."[19] God's love toward the soul was such that he gave his son to conquer the soul's enemies and enable us to be reborn according to the divine image in which we were originally created.

Law also refers to the inner treasure of the soul as a "seed of divine life" and as a "seed that has all the riches of eternity in it." In the same way that the sun nourishes natural seeds in the earth, so Jesus Christ, the sun of righteousness, is always shining on the soul's seed to "kindle and call it forth to the birth."[20]

In an echo of Eckhart, Law expressed his emphasis on the divine aspect of humanity in the idea of the birth of Christ within the soul. Christ, as the Word, existed from the beginning and lives inside us, wanting only our faith and good will in order to have in us "as real a birth and form as He had in the Virgin Mary." We must give ourselves over totally to nurturing the innate desire we have of God: then we will be led to the birth of Jesus "not in a stable at Bethlehem in Judea, but ... in the dark centre of thy fallen soul."[21]

In *The Spirit of Love* Law again contrasts the limited value of "outward, verbal instruction" with the true efficacy of an "inward birth of divine light, goodness, and virtue in our own renewed spirit."[22] Love, he makes clear, is all-inclusive and needs no rewards and makes no demands:

> For as love has no by-ends, wills nothing but its own increase, so everything is as oil to its flame; it must have that which it wills and cannot be disappointed, because everything (including unkindness on the part of those loved) naturally helps it to live in its own way and to bring forth its own work.[23]

The "spirit of love" itself cannot simply be embraced easily and casually: we must deny our creaturely nature absolutely to bring forth its birth within, dying to ourselves through patience, humility, and resignation to the divine will.[24] For Law, the spirit of love is not just the means to personal happiness but a cosmic force, identical with God, bringing peace and harmony wherever it is allowed to blossom. With its birth, "every hunger is satisfied, and all complaining, murmuring, accusing, resenting, revenging, and striving are as totally suppressed and overcome as the coldness, thickness, and horror of darkness are suppressed and overcome by the breaking forth of the light."[25]

LIGHT AND REASON

John Wesley (1703–91)

One of those deeply influenced by William Law was John Wesley, one of the principal founders of Methodism—a movement within the Church of England, from which it eventually separated—and one of the great spiritual figures of the modern era. His status as a mystic is a matter of debate. Although he is usually included in surveys of mysticism, he was not a contemplative, and he is recorded to have been critical of the state of passivity to which some mystical teachings could lead. He was also wary of visions, voices, and revelations—manifestations of the "enthusiasm" that was much despised at the time. On the other hand, as one modern commentator has noted, "At least on a broad definition of mysticism, as communion or union with God, Wesley always showed himself mystical."[26] He was greatly inspired by the simple, otherworldly piety of the Moravians; and he himself enjoyed a profound conversion experience that altered his personal spirituality and paved the way for his immense evangelical activities. He was also an avid reader of mystics, and between 1749 and 1755 he published extracts from his favorite Christian writers in his fifty-volume *Christian Library*, which included the likes of Miguel de Molinos and François Fénelon.

John Wesley was born in 1703 in Epworth in Lincolnshire, the fifteenth child of Samuel and Susannah Wesley. His father was an Anglican clergyman, and the seeds of John's piety were nurtured in his early years by the Bible and the Book of Common Prayer. At Oxford University he and his younger brother Charles formed a religious group of Christians who met to read the Bible and pray together. Others scoffed at the earnestness and "methodical" worship of these sincere, studious individuals and nicknamed them the "Bible Moths," the "Holy Club," and—the name they adopted for themselves—"Methodists."

In 1735 John and his brother left Oxford to go abroad to America to preach the word of God in Georgia, both to the colonists and to the Native Americans. The trip was largely a failure: John fell out with the colonists, whose morality he criticized, and an unhappy love affair did not improve his state of mind. While Charles returned home in August 1736, John remained for more than another year, sailing for England in December 1737. One positive

DAZZLING DARKNESS

outcome for John was his encounter with Moravian missionaries both in America and on the voyage home, when during a violent storm he was impressed by the way they calmly sang hymns. Back home Wesley's spiritual life changed for good after a conversion experience on the evening of May 24, 1738, which he recorded in his journal. It occurred while he was attending a small religious gathering in London. He was listening to a reading of Martin Luther's preface to Paul's Letter to the Romans, when: "I felt my heart strangely warmed. I felt I did trust in Christ, Christ alone for salvation, and an assurance was given me that he had taken away my sins, even mine, and saved me from the law of sin and death."[27]

From then on, Wesley devoted his life to promoting what he called "vital practical religion," and to this end he rode around Britain and Ireland preaching, especially to the rural and urban poor, often in the open fields, where thousands gathered to hear his message. By the time of his death in 1791, there were more than 70,000 Methodists in Britain and 43,000 in America, where Methodism had developed during the 1760s.

The immediate source of Wesley's spiritual vitality was his inner conversion, after which his life became truly Christ centered. As he says in his journal entry for May 25, 1738, the morning after the experience, he found as he woke up that "'Jesus, Master,' was in my heart and in my mouth" and that all his strength "lay in keeping my eye fixed upon Him and my soul waiting on Him continually." In the afternoon he went to a service at Saint Paul's Cathedral, and it was there that a moment of doubt crept in, when an inner voice asked why there was not more of a dramatic change in him: "I answered (yet not I), 'That I know not. But, this I know, I have now peace with God.' And I sin not today, and Jesus my Master has forbidden me to take thought for the morrow."[28]

It was this inner experience of peace and profound sense of release from sin and the anxieties of the future that Wesley felt impelled to convey to his audiences, most of whom were starved for spiritual nourishment. Wesley spoke to them with the authority of one who had himself been reborn in Christ; he was able to impress not by declaiming cold doctrine and creeds but by describing what it was like from the inside to live a completely different life, guided

274

LIGHT AND REASON

by the spirit. In one of his sermons he conveys the excitement and immediacy of what happens to one who is reborn:

> But the "eyes of his understanding are opened." ... He feels "the love of God shed abroad in his heart." ... And now he may be properly said to live. ... From hence it manifestly appears, what is the nature of the new birth. It is a great change ... wrought in the whole soul by the almighty Spirit of God, when it is "created new in Christ Jesus," ... when the love of the world is changed into the love of God; pride into humility; passion into meekness; hatred, envy, malice into a sincere, tender, disinterested love for all mankind.[29]

15

ROMANTICS, NATURE MYSTICS, AND TRANSCENDENTALISTS

Humility like darkness reveals the heavenly lights.

—Henry David Thoreau

The French Revolution, which swept away France's old order and sent seismic tremors throughout Europe, marked a low point for French Catholicism. The revolutionary leaders reorganized the church, prohibited the taking of monastic vows, and sold off church lands. Central clerical appointments were replaced by local clerical elections, and the clergy were obliged to give their assent to the new constitution by oath: the vast majority of bishops refused, as did many local priests. But in 1792 these nonjurors, their loyalty to the new regime suspect, suffered repressive measures, with thousands being deported, executed, or lynched. Later the government tried to replace Catholicism with new, ephemeral cults dedicated to Reason and the Supreme Being. Matters changed, however, when Napoleon Bonaparte (1769–1821), backed by the army, took control of the government in 1799. A religious skeptic himself, Napoleon realized that religion could help to bolster patriotism and social stability, and in 1801 he agreed to a concordat with Pope Pius VII that formally restored Catholicism in the country.

The Revolution is often considered to be a watershed between the so-called Age of Enlightenment and that of Romanticism, which began toward the end of the eighteenth century and continued throughout the nineteenth. Romanticism was not so much a concerted preconceived movement as a distinctive attitude or intellectual cast of mind that informed many influential thinkers and artists of the time. In general, Romantics felt unsatisfied by the Enlightenment's rationalism and its predominant values of balance, harmony, urbanity, and politeness. Instead, they stressed the importance of the imagination, the individual, introspection, the emotions, and nature in its wild, unpredictable aspects. In the English-speaking world this new philosophy of life was pioneered by poets and thinkers such as Samuel Taylor Coleridge, William Wordsworth, William Blake, and Percy Byshe Shelley. In Germany, an even more influential group of Romantics was centered on the university town of Jena and included the philosopher Johann Gottlieb Fichte, the playwright Friedrich Schilling, and Goethe.[1]

Two other early influential figures of Romantic philosophy—although they were sons of the Enlightenment—were the French author Jean-Jacques Rousseau (1712–78) and the German philosopher Immanuel Kant (1724–1804). Rousseau was one of the first to voice the Romantics' suspicion of the artificiality of civilization by championing the "noble savage," the idea that human beings living in a primitive state according to their instincts attain a natural happiness that civilized society corrodes. Kant, meanwhile, had anticipated the Romantics' shift of emphasis from objective to subjective knowledge by his assertion that we cannot gain direct knowledge of the outside world—"things in themselves"—but only of our own perceptions, which we order by imposing on them innate mental structures, such as notions of time and space.

Later, Kant's fellow countryman Friedrich Schleiermacher (1768–1834), a theologian who had been raised by parents who had become Herrnhuter brethren, echoed the Romantic approach to spirituality by emphasizing the place of feeling and intuition as a basis for religion. "I ask, therefore," he once wrote, "that you turn from everything usually reckoned religion, and fix your regard on the *inward emotions and dispositions*, as all utterances and acts of inspired men direct."[2] He later defined religion in terms of the feeling of being absolutely dependent on God.

So whereas the Enlightenment era had proved to be thorny ground for mysticism, Romanticism, with its higher regard for the inner emotional life and greater feeling for spirituality, was much more fertile. Yet the spirit of mysticism seems to have largely passed over the mainstream churches—even though there was a revival

278

ROMANTICS, NATURE MYSTICS, AND TRANSCENDENTALISTS

of Catholicism and a strengthening of the papacy in the nineteenth century—and settled on spiritually-inclined artists and writers. In Germany, for example, there was Novalis, the pen-name of Friedrich von Hardenberg (1772–1801), an early Romantic mystical writer who asserted that "the spirit world is in fact revealed to us; it is always open. Could we suddenly become as sensitive as is necessary, we should perceive ourselves to be in its midst."[3] His best-known works are his *Hymns to the Night*, a mystical rhapsody of death and night prompted by the death of his young fiancée, and *Heinrich von Ofterdingen*, in which the eponymous hero, a medieval poet, searches for a mysterious blue flower, representing spiritual truth.

In England, there was a great flowering of poets who covered the spectrum of Romantic ideals, from Lord Byron's heroic individualism to Keats's melancholic introspections and Shelley's flights of Platonism. Coleridge, the greatest thinker among them, explicitly acknowledged the debt he owed to the mystics of the past, men such as Jacob Boehme, George Fox, and William Law, who had helped him "keep alive the heart in the head" and showed him that "all the products of the mere reflective faculty partook of death."[4] But arguably the two greatest English mystical poets of the time were the early Romantics William Blake and William Wordsworth, the first an artist and visionary with a mystical view of the imagination, the second a subtle, reflective writer who was one of England's most expressive nature mystics.

Nature mysticism was the preserve not only of Romantic poets such as Wordsworth. It was also central to the spiritual and philosophical movement known as Transcendentalism, which flourished in New England in the first half of the 1800s, especially in the lives and works of Ralph Waldo Emerson and Henry David Thoreau. Transcendentalism never had a definitive credo or system. Instead, it emphasized the importance of the individual, as opposed to the masses, and, influenced by the Quakers and the Romantic movement in Europe, believed in the divine immanence, which was especially manifest in nature. They also valued personal emotions and intuitive knowledge more than intellectual rationalism, formal education, and institutionalized religion. Theologically, they "replaced the Calvinist emphasis on sin-sick selves with a view of the 'divine in all.'"[5]

279

DAZZLING DARKNESS

William Blake (1757–1827)

"A true mystic to whom the eternal was the natural and the human indistinguishable from the divine,"[6] William Blake saw visions from an early age. It is said that when he was four he screamed in shock at seeing the face of God at his bedroom window. Some years later, while walking in Peckham, he saw "a tree filled with angels, bright angelic wings bespangling every bough like stars." On another occasion, in summer, he was watching haymakers in the fields when he saw angels walking among them.[7] It is not surprising then that he was later influenced by mystical and unorthodox visionaries such as the alchemist Paracelsus (1493–1541); Jacob Boehme (whom Blake described as "a divinely inspired man"); and the Swede Emanuel Swedenborg (1688–1772). Like Swedenborg, Blake claimed to have constant access to a supramundane reality, communing with spirits and angels who directed his work ("I am under the direction of messengers from Heaven, daily and nightly"[8]).

The son of a hosier, Blake was born in 1757 in London, the city where he lived for almost his entire life. From the age of fourteen to twenty-one he was apprenticed to an engraver, a period when he developed a fascination for Gothic art. After his apprenticeship he studied art at the Royal Academy for a while before setting himself up as an engraver, the profession by which he supported himself for the rest of his life (his poems, nearly all of which he hand-engraved and published himself, brought in little money). In 1782, at the age of twenty-five, he married Catherine Boucher, whom he taught to read and write and who would remain his lifelong companion, helper, and fellow pilgrim on his spiritual journey. In 1789 Blake engraved his *Songs of Innocence*, which, along with the *Songs of Experience*, completed five years later, are his best-known lyrical poems.

In 1800 Blake left London for Sussex to do illustration work for William Hayley at Felpham by the sea. His three-year sojourn there—his only departure from London during his life—was a mixed experience, the joys of nature to some extent compensating for the frustration that working for the domineering Hayley entailed. Four years later, back in the metropolis, Blake began to engrave his long prophetic works *Milton* and *Jerusalem*. These, in common with

ROMANTICS, NATURE MYSTICS, AND TRANSCENDENTALISTS

his other prophetic books, have an arcane, private symbolism and idiosyncratic style that continue to divide readers, although few have failed to be impressed by their scale and originality. For the rest of his life, Blake continued to engrave and write, unfolding his inner vision, while his outward life was seemingly uneventful. When he died in 1827 he was largely unknown except to a small band of admirers. His reputation has grown steadily, however, with W. B. Yeats among the forefront of modern poets who have recognized his genius.

Blake abhorred anything that fettered spiritual energy. Much of his invective was directed against organized religion, with its "Priests in black gowns ... binding with briars my joys,"[9] as well as those he saw as the moving spirits of the Enlightenment's culture of reason and scientific materialism:

> Mock on, mock on, Voltaire, Rousseau;
> Mock on, mock on; 'tis all in vain!
> You throw the sand against the wind,
> And the wind blows it back again.
>
> And every sand becomes a gem
> Reflected in the beams divine;
> Blown back they blind the mocking eye
> But still in Israel's paths they shine.
>
> The Atoms of Democritus
> And Newton's Particles of Light
> Are sands upon the Red Sea shore,
> Where Israel's tents do shine so bright.[10]

Embodying one of Blake's central themes, the poem sets out, with the concision and sharpness Blake valued so much in his engraving, two opposing worldviews, that of the skeptical rationalists and scientists and that of the Bible and "true" religion. The sand that in the first verse is used in the act of childish rejection of true religion (the "wind") becomes in the second verse a numinous, jewel-like reflection of God's creation, seeming to light the path of the tribes of Israel as they make their way across the wilderness toward the promised land of Canaan (the implication being that divinely created nature can lead the soul to its promised land, union with

281

God). This contrast is again brought out in the last verse, in which the scientific—and for Blake reductionist—ideas of the Greek philosopher Democritus and Sir Isaac Newton regarding the nature of matter are set against the image of Israel's tents, suggesting stasis and peacefulness, and especially freedom, since the reference to the Red Sea indicates that the tribes have crossed the sea and escaped Pharaoh's chariots and bondage in Egypt. Again the suggestion is of the soul escaping the bondage of materialism.

For Blake, ever aware of a reality beyond the external world, nature—even in its minutest and seemingly inert form—was an opening to the timeless realm of God, as one of his best-known quatrains suggests:

> To see a World in a grain of sand,
> And a Heaven in a wild flower,
> Hold Infinity in the palm of your hand,
> And Eternity in an hour.[11]

The core of Blake's mysticism was his view of the imagination, which for him was not just a faculty of the mind but a divine reality. He also called it "vision" and compared it favorably to "fable" or "allegory."[12] Whereas allegory is the product of memory, imagination is "surrounded by the daughters of inspiration," who, in Blake's terminology, are collectively called "Jerusalem." That is not to say that allegory cannot have imagination or vision within it— and he cites John Bunyan's *The Pilgrim's Progress* as one such "fable" that contains visions. But essentially the two modes of expression are distinct.

Blake equates imagination with the infinite "world of eternity" into which mortals go after the death of the body; by contrast, the world of generation or, as he calls it, "vegetation," is finite and temporal. Imagination contains "the permanent realities of everything which we see are reflected in this vegetable glass of nature," in which respect it is similar to Plato's world of Forms, the imperfect copies of which can be found in our world. Blake then identifies this realm of imagination with the "divine body of the saviour, the true vine of eternity," rooting his visionary system in Christianity. In the section called "To the Christians" in his book *Jerusalem*, he makes explicit this connection between the imagination and his own brand of the

ROMANTICS, NATURE MYSTICS, AND TRANSCENDENTALISTS

faith: "I know of no other Christianity and of no other Gospel than the liberty both of body and mind to exercise the divine arts of imagination. ... The Apostles knew of no other Gospel."[13]

Blake claimed to be able to apprehend the divine through his visionary powers, and he believed that this gift was natural and open to humanity, but most people are unaware of it because of the habitual and limited way they think and behave: "If the doors of perception were cleansed everything would appear to man as it is, infinite. For man has closed himself up till he sees all things through narrow chinks of his cavern."[14] Blake recognized that people see different things according to their conditioning: to the miser a coin is more beautiful than the sun, a money bag more shapely than a vine full of grapes. One person may delight in a tree, while someone else may think it is just an impediment. Some people think nature is full of ugliness, others scarcely notice it, while to the person of imagination, "Nature is Imagination itself."[15]

Blake himself saw the world through a lens that pierced the ordinary appearances of everyday objects and revealed their inner sacred nature: "'What,' it will be questioned, 'when the sun rises, do you not see a round disc of fire somewhat like a guinea?' Oh! no, no! I see an innumerable company of the heavenly host, crying 'Holy, holy, holy.'"[16] Blake referred to this ability to see outer forms and their inner nature at the same time as "Double Vision." He gives an example of Double Vision in a poem in which he describes a thistle in terms of a grey-haired old man. It's as if Blake saw through the outward surface of the thistle's whiskery spikes, its drooping head and thin body, and his imagination re-shaped it into an old man:

> For double the vision my Eyes do see
> And a double vision is always with me
> With my inward Eye 'tis an old Man grey
> With my outward a Thistle across my way.[17]

For Blake Double Vision was not just what poets should practice, but everybody. His fear and rage against the Single Vision, as he called it, of the Newtonians, of scientific reductionism and literalism, feels like a fight to the death. Another fuller example of his Double Vision can be seen in a poem he wrote to his friend Thomas Butts in the autumn of 1800.[18] Blake had just moved to Felpham with

283

DAZZLING DARKNESS

his wife Catherine to experience three years of a life completely different to the urban compactness and grime he encountered on a daily basis in London. In Sussex he enjoyed the sound of birdsong, trees, fields, and the sea. Not long after his arrival he reported to Butts a vision he had received when sitting on the "yellow sands" of the seashore. As the sun shone on him,

> My Eyes did Expand
> Into regions of air
> Away from all Care
> Into regions of fire
> Remote from Desire ...

The morning light adorned "Heavens Mountains" in jewel-like particles; when Blake stared at them, he was astonished to see that each one had become "a Man / Human formd." These anthropomorphic particles revealed to Blake a holistic vision of creation in which the fundamental material of nature is human, ensouled, animated, vital:

> ... Each grain of Sand
> Every Stone on the Land
> Each rock & each hill
> Each fountain & rill
> Each herb & each tree
> Mountain hill Earth & Sea
> Cloud Meteor & Star
> Are Men Seen Afar ...

The poet's vision is transformed: he sees Felpham as if from an elevated position "Sweet / Beneath my bright feet," and then his "Eyes more & more / Like a Sea without shore" continued expanding the range and depth of their vision until the particles of "Heavenly Men" coalesce into "One Man," a divine Christ-like figure who absorbs the poet into his "beams of bright gold" and purges him of "mire & my clay" until he is "consumd in delight." The divine figure refers to the earth as "his fold," and as his voice fades he leaves the poet in a state of renewed innocence and with a lingering vision of his friend and his wife in paradise:

ROMANTICS, NATURE MYSTICS, AND TRANSCENDENTALISTS

> I remaind as a Child
> All I ever had known
> Before me bright Shone
> I saw you & your wife
> By the fountains of Life
> Such the Vision to me
> Appeard on the Sea.

It is difficult to imagine someone like Blake, or indeed Hildegard, negotiating two levels of reality at the same time, one quotidian, the other visionary. But Blake managed it, and the artistic task he set himself was "to Restore what the Ancients call'd the Golden Age,"[19] or a state of spiritual harmony, and he saw it as his life's work to convey this vision to his fellow human beings, despite the incessant incomprehension and scorn he received from them. As he says in the first chapter of *Jerusalem*: "I rest not upon my great task / To open the Eternal Worlds, to open the immortal Eyes / Of Man inwards into the Worlds of Thought: into Eternity / Ever expanding in the Bosom of God, the Human Imagination."[20] To do this was a gargantuan task, and Blake's prophetic books show the barely subterranean tensions of the times—the oppressiveness of reason and materialism, revolutionary fervor, and increasing dehumanization brought about by the industrial revolution. Yet his unitary vision, often expressed by violent imagery, was always underpinned by his not entirely orthodox faith, and the central place in his life of Christ, his anchor and shepherd, whose relationship with us recalls the reciprocal indwelling described in John's Gospel.

William Wordsworth (1770–1850)

For Blake, as we have seen, nature was a world of divine illumination and boundlessness for those who had exchanged their "vegetable eyes" for the eyes of cleansed perception. His fellow poet and younger contemporary William Wordsworth, arguably the greatest of the English Romantic poets, also found in nature a source of wonder, although the two men differed in their approach to it. Blake was critical of the way Wordsworth saw nature as a divine end in itself, whereas for him nature was a means to entering a further eternal world. Wordsworth's descriptions of nature are less obviously

DAZZLING DARKNESS

visionary than Blake's, but his early devotion toward creation, and the perceptiveness of his own feelings toward it, provide an eloquent record of what is generally known as nature mysticism.

The Christian tradition of celebrating the divine in nature found notable expression in the words of Francis of Assisi, for whom God's creatures were his brothers and sisters. But the idea of the "nature mystic," one who obtains a sense of God *primarily* through nature and not simply as a result of a unitive vision, seems to be a particular phenomenon of post-Reformation times. The vision of divine nature appealed especially to those whose religious instincts were not being satisfied by either the sometimes-passionless established churches or the sometimes-overemotional dissenting groups. In England, Blake, Wordsworth, Coleridge, Keats, and Shelley, and, later, Gerard Manley Hopkins, channeled in different degrees their religiosity through the lens of the created world, and it was Wordsworth—"In aloofness and loneliness of mind he is exceeded by no mystic of the cloister"[21]—who was the most persistent and convincing, with his evocations of nature and his own ecstatic feelings toward it.

For Wordsworth, at least in his youth, nature was animate, a living creature, a manifestation of God. In *The Excursion* (Book 1), for example, he describes how a panoramic sweep of earth, sky, and ocean viewed from a headland imbued him with a sense of "unutterable love" and "sensation, soul, and form":

> All melted into him; they swallowed up
> His animal being; in them did he live,
> And by them did he live; they were his life.[22]

He refers to the experience as "a visitation from the living God" and compares his rapt state of "still communion" favorably with the "imperfect offices of prayer and praise."

The son of a lawyer, Wordsworth was born in Cumberland in northwest England in 1770. After graduating from Cambridge University, he traveled around France, where he had a love affair with a woman named Annette Vallon, by whom he had a daughter. After his return to England in 1792, initially enthusiastic about the French Revolution (before the onset of the carnage of "the Terror")

286

ROMANTICS, NATURE MYSTICS, AND TRANSCENDENTALISTS

and full of political idealism, he began to publish his first poems. In 1798 he and the poet Samuel Taylor Coleridge brought out their highly influential *Lyrical Ballads*, a joint book of poems that proclaimed a new literary aesthetic: the mannered, artificial diction and style typical of the eighteenth century was rejected in favor of what they claimed was a language spoken by ordinary people, especially the humble and uneducated, and an emphasis was placed on nature, introspection, and personal feelings.

In 1799 Wordsworth moved north with his only and beloved sister Dorothy to the Lake District, where he would reside for the rest of his life. Three years later he married a woman named Mary Hutchinson, by whom he had five children (two of whom died young), and settled down to a long and contented domestic life. In fact, by about 1807 he was no longer the adventurous soul and daring original poet of a few years before. By this time he had more or less completed all the poems for which he would be famous, including his great autobiographical work, *The Prelude*, published after his death. From then on his poetic vitality began to wane. He continued to write throughout the rest of his life—indeed he was appointed poet laureate in 1843—but his later work seems more dutiful than inspired, reflecting the worthy sentiments of the establishment figure he had become as a pillar of the Church of England. He died in 1850.

The art of creating poetry, as Wordsworth describes it, is not so remote from the meditative exercises of Ignatius Loyola or Francis de Sales. Poetry is born from "emotion recollected in tranquility," that is, it is re-created from primary experiences (for example, seeing a cascade of wild daffodils) by a sort of controlled meditation in which, during a state of calm, the emotion that was originally felt is allowed to rise to the surface. Yet unlike other Christian mystics, Wordsworth directed his religious gaze not directly at God or Christ but at God's creation. He found his spiritual center at the conjunction of nature—earth, air, light, darkness, sea, rushing streams, mysterious woods, wild mountain crags, which filled him "with joy exalted to beatitude"—and the inner workings of his mind and heart. Perhaps the best example of this nature mysticism can be seen in his poem "Lines Composed a Few Miles above Tintern Abbey" (a ruined monastery lying in a fold of the river Wye in southeast Wales).

287

DAZZLING DARKNESS

Wordsworth's poem recalls the idyllic setting and his feelings toward it during a visit five years before, in 1793. Looking at the scene of woods, orchards, groves, copses, farms, and "wreaths of smoke / Sent up, in silence, from among the trees," he considers how these images have had in the intervening years a vitalizing, even physical, effect on him ("felt in the blood, and felt along the heart") and how the memory of them has helped to create an inner state of peacefulness. He describes such a mood as "serene and blessed" and goes on to say that the "affections," that is, our feelings, "gently lead us on,"

> Until, the breath of this corporeal frame
> And even the motion of our human blood
> Almost suspended, we are laid asleep
> In body, and become a living soul:
> While with an eye made quiet by the power
> Of harmony, and the deep power of joy,
> We see into the life of things.[23]

His words are reminiscent of the medieval mystics' descriptions of "recollection," the gathering in of thoughts and feelings prior to contemplation proper. The lines convey the sense of the body dematerializing and of the spiritual faculties tuned in to a reality normally obfuscated by the excitation of the mind.

It was one of Wordsworth's gifts to be able to make subtle distinctions in the complexities of the inner life, and in the same poem he describes a shift in his attitude toward nature over the years. Whereas on his first trip the Wye valley affected him viscerally as "an appetite; a feeling and a love," now, five years later, older and more sophisticated, he experiences nature with less raw emotion but with a greater sense of spiritual uplift:

> And I have felt
> A presence that disturbs me with the joy
> Of elevated thoughts; a sense sublime
> Of something far more deeply interfused,
> Whose dwelling is the light of setting suns,
> And the round ocean and the living air,
> And the blue sky, and in the mind of man;
> A motion and a spirit, that impels

ROMANTICS, NATURE MYSTICS, AND TRANSCENDENTALISTS

> All thinking things, all objects of all thought,
> And rolls through all things …[24]

For the youthful Wordsworth, this indwelling presence is what he calls in *The Excursion* (Book 4) the "active principle," which informs all parts of creation, subsisting in "the stars of azure heaven" as well as clouds, trees, flowers, and stones: it is a unifying spirit or "the Soul of all the worlds." In *The Prelude* (Book 1), he talks of his ineffable bliss when experiencing "the sentiment of Being spread / O'er all that moves and all that see meth still." In short, nature gave him an entry into a sublime, spiritual world in which everything was infused with a sense of divine harmony and unity. In a journey through the Simplon Pass in the Alps in *The Prelude* (Book 5), he likens the diversity of nature—the waterfalls, torrents, rocks, crags, and sky—to the "workings of one mind, the features / Of the same face, blossoms upon one tree." So potent and luminous do these natural features appear to him that he sees them as "The types and symbols of Eternity."

However, Wordsworth's ecstatic reaction to nature did not last. Like mystics who experience the presence of God only to suffer after the withdrawal of his divine favor, Wordsworth records his own disenchantment with nature in his poem "Intimations of Immortality," in which he states poignantly: "The things which I have seen I now can see no more." The poem, completed in 1806, stands like a dismal arch through which he passed from poetic life on a slow march toward poetic death.

Ralph Waldo Emerson (1803–82)

The British Romantics' belief that nature provided evidence of the glory of the divine was shared by their cousins in America, the Transcendentalists, of whom Ralph Waldo Emerson and Henry David Thoreau were the most prominent. Philosopher, poet, and spiritual and mystical writer, Emerson diffused his ideas throughout the world by means of countless talks and lectures, as well as by essays and books. Influenced by a variety of sources ranging from Plato to Indian philosophy (especially the *Bhagavad Gita*) and the Romantic movement, he emphasized the divine aspect of nature

DAZZLING DARKNESS

and the idea that God resides inside the individual, who therefore has the spiritual wherewithal for salvation. He believed that the "inner light" operated "to bring the universe into the possession of a single soul."[25]

Emerson was born in Boston, the son of a Unitarian minister (the Unitarians rejected the Trinity and the divinity of Christ in favor of a "unified" concept of God). He was educated at Harvard, then subsequently trained to become a minister like his father (who had died while he was a young boy). In 1826 he gained his license to preach and within a couple of years he was practicing as a Unitarian minister in Boston. However, he resigned his position in 1832 over a doctrinal matter involving the Eucharist and decided to broaden his horizons and travel to Europe in the following year. There he sampled British Romanticism at first hand through meetings with William Wordsworth and his fellow poet, Samuel Taylor Coleridge.

On his return from Europe, Emerson moved to Concord, Massachusetts, which would remain his home for the next fifty years. There he would take long walks in the wild landscape of woods and streams and find inspiration in nature. He married his second wife, Lydia Jackson, in 1835 (his first wife had died young), and together they had four children (one of whom, Waldo, died at the age of five).

Emerson spent the bulk of his life walking, talking out his ideas with friends, reading, writing poetry, going on lecture tours, and publishing books. His first work, *Nature*, which sets out his thoughts on humankind's relationship with nature and on other subjects, appeared in 1836. Two collections of influential essays (*First Series* and *Second Series*) appeared in 1841 and 1844. He also became editor of *The Dial*, the Transcendentalist journal, where many of his poems first appeared.

Those in sympathy with the Transcendentalist movement regularly visited his home in Concord to discuss the great issues of the day. They included a fellow Concord resident, Henry David Thoreau, who also advised Emerson on matters of gardening. Emerson was more than a brilliant, original thinker and writer. He also had a strong, reforming, anti-authoritarian instinct and was an active campaigner against slavery and fought for justice for indigenous Americans. He also served on school committees

290

ROMANTICS, NATURE MYSTICS, AND TRANSCENDENTALISTS

and attended Concord town meetings. In 1872 his house was accidentally set on fire and partially destroyed, an event that caused him great sadness. But friends helped to pay for its reconstruction and he died at home, ten years later, in 1882.

Emerson's philosophical ideas blend rationalist thought with mysticism. He did not expound a unified spiritual system but presented his insights piecemeal throughout numerous journals and essays. Fundamental was his idea that salvation is ultimately a personal affair: each of us is endowed with a divine soul, which, if we allow it to, hears the call of divine nature.

Emerson himself seems to have had rapturous moments of one-ness with nature—timeless moments of non-duality. In his journal entry for April 11, 1834, for example, he writes of an experience at Mount Auburn, Cambridge. He was lying down next to a tree, when:

> I opened my eyes and let what would pass through them into the soul. I saw no more my relation, how near & petty, to Cambridge or Boston. I heeded no more what minute or hour our Massachusetts clocks might indicate—I saw only the noble earth on which I was born, with the great star that warms & enlightens it.[26]

At a time when the industrial revolution and the coming of the railroad were beginning to scar national landscapes (Emerson witnessed the worst aspects of this during his trip to England), Emerson tried to convey in his writings the beauty and divinity of nature and the way in which it is the natural habitat of the human soul. The soul, he believed, has a unifying vision of the disparate parts of nature: "We see the world piece by piece, as the sun, the moon, the animal, the tree; but the whole, of which these are the shining parts, is the soul."[27] Elsewhere, he refers to nature as "the apparition of God." It is the "organ through which the universal spirit speaks to the individual, and strives to lead back the individual to it."[28]

In the first chapter of his book *Nature*, he conveys a mystical awe for the cosmos: "But if a man would be alone, let him look at the stars. The rays that come from those heavenly worlds will separate between him and what he touches." Changing his imagery from the stars to the sun, he describes how a true inner awareness of creation comes only through innocence: "The sun illuminates only the eye of the man, but shines into the eye and the heart of the child." Nor does his focus remain solely in the heavens—at the level of the earth, the woods provide us with a place of healing, inducing a condition in which "all mean egotism vanishes." In such an ego-less state the heaviness of flesh may dissolve: "I become a transparent eye-ball; I am nothing; I see all; the currents of the Universal Being circulate through me; I am part or particle of God."[29]

As well as nature, light is also a mystical component in Emerson's thought. Light has a transfiguring quality reminiscent of the light mysticism of Symeon the New Theologian. Beauty is also important: the world, he says, was originally endowed with eternal beauty, but we cannot see it because "man is disunited with himself." Our task is to restore our vision of nature's beauty through love, awareness, and prayer ("a sally of the soul into the unfound infinite").[30]

As soon we conform our lives to the "pure idea" in our minds, the influx of spirit will cause an inner revolution:

> As when the summer comes from the south; the snow-banks melt, and the face of the earth becomes green before it, so shall the advancing spirit create its ornaments along its path, and carry with it the beauty it visits, and the song which enchants it; it shall draw beautiful faces, warm hearts, wise discourse, and heroic acts, around its way, until evil is no more seen.[31]

Henry David Thoreau (1817–62)

An essayist, philosopher, and campaigner, Henry Thoreau could also, like his friend and elder contemporary Ralph Waldo Emerson, lay claim to being a nature mystic. His two years of solitary life in the middle of a forest beside Walden Pond near his home town of Concord, Massachusetts, seem to have given him moments of deep sympathy with the natural world that border on the rapturous. Like Emerson, Thoreau was a literary master, producing memorable images and aphoristic statements such as, "If I were confined to a corner of a garret all my days, like a spider, the world would be just as large to me while I had my thoughts about me"; and, "Humility like darkness reveals the heavenly lights."[32]

Thoreau was the son of a businessman and grew up in the idyllic setting of Concord and its woods. In 1833 (the year Emerson moved

ROMANTICS, NATURE MYSTICS, AND TRANSCENDENTALISTS

to Concord) he went to Harvard, graduating four years later. On returning home, he briefly worked as a teacher and struck up a friendship with Emerson, in whom he saw a kindred spirit, a spiritual seeker, and wise counselor (and Emerson encouraged Thoreau to keep a journal, which he continued to write until his death).

In 1840 Thoreau had his first and last flirtation with matrimony, when he proposed to a young local woman named Ellen Sewall. But her father disliked the idea of having Thoreau as a son-in-law and compelled his daughter to break off the engagement. The following year Thoreau went to live with Emerson and his family for a couple of years, working as a handyman and writing poetry (like Emerson's, his poems were published in *The Dial*). Then, in spring 1845, his hitherto checkered career (which also included working in the family pencil-making business) took an unusual and life-changing turn when he made the decision to live a solitary existence in woods near Walden Pond, a small lake a couple of miles south of Concord. Making himself as self-sufficient as possible (perhaps bearing in mind Emerson's ideal that people should be "self-reliant"), he chopped down trees and built a small wooden house, which was basically one room, with a bed, table and chair, and stove. He gathered wild fruits and nuts, grew beans, fished, swam, fetched his water, and cooked his own food (although once a week he would return to Concord to eat with his family or pick up food supplies). Meanwhile he was reading, meditating, observing nature, and writing down notes for what would become his classic work, *Walden*.

Thoreau remained at Walden Pond for two years. Afterward he continued to live in Concord, taking more responsibility for the family business and also working as a surveyor. He continued to write, and sometimes travel, with notable excursions to Cape Cod, Maine Woods, and Canada. He also gave lectures and became more of a political activist, even spending the night in jail for civil disobedience. He wholeheartedly espoused the abolitionist cause; and it was said that the hanging of the abolitionist John Brown in 1859 caused him such heartache that it hastened his own death, from tuberculosis, in 1862.

Thoreau believed in God, but his concept of him is ambiguous and subtle. In a letter to a friend, written in 1850, he said: "It is

DAZZLING DARKNESS

not when I am going to meet him, but when I am just turning away and leaving him alone, that I discover that God is. I say, God. I am not sure that that is the name. You will know whom I mean."[33] Elsewhere in his writings he talks about the "Great Spirit" and "gods and goddesses."

What was important to Thoreau was not so much metaphysical speculations but a sense of the divine within, as well as living in the present. His religious spirit embodied the way of individualistic non-conformity that was one of the core values of Transcendentalism. Allied with this was his deep and pervasive sense that people lose touch with their natural environment at their own psychic and spiritual peril. His classic book *Walden* relates how at-one-ment with nature can be achieved. It gives an intense psychological and spiritual picture of solitary living that's worthy of that of a medieval hermit.

Thoreau's decision to live by himself was a conscious attempt to see what would happen to him if the trappings of civilization were removed: "I went to the woods because I wished to live deliberately, to front only the essential facts of life, and see if I could not learn what it had to teach, and not, when I came to die, discover that I had not lived."[34] It was a quest for authenticity, an existential experiment to discover the inner core of his being. It was also a one-man protest about the complications of cultivated life: "Our life is frittered away by detail. An honest man has hardly need to count more than his ten fingers, or in extreme cases he may add his ten toes, and lump the rest. Simplicity, simplicity, simplicity!"[35]

Like an early Christian anchorite, Thoreau also experienced doubt or accidie, spiritual listlessness, as a consequence of withdrawing from the world. But, on one occasion, even as he had these misgivings it began to drizzle with rain and he had a profound spiritual awakening, bordering on the mystical:

> I was suddenly sensible of such sweet and beneficent society in Nature, in the very pattering of the drops, and in every sound and sight around my house, an infinite and unaccountable friendliness all at once like an atmosphere sustaining me ... Every little pine needle expanded and swelled with sympathy and befriended me. I was so distinctly made aware of the presence of something kindred to me ... that I thought no place could ever be strange to me again.[36]

ROMANTICS, NATURE MYSTICS, AND TRANSCENDENTALISTS

Indeed, William James (1842–1910), the American psychologist and spiritual writer, referring to this passage, likened Thoreau's state of being to a conversion experience, after which the physical world seems transfigured.[37]

Thoreau seems to have gained a genuine sense of how the soul, renewed by gentle asceticism, gains an empowering, creative vision of reality in which it takes its due place within an orderly dispensation:

> He will put some things behind, will pass an invisible boundary; new, universal, and more liberal laws will begin to establish themselves around and within him; or the old laws be expanded, and interpreted in his favor in a more liberal sense, and he will live with the license of a higher order of beings.[38]

Thoreau can speak with the confidence and certitude of an Old Testament prophet, calling his fellow human beings to action, the action of simplification:

> In proportion as he simplifies his life, the laws of the universe will appear less complex, and solitude will not be solitude, nor poverty poverty, nor weakness weakness. If you have built castles in the air, your work need not be lost; that is where they should be. Now put the foundations under them.[39]

16

MODERN VOICES

Perfect joy excludes even the very feeling of joy, for in the soul filled by the object no corner is left for saying "I."

—Simone Weil

It is tempting to characterize Christianity in the West during the last two centuries as suffering a relentlessly steady decline in churchgoing and, in the face of increasing secularization, a falling away from, or at least a greater questioning of, the faith. But generalizations of this sort have to be modified by acknowledging all sorts of exceptions, such as the rise of Marian piety in nineteenth-century Europe (symbolized by Pope Pius IX proclaiming the doctrine of the Immaculate Conception in 1854), as well as, say, the rise of the vibrant African independent churches in the twentieth century. Nevertheless, the mainstream churches of the West have had to face up to a number of challenges, which to varying degrees have negatively impacted individuals' faith, church attendance, and general morale. For example, scientific advances, from astronomy to genetics, have served to demystify the universe and shift people from relying on God to relying on the intellectual capability of humankind; and the rise of the psychotherapeutic movement has generally had the effect of focusing interest on the human personality, often at the expense of the place of the transcendent. Other changes in modern times that have affected Christianity have been tentatively suggested by the church historian Owen Chadwick: the diminishing specter of mortality through improved medicine; population shifts from country to towns, removing people from the liturgical rhythm connected with the seasons; and

DAZZLING DARKNESS

a growing societal toleration, making alternative belief systems increasingly available.[1]

The challenge to religious faith in the modern era is usually associated with the rise of scientific method in the seventeenth and eighteenth centuries, which gradually began to undermine the traditional authority of the churches and literalist readings of the Bible. In the nineteenth century, the book of Genesis, with its account of Adam and Eve and Noah's Ark, came in for particular attention when theories of evolution seemed to some to turn it from being the repository of sacred literal truth to just another Near Eastern creation myth. Discoveries of fossils of long-extinct animals shook the widespread belief that the earth was just a few thousand years old: James Ussher (1581–1656), the archbishop of Armagh, had confidently assigned the first day of creation to October 23, 4004 BCE.

Although evolution had been in the air for some time before Charles Darwin (1809–82), it was he who, in *The Origin of Species* (1859) and *The Descent of Man* (1871), compellingly presented the idea that animal and plant species evolve through a process of natural selection. For many, descent from apes and not Adam and Eve not only contradicted Genesis but seemed risible. Before the time of Darwin the German philosopher Johann Fichte (1762–1814) had scoffed at the idea that an orangutan might be the ancestor of such distinguished thinkers as Leibniz (1646–1716) and Kant.[2] And in a similar vein, during a debate in Oxford in 1860, Bishop Samuel Wilberforce (1805–73) famously asked the Darwinist T. H. Huxley (1825–95) whether his ape ancestors came from his grandmother's or his grandfather's side of the family. But the evolutionist challenge to the Bible was there to stay.

The integrity of the Bible also came under pressure from the new science of biblical criticism. Protestant biblical scholars, such as the German theologian David Strauss (1808–74), examined and analyzed the Bible as if it were just any other ancient text. In his influential *Life of Jesus Critically Examined*, published in 1835, Strauss denied the historical basis for the miraculous happenings in the scriptures and searched for patterns of myth. The subsequent chorus of outrage led to his being dismissed from his teaching position at Tübingen.

MODERN VOICES

The reactions to these new currents of science and scholarship that appeared to undermine the Bible and the church were various. Some Christians were able to accommodate them into their faith, some ignored them, and some launched a counteroffensive: in 1907 Pius X (pope from 1903–14) issued his decree *Lamentabili*, officially condemning the modernist movement within the Catholic Church. Some, desiring encounters with the supernatural that their churches could not provide, turned to spiritualism, hoping to make contact with the dead through mediums (in Britain, the Society for Psychical Research was founded in 1882). And others, such as Darwin himself, slipped quietly into agnosticism (a word coined by T. H. Huxley) or atheism.

Yet although during the nineteenth century religious skepticism became more commonplace in Western societies, the Christian faith, with its age-old rites and rituals, still formed the focal point of the lives of the majority of people. Indeed, Catholicism in France in the early years of the century experienced something of a renewal. There were also bursts of revivalism, such as those inspired by the Americans Dwight L. Moody (1837–99) and Ira D. Sankey (1840–1908) in the nineteenth century and Billy Graham (1918–2018) in the twentieth. And at a grassroots level, there were many instances of faith being kindled by new and reborn pilgrimages and devotions that have continued to the present. Many of them were founded on the mystical or visionary experiences of individuals, often children, occurring in places that have subsequently become world famous. They include Lourdes in southern France, Knock in the west of Ireland, Fátima in Portugal, Garabandal in northern Spain, and Medjugorje in Bosnia.

Although it is right to stress the continuity of popular piety, it remains true that Christian spirituality had, and has, never before encountered such competition from secular forces and rival faiths—especially those with strong mystical elements, such as Zen and other forms of Buddhism—as well as quasi-religious movements, such as Transcendental Meditation. Yet despite the odds, the Christian mystical tradition was maintained through the late nineteenth and twentieth centuries by mystics such as Thérèse of Lisieux, Charles de Foucauld, Pierre Teilhard de Chardin, Simone Weil, and Thomas Merton.

299

DAZZLING DARKNESS

Thérèse of Lisieux (1873–97)

During her short life of twenty-four years, Thérèse of Lisieux led an unremarkable existence as a nun in a Carmelite convent. But the story of her life, which she wrote down before her death and was characterized by the carrying out of daily duties and performing small tasks in the name of God, struck a chord with people all over the world. Her life showed that even the most "ordinary" and obscure individual could attain sainthood through little acts of devotion and humility. Thérèse is also said to have received direct mystical experiences in the form of raptures—or "transports of love," as she called them. One time, for example, when she was in her convent choir, she felt herself suddenly wounded by a dart of fire so ardent that "I thought I should die. I do not know how to explain this transport; there is no comparison to describe the intensity of that flame. It seemed as though an invisible force plunged me wholly into fire. ... But oh! what fire! what sweetness!"[3]

Baptized Marie Françoise Thérèse Martin, Thérèse was born in 1873 at Alençon in Normandy, northeastern France, the daughter of Louis Martin, a watchmaker. At the age of fifteen she followed two of her four sisters to the Carmelite convent in Lisieux, about sixty miles north of Alençon, where she was given the name Sister Thérèse of the Child Jesus and of the Holy Face. She later described the wrench of leaving the world: "I did not shed a tear, but as I led the way to the cloister door my heart beat so violently that I wondered if I were going to die."[4] Her sister Pauline became prioress of the convent (under the name Mother Agnes) and showed Thérèse no favors. As Thérèse recalled, addressing Pauline: "I remember once I had left a cobweb in the cloister, and you said to me before the whole community: 'It is easy to see that our cloisters are swept by a child of fifteen. It is disgraceful!'"[5] Thérèse continued to live as a Carmelite nun, engaging in a round of work and prayer. After nine years of convent life she contracted tuberculosis and died in 1897 at the age of twenty-four.

Thérèse might have joined the ranks of the thousands of unsung nuns but for the fact that in 1895 she had begun to write, on instruction by Pauline, a memoir recalling episodes of her spiritual

MODERN VOICES

life. This work was edited after her death and circulated to other Carmelite convents as *The Story of a Soul* (*L'Histoire d'une âme*). Filled with homely details and sincere spirituality, the book soon reached a wider audience and over the years became (with variant titles) a religious bestseller. (In the later twentieth century scholars re-examined Thérèse's original manuscripts and produced a version of her story closer to the original.) As her fame increased, pilgrimages were made to Lisieux, prayers were addressed to her, and miracles attributed to her (she was canonized in 1925). In Lisieux itself, a large church was built in 1926 to cater for the increasing numbers of visitors.

Thérèse, who referred to herself as Jesus's "little flower," appealed to ordinary people through her childlike simplicity and sincerity. She did not construct a theological edifice or resort to extremes of asceticism or found a new religious order, as other mystics had done. She was content to live an anonymous life according to the Carmelite Rule, concentrating on what she called "little things" (such as folding the mantles of her sister nuns) rather than overarching ideals. In this she expressed, constantly and consistently, her love for God and Jesus, demonstrating this love in her tenderness and gentleness toward her sister nuns and nature. She once said that her mission was "to make others love God as I love him ... to teach souls my little way ... the way of spiritual childhood, the way of trust and absolute surrender."[6]

Thérèse communicated to the world beyond the cloisters through her writings, and she had a gift for the striking or poetic image. For example, she says that when in her youth she was ill for a while, she disliked seeing "people seated around my bed like a row of onions, looking at me as though I were a strange beast."[7] She described her way to heaven as short, straight, and akin to taking an elevator or lift: "We live in an age of inventions; nowadays the rich need not trouble to climb the stairs, they have lifts instead. Well, I mean to try and find a lift by which I may be raised unto God, for I am too tiny to climb the steep stairway of perfection."[8] About prayer she said: "One could call it a Queen who has at each instant free access to the King and who is able to obtain whatever she asks. To be heard it is not necessary to read from a book some beautiful formula composed for the occasion."[9] Elsewhere, in a letter to her

301

DAZZLING DARKNESS

sister Céline, she tells her she must be like a drop of dew hidden in a beautiful lily-of-the-valley (symbolizing Christ).

> The dew-drop—what could be simpler, what more pure? It is not the child of the clouds; it is born beneath the starry sky, and survives but a night. When the sun darts forth its ardent rays, the delicate pearls adorning each blade of grass quickly pass into the lightest of vapor.[10]

Thérèse's writings do not always bear the innocence of a child. Sometimes her tone is adult and almost peremptory:

> I do not hold in contempt beautiful thoughts which nourish the soul and unite it with God; but for a long time I have understood that we must not depend on them and even make perfection consist in receiving many spiritual lights. The most beautiful thoughts are nothing without good works.[11]

Nor was her life all sweetness and light. In the chapter of her book called "The Night of the Soul" she describes her profound spiritual doubts and anxieties. She talks about "mists" penetrating her soul, of being weary of the enveloping darkness; even the prospect of an afterlife in heaven is gnawed at by an inner demonic voice: "you think one day to escape from these mists where you now languish. Nay, rejoice in death, which will give you, not what you hope for, but a night darker still, the night of utter nothingness!"[12]

Yet ultimately, despite her spiritual questionings and grim final physical illness, she seems to have fulfilled her childhood dream that

> one day I should be set free from this land of darkness ... my heart's most secret and deepest longings assured me that there was in store for me another and more beautiful country—an abiding dwelling-place. I was like Christopher Columbus, whose genius anticipated the discovery of the New World.[13]

Charles de Foucauld (1858–1916)

A wealthy French aristocrat who stripped away the trappings of his privileged life and identified himself with the poorest of society in the desert regions of northern Africa, Charles Eugene de Foucauld was a scholar, mystical writer, hermit, counselor, and man of God.

MODERN VOICES

The essence of his spirituality lay in abandoning the ego through humility, poverty, and simplicity, as well as committing oneself to prayer and to love: "To pray is to think of God with thoughts of love ... The best prayer is the one in which there is the most love. It is so much better because it is loving."[14]

Born into noble family—it is said his ancestors fought in the Crusades and stood beside Joan of Arc at Orleans[15]—Charles de Foucauld grew up to become a dashing, pleasure-loving cavalry officer, serving in northern Africa. In 1883–84 he explored the relatively unknown region of Morocco—disguised as a Jewish merchant to protect himself from anti-Christian fanatics—and later published a book of his findings. A restless soul in search of the meaning of life, de Foucauld found the key to his existence in his African experience. As he wrote to a friend: "Islam has produced in me a profound upheaval. Observing this faith and these souls living with God as a continual presence has allowed me to glimpse something greater and more true than worldly occupations."[16]

On his return to France, de Foucauld wrestled with his lack of faith, on one occasion praying at the altar of a Parisian church with the words: "My God, if you exist, let me know you."[17] Eventually he received guidance from a charismatic priest named Father Henri Huvelin, the curate of the church of Saint-Augustin in Paris. There, on October 30, 1886, de Foucauld had a conversion experience: he poured out his troubled mind in a long confession to Huvelin, who absolved him and gave him Holy Communion. De Foucauld "felt astonishingly light and at the same time possessed by that incomprehensible joy. In one moment, all his doubts had been swept away." On leaving the church he was overcome by "that infinite peace, that dazzling light, that unfailing happiness."[18]

De Foucauld now knew his path in life: total service to God. But he was unsure how to fulfill this vocation. He wanted to join a religious order, but there were many to choose from. His way of dealing with big decisions is indicated in his words: "We must silence our own arguments, lend our ears to the voice of the Spirit, and observe where God is pushing us, obeying his impetus."[19] The impetus of God pushed him first, in 1890, to the Trappist monastery of Notre-Dame-des-Neiges in the Ardèche region, about 100 miles north of Montpellier. But seven years later, deciding he wanted to

303

DAZZLING DARKNESS

live by an even stricter regime, he left the Trappists to join the Poor Clares in the Holy Land, first at Nazareth, where he worked as a gardener and handyman, then Jerusalem. In 1900 he returned to France, where, the following year, he was ordained a priest.

His sojourn in France was only temporary. The call of the desert echoed in his soul and he was anxious to return to Africa to help the poorest of society. He once said: "I do not think there is a Gospel phrase which has made a deeper impression on me and transformed my life more than this one: 'Insofar as you do this to one of the least of these brothers of mine, you did it to me.'"[20] He duly returned to Africa and became a hermit in Algeria at Béni Abbès (from 1901–05), then at the oasis of Tamanrasset in the Sahara, near the imposing Hoggar Mountains. There he immersed himself in the lives and culture of the Tuareg people, learning their language and even compiling a French-Tuareg dictionary. He lived as a hermit, working, praying, and performing acts of charity for the local community, who regarded him as a Marabout, or Muslim holy man. He was visited by the poor, sick, elderly, and women and children in search of help and advice. He stayed in Tamanrasset until his death in 1916, when he was killed by a group of rebel tribesmen during the First World War.

De Foucauld's mystical spirituality had its foundation in self-abasement and an appreciation of the *via negativa*:

> To embrace humility, poverty, renunciation, abjection, solitude, suffering, as did Jesus in the manger. To care not for human grandeur, or rising in the world, or the esteem of men, but to esteem the very poor as much as the very rich. For me, to seek always the last of the last places, to order my life so as to be the last, the most despised of men.[21]

For him, people move toward God through a silent appreciation of creation and ultimate truths; the desert is a paradigm for an inner state of vast godly silence: "The soul is not made for noise, but for meditation." Our lives must be God-centered, a preparation for the life to come; to this end, in addition to the Christian virtues and meritorious works, we must find "peace and recollection in God." De Foucauld was suspicious of political rhetoric and public discourse; what matters is an individual's relationship with God,

304

MODERN VOICES

forged in an interior silence: "But man has launched out into endless discussions: the little happiness he finds in loud debates is enough to show how far they lead him away from his vocation."[22]

De Foucauld also firmly believed that the Gospel was something that should be brought to the people, not confined to pulpits, and that its message was best spread by personal example: kindness and warmth. He knew, for example, from personal experience, that preaching Christianity directly to Muslims would be counterproductive; other faiths had to be respected. During his time as a hermit, he wrote rules for communities of what he called "Little Brothers" and "Little Sisters"—who, he hoped, would put his ideals into action. Although these communities did not materialize in his lifetime, after his death a group of priests led by René Voillaume set up a community of the Little Brothers of Jesus in the Sahara in 1933, but the project foundered during the anarchic years of the Second World War. After the war they renewed their energies and, with other members, founded a number of communities of Little Brothers of Jesus across the world: "They formed workers' fraternities—small groups of men who lived and worked in the slums of Lyons, among the fishermen of Brittany, in the shanty towns of North Africa, and, later, among the miners of Peru and the metal workers of Damascus."[23] In a similar manner, a community of Little Sisters was founded by Madeleine Hutin (who took the name Little Sister Magdeleine) in Touggourt, Algeria, in 1939, and by the early 2000s there were more than sixty communities of Little Sisters throughout the world.

Pierre Teilhard de Chardin (1881–1955)

Like William Wordsworth, Pierre Teilhard de Chardin was fascinated by nature and regarded it with religious awe, but at a literally much more fundamental level than the poet. For Teilhard it was the rocks, soil, minerals, and metals, the very substance of the earth, that were tangibly holy—he once wrote of the world's gradually appearing to him as "fire and light," eventually enveloping him "in one mass of luminosity, glowing from within."[24] As a geologist and paleontologist as well as a priest, he straddled two worlds, and throughout his life he tried to reconcile them, seeing theology and science as

305

complementary partners rather than as warring neighbors. The keystone of his mystical vision was the concept of evolution, which he saw as spiritually purposeful and directed toward a goal.

Teilhard believed that nature was evolving into higher and more complex forms of life, culminating in human beings, with their capacity for self-reflection. Not only that, he thought that humans had the power actually to participate in and influence evolution as it progressed toward a focal terminus that he termed the Omega point and identified with Christ, whom he describes as "a centre of radiation for the energies which lead the universe back to God through his humanity."[25] Yet despite his elevated and cosmic mystical vision, Teilhard was ever conscious of its roots in Christian scriptures: "However far we may be drawn into the divine spaces opened up to us by Christian mysticism, we never depart from Jesus of the Gospels. On the contrary, we feel a growing need to enfold ourselves ever more firmly within his human truth."[26]

Pierre Teilhard de Chardin was born in 1881 near Clermont in the Auvergne in central France. One of eleven children, he developed a love of nature from his father and the wild, rugged scenery of the local countryside, and he became an avid collector of rocks and stones, the beginnings of his love affair with geology. In 1899, at the age of eighteen, he entered the novitiate of the Jesuit order in Aix-en-Provence, later continuing his teacher training and studies—which included natural sciences—in Egypt and England. In 1911 he was ordained a priest, but he continued to pursue his scientific studies in Paris. This came to a halt after the outbreak of the First World War in 1914. Teilhard served as a stretcher bearer and emerged from the experience unshaken in his religious faith and decorated twice for bravery. It was during this difficult period that he experienced a powerful mystical vision while looking at a picture of Christ in a church close to the battlefront. The image seemed to vibrate, blur, dissolve, and take on a life of its own, and the space around the figure of Christ seemed to radiate "outwards to infinity" and was punctuated by "trails of phosphorescence" which he compared to a sort of "nervous system running through the totality of life."[27]

After the war Teilhard again concentrated on his scientific studies, and in 1922 he gained a doctorate from the Sorbonne and became

MODERN VOICES

a geology teacher in the Catholic Institute in Paris. In the following year he embarked on a paleontology trip to China, a country he would spend many years working in and where he would further his professional reputation (he was part of the team that discovered the famous Peking man, or *Sinanthropus*, in 1929). But his success as a paleontologist was balanced by his difficulties as a Catholic priest. His Jesuit superiors became aware of his views on evolution and its challenge to the orthodox teaching on original sin, and they censured him, preventing him from teaching. The Jesuits also refused to give him their approval to publish his theological and philosophical books, which reached the general public only after his death.

However, these restrictions did not affect Teilhard's scientific work, and toward the end of his life he received recognition from academic institutes in France and also America, where he was to die in New York in 1955 shortly before his seventy-fourth birthday. After his death, books such as *The Phenomenon of Man* and *Le Milieu Divin*, written in expressive, often poetic, and sometimes difficult prose, became widely known for their optimistic vision of a world evolving ever more spiritually. They brought him the fame and recognition as a religious thinker that had largely evaded him during his life.

Teilhard stands out in Christian spirituality for his mystical vision of the sacredness of matter and its fundamental place in creation: he talks of "the world [manifesting] itself to the Christian mystic as bathed in an inward light,"[28] and of God penetrating and shaping us through his creation.[29] He recognizes the scientific view of matter, but he expands it, attributing to matter an energy that is spiritual. In other words, it is not an inert substance waiting to be manipulated but an aspect of life itself, and so should be given reverence. He also describes matter theologically as something that not only causes us physical suffering—making us "heavy, paralysed, vulnerable, guilty"—but also as a principle of growth and renewal.[30] Nor does Teilhard maintain an opposition between matter and spirit but sees them as complementary forces together forming a continuum of cosmic energy.[31] He also describes how he experienced God continuously interacting with the world in such a way as to produce "a sudden blaze of such intense brilliance that all the depths of the world were lit up for me."[32]

307

DAZZLING DARKNESS

Allied with Teilhard's vision of matter is his spiritual vision of evolution. He suggests that there are three main stages in the evolutionary process: chemical, organic, and psychosocial. These relate respectively to the formation of the earth itself, the emergence of organic life, and the rise of human beings and their capacity for self-reflection. He also posits the idea of the noosphere (a word he coined from the Greek for "mind"): in the same way that there is the geosphere (the nonliving world) or the lithosphere (the outer layer of the earth) or the biosphere (the realm of living organisms), Teilhard suggests that there will evolve a noosphere, which he describes as a layer of thought enveloping the world and linking human beings to each other (for many people the noosphere has seemed to be prophetic of the Internet, itself a global, interconnecting sphere of "thought").

For Teilhard, the idea that life has evolved to the point of human consciousness only to stop seems implausible. The biosphere is characterized by "a network of divergent lines," but through the agency of reflective thought these lines converge and the noosphere becomes "a single closed system in which each element sees, feels, desires and suffers for itself the same things as all the others at the same time."[33] The noosphere itself is not the final phase of evolution. Teilhard envisages a future when people will develop their human potential fully and will individually and collectively converge toward a point that he calls Omega and identifies with Christ,[34] who is therefore the evolutionary terminus. Alongside this sense of convergence is the Christian ideal that to love Christ is to love one another, and to love one another is to draw closer to Christ.[35]

Teilhard had a holistic vision of the world in which everyone has a part to play, no matter how lowly his or her work or station—God is "at the point of my pen, my pick, my paint-brush, my needle."[36] He balances the traditional strand of Christian teaching that emphasized detachment and avoidance of the world—the ascetic's search for isolation and purity—with the idea that the whole of human life is holy and that we must embrace it, with all of its joys and sufferings. Teilhard, for all his general optimism, fully recognized the reality of suffering, sin, and evil, but he insisted that for those who trust him lovingly, God uses evil as an occasion for a higher good, just as a sculptor will create beauty out of some flaw he might detect

308

MODERN VOICES

in the stone he is working on.[37] Death itself, which from a human perspective is the ultimate "diminishment," is simply the natural and necessary way of preparing the individual for God to enter him or her fully with his divine fire.

Simone Weil (1909–43)

Like Charles de Foucauld and Pierre Teilhard de Chardin, Simone Weil was another unorthodox French mystic of the modern era. Jewish by birth, Weil became renowned as a philosopher and later committed herself to Catholic Christianity (although she never formally converted). She was deeply concerned with the plight of the poor and oppressed—she once did a stint in a Renault car factory, despite frail health, to show her solidarity with the workers—and she went to Spain to help the Republican side during the Spanish Civil War. Like de Foucauld, Weil believed that Christianity was not something that should be kept within church walls or cloisters or Episcopal palaces: "Christ went to bring his presence into those places most polluted with shame, misery, crime, and affliction, into prisons and law courts, into workhouses and shelters for the wretched and the outcast."[38]

Simone Weil was born in Paris in 1909 and showed great intellectual ability from an early age, though she felt crushed by her elder brother, who was regarded as a mathematical genius. By the age of twenty-two she had qualified as a philosophy teacher and began teaching in girls' schools. Her passionate interest in Christianity, and Catholicism in particular, stemmed from certain experiences she had in the mid-to-late-1930s. In 1935 she was on holiday with her parents in Portugal when she visited a small coastal village on a festival day. She witnessed a candlelit procession and singing of ancient hymns of "a heart-rending sadness." In 1937 she visited Assisi and there, in the church of Saint Mary of the Angels, where Francis once prayed, "something stronger than I was, compelled me for the first time in my life to go down on my knees."[39]

The following year she spent ten days, including the week of Easter, at Solesmes in northwestern France. At Solesmes Abbey, despite a splitting headache, she attended services and found "a pure and perfect joy in the unimaginable beauty of the chanting and the

309

words." It was an experience that helped her better understand the possibility of "divine love in the midst of affliction." At Solesmes she also met a young English Catholic who introduced her to the English Metaphysical poets of the seventeenth century. Weil discovered George Herbert's poem "Love (III)," which she learned by heart. Once, when reciting the poem, "Christ himself came down and took possession of me." It was so sudden that "neither my senses nor my imagination had any part." She simply felt the presence of a love, "like that which one can read in the smile on a beloved face."[40]

During the Second World War, Weil left France and after a short stay in the United States eventually made her way to England. There, working for the French provisional government in London, producing reports, she fell ill and, refusing to eat sufficient food out of solidarity with her fellow French citizens under German occupation, died in August 1943.

Weil's thoughts on spirituality were published after her death in books such as *Waiting on God* and *Gravity and Grace*. These works reflect not only her interest in Christian spirituality but also her love of ancient Greek and Hindu thought. She never produced a systematic, unified view of Christian spirituality; her reflections are scattered throughout essays and letters, many having a terse, aphoristic authority, for example: "Humility consists in knowing that in what we call 'I' there is no source of energy by which we can rise."[41] The ego, or I, was at odds with receiving the divine: "Perfect joy excludes even the very feeling of joy, for in the soul filled by the object no corner is left for saying 'I.'"[42]

Weil regarded herself as an outsider looking in on the church, but an outsider with the depth of spiritual feeling and commitment of an insider. For her the church could feel too tribal and exclusive: "The children of God should not have any other country here below but the universe itself, with the totality of all the reasoning creatures it ever has contained, contains, or ever will contain. That is the native city to which we owe our love."[43] She was continually drawn to sources of spirituality other than that of the Gospel, including the *Iliad* and the *Bhagavad Gita*. For her, intellectual concentration merged into religious contemplation and could produce a sense of closeness to the divine. For a while, for example, she studied the Lord's Prayer word by word in the original Greek and would

MODERN VOICES

recite it every day, finding that at times "the very first words tear my thoughts from my body and transport it to a place outside space where there is neither perspective nor point of view." This shift of perspective was accompanied by "a silence which is not an absence of sound but which is the object of a positive sensation, more positive than that of sound." In addition, at other moments, "Christ is present with me in person, but his presence is infinitely more real, more moving, more clear than on that first occasion when he took possession of me."[44]

Weil wrote persuasively about schooling, justice, and suffering, as well as humankind's relationship with nature and art. Other recurring themes are the spiritual benefits that affliction can bring; the necessity to "wait" for God; and to root love in the divine.

Love itself may be rooted in personal friendship, but it should not be discriminatory. It should "stretch as widely across all space, and should be as equally distributed in every portion of it, as is the very light of the sun. Christ has bidden us to attain to the perfection of our heavenly Father by imitating his indiscriminate bestowal of light."[45] Yet no matter how much love we have for the universe—for "the heavens, the plains, the sea, and the mountains, for the silence of nature which is borne in upon us by thousands of tiny sounds, for the breath of the winds or the warmth of the sun,"[46]—that love is always incomplete and painful, because matter cannot reciprocate. Love, she suggests, finds fulfillment in human relationships, especially in those in which divine love has been allowed to flourish: in the parable of the Good Samaritan, the "neighbor" whom the Samaritan helps is someone "of whom nothing is known, lying naked, bleeding, and unconscious on the road. It is a question of completely anonymous, and for that reason completely universal, love."[47]

It is love, too, that allows us to shift away from a self-centered to a God-centered world:

> To empty ourselves of our false divinity, to deny ourselves, to give up being the center of the world in imagination, to discern that all points in the world are equally centers and that the true center is outside the world, this is to consent to the rule of mechanical necessity in matter and of free choice at the center of each soul. Such consent is love.[48]

DAZZLING DARKNESS

Thomas Merton (1915–68)

Like Pierre Teilhard de Chardin, the American monk and writer Thomas Merton was a mystic for the troubled times he lived in. He was born during the First World War, celebrated his twenty-fifth birthday during the Second World War, and died during the height of the Vietnam War. A complex, questing soul, he sought solitude, silence, and detachment from the world in a Trappist monastery. Yet, especially toward the end of his life, he became more involved in social and political issues, including the antiwar movement. A devout Catholic, he explored Eastern religions, especially Zen Buddhism, and he always sought to emphasize the agreements rather than the differences between his and other faiths. His most obvious personal gift was his ability to write—with clarity, honesty, and vitality. He authored some fifty books, including poetry, journals, essays, and works on church history, the Bible, theology, and mysticism. His best-known book, the autobiographical *Seven Storey Mountain*, became an international best-seller: the warts-and-all story of his groping toward his spiritual vocation is a compelling one, and it touched a nerve with readers in America and other countries who were seeking some sort of meaning in life after the traumas of the Second World War.

With Merton we enter a world in which psychology and the psychoanalytic movement have made their mark. He is at home with Freudian terms such as *ego* and *id*, and his distinction between a false self and a true self recalls C. G. Jung's distinction between the persona and the Self. At the heart of Merton's spirituality lies the practice of contemplation. He stressed that contemplation is not synonymous with visions, trances, locutions, raptures, and the like, although they may accompany it. Rather, contemplation is "the union of the simple light of God with the simple light of our spirit, in love."[49]

Thomas Merton was born in Prades in the south of France in 1915. His father was from New Zealand and his mother was American. He suffered the loss of his mother when he was six, and his childhood was constantly disrupted by his artist father's moving from place to place in search of congenial locations in which to live and paint. Merton was educated at boarding schools in France and

MODERN VOICES

in England, where he later went to Cambridge University to study modern languages. His time at university turned out to be short and miserable. By this time his father had died of cancer and his only brother, John Paul, and his maternal grandparents lived thousands of miles away in America. Rootless and confused, Merton threw himself into a wild social life, to the neglect of his studies and the icy reproach of his English godfather and guardian. The final straw occurred when he seems to have gotten a girlfriend pregnant: he left Cambridge after a year's study and settled in America for good.

Merton continued his studies at Columbia University, where he blossomed and made strong friendships. In 1938 his unfulfilled and nagging religious instinct led him to become baptized as a Catholic and to aspire to enter a religious order. Three years later, having taught for a while in a Franciscan college in New York, he finally entered the Order of Cistercians of the Strict Observance, commonly known as the Trappists, at the monastery of Gethsemani near Louisville, Kentucky, where he would remain until his death.

The Trappist way of life was severe, a daily routine of prayer, meditation, reading, and manual work, with communication between the brothers conducted in sign language to preserve the silence. Gethsemani's abbot, however, recognized the gift Merton—or Brother Louis, as he was known—had for words, and he allowed him to continue his writing. In 1948 *The Seven Storey Mountain* was published to great acclaim, bringing Merton into the public eye. Further books on Christian spirituality added to his growing reputation; then in the 1950s his interests broadened to include Eastern religions and social and political issues. This change of direction inevitably alienated some of his earlier readers, but it also brought him a new following, especially in the 1960s during the Vietnam War, when many peace campaigners found inspiration in his writings.

Since his arrival at Gethsemani in 1941, Merton had not ventured from his monastery apart from occasional trips to Louisville for medical reasons. But in 1968, the last year of his life, his abbot allowed him to attend interfaith conferences in India and Thailand. Rejoining the world again, Merton savored the new sights and sounds and engaging with minds of other spiritual persuasions. On December 10, however, after giving a talk in Bangkok, he returned

313

to his room and was later found dead, lying on the floor, having been electrocuted, it seems, by a faulty electric fan.

During his life, Merton had at least two spiritual experiences that affected him profoundly. The first occurred while he was visiting Rome when he was eighteen. One night, in his hotel room, he suddenly felt the presence of his dead father "as vivid and as real and as startling as if he had touched my arm or spoken to me." In that moment he saw into the darkness of his own soul and was filled with revulsion and an intense desire to be liberated from his "misery and corruption." For the first time in his life he prayed to God with his whole being. The experience later seemed to him to be "a grace, and a great grace." It did not save him from his misspent time at Cambridge, but it was nevertheless a memorable landmark toward his spiritual vocation.[50]

The second experience happened in 1940 during a visit to Cuba. One Sunday, while attending Mass in Havana, he heard a group of children at the front of the church cry out the creed in joyful unison and was struck by a sudden awareness of God's presence: "It was a light that was so bright that it had no relation to any visible light and so profound and so intimate that it seemed like a neutralization of every lesser experience." He was sure he had received a divine illumination, and the first articulate thought he had was, "Heaven is right here in front of me: Heaven, Heaven!"[51] Yet in the midst of what appeared to be an extraordinary experience, Merton was also struck by the thought that the light was in fact "ordinary" and open to anybody.

Indeed, it was one of Merton's beliefs that contemplation was not something that only monks and other members of religious orders should practice. All Christians, whether they be monks, teachers, or nurses, single or married, are called to deepen their inner lives, to become "fused into one spirit with Christ in the furnace of contemplation," then benefit others with the fruits of their spirituality.[52]

Merton's thoughts on mysticism and contemplation are scattered throughout his works, including *The Ascent to Truth* and, especially, *New Seeds of Contemplation*. Merton approaches contemplation in different ways, trying to define it and to explain what it is *not* as much as what it is, as well as describing the necessary preparation

MODERN VOICES

for it. He says that contemplation is a type of spiritual vision but that it sees "without seeing" and knows "without knowing."[53] Elsewhere he refers to the "ignorance" of the "true mystic" being not "unintelligence but superintelligence" and says that although "contemplation seems to be a denial of speculative thought, it is really its fulfillment."[54] Contemplation involves dying to our old way of living and uniting our minds and wills with God "in an act of pure love that brings us into obscure contact with him as he really is."[55] Through union with God by love, the soul receives the "hidden" or "secret" knowledge of God.[56]

Fundamental to the practice of contemplation is the destruction of the false self and the emergence of the true self, which participates in God through Christ. The false self is the "I," or the ego, which deals with the outside world, with everyday life, and with which the individual usually identifies himself or herself to the exclusion of the true self. It is my "I" that dominates my life: insofar as I do things— wanting, loving, hating, eating, resting, thinking, and so on—it is my "I" that is in control, experiencing, evaluating, comparing. But in doing so the "I" is strengthened, dominating the personality, leaving no room for the true self, the real spiritual center, to develop and for contemplation to blossom: "As long as there is an 'I' that is the definite subject of a contemplative experience, ... we remain in the realm of multiplicity, activity, incompleteness, stirring and desire."[57]

The key to destroying the false self is humility, which, with faith, is the foundation of the contemplative life. It is pride that bolsters the ego, and it is humility that erodes this sense of self, allowing the divine to shine through. The more we abase ourselves—not through a deliberate process, which can lead to a false humility, but by a genuine abandonment of any sort of self-aggrandizement— the more likely we are to be filled with the happiness that comes with encountering God: "for the only way to enter joy is to dwindle down to a vanishing point and become absorbed in God through the centre of your own nothingness."[58]

Merton did not underestimate traditional attitudes toward, and preparations for, contemplation. Like the mystics of old, he stressed the importance of detachment, not just from material things, but also from more "virtuous" desires, such as for serenity and enlightenment. He also acknowledged to some extent the need

DAZZLING DARKNESS

for solitude and quiet, but he emphasized that they were strictly a means to an end: if solitude is regarded as a way of escaping the world and responsibilities, it cannot serve contemplation. True solitude is "an abyss opening up in the centre of your own soul." And the point of contemplation is that we share its fruits—the inner joy and peace—with others and not simply revel in them narcissistically in a remote cave or desert. Contemplation and the active life are complementary, but activities must be infused with the spiritual energy received in contemplation. Equally, contemplation must be nourished by the right kinds of activities, that is, those that fulfill God's will.[59]

Merton admits that the contemplative path can be long and testing, passing through a wilderness that has no vegetation, beauty, or water—for mysticism is all-demanding, embracing "the whole interior experience of the soul immersed in the Absolute."[60] Yet despite inevitably experiencing confusion and anxiety, the contemplative will sense that "peace lies in the heart of this darkness." Those that persevere will reach the promised land and "taste the peace and joy of union with God" and have "a habitual, comforting, obscure and mysterious awareness of ... God, present and acting in all the events of your life."[61]

EPILOGUE

> We ought not to be weary of doing little things for the love
> of God, Who regards not the greatness of the work, but the
> love with which it is performed.
>
> —Brother Lawrence

At the end of this survey of mystics of the past, it remains to consider briefly what the future holds for Christian contemplation in the twenty-first century. Since the 1960s there has been a considerable growth in the West of a variety of spiritual movements involving personal growth, which might suggest a need for Christian contemplation. Yet it is also clear that the churches have not been automatic beneficiaries of this growth. In the early 2000s a correspondent on religious affairs in the *Irish Times* wrote:

> There probably isn't a shopping centre in Ireland that doesn't have a shop selling incense, candles and statuettes of money frogs. The superfluity of mystic merchandise and fortune-tellers highlights a problem within Christianity. One has to ask why people feel they need the services of mediums, fortune-tellers and card-readers in the 21st century. As churches face dwindling memberships it seems strange that the thirst for matters spiritual is on the increase. In fact it is becoming obvious every day that these practices are replacing traditional religion in our society. The reason could lie in the fact that much of what is being preached by churches is *failing to satisfy the need for spiritual and mystical experience.*[1]

If this observation is true, how can the churches in the West nurture and satisfy the hunger for spiritual and mystical experience?

In fact, in recent times there have been a number of Christian grassroots initiatives that have attempted to address the apparent need for a more engaging and participative spirituality. Many of these movements tap into the Christian mystical tradition, emphasizing the importance of prayer, meditation, and contemplation. Together they may be seen as raising the water table of Christian spirituality, providing a genuinely fertile soil for individuals to grow inwardly toward God.

One such movement is that associated with the Burgundian village of Taizé, where Brother Roger Schutz (1915–2005) founded an ecumenical Christian community during the Second World War. Taizé has become one of the most successful spiritual movements in the West. Every year thousands of Christians from different denominations—from Roman Catholic to Eastern Orthodox— converge on Taizé to attend prayer meetings and talks, sing Taizé's distinctive simple and melodic songs, or meditate in silence. Visitors are then encouraged to return home and put Taizé's values, such as its emphasis on fruitful spiritual reflection and tolerance, into practice.

Similar to Taizé's values are those of the Christian community based on the island of Iona off the west coast of Scotland. In 1938, some 1,500 years after the Irish monk Columba established a monastic presence on the island, a Church of Scotland minister named George Macleod (1895–1991) founded the Iona Community, restoring the dilapidated medieval abbey and making it a center for retreats and programs of spiritual renewal. The community itself has an ecumenical flavor and is dedicated to inner devotion as well as to justice and peace in the world.

The success and popularity of Iona, which now attracts thousands of pilgrims each year, may be partly due to the modern phenomenon of what is called "Celtic Christianity," which has become increasingly popular since the 1980s. Advocates of Celtic Christianity emphasize what they believe to be a distinctive and ancient spiritual tradition, which includes laying great importance on: being aware of the natural world as God's creation; an openness to prophetic or mystical experiences; forms of worship centered around creativity, such as dance and poetry; and loose, informal organizational structures with equality between the genders. (It should be noted, however, that one scholar has argued that the concept of "Celtic Christianity" in modern times has come about

318

EPILOGUE

from a nostalgic or sentimental recasting of Celtic worship and culture based on meager evidence from the distant past.[2])

Pilgrims making their way to Iona are part of a wider pilgrimage movement that has seen a significant revival in modern times. It can be argued that pilgrimage is an exterior, physical equivalent to contemplation: both traditionally involve a number of similar stages, such as withdrawal from the everyday world, the journey to a spiritual center (a pilgrim shrine, or God), arrival, then return to the world. Shrines such as Lourdes in France and the basilicas of Our Lady of Guadalupe and Sainte-Anne-de-Beaupré in Mexico and Canada respectively, receive millions of pilgrims every year. The best-known pilgrimage in the West is arguably the "Camino," the pilgrimage to Santiago de Compostela in Galicia in northern Spain, where well-defined footpaths and numerous hostels help to attract tens of thousands of pilgrims every year.

The biggest-growing area of Christian spirituality in the West, however, may well be the retreat movement, where religious houses and organizations allow laypeople to spend a weekend or longer in peaceful surroundings to pray, read, and reflect on spiritual truths. There are now hundreds of retreat houses in America and Europe catering for different requirements. Some houses offer guided retreats, where a spiritual director will offer spiritual advice, and there are themed retreats, where an issue such as social justice forms the focus for discussion and reflection. Other houses allow participants simply to enjoy silence and the opportunity to read and pray. In some retreats, held in monasteries, visitors can sample the monastic lifestyle.

The spiritual movements and centers mentioned above are positive signs that Christianity is capable of renewing itself spiritually and that its long contemplative tradition still has relevance today—indeed some would say more relevance than ever. But it is noticeable that initiatives for stimulating interest in prayer and contemplation tend to be the result of one person's genius and dynamism and that they remain at the fringes of the churches, almost as if they were add-ons or extracurricular activities.

Yet surely the Christian mystical tradition should not be an optional extra. The experiences and teachings and example of the mystics are crucial to the prosperity, and perhaps even the survival,

DAZZLING DARKNESS

of Christianity. The greatest mystics, as this book has tried to show, demonstrate what it is to be fully Christian—and therefore fully human. They are outstanding examples of individuals whose love of and devotion to God is synonymous with their love of and devotion to humanity. Also, from Paul to Thomas Merton, they were almost without exception loyal members of the church, for whom the sacraments and liturgy were central.

So what in essence can the mystics teach us today? First of all that the spiritual and mystical way is holistic: it is a journey to ultimate reality that involves the whole person—mind, body, soul, the feelings, and the intellect. Mysticism is not simply a mental exercise or a series of physical exercises; nor is it a case of splitting ourselves off from the rest of humanity to find personal ecstasy in a cocoon of peacefulness. Periods of uninterrupted quiet may well be necessary to foster contemplative prayer, but the whole modus operandi of mysticism is engagement with both God and the world to the extent that they become synonymous. As Mechthild of Magdeburg said, taking care of natural, commonplace needs ranks as high in God's sight as the highest states of contemplation.[3]

The mystics also make it clear that ecstasy, the sense of engulfing peace and joy that comes with the awareness of the presence of God, plays a relatively small part in the totality of their spirituality. The crowning moments of rapture cannot be split off from what happens before and afterward in the mystic's life, which is essentially unitive: it cannot be a case of receiving divine illumination out of the blue and then carrying on as if nothing had happened.

True mystical experiences are divine blessings that deepen compassion and give a sense of otherworldly peacefulness, as well as physical energy. They are transformatory points that help to shift a person's life from habitual egotism to selflessness, and they rarely happen, if ever, ex nihilo. They require a spiritual commitment and discipline based on humility and faith, which, as the mystics remind us, form the cornerstone of contemplation; and the result of contemplation is love, a love that makes no distinction between great and small, rich or poor, worthy or unworthy. As Teresa of Ávila wrote: "The Lord does not look so much at the magnitude of anything we do as at the love with which we do it."[4] She is echoed by

320

EPILOGUE

Brother Lawrence, who said that "we ought not to be weary of doing little things for the love of God, Who regards not the greatness of the work, but the love with which it is performed."[5] The mystics teach us how to reach God not through clouds of joy and ecstasy and angelic choirs but through the deepening of love.

APPENDIX

POEMS INSPIRED BY THE MYSTICS

The following poems of mine took their inspiration from some of the mystics (indicated by square brackets) who feature in this book.

[Hildegard of Bingen[1]]

Hildegard and Volmar

We would be sitting in her room
Talking about an illness of the soul
Or inessentials of the day, or listening
To noises in the yard below
Then suddenly a puzzlement
Would creep up on her eyes
Tighten her lips into a patient smile
Or look of mildest irritation
As if she could not quite remember
Some herb, or novice.
I'd test her with a whispered question
And when she did not answer
I knew: her eyes would open deeper,
So blue and with a strange liquidity
As if the Rhine was flowing into them,
Her cheeks relaxing – and her mouth;
Her breathing rhythmic as a cat's,
Exhaling such a peacefulness
I'd hardly want to stir
But stilled my hands and feet
Embarrassed by my grossness
During these times of delicacy;
Within the walls of quietude
My senses opened up or deepened:

DAZZLING DARKNESS

The melancholy call of crows
A breeze escaping round the chapel
Steps fading on the flagstones
A boatman's solitary shout.
We sat alone in different worlds,
I'd watch the sun reduce
The shadow on the ledge
Or wonder where she was,
Perhaps revisiting that valley
So green in its particulars
The air was like the dust of emeralds.
I often questioned why the lord
Selected her not me.
Was it the purity of thought or heart?

And yet I was contented
With what this world provided me,
The river sweeping light downstream
The fragrance of ale, the touch
Of parchment, good ink and pen.
It might be minutes or an hour
Before the lustre left her eyes;
Her fingers were the first to move,
Then blinking, a deflating sigh,
Her look of momentary sadness,
A frown as now, returned to earth,
She attempted to forgive
My pouched world-weary eyes
As I attempted to forgive
Her journey to the indescribable
Which my obedient hand
Was scribbling down.

APPENDIX

[Marguerite Porete[2]]

Sinner

i.m. Marguerite Porete, died in Paris, 1 June 1310

Without a will no one can sin, she said.
Who cannot sin except the Lord?
We didn't want her dead

But she insisted on spreading lies
To simpletons and miscreants;
We had to stop her heresies.

Besides, she was a *pseudo-mulier*
Not fish or fowl, but smelling of them both
In the smoke that purified the square

Her face a wilting fleur-de-lys
Above the sackcloth of her body.
She had some dignity

Until the flames' red claws
Were gripping at her face
And carried out god's law –

Screeching like a thousand geese
The crowd let out a choral groan
When gold broke from her eyes.

But we were sanguine: the pyre
Released the soul she wanted god to enter
And sent it weeping to eternal fire.

That night we dumped her ashes in the Seine –
'Let her preach to fishes
About the will and its annihilation!'

Without a will no one can sin.
We did not sin: our will was god's.
Our work was holy doctrine

Our reasoning was unassailably strong,
We had a thousand years of learning.
Why did she swear that we were wrong?

DAZZLING DARKNESS

Unless her words were not her own —
Then whose? Who spoke that filth?
Who gave her that conviction

If not the devil? No one spouts
With that intensity unless mad, evil;
Or touched by god, which she was not.

We had to safeguard others from her yeast,
Her hatred for us. She had to die.
She had to die—so help me Christ.

APPENDIX

[Jan van Ruysbroeck[3]]

Groenendaal

He sits against a trunk and bends
His knees, a lectern for his book;
Thoughts fly and land like birds around
The glade, unless he makes them still,
When, as they say, a glow appears
Above his head and he reaches for
The spirit tree that's upside down
Its branches fanned towards the earth
Its roots in heaven, so he climbs
Till he can see–above the woods
Of Soignes–the very ends of earth,
Snail weavings of rivers, puddle lakes,
Cities like little castles; and below
A speck of life, a man–himself
His face upturned towards his gaze,
Both paralysed between two worlds
Each one unsure of where he is
Or where he wants to be just then
And waiting for the other to return.

DAZZLING DARKNESS

[John Tauler[4]]

Tauler

Domini canis, he dared
To sniff out the poor,
Administered; the bedside air

Of pestilence hissed
From each half-cautious door
Like malicious gossip.

No use his shining pulpit verses
To swollen heads with turnip tongues.
Yet just his coming, his cloaked darkness

Brought light
And gave the almost dead new lungs
And eyes of evening swallows, alert

Above the tipped horizon
Of fields of swaying radiance.

APPENDIX

[Julian of Norwich[5]]

Visiting Julian of Norwich

We left the glare, the creaking laughter
Of rooks outside the church; stepped in.
No movement, noise, disturbed the dust
Within the banners of light the sun
Shone through the lancets onto stone.

We always felt a presence there,
As if there were an unseen cat
Haloed in a ginger pool of warmth,
Or friendly ghost kneeling at the back.

We found ourselves tip-toeing
Towards her cell, its aperture
An open gate between two worlds.
A cough, a whisper of her name
Seemed a shouted imposition;
Her slow approaching silhouetted hood
Looked like the angel of death's.

She listened to our loose confessions
And tales of lust and petty thieveries
And violence at the hands of others
And let silence be the judge.

It was the words she never said,
The looks we never saw
That clambered through us
As we retreated, met the sudden day
And quickly slipped our penitence,
Relieved to see the sharp horizon,
The spire, the mill, the five-roads' cross,
While she dissolved again to shadow
And a world without circumference.

DAZZLING DARKNESS

[Richard Rolle⁶]

The Song of Richard Rolle

In thinning winter cloud the sun
Finds petals of a Yorkshire rose;
The chapel light softens the stone
Around his knees and calloused toes

And he is deep in holy fire–
Although his nose and fingers freeze
His heart's a furnace and transforms
His godly thoughts to melodies

Of such a sweetness he's impelled
To sing full-chested, eyes shut tight,
Propelling songs to paradise–
Cascades of them–so loud they might

Drown out the angels, wake the saints
As on the last day; yet these psalms
Which shake the galleries of heaven
Lie silent in his prayer-pressed palms.

APPENDIX

[John of the Cross[7]]

Dark Night of the Soul

What are the use of senses
That only magnify
The details of a cell
A cesspit in Toledo
Where jailers have the masks of monks
And beat with famished rage?
A blacker line
Frames the bolted door,
The touch of waste and stone,
Stench of straw, taste
Of sweat, dry body salt,
The sound of steps that mark
Patterns of persecution

Day after day
Or is it
Night after night?

Sometimes, without the stars,
The sun-dial's blade of shadow,
Time flies off from its rhythm
A sort of death, no less,
And in the emptiness
The desolation of nothing
The blindness of a box of night
My soul surges, escapes
The prison in the prison
Soars up and over new worlds
An eagle
Afloat on the breath of life
Like god above creation—

My loved one is the mountains
And lonely wooded valleys
Strange islands
Rushing streams
Whispering sensual winds.

331

DAZZLING DARKNESS

[Brother Lawrence[8]]

Winter Tree

i.m. Nicolas Herman (Brother Lawrence), d. 1691

The forest of Lorraine had died
Of cold; the air, too gripped for snow,
Had frozen tracks of boots to fossils.
He stood there all alone inside
The limbo of eighteen years of life,
Hung between a squandered past
And dread of future days, unfit
For soldiery, books, a wife.
He stared across the field: the tree
Was silhouetted like a gallows,
Its upraised fingers begging God
To start the world again, to free
The warmth. Then as the first snow fell
A realisation thawed his blood—
Though stripped and scourged to death the tree
Was holding tight in every cell
The forms of blossoms, fruits and leaves
All waiting to unfurl their colours
In depths of green. He smiled as if
He were the sun, in such relief
That against appearances and reason
Life can never be extinguished;
Frozen and starved of light it waits
And waits for the right unrolling season.

APPENDIX

[George Fox[9]]

Tobacco, Psalms and Bloodletting

I sometimes think back to my youth
Remembering the heavy sack of sin on my shoulders
And I bent double so it seemed
Across the fields, with scarecrows hung on crosses,
Along straight roads that led to nowhere,
Weighed down in ditches, barns, the hollow trees I slept in;
And how I searched like a pig for acorns
For someone to administer the truth,
To take the sack away;
I tried two men of god:
The first one said *tobacco, that's your man,*
It will not rid you of your weight
But it is good for easing pain;
And you should also sing the psalms,
They will distract you from your ruminations;
How can you sing of Zion and think of sin?
The second holy man suggested *bloodletting,*
It rids the body of its pompous need for god's salvation.
That's what I thought about within
The forest of my transformation,
Spiders threading their rigging across wet blades of grass, *tobacco;*
The wren up-tailed and blown about, *psalms;*
King-cups and wild garlic by the marshy stream, *bloodletting;*

And then that queer old morning
There came the stripes of sun through trees,
Illuminating things by chance it seemed at first.
I stared at leaves, tufts of grass now tipped with fire,
And everything appeared to be connected,
The little bits of world ran into one another
And I was part of that confluence
Standing like an angel on a chequerboard of light
And in a trance or slowing down of time
I moved into another world
My heart unclenching, like a fist becoming hand;
It came to me that nothing need be pressed by sin
In the full opening of the heart,

DAZZLING DARKNESS

And with that realisation
Something like forgiveness poured in, or out,
My shoulders cast their burden off
My back at last began to straighten
And in a state of weightlessness I rose
High above the fields and villages of Leicestershire
High above the curious streets of Lichfield
High above the spires of London
And never really came back.

APPENDIX

[Seraphim of Sarov[10]]

Seraphim of Sarov

*(After a conversation between Nicholas Motovilov
and Seraphim in November 1831)*

The day was born in twilight,
grey above the forest glade,
the earth deepening with snow
as snow kept falling from the sky;
the fields pure white below the hill
beside the River Sarovka.
I sat on a stump opposite him;
all I could smell was fir trees.
'The only thing in life,' he said,
is to make ourselves a home
to welcome the holy spirit.
Nothing more. All else will follow.
Our souls use words for prayer,
but when the spirit descends
we must stay silent ...'
I glanced at him: imagine
staring at the centre of the sun
and there you see someone's face,
lips moving, eyes expressive,
and you hear a voice speaking,
feel your shoulders being held
by hands you cannot see;
in fact you do not even see yourself,
just a dazzling light, diffusing
and making the glade luminous
and the snowflakes layering the snow.
I felt such peace in my soul;
no words could express it.
And such warmth.
No words can express it.

pp. [xiii–20]

NOTES

PREFACE

1. From "The Pram Pusher's Tale," in Harpur, *Angels and Harvesters,* p. 40. Reproduced in Italian and English in *Il vento e la creta*, Venice: Molesini Editore Venezia, 2024.
2. Underhill, *The Mystics of the Church*, p. 17, quoted in Nuth, *God's Lovers* p. 13.

INTRODUCTION

1. Quoted in Happold, *Mysticism*, p. 38.
2. McGinn, *Foundations of Christian Mysticism*, p. xviii.
3. Nuth, *God's Lovers*, p. 15.
4. McGinn, *Foundations of Christian Mysticism*, p. xv.
5. Fallon and Riley, *Religion and Culture*, p. 33.

1. FIRST SEEDS

1. See Lindars, Edwards, and Court, *Johannine Literature,* p. 9ff.
2. Ferguson, *Mysticism and the Mystery Religions*, p. 125.
3. Shewring, trans., *The Passion of SS. Perpetua and Felicity,* p. 26.
4. Chadwick, *Early Church*, p. 56.
5. McGinn, *Foundations of Christian Mysticism*, p. 97.
6. Clement of Alexandria, *Miscellanies* 5.12, in Roberts and Donaldson, *Ante-Nicene Fathers*, vol. 2.
7. Ibid.
8. Williams, *Wound of Knowledge*, p. 26.
9. Quoted in Inge, *Christian Mysticism*, pp. 86–87.
10. McGinn, *Foundations of Christian Mysticism*, p. 104.
11. Clement of Alexandria, *Miscellanies* 7.10.
12. Ibid.
13. See McGinn, *Foundations of Christian Mysticism*, pp. 108–30; Louth, *Christian Mystical Tradition*, pp. 52–74.
14. McGinn, Meyendorff, and Leclerq, *Christian Spirituality*, p. 39.

337

NOTES pp. [21–37]

15. Origen, *On Prayer*, ch. 5. Translated by William Curtis.
16. Ibid., ch. 7.
17. Spencer, *Mysticism in World Religion*, p. 159.
18. Plotinus, *Enneads*, 4.8.1.
19. Quoted in O'Meara, *Plotinus*, p. 6.
20. Plotinus, *Enneads*, 1.6.9.
21. Ibid., 6.9.11.
22. Ibid.

2. DESERTS AND MONASTERIES

1. Louth, *Christian Mystical Tradition*, p. 98.
2. Quoted in Williams, *Wound of Knowledge*, p. 94.
3. Athanasius of Alexandria, *Life of St Anthony,* ch. 7, in Schaff and Wace, *Nicene and Post-Nicene Fathers*, vol. 4.
4. Benedicta Ward, *The Sayings of the Desert Fathers*, p.7.
5. Athanasius, *Life of St Anthony,* ch. 52.
6. Ward, *The Sayings of the Desert Fathers*, p. 3.
7. Pachomius, *The Rules of Pachomius*, Part I.
8. See Watts, *Riot in Alexandria*, p. 103.
9. Lent, *Life of Simeon Stylites*, p. 183.
10. MacCulloch, *A History of Christianity*, p. 208.
11. MacHaffie, *Her Story*, pp. 53–54.
12. Ibid., p. 56.
13. Margot H. King, "The Desert Mothers," p. 5.
14. Ward, *The Sayings of the Desert Fathers*, p. 230.
15. Ibid., p. 229.
16. Ibid., p. 230.
17. Ibid.
18. Ibid., p. 83.
19. Ibid.
20. Ibid., p. 84.
21. Castelli, Elizabeth A., "Pseudo-Athanasius," ch. 11.
22. Ward, *The Sayings of the Desert Fathers*, Syncletica, 1, p. 231.
23. Castelli, Elizabeth A., "Pseudo-Athanasius," chs. 110–113.
24. See Sophronius, *Life of Mary of Egypt* (online edition).
25. Ibid.
26. Gregory of Nyssa, *On Virginity*, ch. 11, in Schaff and Wace, *Nicene and Post-Nicene Fathers*, vol. 5.
27. Ibid.
28. Louth, *Christian Mystical Tradition*, pp. 81–83.

pp. [37–51]   NOTES

29. Gregory of Nyssa, *Life of Moses* 2:162–64, cited in Louth, *Christian Mystical Tradition*, p. 87.
30. McGinn, *Foundations of Christian Mysticism*, p. 151.
31. Evagrius, *On Prayer* 2, in Palmer, Sherrard, and Ware, *Philokalia,* vol. I.
32. Ibid., aphorisms 11, 23.
33. McGinn, *Foundations of Christian Mysticism*, p. 155.
34. See ibid., p. 147ff.
35. See Louth, *Christian Mystical Tradition*, pp. 102–10.
36. Evagrius, *On Prayer*, 71, in Palmer, Sherrard, and Ware, op. cit.
37. Sulpitius [Sulpicius] Severus, *Life of St. Martin*, ch. 3, trans. by Alexander Roberts, in Schaff and Wace, *Nicene and Post-Nicene Fathers of the Christian Church*, vol. 11.
38. Ibid., ch. 26.
39. Ibid., ch. 21.
40. Ibid., ch. 14.
41. Ibid., ch. 27.
42. Augustine, *Confessions*, 1.1, trans. Pine-Coffin.
43. See Augustine, *On the Trinity*, 8; McGinn, *Foundations of Christian Mysticism*, p. 245.
44. Augustine, *Confessions*, 7.10.16, trans. Pusey.
45. See McGinn, *Foundations of Christian Mysticism*, pp. 233–34.
46. E. R. Dodds, cited in Wakefield, *Dictionary*, p. 34: "Augustine of Hippo, St."
47. Augustine, *Confessions*, 9.10.23–24, trans. Pusey (translation slightly modernized by author).
48. Louth, *Christian Mystical Tradition*, 136.
49. See ibid., p. 137; McGinn, *Foundations of Christian Mysticism*, p. 254.
50. Augustine, *Literal Commentary on Genesis*, 12.26, quoted in Graeff, *Light and the Rainbow*, p. 203.
51. Frank Tobin, in Bartlett, *Vox Mystica*, p. 43.
52. See Butler, *Western Mysticism*, p. 103.
53. Ibid., pp. 81–83.

3.   THE EARLY MIDDLE AGES

1. Brown, *World of Late Antiquity*, p. 120.
2. Quoted in Harpur, *The Pilgrim Journey*, p. 41.
3. Fraser, *From Caledonia to Pictland Scotland to 795*, p. 96.
4. Adamnan, *Life of Columba*, ch. 17.
5. Ibid., ch. 21.
6. Ibid., ch. 3.
7. Harpur, *The Pilgrim Journey*, pp. 41–44.

NOTES

pp. [51–68]

8. Elva Johnston, in Flechner and Meeder, eds., *The Irish in Early Medieval Europe,* ch. 2.
9. Jonas of Bobbio, *Life of St. Columban [Columbanus],* ch. 56.
10. Harpur, *The Pilgrim Journey,* pp. 45–46.
11. Sheldrake, *The New SCM Dictionary of Christian Spirituality,* p. 117.
12. Pseudo-Dionysius (Dionysius the Areopagite), *The Complete Works,* p. 135.
13. Dionysius the Areopagite, *Divine Names,* ch. 3.
14. Cited by C. E. Rolt (trans), in Dionysius the Areopagite, *Mystical Theology,* p. 6.
15. Williams, *Wound of Knowledge,* p. 120 (his emphasis); and see McGinn, Meyendorff, and Leclerq, *Christian Spirituality,* p. 134.
16. Dionysius the Areopagite, *Mystical Theology,* ch. 2, trans. C. E. Rolt.
17. Ibid., ch. 1.
18. Ibid.
19. Ibid., ch. 5.
20. Brown, *World of Late Antiquity,* p. 134.
21. Gregory the Great, *Dialogues,* i., preface, quoted in Butler, *Western Mysticism,* 130.
22. Gregory the Great, *Moralia on Job,* 6.58, in Butler, *Western Mysticism.*
23. Gregory the Great, *Homilies on Ezekiel,* 2.5.9, cited in McGinn, *Growth of Mysticism.*
24. Ibid., 2.2.13.
25. Ibid., 2.2.12.
26. Gregory the Great, *Dialogues,* 2.35.
27. Gregory the Great, *Homilies on Ezekiel,* 40.17.
28. Ibid., 2.2.12.
29. Gregory the Great, *Moralia on Job,* 31.101.
30. John the Scot, *Periphyseon,* trans. Uhlfelder, Book 1, 1.
31. Luscombe, *Medieval Thought,* p. 35.
32. McGinn, *Growth of Mysticism,* p. 116.
33. Leff, *Medieval Thought,* p. 69.

4.   THE TWELFTH CENTURY

1. Quoted in Coulton, *Life in the Middle Ages,* p. 3.
2. Marks, *Stained Glass in England,* p. 111.
3. Licence, *Hermits and Recluses in English Society,* chs. 5 and 6.
4. Deanesly, *Medieval Church,* p. 119.
5. See Butler, *Western Mysticism,* pp. 154–80; McGinn, *Growth of Mysticism,* pp. 158–224.
6. Bernard of Clairvaux, *Sermons on the Song of Songs,* 23.15, quoted in Graef, *Light and the Rainbow,* p. 222.

340

pp. [68–78] NOTES

7. Bernard of Clairvaux, *Sermons on the Song of Songs*, 74.6, in *Selected Works*.
8. Ibid., 46.5.7; quoted in Butler, *Western Mysticism*, p. 158.
9. Bernard of Clairvaux, *Sermons on the Songs of Songs*, 57.8.
10. Bernard of Clairvaux, *On Loving God*, ch. 10, quoted in Butler, *Western Mysticism*, pp. 168–69.
11. Bernard of Clairvaux, *Sermons on the Song of Songs*, 18.6, quoted in Butler, *Western Mysticism*, p. 179.
12. Bernard of Clairvaux, *On Loving God*, 11:33, quoted in Williams, *Wound of Knowledge*, p. 114.
13. Thomas Merton, *In the Valley of Wormwood*, p. 336.
14. William of Saint Thierry, *The Golden Epistle*, p. 3.
15. Ibid., pp. 51–52.
16. See Ian P. Wei, *Twelfth-century Monasteries and Hugh of Saint Victor in Intellectual Culture in Medieval Paris*, p. 66.
17. William of Saint Thierry, *The Golden Epistle*, pp. 92–94.
18. See Anne Hunt, *The Trinity: Insights from the Mystics*, pp. 26–27.
19. Richard of Saint-Victor, *Benjamin Minor*, 73, quoted in McGinn, *Growth of Mysticism*, p. 404.
20. Richard of Saint-Victor, *The Mystical Ark* 1.6, trans. By Grover A. Zinn.
21. Ibid., 5.
22. McGinn, *Growth of Mysticism*, p. 413.
23. See abridgement in Happold, *Mysticism*, pp. 211–17, from Clare Kirchberger, trans., *Richard of St. Victor: Writings on Contemplation* (London: Faber and Faber, 1957).
24. Newman, *Sister of Wisdom*, p. 4.
25. Cited in Beer, *Women and Mystical Experience*, p. 28.
26. Hildegard, *Selected Writings*, translated by Mark Atherton, p. 9.
27. Ibid., p. 21.
28. Hildegard, *Scivias*, trans. by Hart and Bishop, p. 59.
29. Hildegard, *Selected Writings*, p. 4.
30. Dronke, *Women Writers*, p. 203.
31. Petroff, *Medieval Women's Visionary Literature*, p. 6.
32. Hildegard, *Selected Writings*, p. 60.
33. Quoted in Beer, *Women and Mystical Experience*, p. 28.
34. Hildergard, *Selected Writings*, pp. 9–10.
35. Newman, *Sister of Wisdom*, p. 247.
36. Hildegard, *Scivias*, trans. by Hart and Bishop, p. 67.
37. Hildegard, *Symphonia* No. 28, "O ignis Spiritus," translated by author. For the Latin original, see; http://www.hildegard-society.org/2014/11/o-ignis-spiriti-paracliti-sequence.html (last accessed 27/10/24).
38. Barbara J. Newman in the introduction to *Scivias*, trans. by Hart and Bishop, p. 25.

NOTES

pp. [78–97]

39. Victoria Sweet, "Hildegard of Bingen and the Greening of Medieval Medicine," pp. 381–403.
40. Hildegard, "O nobilissima viriditas," translated by author. For the Latin original, see: http://www.hildegard-society.org/2017/04/o-nobilissima-viriditas-responsory.html (last accessed 27/10/24).
41. Hildegard, *The Book of Divine Works*, 1.i., in *Selected Writings*, pp. 32–33.
42. See McGinn, *Growth of Mysticism*, pp. 333–36; Caroline Bynum Walker, Preface to *Scivias*, trans. by Hart and Bishop, pp, 2–3.
43. Christina of Markyate, *Life of Christina Markyate,* trans. by Talbot and edited by Fanous and Leyser, p. xiii.
44. Christina of Markyate, *Life of Christina of Markyate,* p. 9.
45. Ibid., p. xi.
46. Ibid., p. 117.
47. Ibid., p. 68.
48. Ibid., p. 37.
49. Ibid., p. 48.
50. Ibid., pp. 37, 39.
51. Ibid., p.77.
52. Ibid., 107, 111.
53. Katie Bugyis, "Envisioning Episcopal Exemption: The Life of Christina of Markyate," pp. 44–5.
54. Ibid., pp. 53–54.
55. Ibid., p. 54.

5. PREACHERS AND POETS: THE FRANCISCANS

1. Southern, *Church in the Middle Ages*, p. 273.
2. Ibid., p. 285.
3. Francis of Assisi, *Life of St. Francis*, ch. 13 in *The Little Flowers*.
4. Armstrong and Brady, introduction to *Francis and Clare*, p. 5.
5. Francis of Assisi, *Life of St. Francis*, ch. 12, in *The Little Flowers*.
6. Francis of Assisi, "Canticle of the Sun," in *Francis and Clare*, p. 39.
7. Quoted in Francis of Assisi, *Francis and Clare*, p. 19.
8. Robinson, *Writings of Saint Francis*, p. 150. Translation adapted by author.
9. Armstrong, *The Lady: Clare of Assisi*, p. 14.
10. McGinn, *Flowering of Mysticism*, pp. 65–66.
11. See Mueller, *Clare's Letters to Agnes*.
12. Ibid., 2:20, author's translation.
13. Armstrong, *The Lady: Clare of Assisi*, p. 52.
14. Bonaventure, *Life of St Francis*, p. 3.
15. Bonaventure, *Sentences* 35.1, quoted in Wakefield, *Dictionary*, p. 54.
16. Bonaventure, *Journey*, 4.3.

342

pp. [97–109]   NOTES

17. Ibid., 5.1.
18. Ibid., 7.6.
19. *The Threefold Way*, 1.17, quoted in Graeff, *Light and the Rainbow*, p. 236.
20. Underhill, *Jacopone da Todi*, p. 50. (Translations from the Italian in Underhill's book are by Theodore Beck.)
21. Ibid., p. 52.
22. Ibid., pp. 268–73.
23. Ibid., p. 269, translation adapted by author.
24. Ibid., pp. 356–61.
25. Ibid., p. 128.
26. Ibid., pp. 362–83.
27. Jacopone da Todi, *The Lauds*, trans. by Hughes and Hughes, pp. 265ff.
28. Ibid.
29. Underhill, *Jacopone da Todi*, p. 460.
30. Ibid., p. 469, translation adapted by author.
31. Dronke, *Women Writers*, p. 216.
32. Angela of Foligno, *Complete Works*, p. 302.
33. Ibid., p. 236.
34. Ibid., pp. 252–53.
35. Quoted in Underhill, *Mysticism*, p. 252 (translation slightly adapted by author).
36. Angela of Foligno, *Complete Works*, pp. 151–52.
37. Ibid., pp. 181–83.
38. Quoted in Underhill, *Mysticism*, p. 351.
39. Quoted in McGinn, *Flowering of Mysticism*, p. 151.

6. HOLY WOMEN: THE BEGUINES

1. Furlong, *Medieval Women Mystics*, p. 13.
2. Margot H. King, "The Desert Mothers: from Judith to Julian of Norwich," p. 4.
3. Southern, *Church in the Middle Ages*, p. 314.
4. McGinn, *Flowering of Mysticism*, p. 32.
5. Ibid., p. 321.
6. Bowie, *Beguine Spirituality*, p. 19.
7. Swan, *The Wisdom of the Beguines*, p. 2.
8. Matthew Paris, *Chronica Majora*, 4.278, quoted in Southern, *Church in the Middle Ages*, p. 319.
9. See Marie of Oignies, *Vita*. (Latin text by Jacques de Vitry. A translation of this by Margot King can be found in Mulder-Bakker, Anneke B., ed., *Mary of Oignies*).
10. Perrin, ed., *Women Mystics Speak*, p. 74.

343

NOTES pp. [109–118]

11. Translation by Kisha G. Tracy and Alicia Protze from "Life of Mary of Oegines (or Oignies)" in McNabb, *Medieval Disability Sourcebook,* p. 227.
12. Marie of Oignies, *Vita.*, 2.91.
13. Ibid., 1.25.
14. "Spirit of fear of the Lord," ibid., 2.43–49.
15. "Spirit of piety," ibid., 2.50–63.
16. "Spirit of knowledge," ibid., 2.64–72.
17. "Spirit of fortitude," ibid., 2.73–75.
18. "Spirit of counsel," ibid., 2.76-77.
19. "Spirit of understanding," ibid., 2.81-86.
20. "Spirit of wisdom," ibid., 2.87–92.
21. Quoted in Petroff, *Body and Soul,* p. 14.
22. Vision 7, cited in Malone, *Women and Christianity*, p. 147.
23. Letter 9, quoted in Petroff, *Body and Soul*, p. 61.
24. Letter 6 and Poems in Couplets 5 and 6, in Bowie, *Beguine Spirituality*, pp. 106, 98–99.
25. Letter 30, in ibid., p. 113.
26. Letter 6, in Malone, *Women and Christianity*, p. 146.
27. Letters 10 and 20, in Bowie, *Beguine Spirituality*, pp. 109, 112.
28. Letter 19, quoted in Petroff, *Body and Soul*, p. 61.
29. "Poems in Couplets" 13, in Bowie, *Beguine Spirituality*, p. 101.
30. "Poems in Stanzas" 17, in ibid., p. 120.
31. Mechthild of Magdeburg, *Flowing Light of the Godhead*, 5.13, in ibid, p. 74.
32. Mechthild of Magdeburg, *Flowing Light*, 5.32, trans. by Frank Tobin, p. 214.
33. *Flowing Light*, 1.2, in Beer, *Women and Mystical Experience*, p. 80.
34. Malone, *Women and Christianity*, p. 166.
35. *Flowing Light*, 1.44, quoted in Beer, *Women and Mystical Experience*, p. 94.
36. *Flowing Light*, 5.30, in Bowie, *Beguine Spirituality*, translations by Oliver Davies, p. 76.
37. Ibid., 5.4, p. 71.
38. Ibid., 1.26, p. 61.
39. Ibid., 1.23. p. 57.
40. Mechthild of Magdeburg, *Flowing Light*, 1.13, trans. by Frank Tobin. p. 47.
41. Ibid., 3.7, p. 113.
42. *Flowing Light* 5.4, in Bowie, *Beguine Spirituality*, p. 72.
43. Ibid., 1.35, p. 63.
44. *Flowing Light* 7.61, quoted in Beer, *Women and Mystical Experience*, p. 107.
45. Porete, *Mirror of Simple Souls*, ch. 118, trans. Colledge, Marler, and Grant, p. 140ff.

344

pp. [118–130]   NOTES

46. Ibid., ch. 51.
47. Ibid., ch. 13.
48. Ibid., ch. 121.
49. Ibid., ch. 68.
50. Ibid., ch. 29.
51. Ibid., ch. 6.
52. Porete, *Mirror of Simple Souls*, ch. 28, quoted in Dronke, *Women Writers*, p. 219.
53. McGinn, *Flowering of Mysticism*, p. 166.
54. Bowie, *Beguine Spirituality*, p. 86.
55. E. Rozanne Elder, in Bruun, ed., *Cambridge Companion to the Cistercian Order*, p. 209.
56. See de Ganck, trans., *Life of Beatrice of Nazareth*.
57. Veerle Fraeters, in Hollywood and Beckman, eds., *Cambridge Companion to Christian Mysticism*, p. 186.
58. Bowie, *Beguine Spirituality*, p. 89, translation by Oliver Davies.
59. Van den Dungen, *Beatrice of Nazareth*, p. 1; see also E. M. W. Pedersen, "Beatrice of Nazareth," in Schaus, ed., *Women and Gender in Medieval Europe*.
60. McGinn, *Flowering of Mysticism*, p. 168.
61. This summary of the seven stages is mainly based on Beatrice of Nazareth's *On Seven Ways of Holy Love* translated by Wim van den Dungen.
62. Bowie, *Beguine Spirituality*, p. 88.

7. MYSTICS OF THE RHINELAND

1. Quoted in Huxley, *Perennial Philosophy*, p. 125.
2. Quoted in ibid., p. 145.
3. Quoted in ibid., p. 358.
4. Eckhart, Sermon 12, in *Selected Writings*, p. 179.
5. Eckhart, Sermon 22, quoted in Stace, *Teachings of the Mystics*, p. 156.
6. Quoted in Huxley, *The Perennial Philosophy*, p. 51.
7. Eckhart, German Sermon 38, in *Selected Writings*, pp. 112–13.
8. German Sermon 2, in ibid., pp. 216, 221.
9. German Sermon 48, in ibid., pp. 135–36.
10. German Sermon 83, in ibid., p. 239.
11. German Sermon 52, in ibid., p. 204.
12. Eckhart, *The Talks of Instruction* 6, in ibid., p. 9.
13. Quoted in Huxley, *Perennial Philosophy*, p. 103.
14. The words of the medieval Dominican nun, Christina Ebner, quoted in Clark, *The Great German* Mystics, p. 39.
15. Tauler, *Spiritual Conferences*, Ch. 6, p. 153 ff.

345

NOTES
pp. [130–139]

16. Tauler, Sermon 11, in Woods, *Mysticism and Prophecy*, p. 114.
17. Tauler, Sermon 76, quoted in ibid., p. 115.
18. Tauler, *Spiritual Conferences*, Ch. 7, p. 172 ff.
19. Inge, *Christian Mysticism*, p. 186.
20. Ibid., p. 189.
21. Tauler, Sermon 7, in *The Inner Way*, pp. 63–64.
22. Quoted in Ferguson, *Illustrated Encyclopedia of Mysticism*, p. 190.
23. Tauler, Sermon 35, in *Inner Way*.
24. Quoted in Ferguson, *Illustrated Encyclopedia of Mysticism*, p. 191.
25. Suso, *The Exemplar*, p. 66.
26. Ibid.
27. Suso, *The Life of Blessed Henry Suso*, p. 20.
28. Quoted in Wakefield, *Dictionary*, p. 366.
29. Suso, *The Exemplar*, p. 198.
30. Ibid.
31. Suso, *The Life of Blessed Henry Suso*, p. 138.
32. Suso, *The Exemplar*, p. 314.
33. Suso, *Little Book of Truth*, p. 185, quoted in Zaehner, *Mysticism*, p. 21.
34. Warnar, *Ruusbroec*, p. 39.
35. Ruysbroeck, *The Spiritual Espousals,* p. xiii.
36. Quoted in Raitt, *Christian Spirituality*, p. 165.
37. Warnar, *Ruusbroec*, p. 7.
38. Ruysbroeck, *Spiritual Marriage*, 1.26. p. 47.
39. Ruysbroeck, *The Spiritual Espousals,* p. 71–72.
40. Ruysbroeck, *Spiritual Marriage*, 2.65. p. 151.
41. Ibid., 3.1. p. 170.
42. Ibid.
43. Ibid., 3.4. p. 178.
44. It should be noted that there has been scholarly debate as to whether Thomas was the author of the *Imitation of Christ*, but the consensus is that he was in all probability.
45. Bigg, in the introduction to his translation of the *Imitation*, p. xxxvii.
46. Ibid., pp. xxxviii-xxxix.
47. MacCulloch, *A History of Christianity*, p. 567.
48. Translated by Croft and Bolton, adapted by author.
49. Bigg, introduction to his translation of the *Imitation*, p. xli.
50. Kettlewell, *Thomas à Kempis and the Brothers of the Common Life*, pp. 358–360.
51. Ibid., p. 363.
52. Thomas à Kempis, *Imitation of Christ*, 2.12., translated by Croft and Bolton.
53. Ibid., 3.23.

pp. [140–155]   NOTES

54. Ibid., 1.23, translated by Bigg and adapted by author.
55. Ibid., 3.5, translated by Bigg.
56. Ibid., 2.4, translated by Croft and Bolton.
57. Ibid., 3.23.
58. Ibid., 3.34.
59. Ibid., 3.5, translated by Bigg.

8.   THE FLAME OF ENGLISH MYSTICISM

1. See Bernard McGinn, "The English Mystics," in Raitt, *Christian Spirituality*, p. 195.
2. Rolle, *Fire of Love*, trans. Wolters, ch. 5.
3. Ibid., ch. 29.
4. Ibid., ch. 39.
5. Rolle, *Fire of Love*, trans. Misyn, ch. 15.
6. Ibid.
7. Ibid., ch. 7.
8. Ibid., ch. 28.
9. Ibid.
10. Ibid.
11. Underhill, *Cloud of Unknowing*, introduction, p. 5.
12. Del Corra, "Female Authorship: Cloud of Unknowing."
13. Underhill (ed.), *Cloud of Unknowing*, ch. 53.
14. Ibid., ch. 3.
15. Ibid., ch. 5.
16. Ibid., ch. 9.
17. Ibid., ch. 37.
18. Ibid., ch. 4.
19. Ibid., ch. 20.
20. Hilton, *Ladder of Perfection* 1.4.
21. Ibid., 1.5.
22. Ibid., 1.8.
23. Ibid., 2.5.
24. Ibid., 2.32.
25. Ibid., 2.21.
26. Ibid., 2.24.
27. Julian of Norwich, *Revelation of Love*, ch. 27.
28. MacHaffie, *Her Story*, p. 56.
29. Julian of Norwich, *Revelation of Love*, ch. 4 and 7.
30. Ibid., ch. 37.
31. Ibid., ch. 29.
32. Quoted in Nuth, *God's Lovers*, p. 119.

NOTES

pp. [155–170]

33. Julian of Norwich, *Revelation of Love*, ch. 41.
34. Ibid., ch. 5.
35. Ibid., ch. 86.
36. Kempe, *The Book of Margery Kempe*, Bk. 1.1. I have used translations by W. Butler-Bowdon and B. A. Windeatt.
37. Ibid., 1.3.
38. Ibid., 1.30.
39. Ibid., 1.18.
40. Ibid., 1.35.
41. Ibid., 1.62.
42. Ibid., 1.35–36.
43. Ibid., 1.37.

9.   WOMEN MYSTICS OF ITALY AND SWEDEN

1. MacCulloch, *A History of Christianity*, p. 560.
2. Scott, *Medieval Europe*, p. 366.
3. Hay, *Medieval Centuries*, p. 138.
4. Birgitta of Sweden: *Life and Selected Revelations*, trans. Kezel, 6, p. 72.
5. Ibid., 10, p. 73.
6. Birgitta of Sweden: *Revelations of St. Birgitta*, trans. Searby, vol. 1, introduction, p. 8.
7. Ibid., vol. 2, p. 8.
8. Birgitta of Sweden: *Life and Selected Revelations*, trans. Kezel, 27, p. 78.
9. Ibid., 65, p. 92.
10. Morris, *St Birgitta of Sweden*, p. 140.
11. Quoted in Ferguson, *Illustrated Encyclopedia of Mysticism*, p. 37.
12. Underhill, *Mysticism*, p. 365.
13. Catherine of Siena, *Dialogue*, ch. 79, cited in ibid.
14. Catherine of Siena, *Dialogue*, ch. 4, in Graeff, *Light and the Rainbow*, p. 258.
15. Catherine of Siena, letters 189 and 226, cited in Woods, *Mysticism and Prophecy*, p. 103.
16. Catherine of Siena, *Dialogue*, ch. 63, trans. Suzanne Noffke.
17. Ibid., ch. 78, p. 145.
18. Underhill, *Mysticism*, p. 441.
19. Cited in ibid., pp. 181–82.
20. Quoted in Huxley, *Perennial Philosophy*, p. 122.
21. Catherine of Genoa, *Purgation and Purgatory*, p. 81.
22. Catherine of Genoa, *Spiritual Dialogue*, p. 109.
23. Cited in Underhill, *Mysticism*, p. 441.
24. Catherine of Genoa, *Purgation and Purgatory*, p. 81.

pp. [170–184] NOTES

25. Ibid., p. 72.
26. Ibid., p. 78.
27. Quoted in Huxley, *Perennial Philosophy*, p. 99.
28. Catherine of Genoa, *Spiritual Dialogue*, p. 109.

10. EASTERN ORTHODOX MYSTICISM

1. Runciman, *History of the Crusades*, Volume III, p. 123.
2. Lossky, *Mystical Theology*, p. 218.
3. Ibid., p. 227.
4. Kallistos Ware, "Prayer of the Heart," in Wakefield, *Dictionary*, p. 315.
5. French (trans.), *Way of a Pilgrim*, p. 56.
6. Chryssavgis, *John of Climacus*, pp. 18–19.
7. John Climacus, *The Ladder of Divine Ascent*, 27:47.
8. Ware, *The Inner Kingdom*, p. 97.
9. John Climacus, *The Ladder of Divine Ascent*, 29:2.
10. Ibid., 29:14.
11. Ibid., 30:35.
12. Ibid., 30:36.
13. Quoted in Spencer, *Mysticism in World Religion*, p. 227.
14. Quoted in Chadwick, *Early Church*, p. 211.
15. Palmer, Sherrard, and Ware, *Philokalia* vol. 2, p.173.
16. Ibid., p. 178.
17. Ibid., p. 240.
18. Ibid., p. 263.
19. St. Maximus the Confessor, *The Ascetic Life*, Polycarp Sherwood (ed.), p. 91.
20. Maximus the Confessor, *Selected Writings*, trans. by George Berthold, p. 36.
21. Ibid., p. 108.
22. Quoted in Sidney Spencer, *Mysticism in World Religion,* p. 229.
23. Ware, *The Orthodox Church*, p. 75.
24. Symeon the New Theologian, *Mystical Life*, vol. 2, p. 106.
25. Symeon the New Theologian, Homily 29.2, quoted in Lossky, *Mystical Theology,* p. 218.
26. Symeon the New Theologian, *Discourses*, pp. 364–65; Lossky, ibid., p. 226.
27. Symeon the New Theologian, ibid., p. 245.
28. Quoted in Lossky, *Mystical Theology,* p. 181.
29. Lossky, *Mystical Theology,* p. 209.
30. Symeon the New Theologian, *Discourses*, p. 80.
31. Ibid., p. 292.

NOTES pp. [184–204]

32. Ibid., pp. 187–88.
33. Symeon the New Theologian, *Mystical Life*, vol. 2, pp. 109–10.
34. Symeon the New Theologian, *Discourses*, pp. 219–20.
35. Symeon the New Theologian, Homily 19.2, quoted in Lossky, *Mystical Theology*, p. 219.
36. Lossky, *Mystical Theology*, p. 219.
37. Symeon the New Theologian, *Discourses*, p. 365.
38. Ibid., p. 236.
39. Gregory Palamas, quoted in Ware, *The Orthodox Church*, p. 77.
40. Quoted in Lossky, *Mystical Theology*, p. 72.
41. Quoted in Spencer, *Mysticism in World Religion*, p. 226.
42. Palamas, *Antirrhetic against Akindynos* 4.14.36, quoted in Raitt, *Christian Spirituality*, p. 213.
43. Palamas, Homily 16, quoted in Ware, *The Orthodox Church*, p. 77.
44. Palamas, *Triads* 1.3.47, quoted in Raitt, *Christian Spirituality*, p. 219.
45. Fedotov, *A Treasury of Russian Spirituality*, pp. 69–70.
46. MacCulloch, *History of Christianity*, p. 520.
47. Ibid., p. 61.
48. Strezova, *Hesychasm and Art*, p. 184.
49. Fedotov, *A Treasury of Russian Spirituality*, pp. 76–77.
50. Strezova, *Hesychasm and Art*, p. 185.
51. Fedotov, *A Treasury of Russian Spirituality*, pp. 80–81.
52. See Dobbie-Bateman, "St. Seraphim of Sarov," in Fedotov, ibid., pp. 246ff.
53. Ibid., p. 274.

11. MYSTICS OF SPAIN

1. Ignatius of Loyola, *Autobiography*, pp. 40–41.
2. Ibid., pp. 53–56.
3. Ibid., pp. 56–57.
4. Caraman, *Ignatius Loyola*, p. 52.
5. Ignatius of Loyola, *Spiritual Exercises*, p. 46.
6. Ibid., p. 36.
7. Teresa of Ávila, *Life of St Teresa*, ch. 20.
8. Quoted in Huxley, *Perennial Philosophy*, p. 115.
9. Teresa of Ávila, *Life of St Teresa*, ch. 11.
10. Ibid., chs. 14–15.
11. Ibid., chs. 16–17.
12. Ibid., ch. 18.
13. Teresa of Ávila, *Interior Castle*, 5.2., in *Complete Works*.
14. Ibid., 7.2.

pp. [204–228]   NOTES

15. John of the Cross, *Mystical Doctrine*, p. 130.
16. Quoted in Huxley, *Perennial Philosophy*, p. 100.
17. John of the Cross, *Ascent of Mount Carmel* 1.13, in *Complete Works*.
18. John of the Cross, *Mystical Doctrine*, pp. 144–45.
19. "Spiritual Canticle," stanza 14 (author's translation).
20. John of the Cross, *Dark Night of the Soul*, 1.9.4, in *Complete Works*.
21. John of the Cross, *Mystical Doctrine*, p. 104.
22. Ibid., p. 118.
23. Ibid., pp. 127–28.
24. John of the Cross, *Living Flame of Love*, stanza 2, in *Complete Works*.

12. PROTESTANT MYSTICS OF THE SEVENTEENTH CENTURY

1. In Harries and Mayr-Harting (eds), *Christianity*, p. 143.
2. See Rhodes, "Some Writings of a Seventeenth-Century English Benedictine."
3. MacCulloch, *A History of Christianity*, p. 652.
4. Quoted in Jordan, "Thomas Traherne," p. 382.
5. Husain, *The Mystical Element*, p. 20.
6. Weeks, *Boehme*, p. 40.
7. Ibid., p. 2.
8. Ibid., p. 218.
9. Quoted in Inge, *Christian Mysticism*, p. 278.
10. Boehme, *Of the Supersensual Life*, I, pp. 233–34, in Boehme, *Signature*.
11. Ibid., p. 243.
12. *Of the Supersensual Life* II, p. 247, in Boehme, *Signature*.
13. Ibid., p. 253.
14. Ibid., pp. 255–56.
15. Quoted in Husain, *The Mystical Element,* p. 21.
16. Kelleher, "Light thy Darknes is," pp. 47–64.
17. Husain, *The Mystical Element,* pp. 125–58.
18. Deane, *The Works of Love*, pp. 125–26.
19. Dury, *Music at Midnight*, p. 244.
20. Thompson, "Mysticism in Seventeenth-Century English Literature," p. 207.
21. Oliver, *Journal of English*, p. 354.
22. Quotations from Vaughan's work are taken from *Poems of Henry Vaughan*, edited by E. K. Chambers.
23. Durr, *Mystical Poetry of Henry Vaughan*, p. 9.
24. Post, *Henry Vaughan: The Unfolding Vision,* p. xv.
25. Fox, *Journal*, ch. 2.
26. Eamon Duffy, "Fox," in Wakefield, *Dictionary*, p. 156.

351

NOTES pp. [228–249]

27. Fox, *Journal*, ch. 1.
28. Ibid.
29. Ibid.
30. Ibid., ch. 2.
31. Ibid.
32. Ibid.
33. Bunyan, *Grace Abounding*, ch. 4.
34. Ibid., ch. 5.
35. Ibid., ch. 22.
36. Ibid., ch. 135.
37. Bunyan, *The Pilgrim's Progress* (1853 edition), First Stage.
38. Ibid., Sixth Stage.
39. Ibid., Tenth Stage.
40. Ibid.
41. In Julia J. Smith, "Thomas Traherne," *Oxford Dictionary of National Biography* (ODNB), online edition.
42. Clements, *The Mystical Poetry of Thomas Traherne*, p. 275.
43. Osmond, *The Mystical Poets*, 236.
44. In Smith, "Thomas Traherne," ODNB.
45. Traherne, *Centuries of Meditation*, 3, 17.
46. From "Rapture" parts I and II; poems quoted are from Traherne, edited by Dobell.
47. In Smith, "Thomas Traherne," ODNB.
48. Traherne, *Centuries of Meditation*, 3, 60.
49. Jordan, "Thomas Traherne," p. 402.
50. Traherne, *Centuries of Meditation*, 3, 16.
51. Ibid., 3.3.
52. Ibid., 2.78.

13. EARLY MODERN FRENCH MYSTICS

1. Daniel Didomizio, "French Spirituality," in Wakefield, *Dictionary*, p. 163.
2. Brémond, Henri. *A Literary History of Religious Thought*, p. 115.
3. Grant, *Images and Ideas*, p. 98.
4. Canfield, *Rule of Perfection*, p. 117.
5. Ibid., p. 23 and p. 54, with modified spellings.
6. See O'Donnell, "Apostolic Reflection."
7. Cited in Groschel, *I Am with You Always*, p. 238.
8. Bowles, *A Gracious Life*, p. 118.
9. Deville, *L'École française de spiritualité*, p. 37.
10. Thompson (ed.), *Bérulle and the French School*, p. 195.

pp. [249–263]   NOTES

11. Ibid., p. 33.
12. See Reid (ed.), *From Eucharistic Adoration to Evangelisation*, p. 9.
13. Quoted in Ferguson, *Illustrated Encyclopedia of Mysticism*, p. 63.
14. See Michael J. Buckley, "Seventeenth-Century French Spirituality," in Dupré and Saliers, *Christian Spirituality*, p. 35.
15. Francis de Sales, *Devout Life* 1.1.
16. Ibid., 2.2.
17. Ibid., 2.5.
18. Ibid., 2.6.
19. Ibid., 2.7.
20. Francis de Sales, *Treatise on Love*, 6.3, in Mursell, *Christian Spirituality*, p. 225.
21. Ibid., 6.9.
22. Lawrence, *Presence of God*, Second Letter.
23. Ibid., First Conversation.
24. Ibid., Fourth Conversation.
25. Ibid., Second Conversation.
26. Pascal, *Pensées*, 913, trans. by A. J. Krailsheimer. Note: the numbering of the *Pensées* differs in different translations.
27. *Pensées*, 17, in *Pascal's Pensées*, trans. by W. F. Trotter.
28. Ibid., 66.
29. Ibid., 205.
30. Ibid., 206.
31. Ibid., 194.
32. Ibid., 278.
33. Ibid., 552.
34. Ibid.
35. Ibid.
36. Guyon, *Autobiography*, part 1, ch. 8.
37. See Louis Dupré, "Jansenism and Quietism," in Dupré and Saliers, *Christian Spirituality*, pp. 136–37.
38. Fénelon, *Maxims of the Saints*, article 30, p. 45.
39. Ibid., article 45, pp. 58–60.
40. Quoted in "Fénelon," Wakefield, *Dictionary*, p. 150.
41. Fénelon, *Maxims of the Saints*, article 5, p. 14.
42. Ibid., article 36, p. 52.
43. Ibid., article 3, p. 12.
44. Ibid., article 35, p. 52.

14. LIGHT AND REASON

1. Wulf, *Magnificent Rebels*, p. 12.

353

NOTES pp. [264–281]

2. Jane Shaw, in Harries and Mayr-Harting (eds), *Christianity*, p. 173.
3. Quoted in Bainton, *Penguin History of Christianity*, p. 218.
4. Quoted in Graeff, *Light and the Rainbow*, p. 382.
5. De Caussade, *Present Moment*, p. 31.
6. De Caussade, *Abandonment to Divine Providence*, 1.2.3.
7. Ibid., 1.2.7.
8. Ibid., 1.2.1.
9. Ibid., 1.2.8–10.
10. De Caussade, *Present Moment*, p. 25.
11. De Caussade, *Abandonment to Divine Providence*, 2.2.6.
12. Ibid., 2.2.7.
13. Ibid.
14. Sampson, *History of English Literature*, p. 409.
15. Law, *Spirit of Love*, 2.3.78.
16. Law, *Spirit of Prayer*, 1.2.8.
17. Law, *Spirit of Love*, 2.3.33.
18. Law, *Spirit of Prayer*, 1.2.10.
19. Ibid., 1.2.16.
20. Ibid.
21. Ibid., 1.2.52.
22. Law, *Spirit of Love*, 2.3.37.
23. Quoted in Huxley, *Perennial Philosophy*, p. 114.
24. Law, *Spirit of Love*, 2.3.49–50.
25. Ibid., 2.3.46.
26. Parrinder, *Mysticism*, p. 158.
27. Quoted in McManners (ed.), *Oxford History of Christianity*, p. 303.
28. Wesley, *Journal*, May 25, 1738.
29. Quoted in Bainton, *Penguin History of Christianity*, pp. 219–20.

15. ROMANTICS, NATURE MYSTICS, AND TRANSCENDENTALISTS

1. Wulf, *Magnificent Rebels*, p. 10.
2. Quoted in Mursell, *Christian Spirituality*, p. 189 (author's emphasis).
3. Quoted in Ferguson, *Illustrated Encyclopedia of Mysticism*, p. 134.
4. Coleridge, *Biographia Literaria*, ch. 9.
5. Wiley, *Angels and Troublemakers*, p. 17.
6. Sampson, *History of English Literature*, p. 490.
7. Ackroyd, *Blake*, p. 23.
8. Letter to Thomas Butts, January 10, 1802, in Blake, *Selected Poems*, p. 297.
9. Blake, "The Garden of Love," in *Selected Poems*, p. 65.

pp. [281–298] NOTES

10. Blake, "Mock on, mock on, Voltaire, Rousseau," from "Poems from the Rossetti Ms.," in *Selected Poems*, p. 79.
11. Blake, opening to "Auguries of Innocence," in *Selected Poems*, p. 107.
12. See prose note to "A Vision of the Last Judgment" in "Poems from the Rossetti Ms.," in the *Complete Poetry and Prose of William Blake*, edited by David V. Erdman, p. 554.
13. Blake, "To the Christians," from *Jerusalem*, in *Selected Poems*, p. 251.
14. Blake, "The Marriage of Heaven and Hell," in *Selected Poems*, p. 146.
15. Quoted in Underhill, *Mysticism*, p. 259.
16. From "Descriptive Catalogue," in Blake, *Selected Poems*, p. x.
17. To Thomas Butts, November 22, 1802 in Erdman (ed.), *The Complete Poetry & Prose of William Blake*, p. 721.
18. To Thomas Butts, October 2, 1800 in ibid., pp. 711–714.
19. Quoted by Northrop Frye, in Abrams, *English Romantic Poets*, p. 60.
20. Blake, lines from "Jerusalem," in *Poems of William of Blake*, p. 56.
21. Inge, *Christian Mysticism*, p. 307.
22. Wordsworth, "The Pedlar," ll. 104–106.
23. "Tintern Abbey," ll. 43–49.
24. Ibid., ll. 93–102.
25. Richardson, *Emerson*, p. 162.
26. Emerson, *Emerson in his Journals,* p. 122.
27. *Essays Series One*, Ch. IX, in Emerson, *The Portable Emerson,* pp. 210–225.
28. Emerson, *Nature*, ch. 7.
29. Ibid., ch. 1.
30. Ibid., ch. 8.
31. Ibid., ch. 8.
32. Thoreau, *Walden*, ch. 18.
33. Thoreau, "Letter to Harrison Blake," April 3, 1850, in *Familiar Letters,* p. 178.
34. Thoreau, *Walden*, ch. 2.
35. Ibid.
36. Ibid., ch. 5.
37. James, *Varieties of Religious Experience*, p. 275.
38. Thoreau, *Walden*, Ch. 18.
39. Ibid.

16. MODERN VOICES

1. Owen Chadwick, "Science and Religion," in McManners (ed.), *Oxford History of Christianity*, pp. 352–53.
2. Hampson, *Enlightenment*, p. 278.

NOTES   pp. [300–310]

3. Thérèse of Lisieux, *Soeur Thérèse of Lisieux*, "Epilogue: A Victim of Divine Love."
4. Ibid., ch. 7, "The Little Flower Enters the Carmel."
5. Ibid.
6. Ibid., "Epilogue: A Victim of Divine Love."
7. Thérèse of Lisieux, *Story of a Soul*, p. 63.
8. Thérèse of Lisieux, *Soeur Thérèse of Lisieux*, ch. 9, "The Night of the Soul."
9. Thérèse of Lisieux, *Story of a Soul*, p. 243.
10. Thérèse of Lisieux, *Soeur Thérèse of Lisieux*, Letter 14, "To Celine."
11. Thérèse of Lisieux, *Story of a Soul*, p. 234.
12. Thérèse of Lisieux, *Soeur Thérèse of Lisieux*, ch. 9, "The Night of the Soul."
13. Ibid.
14. Antier, *Charles de Foucauld*, p. 154.
15. Charles de Foucauld, *Writings*, selected by Robert Ellsberg, p. 14.
16. Antier, *Charles de Foucauld*, p. 93.
17. Ibid., p, 97.
18. Ibid., pp. 98–102.
19. Ibid., p. 112.
20. Charles de Foucauld, *Writings*, selected by Robert Ellsberg, p. 41.
21. Antier, *Charles de Foucauld*, p. 152.
22. Bazin, *Charles de Foucauld*, p. 297.
23. Preminger, *The Sands of Tamanrasset*, p. 273.
24. Teilhard de Chardin, *Le Milieu Divin*, p. 13.
25. Ibid., p. 123.
26. Ibid., p. 117.
27. From "Christ in the World of Matter," in Teilhard de Chardin, *Hymn of the Universe*, p. 41.
28. Teilhard de Chardin, Pensée 15, in *Hymn of the Universe*, p. 81.
29. Teilhard de Chardin, *Le Milieu Divin*, p. 112.
30. Ibid., pp. 106–7.
31. Ibid., pp. 21–22; Teilhard de Chardin, Pensée 13, in *Hymn of the Universe*, p. 80.
32. Teilhard de Chardin, *Le Milieu Divin*, p. 37.
33. Teilhard de Chardin, *Phenomenon of Man*, p. 251.
34. Teilhard de Chardin, *Le Milieu Divin*, p. 38.
35. Ibid., p. 144.
36. Teilhard de Chardin, Pensée 9, in *Hymn of the Universe*, p. 77.
37. Teilhard de Chardin, *Le Milieu Divin*, p. 86.
38. Weil, *Waiting for God*, p. 198.
39. Ibid., p. 67–68.
40. Ibid., p. 68–69.
41. Weil, *Gravity and Grace*, p. 76.

NOTES

pp. [310–335]

42. Ibid., p. 77.
43. Weil, *Waiting for God*, p. 97.
44. Ibid., pp. 71–72.
45. Ibid., p. 97.
46. Ibid., p. 171.
47. Ibid., p. 98.
48. Weil, *Waiting for God*, p. 159.
49. Merton, *New Seeds of Contemplation*, p. 189.
50. Merton, *Seven Storey Mountain*, pp. 138–39.
51. Ibid., pp. 341–42.
52. Ibid., p. 501.
53. Merton, *New Seeds of Contemplation*, p. 13.
54. Merton, *Ascent to Truth*, p. 44.
55. Merton, *New Seeds of Contemplation*, pp. 13, 144.
56. Merton, *Ascent to Truth*, p. 46.
57. Merton, *New Seeds of Contemplation*, p. 181.
58. Ibid., p. 125.
59. Ibid., pp. 130–31.
60. Merton, *Ascent to Truth*, p. 46.
61. Merton, *New Seeds of Contemplation*, pp. 156–58.

EPILOGUE

1. "Thinking Anew," *Irish Times*, October 25, 2003 (author's emphasis).
2. Bradley, *Celtic Christianity*.
3. Mechthild of Magdeburg, *Flowing Light*, 1.27.
4. Teresa of Ávila, *Interior Castle* 7.4, quoted in Graeff, *Light and the Rainbow*, p. 331.
5. Lawrence, Fourth Conversation, in *Presence of God*, p. 21.

APPENDIX

1. Harpur, *Angels and Harvesters*, p. 57.
2. Ibid., p. 52; Harpur, *Il venta e la creta*, p. 126.
3. Harpur, *Angels and Harvesters*, p. 37.
4. Ibid., p. 54.
5. Ibid., p. 49.
6. Ibid., p. 51.
7. Ibid., p. 59.
8. Ibid., p. 61.
9. Ibid., p. 55.
10. Harpur, *The White Silhouette*, p. 91.

BIBLIOGRAPHY

Abrams, M. H., ed. *English Romantic Poets: Modern Essays in Criticism*. New York: Oxford University Press, 1960.

Ackroyd, Peter. *Blake*. London: Minerva, 1996.

Adamnan. *Life of Columba*. Edited by William Reeves. Edinburgh: Edmonton and Douglas, 1874.

Angela of Foligno. *Angela of Foligno: Complete Works*. Translated by Paul Lachance. New York: Paulist Press, 1993.

Antier, Jean-Jacques. *Charles de Foucauld*. Translated by Julia Shirek Smith. San Francisco: Ignatius Press, 1999.

Armstrong, Regis. J., ed. and trans. *The Lady: Clare of Assisi: Early Documents*. New City Press: New York, rev. ed., 2006.

Augustine. *The Confessions*. Translated by R. S. Pine-Coffin. Harmondsworth, UK: Penguin Books, 1961.

————. *The Confessions*. Translated by E. B. Pusey. New York: J. M. Dent and Sons, 1953.

Bainton, Roland. *The Penguin History of Christianity*. Harmondsworth, UK: Penguin Books, 1967.

Baker, Augustine. *Holy Wisdom*. Edited by Serenus Cressy and Abbot Sweeney. London: Burns & Oates, 1911.

Bartlett, Anne Clark, ed. *Vox Mystica: Essays on Medieval Mysticism*. Cambridge: D. S. Brewer, 1995.

Bazin, René. *Charles de Foucauld: Hermit and Explorer*. Translated by Peter Keelan. New York: Benziger Brothers, 1923.

Beatrice of Nazareth. *On Seven Ways of Holy Love*. Translated by Wim van den Dungen. Taurus Books, 2016. Available at: http://www.sofiatopia.org/equiaeon/7ways.htm (last accessed 27/10/24).

Beer, Frances. *Women and Mystical Experience in the Middle Ages*. Woodbridge, UK: Boydell Press, 1992.

Bernard of Clairvaux. *Selected Works*. Translated by G. R. Evans. New York: Paulist Press, 1987.

BIBLIOGRAPHY

Birgitta of Sweden. *Life and Selected Revelations*. Translated by Albert Ryle Kezel. Edited by Marguerite Tjader Harris. New York: Paulist Press, 1990.

————. *The Revelations of St. Birgitta of Sweden, Vols. 1 and 2*. Translated by Denis Searby. Edited by Bridget Morris. Oxford: Oxford University Press, 2006.

Blake, William. *Selected Poems of William Blake*. Oxford: Oxford University Press, 1927.

————. *Poems of William Blake*. Selected and introduced by Peter Ackroyd. London: Sinclair-Stevenson, 1995.

————. *The Complete Poetry and Prose of William Blake*. Edited by David V. Erdman. Newly rev. ed. New York: Anchor-Random House, 1988.

Boehme, Jacob. *The Signature of All Things and Other Writings*. Cambridge: James Clarke and Co., 1969.

Bolshakoff, Sergius. *Russian Mystics*. Kalamazoo, MI: Cistercian Publications, 1977.

Bonaventure. *The Mind's Road to God*. Translated by George Boas. New York: Library of Liberal Arts, 1953.

————. *Life of St Francis*. Translated by E. Gurney Salter. London: J.M. Dent, 1904.

Bowie, Fiona, ed. *Beguine Spirituality: an Anthology*. Translations by Oliver Davies. London: SPCK, 1989.

Bowker, John, ed. *Dictionary of World Religions*. Oxford: Oxford University Press, 1997.

Bowles, Emily. *A Gracious Life: Being the Life of Barbara Acarie (Blessed Mary of the Incarnation)*. London: Burns and Oates, 1879.

Bradley, Ian. *Celtic Christianity: Making Myths and Creating Dreams*. New York: St Martin's, 1999.

Bremond, Henri. *A Literary History of Religious Thought in France from the Wars of Religion Down to Our Own Times, Volume 2: the Coming of Mysticism (1590–1620)*. London: SPCK, 1930.

Bridget of Sweden, see Birgitta of Sweden.

Brown, Peter. *The World of Late Antiquity*. London: Thames and Hudson, 1971.

Bruun, Mette Birkedal, ed. *The Cambridge Companion to the Cistercian Order*. Cambridge: Cambridge University Press, 2013.

Bugyis, Katie. "Envisioning Episcopal Exemption: The Life of Christina of Markyate." *Church History*, vol. 84, no. 1, 2015, pp. 32–63.

360

BIBLIOGRAPHY

Bunyan, John. *Grace Abounding to the Chief of Sinners*. London: The Religious Tract Society, 1905.

———. *The Pilgrim's Progress From This World to That Which is to Come*. Buffalo: Geo. H. Derby and Co. 1853.

———. *The Pilgrim's Progress*. Edited by Roger Sharrrock. Harmondsworth: Penguin Books, 1987.

Butler, Cuthbert. *Western Mysticism*. 2nd ed. London: Arrow Books, 1960.

Canfield, Benet. *The rule of perfection contayning a breif and perspicuous abridgement of all the wholle spirituall life, reduced to this only point of the (will of God)*. Early English Books Online, at https://quod.lib.umich.edu/e/eebo/A68048.0001.001/1:8.1.8?rgn=div3;view=toc (last accessed 27/10/24).

Caraman, Philip. *Ignatius Loyola*. London: Collins, 1990.

Castelli, Elizabeth A. "Pseudo-Athanasius: the Life and Activity of the Holy and Blessed Teacher Syncletica," in *Ascetic Behavior in Greco-Roman Antiquity: A Sourcebook*. Edited by Vincent Wimbush. Minneapolis: Fortress, 1990.

Catherine of Genoa. *Purgation and Purgatory, The Spiritual Dialogue*. Translated by Serge Hughes. New York: Paulist Press, 1979.

Catherine of Siena. *Catherine of Siena: The Dialogue*. Translated by Suzanne Noffke. New York: Paulist Press, 1980.

Chadwick, Henry. *The Early Church*. Rev. ed. London: Penguin Books, 1993.

Chryssavgis, John. *In the Heart of the Desert: The Spirituality of the Desert Fathers and Mothers* (rev. ed.). Bloomington, Indiana: World Wisdom, 2008.

———. *John Climacus: From the Egyptian Desert to the Sinaite Mountain*. New York: Routledge, 2016.

Christina of Markyate. *The Life of Christina Markyate*. Translated by C. H. Talbot. Edited by Samuel Fanous and Henrietta Leyser. Oxford: Oxford University Press, 2008.

Clark, James M. *The Great German Mystics: Eckhart, Tauler, and Suso*. Oxford: Basil Blackwell, 1949.

Clements, A. L. *The Mystical Poetry of Thomas Traherne*. Cambridge, Mass.: Harvard University Press, 1969.

Coleman, T. W. *English Mystics of the Fourteenth Century*. London: Epworth Press, 1938.

Coleridge, Samuel Taylor. *Biographia Literaria*. London: Dent, 1965.

BIBLIOGRAPHY

Coulton, G. G., *Life in the Middle Ages*. New York: Macmillan, 1931.

Cox, Michael. *Mysticism: The Direct Experience of God*. Wellingborough, UK: Aquarian Press, 1983.

Davis, Natalie Zemon. *Women on the Margins: Three Seventeenth-century Lives*. Cambridge, Mass: Harvard University Press, 1995.

Deane, John F. *The Works of Love: Incarnation, Ecology and Poetry*. Dublin: The Columba Press, 2010.

Deanesly, Margaret. *A History of the Medieval Church: 590–1500*. London: Methuen, 1973.

de Beausobre, Julia. *Flame in the Snow: A Life of St. Serafim of Sarov*. Springfield, Il: Templegate, 1996.

de Caussade, Jean Pierre. *Abandonment to Divine Providence*. Translated by E. J. Strickland. St. Louis, MO: B. Herder Book Co., 1921.

———. *The Sacrament of the Present Moment*. Translated by K. Muggeridge. London: Fount Paperbacks, 1981.

de Foucauld, Charles. *Charles de Foucauld: Writings*. (Modern Spiritual Masters). Selected and with an Introduction by Robert Ellsberg. New York: Orbis Books, 1998.

de Ganck, Roger, trans. *The Life of Beatrice of Nazareth*. (Cistercian Fathers Series, 50). Kalamazoo, MI: Cistercian Publications, 1991.

del Corra, Ana Salto Sánchez, "Female Authorship: Cloud of Unknowing," in *Revista de Antropología y Filosofía de lo Sagrado* (*Review of Anthropology and Philosophy of the Sacred*) Vol 5. No. 1, (2021) pp.: 119–138.

Deville, Raymond. *L'École française de spiritualité*. Paris: Desclée de Brouwer, 2008.

Dionysius the Areopagite. *The Divine Names and The Mystical Theology*. Translated by C. E. Rolt. London: SPCK, 1940. See also "Pseudo-Dionysius."

Dronke, Peter. *Women Writers of the Middle Ages*. Cambridge: Cambridge University Press, 1984.

Drury, John. *Music at Midnight: The Life and Poetry of George Herbert*. London: Allen Lane, 2013.

Dupré, Louis, and Don E. Saliers, eds. *Christian Spirituality III: Post-Reformation and Modern*. New York: Crossroad, 1989.

Durr, R. A. *On the Mystical Poetry of Henry Vaughan*. Cambridge, Mass: Harvard University Press, 1962.

Eckhart, Meister. *Selected Writings*. Translated by Oliver Davies. London: Penguin Books, 1994.

Emerson, Ralph Waldo. *Nature*. Boston: James Munroe, 1849.

BIBLIOGRAPHY

————. *Emerson in his Journals*. Edited by Joel Porte. Cambridge, Mass: Harvard University Press, 1982.

————. *The Portable Emerson*. Edited by Jeffrey S. Kramer. New York: Penguin Books, 2014.

Erdman, David V., ed. *The Complete Poetry and Prose of William Blake*. Newly rev. ed. New York: Anchor-Random House, 1988.

Evdokimov, Paul. "Saint Seraphim: An Icon of Orthodox Spirituality," *Ecumenical Review* 15:3, April 1963.

Fallon, Timothy P., and Riley, Philip Boo, eds. *Religion and Culture: Essays in Honor of Bernard Lonergan, SJ*. Albany: State University of New York Press, 1987.

Fanning, Steven. *Mystics of the Christian Tradition*. London: Routledge, 2001.

Fanous, Samuel, and Leyser, Henrietta, eds. *Christina of Markyate: A Twelfth-Century Holy Woman*. New York: Routledge, 2005.

Fedotov, G. P., ed. *A Treasury of Russian Spirituality*. London: Sheed and Ward, 1952.

Fénelon, Archbishop François. *The Maxims of the Saints*. London: H. R. Allenson, 1903.

Ferguson, John. *An Illustrated Encyclopedia of Mysticism and the Mystery Religions*. London: Thames and Hudson, 1976.

Flechner, Roy, and Sven Meeder, eds. *The Irish in Early Medieval Europe: Identity, Culture and Religion*. New York: Palgrave, 2016.

Forman, Robert K. C. *Meister Eckhart: Mystic as Theologian*. Shaftesbury, UK: Element, 1991.

Fox, George. *Journal*. Edited by Rufus M. Jones. New York: Capricorn Books, 1963.

Francis de Sales. *Introduction to the Devout Life*. Translated by John K. Ryan. New York: Image Books, 1972.

————. *Treatise on the Love of God*. Translated by Henry Benedict Mackey. Rockford, IL: Tan Books, 1997.

Francis of Assisi. *Francis and Clare: The Complete Works*. Translated by Regis J. Armstrong and Ignatius C. Brady. New York: Paulist Press, 1982.

————. *The Little Flowers of St. Francis, The Mirror of Reflection, The Life of St. Francis*. London: J. M. Dent, 1910.

Fraser, James E. *From Caledonia to Pictland Scotland to 795*. Edinburgh: Edinburgh University Press, 2009.

French, R. M., trans. *The Way of a Pilgrim*. London: SPCK, 1941.

Furlong, Monica. *Medieval Women Mystics*. London: Mowbray, 1966.

BIBLIOGRAPHY

Gascoigne, Bamber. *The Christians*. London: Granada, 1978.

Glasscoe, Marion. *English Medieval Mystics: Games of Faith*. Harlow: Longman, 1993.

Graeff, Hilda. *The Light and the Rainbow*. London: Longmans, Green and Co., 1959.

Grant, Patrick. *Images and Ideas in the Literature of the English Renaissance*. London: Macmillan, 1979.

Greenberg, Mitchell. *Baroque Bodies: Psychoanalysis and the Culture of French Absolutism*. Ithaca: Cornell University Press, 2001.

Groschel, Benedict. *I Am with You Always: A Study of the History and Meaning of Personal Devotion to Jesus Christ*. San Francisco: Ignatius Press, 2010.

Guyon, Madame. *Autobiography of Madame Guyon*. Chicago: Moody Press, 1985.

Harpur, James. *Angels and Harvesters*. London: Anvil Press, 2012.

————. *The Pilgrim Journey*. New York: BlueBridge, 2016.

————. *The White Silhouette*. Manchester: Carcanet Press, 2018.

————. *Il vento e la creta*. Translated by Francesca Diano. Venice: Molesini Editore Venezia, 2024.

Harries, Richard, and Henry Mayr-Harting, eds. *Christianity: Two Thousand Years*. Oxford: Oxford University Press, 2001.

Hay, Denys. *The Medieval Centuries*. London: Methuen, 1964.

Hildegard of Bingen. *Scivias*. Translated by Columba Hart and Jane Bishop. New York: Paulist Press, 1990.

————. *Selected Writings*. Translated by Mark Atherton. London: Penguin Classics, 2001.

Hilton, Walter. *The Ladder of Perfection*. Translated by Leo Sherley-Price. Harmondsworth, UK: Penguin Books, 1957.

Hollywood, Amy, and Beckman, Patricia Z., eds. *Cambridge Companion to Christian Mysticism*. New York: Cambridge University Press, 2012.

Hunt, Anne. *The Trinity: Insights from the Mystics*. Collegeville, MN: Michael Glazier, 2010.

Husain, Itrat. *The Mystical Element in the Metaphysical Poets of the Seventeenth Century*. New York: Biblo and Tannen, 1966.

Huxley, Aldous. *The Perennial Philosophy*. London: Triad Grafton, 1985.

Ignatius of Loyola. *The Autobiography*. Edited by J. F. X. O'Conor. New York: Benziger Brothers, 1900.

————. *The Spiritual Exercises*. Translated by Fr. Elder Mullan. New York: P. J. Kenedy & Sons, 1914.

Inge, W. R. *Christian Mysticism*. London: Methuen, 1899.

BIBLIOGRAPHY

———. *Light, Life, and Love: Selections from the German Mystics of the Middle Ages*. London: Methuen, 1904.

Jacopone da Todi. *The Lauds*. Translated by Serge Hughes and Elizabeth Hughes. Preface by Elémire Zolla. New York: Paulist Press, 1982.

James, William. *The Varieties of Religious Experience: A Study in Human Nature*. New York: Longmans, Green, and Co., 1917.

John Climacus. *The Ladder of Divine Ascent*. Translated by Archimandrite Lazarus Moore. New York: Harper & Brothers, 1959.

John of the Cross. *Complete Works*. Translated and edited by E. Allison Peers. London: Burns & Oates, 1934.

———. *The Mystical Doctrine of St. John of the Cross*. Translated by David Lewis, revised by Benedict Zimmerman. London: Sheed and Ward, 1934.

———. *Poems*. Translated by Roy Campbell. Harmondsworth, UK: Penguin Books, 1960.

John the Scot. *Periphyseon on the Divine Nature*. Translated by Myra L. Uhlfelder. Eugene, OR: Wipf and Stock, 2011.

Johnson, Paul. *A History of Christianity*. London: Penguin Books, 1976.

Johnston, William M., and Kleinhenz, Christopher. *Encyclopedia of Monasticism*. New York: Routledge, 2015.

Jonas of Bobbio, *Life of St. Columban*. Translated by Dana Carleton Munro. Philadelphia: University of Pennsylvania Press, 1895 (various reprints).

Jordan, Richard Douglas. "Thomas Traherne and the Art of Meditation." *Journal of the History of Ideas*, vol. 46, no. 3, 1985, pp. 381–403.

Julian of Norwich. *A Revelation of Love*. Edited by Marion Glasscoe. Exeter, UK: University of Exeter Press, 1986.

———. *Revelations of Divine Love*. Edited by Grace Warrack. London: Methuen and Co., 1901.

Kelleher, Hillary. "'Light thy Darknes is': George Herbert and Negative Theology." *George Herbert Journal*, Vol. 28, Nos. 1 and 2: Fall 2004/Spring 2005.

Kempe, Margery. *The Book of Margery Kempe*. Translated by W. Butler-Bowdon. London: Jonathan Cape, 1936.

———. *The Book of Margery Kempe*. Translated by B.A. Windeatt. London: Penguin Books, 1985.

Kettlewell, Rev. S. *Thomas à Kempis and the Brothers of the Common Life*. London: Kegan Paul, Trench, & Co., 1882.

BIBLIOGRAPHY

King, Margot H. *The Desert Mothers: A Survey of the Feminine Anchoretic Tradition in Western Europe*. Toronto: Peregrina Publishing Co., 1984.

———. "The Desert Mothers: from Judith to Julian of Norwich." *14th Century English Mystics Newsletter*, vol. 9, no. 1, 1983, pp. 12–25.

King, Ursula. *Christian Mystics: Their Lives and Legacies throughout the Ages*. Mahwah, NJ: Hidden Spring, 2001.

Law, William. *Spirit of Love*. London: G. Robinson and J. Roberts, 1752.

———. *Spirit of Prayer*. 4th ed. London: J. Richardson, 1758.

Lawrence, Brother. *The Practice of the Presence of God*. Translated by Donald Attwater. Oxford: Oneworld, 1993.

Leff, Gordon. *Medieval Thought: St Augustine to Ockham*. Harmondsworth, UK: Penguin Books, 1958.

Lent, Frederick. "The Life of St. Simeon Stylites: A Translation of the Syriac Text in Bedjan's Acta Martyrum et Sanctorum, Vol. IV." *Journal of the American Oriental Society*, vol. 35, 1915, pp. 103–98.

Leonardi, Matteo and Vettori, Alessandro (eds.). *The Power of Mysticism and the Originality of Franciscan Poetry*. Volume 23 of *The Medieval Franciscans*. Leiden: Brill, 2023.

Licence, Tom. *Hermits and Recluses in English Society, 950–1200*. Oxford: Oxford University Press, 2011.

Lindars, Barnabas; Edwards, Ruth B.; Court, John M. *The Johannine Literature*, Sheffield: Sheffield Academic Press, 2000.

Lossky, Andrew. *The Mystical Theology of the Eastern Church*. Cambridge, UK: James Clarke and Co., 1991.

Louth, Andrew. *The Origins of the Christian Mystical Tradition*. Oxford: Clarendon Press, 1981.

Luscombe, David. *Medieval Thought*. Oxford: Oxford University Press, 1997.

MacCulloch, Diarmaid. *A History of Christianity: The First Three Thousand Years*. London: Allen Lane, 2009.

MacHaffie, Barbara J. *Her Story: Women in Christian Tradition* (Second Edition). Minneapolis: Augsburg Fortress, 2006.

Maddocks, Fiona. *Hildegard of Bingen: The Woman of Her Age*. London: Headline, 2001.

Malone, Mary T. *Women and Christianity*. Vol. 2, *The Medieval Period, AD 1000–1500*. Dublin: Columba Press, 2001.

Marie de l'Incarnation: *The Selected Letters of Marie de l'Incarnation to Claude Martin*. Translated by Mary Dunn. Oxford: Oxford University Press, 2014.

BIBLIOGRAPHY

Marie of Oignies. *Vita* (Latin text of her *Life* by Jacques de Vitry): available at http://www.umilta.net/MarieOignes.html (last accessed 27/10/24).

Marks, Richard. *Stained Glass in England During the Middle Ages.* London: Routledge, 1993.

Maximus the Confessor. *Selected Writings.* Translated by George Berthold. Mahwah, NJ: Paulist Press, 1985.

————. *St. Maximus the Confessor. The Ascetic Life, The Four Centuries on Charity (Ancient Christian Writers).* Edited by Polycarp Sherwood. New York: Paulist Press, 1955.

McGinn, Bernard. *The Flowering of Mysticism.* New York: Crossroad, 1998.

————. *The Foundations of Christian Mysticism.* New York: Crossroad, 1992.

————. *The Growth of Mysticism.* New York: Crossroad, 1994.

————, ed. *Meister Eckhart and the Beguine Mystics.* New York: Continuum, 1997.

McGinn, Bernard, John Meyendorff, and Jean Leclerq, eds. *Christian Spirituality I: Origins to the Twelfth Century.* New York: Crossroad, 1985.

McManners, John, ed. *The Oxford History of Christianity.* Oxford: Oxford University Press, 1993.

McNabb, Cameron Hunt, ed. *Medieval Disability Sourcebook.* Punctum Books (Open Access Publisher), 2020. At https://punctumbooks.com/ (last accessed 27/10/24).

Mechthild of Magdeburg. *The Revelations of Mechthild of Magdeburg, or The Flowing Light of the Godhead.* Translated by Lucy Menzies. London: Longmans, Green and Co., 1953.

————. *The Flowing Light of the Godhead.* Translated by Frank Tobin. New York: Paulist Press, 1997.

Merton, Thomas. *The Ascent to Truth.* London: Hollis and Carter, 1951.

————. *New Seeds of Contemplation.* London: Burns & Oates, 1962.

————. *The Seven Storey Mountain.* New York: Signet Books, 1952.

————. *In the Valley of Wormwood: Cistercian Blessed and Saints of the Golden Age.* Collegeville, MN: Liturgical Press, 2013.

Moore, Lazarus. *St. Seraphim of Sarov: A Spiritual Biography.* Blanco, TX: New Sarov Press, 1994.

Morris, Bridget. *St Birgitta of Sweden.* Woodbridge: The Boydell Press, 1999.

Mueller, Joan. *Clare's Letters to Agnes: Texts and Sources.* New York: The Franciscan Institute, 2001.

BIBLIOGRAPHY

Mulder-Bakker, Anneke B., ed., Margot H. King and Hugh Feiss, trans. *Mary of Oignies: Mother of Salvation* (Medieval Women: Texts and Contexts 7). Turnhout: Brepols, 2007.

Newman, Barbara. *Sister of Wisdom: St. Hildegard's Theology of the Feminine.* Berkeley and Los Angeles: University of California Press, 1987.

O'Brien, Kate. *Teresa of Avila.* Cork: Mercier Press, 1951.

O'Donnell, Hugh C. M. "Apostolic Reflection," in *Vincentian Heritage Journal*: Vol. 16: Issue 2, Article 2. (1995) Available at http://via.library.depaul.edu/vhj/vol16/iss2/2 (last accessed 27/10/24).

Offor, George. *The Whole Works of John Bunyan*, 3 Vols. London: Blackie, 1862.

Oliver, H. J. *The Journal of English and Germanic Philology* Vol. 53, No. 3 (July 1954) pp. 352–60.

O'Meara, Dominic J. *Plotinus: An Introduction to the Enneads.* Oxford: Clarendon Press, 1995.

Origen. *On Prayer.* Translated by William A. Curtis. Published online by Christian Classics Ethereal Library, at: https://www.ccel.org/ccel/o/origen/prayer/cache/prayer.pdf (last accessed 27/10/24).

Osmond, Percy H. *The Mystical Poets of the English Church.* London: SPCK, 1919.

Ozanam, Frederick. *The Franciscan Poets of the Thirteenth Century.* Translated by A. E. Nellen and N. C. Craig. London: David Nutt, 1914.

Pachomius. *The Rules of Pachomius: Saint Pachomius.* Translated by G. H. Schodde. London: T&T Clarke, 1885.

Palmer, G. E. H., Philip Sherrard, and Kallistos Ware, trans. and eds. *The Philokalia: The Complete Text.* Vols. 1 and 2. London: Faber and Faber, 1979 and 1981.

Parrinder, Geoffrey. *Mysticism in the World's Religions.* London: Sheldon Press, 1976.

Pascal, Blaise. *Pascal's Pensées.* Translated by W. F. Trotter. New York: E. P. Dutton & Co., 1931.

———. *Pensées.* Translated by A. J. Krailsheimer. Harmondsworth: Penguin Books, 1966.

Peck, George T. *The Fool of God: Jacopone da Todi.* Alabama: University of Alabama Press, 1980.

Petroff, Elizabeth Alvilda. *Medieval Women's Visionary Literature.* Oxford: Oxford University Press, 1986.

———. *Body and Soul: Essays on Medieval Women and Mysticism.* Oxford: Oxford University Press, 1994.

BIBLIOGRAPHY

Perrin, David B., ed. *Women Mystics Speak to our Times*. Franklin, WI: Sheed & Ward, 2001.

Plotinus. *The Works of Plotinus*, trans. Stephen Mackenna. Boston: Charles T. Branford Company, 1916–1930.

Pollard, William F., and Robert Boenig. *Mysticism and Spirituality in Medieval England*. Cambridge: D. S. Brewer, 1997.

Porete, Marguerite. *The Mirror of Simple Souls*. Translated by Edmund Colledge, J. C. Marler, and Judith Grant. Notre Dame, IN: University of Notre Dame Press, 1999.

————. *The Mirror of Simple Souls*. Translated by Ellen L. Babinsky. Mahwah, NJ: Paulist Press, 1993.

Post, Jonathan F. S. *Henry Vaughan: The Unfolding Vision*. Princeton: Princeton University Press, 1982.

Preminger, Marion Mill. *The Sands of Tamanrasset: The Story of Charles de Foucauld*. Fresno, CA: Craven Street, 2002.

Pseudo-Dionysius. *Pseudo-Dionysius: the Complete Works*. Translated by Colm Luibheid with Paul Rorem, ed. Mahwah, NJ: Paulist Press, 1987.

Puttick, Elizabeth; Clarke, Bernard, eds. *Women as Teachers and Disciples in Traditional and New Religions*. Lewiston, NY: Edwin Mellen Press, 1993.

Raitt, Jill, ed. *Christian Spirituality II: High Middle Ages and Reformation*. New York: Crossroad, 1988.

Reid, Alcuin, ed. *From Eucharistic Adoration to Evangelisation*. London: Burns & Oates, 2012.

Rhodes, J. T. "Some Writings of a Seventeenth-Century English Benedictine: Dom Augustine Baker O.S.B." *The Yale University Library Gazette*, vol. 67, no. 3/4, 1993, pp. 110–17.

Richard of St. Victor. *Richard of St. Victor: The Twelve Patriarchs, The Mystical Ark, Book Three of the Trinity*. Translated by Grover A. Zinn. New York: Paulist Press, 1979.

Richardson, Jr., Robert D. *Emerson: The Mind on Fire*. Berkeley: University of California Press, 1995.

Roberts, Alexander, and James Donaldson, eds. *The Ante-Nicene Fathers: The Writings of the Fathers Down to AD 325*. 10 vols. Grand Rapids, MI: William B. Eerdmans Publishing (various reprints).

Robinson, Paschal. *The Writings of Saint Francis of Assisi*. Philadelphia: The Dolphin Press, 1906.

BIBLIOGRAPHY

Rolle, Richard. *The Fire of Love*. Translated by Clifton Wolters. Harmondsworth, UK: Penguin Books, 1972.

————. *The Fire of Love*. Translated by Richard Misyn. 2nd ed. London: Methuen and Co., 1920.

Rousseau, Philip. *Ascetics, Authority, and the Church in the Age of Jerome and Cassian*. Oxford: Oxford University Press, 1978.

Runciman, Stephen. *A History of the Crusades, Vols I-III*. Harmondsworth: Penguin Books, 1981.

Ruysbroeck, Jan van. *The Spiritual Espousals, The Sparkling Stones, and Other Works*. Translated by James A. Wiseman, O.S.B. New York: Paulist Press, 1985.

————. *The Adornment of the Spiritual Marriage*. Translated by C. A. Wynschenck. London: J. M. Dent and Sons, 1916.

Sampson, George. *The Concise Cambridge History of English Literature*. Cambridge: Cambridge University Press, 1970.

Schaff, P., and H. Wace, eds. *A Select Library of the Nicene and Post-Nicene Fathers of the Christian Church*. Vols 1–14. Second Series. Grand Rapids, MI: William B. Eerdmans Publishing (various reprints).

Schaus, Margaret, ed. *Women and Gender in Medieval Europe: An Encyclopedia*. London: Routledge, 2006.

Scott, Martin. *Medieval Europe*. London: Longmans, Green and Co., 1964.

Sheldrake, Philip, ed. *The New SCM Dictionary of Christian Spirituality*. London: SCM Press, 2005.

Shewring, W. H., trans., *The Passion of SS. Perpetua and Felicity*. London: Sheed and Ward, 1931.

Sophronius, *Life of Mary of Egypt*. Available at: https://stmaryofegypt. org/files/library/life.htm (last accessed 27/10/24).

Southern, R. W. *Western Society and the Church in the Middle Ages*. Harmondsworth, UK: Penguin Books, 1970.

Spencer, Sidney. *Mysticism in World Religion*. Harmondsworth, UK: Penguin Books, 1963.

Stace, Walter T. *The Teachings of the Mystics*. New York: Mentor Books, 1960.

Strezova, Anita. *Hesychasm and Art: The Appearance of New Iconographic Trends in Byzantine and Slavic Lands in the 14th and 15th Centuries*. Canberra: ANU Press, 2014.

Suso, Henry. *The Exemplar, with Two German Sermons*. Edited and translated by Frank Tobin. New York: Paulist Press, 1989.

————. *The Life of Blessed Henry Suso by Himself*. Translated by Thomas Francis Knox. London: Burns, Lambert, and Oates, 1865.

BIBLIOGRAPHY

————. *Little Book of Eternal Wisdom and Little Book of Truth*. Translated and edited by James M. Clark. London: Faber and Faber, 1953.

Swan, Laura. *The Forgotten Desert Mothers: Sayings, Lives, and Stories of Early Christian Women*. Mahwah, NJ: Paulist Press, 2001.

————. *The Wisdom of the Beguines: The Forgotten Story of a Medieval Women's Movement*. Katonah, NY: BlueBridge, 2016.

Sweet, Victoria. "Hildegard of Bingen and the Greening of Medieval Medicine." *Bulletin of the History of Medicine*, vol. 73, no. 3, 1999, pp. 381–403.

Symeon the New Theologian. *The Discourses*. Translated by C. J. de Catanzaro. New York: Paulist Press, 1980.

————. *On the Mystical Life: The Ethical Discourses*. Vol. 2. Translated by Alexander Golitzin. Crestwood, NY: St. Vladimir's Seminary Press, 1996.

Talbot, C. H., ed. *The Life of Christina of Markyate: A Twelfth-Century Recluse*. Oxford: Oxford University Press, 1959.

Tauler, John. *The Inner Way: 36 Sermons for Festivals*. 2nd ed. Translated by Arthur Wollaston Hutton. London: Methuen and Co., 1909.

————. *Johannes Tauler: Sermons*. Translated by Maria Shrady. New York: Paulist Press, 1985.

————. *Spiritual Conferences*. Translated by Eric Colledge and Sister M. Jane. Rockford, Ill.: Tan Books, 1978.

Teilhard de Chardin, Pierre. *Hymn of the Universe*. Translated by Gerald Vann. London: Fontana, 1970.

————. *Le Milieu Divin*. Edited by Bernard Wall, et al. London: Fontana, 1960.

————. *The Phenomenon of Man*. Translated by Bernard Wall. London: Collins, 1961.

Teresa of Ávila. *Complete Works*. Translated and edited by E. Allison Peers. New York: Sheed and Ward, 1946.

————. *The Life of Saint Teresa of Ávila by Herself*. Translated by J. M. Cohen. Harmondsworth, UK: Penguin Books, 1957.

Thérèse of Lisieux. *Soeur Thérèse of Lisieux: The Little Flower of Jesus*. Edited by Rev. T. N. Taylor. London: Burns, Oates & Washbourne, 1912; 8th ed., 1922.

————. Story of a Soul: *The Autobiography of St. Thérèse of Lisieux*. Edited by John Clarke, O.C.D. Washington, D.C.: ICS Publications, 1996.

Thomas à Kempis. *The Imitation of Christ*. Translated by Leo Sherley-Price. Harmondsworth: Penguin, 1952.

BIBLIOGRAPHY

————. *The Imitation of Christ*. Translated by C. Bigg. London: Methuen, 1901.

————. *The Imitation of Christ*. Translated by Joseph N. Tylenda. London: Vintage, Revised edition, 1998.

————. Thomas à Kempis. *The Imitation of Christ*. Translated by Aloysius Croft and Harold Bolton. Milwaukee: Bruce Publishing, 1940. / Christian Classics Etherial Library, online https://www.ccel.org/ccel/k/kempis/imitation/cache/imitation.pdf (last accessed 27/10/24).

Thompson, Elbert N. S. "Mysticism in Seventeenth-Century English Literature." *Studies in Philology*, April, 1921, Vol. 18, No. 2, pp. 170–223.

Thompson, William M., ed., and Lowell M. Glendon, trans. *Bérulle and the French School: Selected Writings*. New York: Paulist Press, 1989.

Thoreau, Henry David. *Walden*. London: Penguin, 2016.

————. *The Portable Thoreau*. Edited by Jeffrey S. Kramer. London: Penguin Books, 2017.

————. *Familiar Letters*. Edited by F. B. Sanborn. Boston: Houghton Mifflin, 1906.

Traherne, Thomas. *The Poetical Works*. Edited by Bertram Dobell. Privately Published. 1906.

————. *Centuries of Meditations*. Edited by Bertram Dobell. Privately Published. 1908.

————. "Thomas Traherne" by Julia J Smith in *Oxford Dictionary of National Biography*. Oxford: Oxford University Press, 2004.

————. *Select Meditations*. Edited by Julia J. Smith. Manchester: Fyfield Books, 2009.

Underhill, Evelyn, ed. *The Cloud of Unknowing*. London: John M. Watkins, 1922.

————. *Mysticism*. Oxford: Oneworld, 1991.

————. *Jacopone da Todi, 1228–1306*. London: J. M. Dent & Sons, 1919.

Upham, T. C. *The Story of Madame Guyon's Life*. Atlanta, GA: Christian Books, 1984.

Van den Dungen, Wim. *Beatrice of Nazareth: On Seven Ways of Holy Love*. Brasschaat, Belgium: Taurus Press, 2016.

Vaughan, Henry. *Poems of Henry Vaughan, Silurist,* Vol. 1., edited by E. K. Chambers. London: Routledge, 1890.

Vryonis, Speros. *Byzantium and Europe*. London: Thames and Hudson, 1967.

BIBLIOGRAPHY

Wakefield, Gordon S., ed. *A Dictionary of Christian Spirituality*. London: SCM Press, 1983.

Ward, Benedicta (trans. and ed.). *The Sayings of the Desert Fathers*. Kalamazoo, Michigan: Cistercian Publications, 1975.

Ware, Timothy. *The Orthodox Church*. Harmondsworth, UK: Penguin Books, 1963.

———. *The Inner Kingdom*. Crestwood, NY: St. Vladimir's Seminary Press, 2001.

Warnar Geert. *Ruusbroec: Literature and Mysticism in the Fourteenth Century*. Translated by Diane Webb. Leiden: Brill, 2007.

Watts, Edward J. *Riot in Alexandria: Tradition and Group Dynamics in Late Antique Pagan and Christian Communities*. Berkeley: University of California Press, 2010.

Weeks, Andrew. *Boehme: An Intellectual Biography of the Seventeenth-Century Philosopher and Mystic*. Albany: State University of New York Press, 1991.

Wei, Ian P. *Intellectual Culture in Medieval Paris: Theologians and the University, c. 1100–1330*. Cambridge, UK: Cambridge University Press, 2012.

Weil, Simone. *Waiting for God*. Translated by Emma Craufurd. New York: Harper & Row, 1951.

———. *Gravity and Grace*. Translated by Arthur Wills. Lincoln: University of Nebraska Press, 1997.

Wesley, John. *The Journal of John Wesley*. Edited by Percy Livingstone Parker. Chicago: Moody Press, 1951.

Wiley, A. Terrance. *Angelic Troublemakers: Religion and Anarchism in America*. New York: Bloomsbury, 2014.

William of St-Thierry, *The Golden Epistle: A Letter to the Brethren at Mont Dieu*. Translated by T. Berkeley. Cistercian Fathers Series, 12. Spencer, MA: 1971.

Williams, Rowan. *The Wound of Knowledge*. London: Darton, Longman and Todd, 1979.

Wolters, Clifton, trans. *The Cloud of Unknowing*. Harmondsworth, UK: Penguin Books, 1961.

Woods, Richard. *Mysticism and Prophecy: The Dominican Tradition*. London: Darton, Longman and Todd, 1998.

———, ed. *Understanding Mysticism*. London: Athlone Press, 1981.

Wordsworth, William. *The Poetical Works*. Oxford: Clarendon Press, 1947.

Wulf, Andrea. *Magnificent Rebels*. London: John Murray, 2023.

BIBLIOGRAPHY

Zaehner, R. C. *Mysticism: Sacred and Profane*. Oxford: Oxford University Press, 1961.

Zander, Valentine. *St. Seraphim of Sarov*. Translated by Sr. Gabriel Anne, S.S.C. Crestwood, NY: St. Vladimir's Seminary Press, 1975.

INDEX

Bold numerals indicate an extended entry

Abandonment to Divine Providence
(Caussade), 267
Abbey of Saint Albans, 80
Abbey of Saint-Nicasius, Reims,
70
Abbey of Saint-Victor, Paris, 64,
72
Abelard, Peter, 67, 71
abolitionism, 293
Acarie, Madame, 244, **245–7**, 248
Act of Uniformity (1662), 212
Acts of the Process (life of Clare of
Assisi), 92
Acts of the Apostles, 54
Adam, 59, 152, 298
Adamnán, 47, 50
Adorno, Giuliano, 168–9
Adrian V, Pope, 168
affirmative theology, 53
Age of Enlightenment (c. 1685–
1815), 6, 263–75, 277–8,
281
Agnes of Bohemia, 94–5
Agnietenberg, monastery of,
Windesheim, 138
agnosticism, 299
Albertus Magnus, 86, 124
Albigenses, 87, 107, 109, 123

alchemy, 214, 216
Aldrin, Buzz, 1
Alexander III, Pope, 87
Alexander V, Antipope, 160
Alexandria, Egypt, 15–24, 25,
33–4, 171, 180
Alfred, King of the Anglo-Saxons,
60
Alfwen, 80
Algeria, 42, 304
Alonso de Cepeda, 200
Alumbrado movement, 196
Ambrogio Traversari, 161
Ambrose of Milan, 42–3
American colonies (1607–1776),
230, 264, 265, 273
Amiens, France, 40, 247
Ammonius Saccas, 19, 21
Anacletus II, Antipope, 67
anchoresses, 153–4
see also hermits
anchorites, 31, 32, 66
al-Andalus (711–1492), 49, 124
Angela of Foligno, 3, **101–4**
angels, 27, 29, 34, 50, 55, 77,
237, 280
cherubim, 55, 237
seraphim, 89, 96

375

INDEX

Anglican Church, 211, 212, 218, 222, 223, 228, 232, 243, 269

Anglo-Saxon Chronicle, 49

Anglo-Saxon England (410–1066), 49–50, 58, 60

animals, communion with, 27, 189, 191

Annecy, Savoy, 250

Annegray, France, 52

antihesychasts, 187

Antioch, 171

Antony of Egypt, 26, **27–9**

apatheia, 39, 178, 179

apokatastasis, 38

apophatic theology, 5, 53, 55, 100, 133, 148, 186, 223, 244

Apophthegmata Patrum, see *Sayings of the Desert Fathers*

apostles, 9–11

Arianism, 25, 36, 47

Aristotle, 65–6, 124

Ark of the Covenant, 73

Armstrong, Neil, 1

Ascent of Mount Carmel, The (John of the Cross), 206

Ascent to Truth, The (Merton), 314

Ascetic Life, The (Maximus the Confessor), 180, 182

asceticism, 2, 39, 60, 66
  Benedict of Nursia, 48, 59
  Bernard of Clairvaux, 67
  Catherine of Genoa, 167
  Catherine of Siena, 165
  Christina of Markyate, 79–83
  Cistercian order, 67, 107
  Clare of Assisi, 93–5
  Desert Fathers/Mothers, 26–35

Evagrius Ponticus, 27, 37–9

de Foucauld, 299, 302–5

Fox, 228

Francis of Assisi, 88–90

Franciscan order, 85–7, 88–95, 98–9, 101

Gregory I and, 58

Gregory Palamas, 186

Julian of Norwich, 153–5, 157

Law (William), 270

Marie of Oignies, 110

Maximus the Confessor, 180

Rolle, 145–6

Seraphim of Sarov, 191

Sergius of Radonezh, 189

Suso, 132

Symeon the New Theologian, 184

Teilhard de Chardin, 308

Thoreau, 295

Assisi, Umbria, Italy, 88, 89, 156, 309

astrology, 14, 214, 216

Athanasius of Alexandria, 28, 33

atheism, 299

Athonite order, 176, 186

Augustine of Hippo, 21, 25, 27, **41–6**, 57, 95, 151, 224

Augustinian order, 64, 85, 123, 151

Augustus, Roman Emperor, 11

Aurora (Boehme), 215

Avignon Papacy (1309–76), 124–5, 126, 144, 159, 162–4, 165–6

Ávila, Spain, 200, 205

Baker, Augustine, 211–12

INDEX

Baldwin, Count of Flanders, 173

Bangor, Ireland, 48, 51

baptism, 55, 128, 152

Baptists, 213, 228, 232

Barlaam, 186–8

Barth, Karl, 26

Basil of Caesarea, 26

Basil the Great, 18, 35, 38, 187

Bastia Umbra, Italy, 92

Battle of Kulikovo (1380), 190

Battle of Pamplona (1521), 197

Battle of Poitiers (732), 49

Bavaria, Germany, 52

Beatrice of Nazareth, 108, 113, **119–21**

de Beaufort, Joseph, 253

Bedford, England, 231, 232–3

Beguine order, 72, **105–21**

Belgium, 70, 107, 116

Bemerton, England 218

Benedict XI, Pope, 99

Benedict XVI, Pope, 74–5

Benedict of Nursia, 48, 59

Benedictine order, 48, 64, 70–71, 75, 80, 92, 212, 246

Benet Canfield, **243–5**, 246

Béni Abbès, Algeria, 304

Benincasa, Giacomo, 165

Benjamin Major (Richard of Saint-Victor), 73

Beorhtred, 80–81, 82

Bernard of Clairvaux, 5, 20, 65, **66–70**, 76, 106, 151

Bernardino of Siena, 161

Beroea, Greece, 186

Bethlehem, Pennsylvania, 265

Bhagavad Gita, 289, 310

Bingen, Germany, 76

Birgitta of Sweden *see* Bridget of Sweden

Black Death (1346–53), 6, 129, 143, 146

Blake, William, 7, 79, 214, 236, 278, 279, **280–85**

Bloemendaal, monastery of, Holland, 119

Bobbio, Italy, 49, 52

Boccaccio, Giovanni, 144

Boehme, Jacob, 210, 213, **214–18**, 227, 270, 271, 279, 280

Bohemia, 94, 126, 160

Bohemian brethren, 265, 273, 274

Bonaventure, 6, 86, **95–7**

Bonhoeffer, Dietrich, 137

Boniface VIII, Pope, 99, 124

Book of Common Prayer, 212, 273

Book of Divine Works, The (Hildegard), 77, 78

Book of Foundations (Teresa of Ávila), 201

Book of Martyrs (Foxe), 231

Bossuet, Jacques-Bénigne, 259, 260

Boston, Massachusetts, 290

Boucher, Catherine, 280

Brecknockshire, Wales, 223

Brémond, Henri, 244

Brendan of Clonfert, 51

Breuil, France, 52

Bridgeman, Sir Oliver, 235

Bridget (Birgitta) of Sweden, **161–4**

Bridgettine order, 162

Brittany, 51

377

INDEX

Brown, John, 293

Brown, Peter, 47

Bruges, Flanders, 65, 108

Brussels, 135

Buddhism, 253, 299, 312

Bulgaria, 175

Bunyan, John, 212, **231–4**, 282

Burgundy, France, 52, 63, 67, 318

Butler, Cuthbert, 42

Butler, Joseph, 265

Butts, Thomas, 283–4

Byron, George Gordon, 6th
   Baron, 279

Byzantine Empire (330–1453),
   48, 57, 171–3, 180–88

Byzantium, 25, 171

Caesarea, Cappadocia, 16, 36

Caesarea, Palestine, 19

Calvin, John, 209, 211

Calvinism, 211, 212, 250, 265,
   279

Cambrai, France, 116, 212, 253,
   259

Cambridge, England, 151, 218,
   228, 313, 314

Cambridge, Massachusetts, 291

Camino de Santiago, 319

Campania, Italy, 22

Canada, 319

Candes, France, 40

Canterbury Tales, The (Chaucer),
   144

"Canticle of the Sun" (Francis of
   Assisi), 90, 93

Cappadocia, 16, 27, 35

Cappadocian Fathers, 18, 26,
   35–9, 174

Capuchin order, 195, 244

Carmelite order, 2, 197, 200,
   201, 204, 205, 245, 247, 248,
   253, 300

Carolingian Empire (800–887),
   48

Carthage, 13, 42, 180

Carthusian order, 71

Cassian, John, 27

cataphatic (kataphatic) theology,
   53

Cathars, 87, 107, 109, 123

Catherine of Genoa, 2, 5, 159,
   167–70

Catherine of Siena, 6, 159, **164–7**

Catherine of Sweden, 162

Catholic Church, 47–8, 57–8, 63,
   124, 144, 159, 171–2, 241–2,
   263

   Avignon Papacy (1309–76),
      124–5, 126, 144, 159,
      162–4, 165–6

   Counter Reformation (1545–
      1648), 195

   Great Schism (1378–1417),
      144, 159–61, 166

   Immaculate Conception, 297

   Index of Prohibited Books,
      196, 244

   Inquisition, 116, 196

   Quietism, 242–3, 244, 253,
      254–5, 257, 259, 266, 267

   reform movements, 64–5, 70,
      85

   Reformation (1517–1648),
      4, 108, 124, 129, 195,
      209–11

   revival (1800s), 279

INDEX

Catholic Institute, Paris, 307

Catholic League, 246

de Caussade, Jean-Pierre, **266–9**

Celestial Hierarchy, The (Dionysius), 54

Celestine, Pope, 49

Celtic Christianity, 318–19

cenobitical monasticism, *see under* monasticism

Centuries of Meditations (Traherne), 235, 237

Chadwick, Owen, 297

de Chantal, Jeanne, 250, 266

Charlemagne, Holy Roman Emperor, 48, 172

Charles I, King of England, 212, 235, 248

Charles II, King of England, 212, 233, 235

Charles V, Holy Roman Emperor, 196

Charles the Bald, Carolingian emperor, 60

Chaucer, Geoffrey, 144

cherubim, 55, 237

China, 307

Christian Library, 273

Christianity Not Mysterious (Toland), 264

Christina of Markyate, 66, **79–83**, 109

Chrysopolis, monastery of, 180

Cistercian order, 64–5, 66, 67, 70–71, 85, 106, 107, 114, 119

Trappists, 303–4, 313

Cîteaux, France, 64, 67

City of God, The (Augustine), 27, 41, 43

clairvoyance, 2, 28, 81, 110, 190, 192

Clare of Assisi, 85, 89, 90, **92–5**

Clement IV, Pope, 96

Clement V, Pope, 125

Clement VI, Pope, 162

Clement VII, Antipope, 160

Clement of Alexandria, 9, 12, **14–17**

clerical marriage, 63

Clermont College, Paris, 249

Clonard, Ireland, 48

Clonfert, Ireland, 51

Clonmacnoise, Ireland, 48

Cloud of Unknowing, 143, 148–50, 223

Clovis, King of the Franks, 47

Cluny, France, 64

Cnoc an t-Sidhein, Iona, Scotland, 50

Coleridge, Samuel Taylor, 278, 279, 286, 287, 290

Colga (Irish monk), 50

Collazzone, Italy, 99

Cologne, Germany, 65, 108, 126

Columba (Columcille) of Iona, 47, 48, **50–51**

Columbanus, 48, **51–2**

Columbia University, 313

Communion, 12, 55, 72, 108, 110, 112, 118, 165

Concord, Massachusetts, 290–91, 292–3

Concordat of Worms (1122), 64

Conference of Issy (1695), 258

Confessions (Augustine), 41, 43, 44

Congregationalists, 228

Conrad III, King of Germany, 76

379

INDEX

Constance, Germany, 160

Constans II, Byzantine Emperor, 181

Constantine I, Roman Emperor, 12, 25–6, 171

Constantinople, 25, 124, 171, 172, 176

"Constellation, The" (Vaughan), 225

contemplative prayer, *see under* prayer

Convent of the Incarnation, Ávila, 200, 201, 205

convents
    Middle Ages, 76, 92–3, 106–8, 111, 114, 115, 129, 146, 173
    Modern period, 242–3, 246, 247, 300–301
    Renaissance period, 161, 168, 200, 201, 205, 212
    see also monasticism

Conventual Franciscans, 86, 96

Corinthians, Letter to the, 10, 45, 70, 147

cosmic rhythm, 120

van Coudenberg, Francis, 135

Council of Basel (1431–49), 161

Council of Chalcedon (451), 180

Council of Constance (1414–18), 160

Council of Constantinople
    First (381), 25, 36
    Second (553), 38

Council of Lyon (1272), 96

Council of Nicaea (325), 25

Council of Pavia (1423), 161

Council of Pisa (1409), 160

Council of Trent (1545–63), 195–6

Council of Vienne (1311–12), 108, 125

Counter Reformation (1545–1648), 195

courtly love, 105

Cromwell, Oliver, 212

Crucifixion, 74, 88–9, 96, 153, 251

Crusades, 65, 107, 124, 303
    Fifth (1217–21), 89
    First (1096–9), 65
    Fourth (1202–4), 124, 172
    Second (1147–50), 67

Cybele, 11, 12

Daniel of Raithou, 177

Dante, 36, 67, 73, 95, 114

Danvers, Jane, 218

Danzig, Prussia, 157

Dark Ages (c. 500–1000), 47

Dark Night of the Soul, The (John of the Cross), 6, 152, 167, 204, 206

Darwin, Charles, 7, 298, 299

Deane, John F., 219

Decameron (Boccaccio), 144

Decius, Roman Emperor, 12, 19

Defensor Pacis (Marsilius of Padua), 125

deification, 181

Deism, 264, 269

Demetrius, 19

Democritus, 281, 282

demons, 27, 28, 31, 32, 38–9, 179, 302

INDEX

exorcisms, 40, 76, 90
Derry, Ireland, 48
Descartes, René, 241, 254, 263
Descent of Man, The (Darwin), 298
Desert Fathers, **26–30**
Desert Mothers, 26–7, **31–5**
Deventer, Salland, 138
Devil, 77, 201, 227
    salvation of, 18, 38
    visions of, 28, 30, 33, 40, 66,
        106, 139, 156
Devotio Moderna, 138
Devout Soul, The (Bishop Hall), 213
Dhammapada, xiii
Dial, The (Transcendentalist
    journal), 290, 293
Dialogue, The (Catherine of Siena),
    166
Dialogues (Pope Gregory the
    Great), 58
Diderot, Denis, 263
Diggers (radical Protestants),
    213
Diocletian, Roman Emperor, 12
Dionysus (Greek deity), 11, 12
Dionysius the Areopagite, 5, 15,
    20, 22, **53–6**, 148, 174
    Angela of Foligno and, 104
    Benet Canfield and, 244
    Bernard of Clairvaux and, 69
    Bonaventure and, 95, 97
    Eckhart and, 127
    Gregory Palamas and, 186
    Gregory the Great and, 57
    Jan van Ruysbroeck and, 134
    John of the Cross and, 206
    John Scotus Erigena and, 60
    Law (William) and, 270

    Maximus the Confessor and,
        180
    Pierre de Bérulle and, 249
    Vaughan and, 223
Discalced Carmelites, 201, 204,
    205, 245, 247, 248
Disibodenberg, monastery of,
    Speyer, Germany 75
"Distraction" (Vaughan), 226
ditheism, 187
Divine Comedy (Dante), 36, 67, 95,
    114
divine darkness, 37, 53–6, 104,
    134, 137
divine image, 42, 94, 97, 128,
    152, 272
divine light, 174
    Boehme and, 215, 217
    Bonaventure and, 97
    Catherine of Genoa and, 169
    Columba and, 51
    Dionysius the Areopagite and,
        53
    Fox on, 229
    Gregory of Nyssa and, 36
    Gregory Palamas and, 185
    Gregory the Great and, 59
    Ignatius of Loyola and, 198
    Jacopone da Todi and, 98, 100
    John of the Cross and, 207
    Law (William) on, 271–2
    Merton and, 314
    Plotinus and, 24
    Porete and, 117
    Richard of Saint-Victor and,
        73–4
    Seraphim of Sarov and, 193
    Suso and, 133

381

INDEX

Symeon and, 182–5
Thomas à Kempis and, 141
divine love, *see under* love
Divine Names, The (Dionysius the Areopagite), 54
divine providence, 253, 261, 267
divine union, 2, 5, 6
    Angela of Foligno on, 104
    Augustine of Hippo on, 45
    Beatrice of Nazareth on, 120–21
    Bernard of Clairvaux on, 68–70
    Blake on, 281–2
    Bonaventure on, 97
    de Caussade on, 267
    Clare of Assisi, 92
    Clement of Alexandria on, 15
    Dionysius the Areopagite on, 55–6
    Eckhart on, 127–9
    Francis of Assisi on, 90
    Hadewijch of Brabant on, 112
    Jacopone da Todi, 99–100
    Jan van Ruysbroeck on, 136–7
    John Climacus on, 179
    John Scotus Erigena on, 62
    Mechthild of Magdeburg on, 114–16
    Paul the Apostle on, 10
    Plotinus on, 24
    Porete on, 117–19
    Suso on, 134
    Syncletica of Alexandria on, 33
    Tauler on, 130–31
    Traherne on, 235
    William of Saint-Thierry on, 72

Dmitry Donskoy, Prince of Moscow, 190
Dominic de Guzman, 123
Dominican order, 85–6, 106, 113, 123, 127, 129, 165, 195
Donatism, 43
Dordogne, France, 259
Douai, France, 212, 244
"Double Vision" (Blake), 283
Duns Scotus, 124
Durrow, Ireland, 50

Eastern Orthodox Church, *see* Orthodox Church
Ecclesiastical Hierarchy, The (Dionysius the Areopagite), 54
Eckhart, Meister, 3, 5, 54, 123, **125–9**, 214
"Eclipse, The" (Vaughan), 222
ecstasies, 2
    Acarie, 246
    Augustine of Hippo, 45
    Beatrice of Nazareth, 119
    Beguines, 108
    Bonaventure, 97
    Catherine of Siena, 166
    Christina of Markyate, 81
    Cloud of Unknowing, 150
    Hildegard of Bingen, 79
    Jacopone da Todi, 100, 101
    John Climacus, 178
    John of the Cross on, 204
    Mechthild of Magdeburg, 114
    Paul the Apostle, 10, 45, 147
    Plotinus, 22
    Richard of Saint-Victor, 73
    Rolle, 146–7

382

INDEX

Sergius of Radonezh, 190
Suso, 132–3
Symeon on, 184
Vaughan, 225
"Eden" (Traherne), 236
Edward VI, King of England, 211
Edwards, Jonathan, 265
Egypt, 15–24, 25, 27–35, 38, 89
Eibingen, Germany, 76
Eisleben, Germany, 114
Eliot, Thomas Stearns, xiii, 153
Elizabeth I, Queen of England, 211
Emerson, Ralph Waldo, 279, 289–92
England
    Anglo-Saxon England (410–1066), 49–50, 58, 60
    Kingdom of England (927–1707), see Kingdom of England
    see also Kingdom of Great Britain; United Kingdom
Enlightenment (c. 1685–1815), 6, 263–75, 277–8, 281
Enneads (Plotinus), 21–4
epektasis, 37, 38, 70
Ephesians, 174
L'Estat de Jésus (Pierre de Bérulle), 248
Eucharist, 12, 55, 72, 108, 110, 112, 118, 144, 172, 183, 221, 290
Eugenius III, Pope, 68
Eusebius, 18, 19
Evagrius Ponticus, 27, **37–9**, 175
Eve, 105, 298
evolution, 298

Excursion, The (Wordsworth), 286
Exemplar, The (Suso), 133
exorcisms, 40, 76, 90
Explanation of the Maxims (Fénelon), 260

Fall, the, 59, 105, 154, 221
Fátima, Portugal, 299
Faust (Goethe), 34
Fell, Thomas, 229
Felpham, England, 280, 283–4
Fénelon, François, 6, 243, 253, **259–61**, 270, 273
Ferdinand, King of Aragon, 196
Ferrières, France, 49
Fiachra (Irish saint), 52
Fichte, Johann Gottlieb, 278, 298
Fieschi family, 168
Fifth Monarchy Men, 213
Fire of Love, The (Rolle), 145, 147
First Book of the Christian Exercise, The (Robert Persons), 244
First World War (1914–18), 304, 312
Flambard, Ranulf, 80
Flamstead, England, 80
Florentine Republic (1115–1569), 165, 195
Flores Fortitudinis (Vaughan), 222
Flowing Light of the Godhead, The (Mechthild), 113
Fontaine, France, 52
de Foucauld, Charles, 299, **302–5**
Four Degrees, The (Richard of Saint-Victor), 73, 74
Four Hundred Chapters on Love (Maximus the Confessor), 180, 181

INDEX

Four Quartets (T.S. Eliot), xiii
Fox, George, 209, 210, 213,
  227–31, 279, 333–4
Foxe, John, 231
France
  Kingdom of France (843–
    1792), *see* Kingdom of
    France
  Republic of France, First
    (1792–1804), 277
  Republic of France, Third
    (1870–1940), 300–11
Francia (c. 509–987), 51–2, 58,
  60, 172
Francis de Sales, xv, 241, 246,
  249–52, 266, 287
Francis of Assisi, 2, 85, **87–91**,
  92–4, 95, 189
Franciscan order, 85–104, 106,
  124, 168
  Conventuals, 86, 96
  Spirituals, 86–7, 96, 99, 125
  Third Order, 102
Francke, August, 265
Franks, 47, 48, 60, 172
Frederick II, Holy Roman
  Emperor, 94
Frederick II, King of Prussia, 264
Free Spirit, 108
Freud, Sigmund, 312
Fursey (Irish saint), 52

Galatians, Letter to the, 10
Galilei, Galileo, 263
Gallienus, Roman Emperor, 22
Garabandal, Spain, 299
Gaul, 27, 40, 51–2
Geert de Groote, 138

Geneva, Switzerland, 211, 250
Geoffrey de Gorran, 81
Germany, 52, 75, 108, 113–16,
  123–41, 157, 214–18
  Pietism in, 264–5
  Reformation in, 129, 195,
    209, 210, 214
  Rhineland mystics, 123–41,
    213, 214
  Romanticism in, 278, 279
de Gerson, Jean, 161
Gethsemani, Kentucky, 313
Ghent, Flanders, 65
Gibbon, Edward, 270
Glaber, Radulfus, 63
Gnosticism, 14–17, 24
God, 1–6, 18, 46, 61–2
  direct experiences of, 1–6, 79
  divine image, 42, 94, 97, 128,
    152, 272
  divine union, *see* divine union
  negative theology, 5, 53, 55,
    100, 133, 148, 186, 223,
    244
  oneness of, 21–4, 44, 55
Godhead, 127, 130, 131, 136,
  137, 157, 175, 214
Goethe, Johann Wolfgang, 34, 278
van Gogh, Vincent, 137
Golden Epistle (William of Saint-
  Thierry), 71
Good Samaritan parable, 311
Gordian III, Roman Emperor, 22
Görlitz, Germany, 214
Goths, 47
Grace Abounding (Bunyan), 231
Graham, Billy, 299
Gravity and Grace (Weil), 310

INDEX

Great Awakening (c. 1730–55), 265

Great Britain, Kingdom of, *see* Kingdom of Great Britain

Great Rebellion (66–74), 11

Great Schism (1378–1417), 144, 159–61, 166

Greek Orthodox Church, 96, 171–3

Greek religion, 4, 11, 310

Gregory I, Pope, 48, 56–62, 69

Gregory IX, Pope, 93

Gregory VII, Pope, 63

Gregory X, Pope, 96

Gregory XI, Pope, 159, 161

Gregory XVI, Pope, 132

Gregory of Nazianzus, 18, 26, 35, 38, 183

Gregory of Nyssa, 18, 20, 26, **35–7**, 38, 54, 55, 70, 175

Gregory Palamas, 174, **185–8**

Gudmarsson, Ulf, 161

Guyon, Madame, 243, **257–8**, 260

Hadewijch of Brabant, 105, 108, **111–13**

Hagia Sophia, Constantinople, 172, 188

Hainaut, Wallonia, 116

Hall, Joseph, 213

Hammarskjöld, Dag, 137

Harding, Stephen, 65

Hayley, William, 280

healing, 28, 76, 192

heart (in hesychasm), 175–6

Hegel, Georg Wilhelm Friedrich, 214

Heinrich von Ofterdingen (Novalis), 279

Helfta, Germany, 114

Hell, 52, 114, 139, 163, 199, 251

Henrietta Maria, Queen of England, 248

Henry II, King of England, 76, 81

Henry IV, Holy Roman Emperor, 63

Henry IV, King of France, 242, 244, 246, 248

Henry V, King of England, 145

Henry VIII, King of England, 211

Henry of Halle, 113–14

Henry of Virneburg, 126

Heraclius, Byzantine Emperor, 180

Herbert, George, xiii, 213, **218–21**, 224, 310

Hereford, England, 235

hermits, 26–35, 60, 66
  Benedict of Nursia, 48, 59
  Christina of Markyate, 79–83
  Desert Fathers, 26–30
  Desert Mothers, 26–7, 31–5
  de Foucauld, 299, 302–5
  Gregory Palamas, 186
  Julian of Norwich, xv, 1, 6, 143, 153–5, 157
  Rolle, 145–6
  Seraphim of Sarov, 190–93
  Sergius of Radonezh, 188–90

Herrnhut, Germany, 265

hesychasm, 175–6, 178, 185–8, 190

Hilary of Poitiers, 40

Hildegard of Bingen, 3, 63, 66, **74–9**, 323–4

385

INDEX

Hilton, Walter, 3, 143, **151–3**

Hinba (island near Iona), 51

Hinckaert, Jan, 135

Hinduism, 310

Hippo Regius, 41, 43

Hochheim, Germany, 126

Holy Roman Empire (800–1806), 48, 63, 94, 172, 196, 242

Holy Trinity, 38–9, 42, 54, 77, 96, 127

Holy War, The (Bunyan), 233

Holy Wisdom (Baker), 212

Homilies on Ezekiel (Gregory), 58

Honorius III, Pope, 107

Hopkins, Gerard Manley, 286

von Hügel, Baron Friedrich, 169

Hugh of Saint Victor, 72, 95

Huguenots, 241–2, 246

Humbert of Silva Candida, 172

humility, 2

    Angela of Foligno on, 101, 103

    Bernard of Clairvaux on, 68, 69

    Catherine of Siena on, 166, 167

    Clare of Assisi on, 95

    de Foucauld on, 302, 304

    Francis of Assisi on, 88, 90, 91

    Gregory the Great on, 58

    Hadewijch of Brabant, 113

    John Climacus on, 178

    Julian of Norwich, 153

    Law (William) on, 270, 272

    Mechthild of Magdeburg on, 115

    Merton on, 315

    Richard of Saint-Victor on, 74

    Rolle on, 145, 148

    Symeon on, 182, 184

    Teresa of Ávila on, 200, 203

    Theodora on, 32–3

    Thérèse of Lisieux on, 300

    Thoreau on, 277, 292

    Weil on, 310

Hundred Years' War (1337–1453), 143, 144

Huntingdon, England, 79

Hus, Jan, 160–61, 209

Hutin, Madeleine, 305

Huvelin, Henri, 303

Huxley, Thomas Henry, 298, 299

Hymns to the Night (Novalis), 279

Ignatius of Loyola, xv, 137, 195, **197–9**, 248, 287

Iliad (Homer), 310

Illuminated movement, 196

Imitation of Christ, The (Thomas à Kempis), xiii, 137–41

Immaculate Conception, 297

Incarnation, 42, 44, 61–2, 128, 163, 180, 181, 187

Independents, 213

Index of Prohibited Books, 196, 244

India, 289, 313

indulgences, 160, 210

Inge, Dean, 73

innocence, 235–7, 301–2

"Innocence" (Traherne), 236

Innocent II, Pope, 67

Innocent III, Pope, 87, 89

Innocent IV, Pope, 92, 168

Inquisition, 116, 196

Interior Castle, The (Teresa of Ávila), 201, 203

INDEX

Internet, and the noosphere, 308
Introduction to the Devout Life
  (Francis de Sales), 249, 250
Inverness, Scotland, 50
Iona, Scotland, 50
Iona Community, 318–19
Ireland, 48, 49, 50, 51, 60, 299
Irish Times, 317
Isabella, Queen of Castile, 196
Isis (Egyptian goddess), 11
Islam, 48, 49, 65, 303–5
Island Promised to the Saints, 51
Italy
  Middle Ages, 52, 57, 58,
    88–104, 159–70
  Roman period, 12–13, 15, 22,
    42, 44

Jackson, Lydia, 290
Jacob's ladder, 151
Jacopone da Todi, 87, **97–101**
Jacquérie revolt (1358), 144
Jacques de Vitry, 109, 110
James II, King of England, 270
James, William, 295
Jan van Ruysbroeck, 5, 54, 69,
  123, **134–7**, 248, 270, 327
Jansen, Cornelius, 242
Jansenism, 242–3, 244, 253,
  254–5, 257, 259, 266, 267
Jerusalem, 11, 34, 38, 49, 304
  Crusade, Fifth (1217–21), 89
  Crusade, First (1096–9), 65
  Crusade, Second (1147–50),
    67
  pilgrimage to, 152, 156, 162,
    198
Jerusalem (Blake), 280, 282–3

Jesuits, 137, 195, 197, 205, 242,
  244, 248, 249, 266, 306
Jesus Christ, 9–12, 38, 59, 271–2
  Crucifixion, 74, 88–9, 96,
    153, 251
  Eucharist, 12, 55, 72, 108,
    110, 112, 118, 144, 172,
    183, 221, 290
  Incarnation, 42, 44, 61–2,
    128, 163, 180, 181, 187
  Monothelitism and, 180–81
  Passion, 112, 115, 139, 153
  Sermon on the Mount, 17
  Song of Songs and, 68–9,
    114–15
  Transfiguration, 174, 187
  visions of, 40, 68, 82, 153,
    154, 156, 163, 165
Jesus prayer, 175, 176, 186
Jiménez de Cisneros, Francisco,
  195
Joan of Arc, 303
John VI Cantacuzenus, Byzantine
  Emperor, 188
John XXII, Pope, 87, 108, 125,
  126
John Climacus, 13, 151, 175,
  177–9
John of the Cross, xv, 1, 3, 20, 54,
  69, 152, 195, 197, **204–8**, 331
John Scotus Erigena, **60–62**, 70
John the Evangelist, 9, 10–11,
  154, 181, 190
Johnson, Samuel, 265, 270
Journey of the Mind to God, The
  (Bonaventure), 96
Judaism, 14, 16, 114, 303, 309
Julian, Roman Emperor, 26

INDEX

Julian of Norwich, xv, 1, 6, 143, **153–5**, 157, 329

Jung, Carl Gustav, 312

Jutta (Benedictine nun), 75

Kant, Immanuel, 298

kataphatic (cataphatic) theology, 53

Keats, John, 279, 286

Kellia, Egypt, 38

Kells, Ireland, 50

Kempe, John, 156

Kempe, Margery, 109, 143, **155–8**, 161

Kilian (Irish saint), 52

Kingdom of England (927–1707), 60, 66, 79–83, 143–58, 218–39

  Anglican Church, 211, 212, 218, 222, 223, 228, 232, 243

  Calvinism in, 211, 212, 250

  Civil War (1642–51), 212, 223, 227, 232, 235

  Hundred Years' War (1337–1453), 143, 144

  Lollard movement (1380s–1560s), 144–5, 157

  Peasants Revolt (1381), 144

  Reformation (1534–1603), 211

Kingdom of France (843–1792), 67, 70–74, 241–61

  Beguines, 72, 105–11, 116–19

  Calvinism in, 211

  Cathar Crusade (1209–29), 87, 109, 123

  Council of Lyon (1272), 96

  Huguenots, 241–2, 246

  Hundred Years' War (1337–1453), 143, 144

  Jacquérie revolt (1358), 144

  Quietism, 242–3, 244, 253, 254–5, 257, 259, 266, 267

  Revolution (1789), 108, 277, 286

  Thirty Years' War (1618–48), 241, 242

  Waldenses, 87

  Wars of Religion (1562–98), 241–2, 246, 249

Kingdom of Great Britain (1707–1800), 137, 265, 269–75, 278, 279, 280–89

Kirkby, Margaret, 146

Knights Templar, 117, 125

Knock, Ireland, 299

Knox, Alexander, 260

Kuntzschmann, Katharina, 214

Kyiv, 173–4

Kyivan Rus' (c. 880–1240), 173

Lacombe, Père, 257

Ladder of Divine Ascent (John Climacus), 13, 151, 177

Ladder of Perfection, The (Hilton), 151–3

Lagny-sur-Marne, France, 52

Lamentabili (Pius X), 299

Langland, William, 143, 144

Latin Vulgate Bible, 196

Lauda XCI (Jacopone da Todi), 100

Lausiac History (Palladius), 31

Law, William, 6, 214, 263, **269–72**, 279

388

INDEX

Lawrence, Brother, 241, **252–4**, 266, 317, 320–21, 332

Lazirists, 244

Leibniz, Gottfried Wilhelm, 298

Leo I, Pope, 48

Leo III, Pope, 48

Leo IX, Pope, 63

leprosy, 90, 109, 165

Liège, Wallonia, 107, 109

Life of Antony (Athanasius), 28

Life of Jesus Critically Examined (Strauss), 298

Ligugé, France, 40

Lisieux, France, 300

literacy, 60, 165

Literal Commentary on Genesis (Augustine), 44–5

Little Brothers of Jesus, 305

"Little Gidding" (T.S. Eliot), 153, 225

Little Sisters of Jesus, 305

Living Flame of Love, The (John of the Cross), 204

locutions, 2, 3, 210, 265

    Boehme, 216

    Bridget of Sweden, 163–4

    Bunyan, 232

    Fox, 231

    Francis of Assisi, 88

    Hildegard of Bingen, 76–7

    John of the Cross, 207

    Mary of Egypt, 34

    Ortulana (mother of Clare of Assisi), 92

    Teresa of Ávila, 200, 201

    Thérèse of Lisieux, 302

    Vaughan, 226

logikoi, 38

Logos, 20, 61

Lollard movement (1380s–1560s), 144–5, 157

Lombard Kingdom (568–774), 57, 172

Longchamp, Paris, 246

Lord's Prayer (and Simone Weil), 310

Lord's Supper, *see* Communion

Lorraine, France, 266

Lossky, Vladimir, 175

Louis IX, King of France, 107

Louis XIV, King of France, 241, 242, 257

Louis, Duke of Burgundy, 260

Lourdes, France, 299, 319

Louth, Andrew, 44

love

    Augustine of Hippo on, 43, 45

    Beatrice of Nazareth on, 119–21

    Bernard of Clairvaux on, 68–9

    Catherine of Siena on, 166–7

    de Caussade on, 267

    Clement of Alexandria on, 17

    Fénelon on, 259–61

    Fox on, 229

    Gregory the Great on, 58

    Hadewijch of Brabant on, 111–12

    Herbert on, 220–21, 310

    Jacopone da Todi on, 99, 101

    John Climacus on, 178, 179

    Julian of Norwich on, 154

    Law (William) on, 272

    Maximus the Confessor on, 181–2

INDEX

Origen on, 20
Plotinus on, 23, 120
Porete on, 117
Richard of Saint-Victor on, 73–4
Rolle on, 147–8
Thomas à Kempis on, 140
Traherne on, 238
Weil on, 311
"Love (III)" (Herbert), 220–21, 310
Lucifer, 77, 114
    see also Devil
Lucius III, Pope, 87
Luke the Evangelist, 9, 20, 136
Luther, Martin, 129, 195, 209, 210, 274
Lutheranism, 211, 214
Luxeuil, France, 49, 52
Lyrical Ballads (Coleridge and Wordsworth), 287

Macarius of Corinth, 176
MacCulloch, Diarmaid, 210
Macleod, George, 318
Magdeburg, Germany, 113
Magnus II, King of Sweden, 162
Magyars, 48
Mahler, Gustav, 34
Maintenon, Madame de (Françoise d'Aubigné, Marquise,) 257
Malik-al-Kamal, Sultan of Egypt, 89
"Man" (Vaughan), 224–5
Manichaeism, 42, 43
Manresa, Catalonia, 197
Marabotto, Cattaneo, 169

Marie of Oignies, 108, **109–11**, 158
Mark, the Evangelist, 9
Markyate, England, 80–83
Marmoutier, monastery of, Tours, France, 40
marriage, 31, 63, 80–81, 92, 107
marriage, spiritual, *see* spiritual marriage
Marsilius of Padua, 125
Martin of Tours, 26–7, **39–41**
Martin V, Pope, 160
Martinian of Palestine, 106
martyrdom, 12–13, 26
Mary I, Queen of England, 211, 228
Mary of Egypt, 26, 33, **34–5**
Mary, Mother of Jesus, 67, 78, 82, 94, 98, 105, 131, 144, 163, 248
    Immaculate Conception, 297
    visions of, 81, 82, 138, 156, 165, 189, 190, 191
Mass, 110–11, 154, 209
Matthew the Evangelist, 9, 19, 27, 88, 93
Maxentius, Roman Emperor, 25
Maximus the Confessor, 60, 62, 171, 174, 175, **180–82**
McGinn, Bernard, 2, 3, 59
Mechthild of Magdeburg, 108, **113–16**
de Médici, Marie, 247
meditation, 4, 243
    Angela of Foligno, 103
    Baker, 212
    Christina of Markyate, 79
    Clare of Assisi, 93

390

INDEX

Evagrius Ponticus, 38
Francis de Sales, 250–52
Ignatius of Loyola, 199
John of the Cross, 206–7
Law (William), 270
Richard of Saint-Victor, 74
Rolle, 146
Suso, 133
Teresa of Ávila, 203
Thomas à Kempis, 138
Traherne, 236
Medjugorje, Bosnia, 299
Meister Eckhart, *see* Eckhart,
Meister
mendicants, 85–7, 96, 99, 125
Merton, Thomas, xv, 70, 299,
312–16
Metaphysical poets, 310
Methodism, 137, 264, 265,
273–5
Michael VIII Palaiologos,
Byzantine Emperor, 173
Milan, Italy, 65
Milieu Divin, Le (Teilhard de
Chardin), 307
Milton (Blake), 280
Minnesänger, 105
Mirror of Simple Souls (Porete), 116
misogyny, 105, 146
Misyn, Richard, 146
Mithras, 4, 11
de Molinos, Miguel, 243, 257,
273
Monastery of the Caves, Kyiv, 174
monasticism
Early Modern period, 247
Middle Ages, 48, 49, 56–7, 59,
64, 67, 70–72, 162

Modern period, 303–4
Orthodox Church, 174, 175
Renaissance period, 205, 210
Roman period, 26–7, 29–30,
35–46
see also convents
Mongols, 174, 189, 190
Monothelitism, 180–81
Monte Cassino, Italy, 59
Montgomery, Wales, 218
Montserrat, Catalonia, Spain, 197
Moody, Dwight, 299
Moralia on Job (Gregory the
Great), 58
Moravian brethren, 265, 273, 274
Morocco, 89, 303
mortification, 6, 212, 254
Moses, 16, 36, 55–6
Motovilov, Nicolas, 192–3
Mount Athos, Greece, 175, 186
Mount Auburn, Cambridge,
Massachusetts, 291
Mount La Verna, Italy, 89, 95
Mount of Olives, The (Vaughan),
222
Mount Sinai, 36, 55, 177
Muggletonians, 213
Muhammad, Prophet of Islam,
49
"My Spirit" (Traherne), 238
mystery religions, 4, 11
Mystical Element of Religion (von
Hügel), 169
Mystical Theology (Dionysius the
Areopagite), 53, 54, 55, 148
mysticism, definitions of, 1–2

Nancy, France, 266

391

INDEX

Napoleon I, Emperor of the French, 277
nature, 282–95, 305
   animals, communion with, 27, 189, 191
Nature (Emerson), 291
Nazareth, 119, 304
negative theology, 5, 53, 55, 100, 133, 148, 186, 223, 244
Neoplatonism, 5, 16, 60, 120
   Augustine of Hippo, 42, 43–4, 57
   Bonaventure, 95
   Clement of Alexandria, 14, 15
   Dionysius the Areopagite, 54
   Eckhart, 127
   Gregory of Nyssa, 36–7
   Gregory the Great, 57
   John Scotus Erigena, 60, 61
   Origen, 18, 19
   Pierre de Bérulle, 249
   Plotinus, 21, 22, 23, 57, 120
Neri, Philip, 248
Nero, Roman Emperor, 12
Netherlands, 119, 138, 211, 230
New England, 265, 279
New Seeds of Contemplation (Merton), 314
New Testament, 9–12, 19, 174
Newton-by-Usk, Wales, 223
Newton, Isaac, 263, 281, 282
Niall of the Nine Hostages, 50
Nicaea, 173
Nicholas of Cusa, 161
Nicodemus, 176
Nitria, Egypt, 38
Nivelles, Wallonia, 107, 109
Nonjurors, 270

noosphere, 308
Norman England (1066–1154), 66, 79–83
Notre-Dame-des-Neiges, France, 303
Novalis, 279
Nuth, Joan, 2

Of the Supersensual Life (Boehme), 216
Oignies, France, 109
omphalopsyches, 187
On Loving God (Bernard of Clairvaux), 68, 69–70
On the Division of Nature (John Scotus Erigena), 60–61
On the Greatness of the Soul (Augustine), 45
Oratory of Jesus Christ, 247, 248
Order of Poor Ladies, 89, 92–5, 106, 246, 304
Origen, 5, 15, **17–21**, 38, 69
Origin of Species, The (Darwin), 298
original sin, 307
Orpheus, 4, 11
Orthodox Church, 11, 14, 96, 171–93
Osiris, 11
Ostia, Italy, 44
Ottoman Empire (1299–1922), 48, 124, 172–3
Our Lady of Guadalupe, Mexico, 319

Pachomius, 26, **29–30**, 189
Padua, Italy, 212, 250

INDEX

Palestine, 15, 19, 49
   Crusade, Fifth (1217–21), 89
   Crusade, First (1096–9), 65
   Crusade, Second (1147–50), 67
   Desert Fathers/Mothers, 27, 30, 31
   Great Rebellion (66–74), 11
   pilgrimage to, 152, 156, 162, 198
Palladius, 31, 49
Pantaenus, 16
pantheism, 264
papacy, 48, 57–8, 63, 67, 124, 171–2, 279
   Avignon papacy (1309–76), 124–5, 126, 144, 159, 162–4, 165–6
   Great Schism (1378–1417), 144, 159–61, 166
Papal States (756–1870), 165–6
Paracelsus, 214, 280
Paradiso (Dante), 67, 95
Paris, France, 64, 246, 249, 253, 259, 303
Paris, Matthew, 108
Pascal, Blaise, 234–5, 241, 242, **254–6**
Pastoral Rule (Gregory), 58
Patrick, Saint, 48, 49
Paul III, Pope, 195, 198
Paul the Apostle, 10, 12, 45, 54, 154, 176, 210, 274
Peace of Augsburg (1555), 211
Peace of Westphalia (1648), 242
"Peace" (Vaughan), 226
Peasants Revolt (1381), 144

Peckham, London, 280
Peking man, 307
Pelagianism, 43
Pelagius II, Pope, 57
Pensées (Pascal), 255
Pépin, King of the Franks, 172
peregrini, **49–53**
Périgord, France, 259
Periphyseon (John Scotus Erigena), 60–61
Perpetua, 13, 151
Persia, 14, 22, 49, 180
Persons, Robert, 244
Perugia, Italy, 99
Peter of Alcántara, 201
Peter the Apostle, 181, 190
Phenomenon of Man, The (Teilhard de Chardin), 307
Philip II, King of Spain, 201
Philip IV, King of France, 117, 124, 125
Philo of Alexandria, 54
Philokalia, 176
Picts, 50
Pierre de Bérulle, 244, 245, 246, **247–9**
Piers Plowman (Langland), 143
Pietism, 264–5
Pilate, Pontius, 9
Pilgrim's Progress (Bunyan), 212, 231, 233–4, 282
pilgrimage, 48–50, 65, 152–3, 156–7, 162, 198, 209, 319
piracy, 48
Pius II, Pope, 161
Pius V, Pope, 211
Pius VII, Pope, 277
Pius X, Pope, 299

393

INDEX

Plato, 15, 16, 21, 22, 23, 131, 222, 225, 279, 282, 289

Platonism, *see* Neoplatonism

Plotinus, 5, 15, 19, **21–4**, 44, 55, 57, 120, 127

Pontoise, France, 247

Poor Clares, 89, 92–5, 106, 246, 304

Pope Pius IX, 297

Porete, Marguerite, xv, 6, 108, **116–19**, 325–6

Porphyry, 21

Port-Royal, France, 242–3, 255

Portiuncula, Assisi, 88, 89, 90, 92, 309

poverty, 27, 33, 64, 66, 129, 152
 Franciscan order, 85–95, 98–9, 101, 125

Practice of the Presence of God, The (Beaufort), 253

Prague, Bohemia, 94, 160

prayer, contemplative, 2, 4, 9, 320
 Angela of Foligno on, 103
 Antony of Egypt on, 29
 Benet Canfield on, 244–5
 Bernard of Clairvaux, 67, 68
 Bonaventure on, 96–7
 Cloud of Unknowing, 148–50
 Eckhart on, 130
 Evagrius Ponticus on, 37–9
 Francis de Sales on, 251–2
 Gregory I on, 58
 Guyon on, 248
 Herbert on, 220
 Hilton on, 151
 Jan van Ruysbroeck on, 136
 John Climacus on, 178
 Julian of Norwich on, 153–5

Martin of Tours on, 41
 Merton on, 312, 314–16
 Origen on, 18, 21
 Porete on, 117
 Seraphim of Sarov on, 192
 Suso on, 133
 Tauler on, 131
 Teresa of Ávila on, 201–2
 Theodora on, 32
 Way of a Pilgrim on, 176

prayer of the heart, 176

Prelude, The (Wordsworth), 287, 289

"Preparative, The" (Traherne), 238

Presbyterianism, 212

Priest to the Temple, A (Herbert), 219

Proclus, 54

prophecy, 79, 81, 108, 179, 280–81

Protestantism, 4, 108, 124, 129, 195–6, 209–39, 263, 269–75
 Calvinism, 211, 212, 250, 265
 Huguenots, 241–2, 246
 Methodism, 137, 264, 265, 273–5
 Pietism, 264–5
 Quakers, 213, 227–31

Provence, France, 105

Provincial Letters (Pascal), 242, 255

Psalms, 1, 45, 146, 192, 220

Pseudo-Athanasius, 33

purgatory, 110, 114, 160, 163, 169, 170, 196

Puritanism, 211, 212, 229, 232

Quakers, 213, 227–31, 279

INDEX

Quietism, 242–3, 244, 253, 254–5, 257, 259, 266, 267

Ramière, Henri, 266
Ranters, 213
Reformation (1517–1648), 4, 108, 124, 129, 195, 209–11
Reims, France, 70, 71, 212
relics, 52, 110, 144, 196, 209
"Religion" (Vaughan), 225
Renaissance (c. 1350–1650), 186
repentance, 178, 185
Revelations of Divine Love (Julian of Norwich), 153
Rhineland mystics, **123–41**, 213, 214
Richard of Saint-Victor, 64, **72–4**, 95
Richter, Gregorius, 215
Robert of Geneva, 160
Robert of Molesme, 64
Rolle, Richard, 5, 143, **145–8**, 158, 330
Roman Empire (27 BCE–CE 476), 11, 47, 60
Romantic Period (c. 1798–1837), 7, 277–89
Rome, city of, 12, 22, 27, 42, 49, 57, 156, 159, 162–4, 314
Romulus Augustulus, Roman Emperor, 47
Rousseau, Jean-Jacques, 281
Rublev, Andrei, 174
Rule of Perfection (Benet Canfield), 244–5
Runciman, Stephen, 172
Rupertsberg, Germany, 76
Russia, 173–4, 175, 176, 188–93

Sabaria (modern Szombathely), Hungary, 39
Saint Andrew's monastery, Rome, 57
Saint Andrew's Church, Bemerton, England, 218
Saint Angelo convent, Assisi, 92
Sainte-Anne-de-Beaupré, Canada, 319
Saint-Augustin's church, Paris, 303
Saint Catherine's monastery, Mount Sinai, 177
Saint Damian's church, Assisi, 88, 92
Saint Gall, Switzerland, 49
Saint Mamas monastery, Constantinople, 183–4
Saint Mary of the Angels, Assisi, 88, 89, 90, 92, 309
Saint-Nicholas-de-Port, France, 247
Saint Paul's Cathedral, London, 274
Saint-Sulpice seminary, Paris, 259
Saint-Thierry monastery, Reims, 71
Sancta Sophia (Baker), 212
Sankey, Ira, 299
Santiago de Compostela, Spain, 65, 157, 319
Sarah, Amma, 31–2
Satan, *see* Devil
Savonarola, Girolamo, 195
Sawtry, William, 144
Sayings of the Desert Fathers, 27, 28, 31, 33
Scetis, Egypt, 32

395

INDEX

Schilling, Friedrich, 278

Scholasticism, 6, 65–6, 73, 95, 117, 124, 187

Schutz, Brother Roger, 318

Scivias (Hildegard), 75

"Search, The" (Vaughan), 226

Second World War (1939–45), 310, 312, 318

Seekers (radical Protestant sect), 213

Select Meditations (Traherne), 234

Seljuk Empire (1037–1194), 65

seraphim, 89, 96

Seraphim of Sarov, 174, 176, **190–93**, 335

Sergius of Radonezh, 174, **188–90**

Serious Call, A (William Law), 270

Sermon on the Mount, 17

Seven Storey Mountain, The (Merton), 313

Seven Ways of Holy Love (Beatrice of Nazareth), 120

Severus, Roman Emperor, 13, 16, 17–18

Sewall, Ellen, 293

Shelley, Percy Byshe, 278, 286

Shillington, England, 80, 82

Short and Easy Method of Prayer (Guyon), 257

Siena, Italy, 165

Sigismund, Holy Roman Emperor, 160

Signy, France, 71

Silex Scintillans (Vaughan), 222, 224

Silures (Celtic tribe), 225

Simeon Stylites, 30

simony, 63

Simplon Pass, 289

sin, 31, 66
  Augustine of Hippo on, 42
  Bernard of Clairvaux on 69
  Bunyan on, 232, 233
  Catherine of Genoa on, 170
  Cloud of Unknowing on, 150
  Fénelon, 260
  Francis de Sales on, 251
  Gregory the Great on, 59
  Hilton on, 152
  Julian of Norwich on, 154–5
  Kempe on, 158
  Law (William) on, 269
  Mechthild of Magdeburg on, 114, 115
  Pascal, 256
  Porete on, 118
  Rolle on, 148
  Teilhard de Chardin on, 307
  Vaughan on, 224
  Wesley on, 274

Sinanthropus, 307

Sisters of Charity, 244

slavery, 40, 290, 293

Slavic desert fathers, 189

Society for Psychical Research, 299

Society of Friends, 213, 227–31, 279

Society of Jesus, 137, 195, 197, 205, 242, 244, 248, 249, 266, 306

Solesmes, France, 309–10

Song of Songs, 20, 37, 67, 68–9, 71, 72, 141, 205

Songs of Innocence (Blake), 280

INDEX

Sophronius, Patriarch of
Jerusalem, 34, 35
soul
Angela of Foligno on, 104
Augustine of Hippo on, 42, 43,
44, 45–6
Beatrice of Nazareth on,
120–21
Beguine order and, 105, 108
Bernard of Clairvaux on,
68–70
Blake on, 281–2
Boehme on, 216
Bonaventure on, 96, 97
Catherine of Genoa on, 170
de Caussade on, 267, 269
Clare of Assisi, 92
Clement of Alexandria on, 15
Dionysius the Areopagite on,
55–6
Eckhart on, 127–9
Emerson on, 291
Evagrius on, 38–9
Fox on, 230
Francis of Assisi on, 90
Gregory of Nyssa on, 36–7
Gregory the Great on, 58–9
Hadewijch of Brabant on, 112
Herbert on, 221
Jacopone da Todi, 99–100
John of the Cross on, 204,
206–8
John Scotus Erigena on, 62
Law (William) on, 271–2
Mechthild of Magdeburg on,
114–16
Origen on, 18
Paul the Apostle on, 10

Plotinus on, 23–4
Porete on, 117–19
Syncletica of Alexandria on, 33
Tauler on, 130–31
Teresa of Ávila on, 202–4
Thoreau on, 295
Traherne on, 235
William of Saint-Thierry on,
72
Spain, 49, 58, 65, 195–208, 299
Alumbrado movement, 196
al-Andalus (711–1492), 49,
124
Armada (1588), 211
Civil War (1936–9), 309
Inquisition, 196
Spener, Philipp Jakob, 264–5
Spirit of Love, The (Law), 271, 272
"Spiritual Canticle" (John of the
Cross), 205
Spiritual Espousals, The
(Ruysbroeck), 136
Spiritual Exercises (Ignatius), xv,
199
Spiritual Franciscans, 86–7, 96,
99, 125
Spiritual Instructions (Caussade),
267
spiritual marriage, 2, 69, 72, 108,
136–7, 157, 165, 202–4
Song of Songs, 20, 37, 67,
68–9, 71, 72, 141, 205
spiritualism, 299
St Albans, England, 79, 80, 81
Stabat Mater, 98
starets, 174, 188, 190
Stephen II, Pope, 172
stigmata, 88, 89–90, 165

INDEX

Story of a Soul, The (Thérèse of Lisieux), 301
Strasbourg, 126, 129
Strauss, David, 298
Stuart dynasty, 270
Studion Monastery, Constantinople, 183
Sulpicius Severus, 39, 41
Summa Theologiae (Thomas Aquinas), 124
supernatural experiences, 2, 108
  clairvoyance, 2, 28, 81, 110, 190, 192
  ecstasies, *see* ecstasies
  healing, 28, 76, 192
  locutions, *see* locutions
  prophecy, 79, 81, 108, 179, 280–81
  visions, *see* visions
Suso, Henry, 6, 123, 127, 129, **131–4**
Suzuki, Daisetsu Teitaro, 126
Swarthmoor, England, 229
Sweden, 161–4
Swedenborg, Emanuel, 280
Switzerland, 49, 211
Symeon the New Theologian, 141, 174, **182–5**, 292
Syncletica of Alexandria, 26, 31, 33–4
Synod of Béziers (1299), 108
Syria, 26, 27, 30, 31, 49, 89
Szombathely, *see* Sabaria

Tabennisi, Egypt, 29
Tacitus, 12
Tagaste, Algeria, 42
Taizé Community, 318

Tamanrasset, Algeria, 304
Tauler, John, 123, 127, **129–31**, 270, 328
Tavener, John, 34
"Te Deum Laudamus", 82
Teilhard de Chardin, Pierre, 7, 299, **305–9**
Tennyson, Alfred, 30
Teresa of Ávila, xv, 2, 3, 20, 69, 164, 197, **200–204**, 247, 248, 320
Tertullian, 12–13
Thailand, 313–14
Theatine order, 195
Thebes, Egypt, 26, 29
Theodora, Amma, 31, 32–3
Theodosius I, Roman Emperor, 26, 36
Theophilus of Alexandria, 32
Thérèse of Lisieux, 299, **300–302**
Thirty Years' War (1618–48), 241, 242, 249
Thirty-Nine Articles (1563), 211
Thomas à Kempis, xiii, 123, **137–41**, 224
Thomas Aquinas, 86, 124
Thoreau, Henry David, 277, 279, 289, 290, **292–5**
Threefold Way, The (Bonaventure), 96, 97
Thurgarton, Nottinghamshire, England, 151
Tienen, Flanders, 119
Tobin, Frank, 45
Toland, John, 264
Toledo, Spain, 205
Touggourt, Algeria, 305
Toulouse, France, 266

INDEX

Tours, France, 40

Traherne, Thomas, 213, **234–9**

Transcendental Meditation, 299

Transcendentalism, 279, 290, 294

Transfiguration (of Christ), 174, 187

Trappists, 303–4, 313

Treatise on the Love of God (Francis de Sales), 250

Trebizond (on the Black Sea), 173

Triune God, *see* Holy Trinity

troubadours, 105

True Cross, 110

Tyler, Wat, 144

Ulm, Germany, 132

Umayyad Caliphate (661–750), 49

Underhill, Evelyn, xiv, 2, 167–8

Ungrund, 214

Unitarians, 213, 290

United Kingdom, 278, 279, 280–89, 298, 299

United States, 264, 289–95, 312–16

universities, 86

University of Alcalá, 195

University of Bologna, 86, 98, 123

University of Cambridge, 151, 218, 228, 313, 314

University of Oxford, 86, 123, 228, 270, 273

University of Paris, 86, 96, 116, 123, 126, 198

University of Salamanca, 205

University of Tübingen, 298

University of Wittenberg, 210

Urban II, Pope, 65

Urban VI, Pope, 160, 166

Urban VIII, Pope, 248

Ursuline order, 246, 247

Ussher, James, 298

Vadstena monastery, Stockholm, 163

Valdes, Peter, 87

Vallon, Annette, 286

Vandals, 43, 47

Vaughan, Henry, 213, **221–7**

Venice, Italy, 156, 157

Vermeer, Johannes, 219

Vie de Jésus (Pierre de Bérulle), 248

Vietnam War (1955–75), 312, 313

Vikings, 48, 64

Vincent de Paul, 244

Virgin Mary, *see* Mary, Mother of Jesus

viriditas, 78

Visigoths, 27

visions, 1, 2–3, 299

    Angela of Foligno, 102–3

    Antony of Egypt, 28–9

    Augustine of Hippo, 44–5

    Birgitta of Sweden, 163

    Blake, 280, 283–5

    Bonaventure, 95

    Bunyan, 231–2

    Catherine of Siena, 165

    Christina of Markyate, 66

    Clare of Assisi, 94

    Columbanus, 52

    Constantine, 25

    Francis of Assisi, 89–90

    Hildegard of Bingen, 74–9

399

INDEX

Ignatius of Loyola, 197–8
Julian of Norwich, 153, 154
Kempe, 156
Martin of Tours, 40
Mechthild of Magdeburg, 113, 114
Merton, 314
Paul the Apostle, 10
Perpetua, 13, 151
Seraphim of Sarov, 191
Sergius of Radonezh, 189
Suso, 132
Thomas à Kempis, 138–9
Wesley on, 265, 273
Visitation order, 250, 266
Vladimir of Kyiv, 173
Voillaume, René, 305
Volmar, 75
Voltaire, 263, 264, 281
Vulgate Bible, 196

Waiting on God (Weil), 310
Walden (Thoreau), 293, 294
Walden Pond, Massachusetts, 292–3
Waldenses, 87, 106
Wales, 218, 223
Warburton, William, 216
Wars of Religion (1562–98), 241–2, 246, 249
Way of a Pilgrim, The, 176
Weil, Simone, 220, 297, 299, **309–11**
Wesley, Charles, 273
Wesley, John, 137, 265, 270, **273–5**

Western Roman Empire (395–476), 47
Western Schism (1378–1417), 144, 159–61, 166
white martyrdom, 26
Whitefield, George, 265
Wilberforce, Samuel, 298
Willambroux, Wallonia, 109
William of Ockham, 86, 124
William of Saint-Thierry, 65, 66, **70–72**
Wise, Catherine, 223
women, 31, 105–21, 146
Beguine order, 72, 105–21
Desert Mothers, 26–7, 31–5
misogyny, 105, 146
Poor Clares, 89, 92–5, 106, 246, 304
Rolle on, 146
"Wonder" (Traherne), 236
Wordsworth, William, 278, 279, **285–9**, 290
"World, The" (Vaughan), 226
Würzburg, Germany, 52
Wycliffe, John, 144, 160–61, 209
Wye valley, 287–9

Yeats, William Butler, xiv, 281

Zacchaeus, 136
Zen Buddhism, 253, 299, 312
von Zinzendorf, Nikolaus Ludwig, 265
Zosima (monk), 35
Zwingli, Huldrych, 209, 211

400